ARMY LINEAGE SERIES

ARMOR-CAVALRY

Part I:
Regular Army
and
Army Reserve

by
Mary Lee Stubbs
and
Stanley Russell Connor

MILITARY INSTRVCTION

OFFICE OF THE CHIEF OF MILITARY HISTORY
UNITED STATES ARMY
WASHINGTON, D.C., 1969

Library of Congress Catalog Card Number: 69–60002

First Printing

For sale by the Superintendent of Documents, U.S. Government Printing Office
Washington, D.C. 20402 - Price: $6.75

ARMY LINEAGE SERIES

Stetson Conn, General Editor

Advisory Committee
(as of 14 June 1968)

Walter C. Langsam
University of Cincinnati

Charles P. Roland
Tulane University

Charles B. Burdick
San Jose State College

Maj. Gen. Glenn D. Walker
U.S. Continental Army Command

James A. Field, Jr.
Swarthmore College

Brig. Gen. David S. Henderson
U.S. Army Command and General
Staff College

Richard W. Leopold
Northwestern University

Col. M. J. L. Greene
U.S. Army War College

Ernest R. May
Harvard University

Col. Thomas E. Griess
United States Military Academy

Office of the Chief of Military History

Brig. Gen. Hal C. Pattison, Chief of Military History

Chief Historian
Chief, Historical Services Division
Chief, Histories Division
Editor in Chief

Stetson Conn
Col. Herman S. Schmidt
Col. Wolfred K. White
Joseph R. Friedman

Foreword

Successful military organizations are solidly founded upon the pride of their members—soldiers with a strong sense of belonging to their unit and enthusiastic about its being their own. Good military leaders always strive to attain this intangible quality—generally known as *esprit de corps*. Anything that helps an army to achieve it contributes to better units.

As the authors trace the evolution of cavalry into today's armor branch, their narrative presents a broad history of the growth of the entire U.S. Army. It gives an insight into the reasoning and considerations behind most of the organizational changes the Army has undergone, lending clarity and perspective to the unit lineages that follow.

The Army Lineage Series is designed to foster the *esprit de corps* of United States Army units. It is intended for use at all levels of command, in service schools, and in various training programs. *Armor-Cavalry,* the second volume in the series, is designed as a tool to perpetuate the rich tradition of cavalry and the brilliant record of modern armor.

Washington, D.C.
14 June 1968

HAL C. PATTISON
Brigadier General, USA
Chief of Military History

The Authors

Mary Lee Stubbs, a graduate of Alabama State Teachers College, is Chief of the Organizational History Branch of the Office of the Chief of Military History. Before joining the office in 1947, she taught in the public schools of Alabama and in the Indian Service schools of the Navajo Agency in New Mexico.

Stanley Russell Connor, a graduate of Mississippi State College, served during World War II as a company commander of rifle and heavy weapons companies and as a battalion executive officer. He had tours of duty as a historian with the Office of the Chief of Military History and the United Nations Command element of the Military Armistice Commission in Korea. He holds the Silver Star and Bronze Star Medals. After 20 years of active duty as an infantry officer, he retired in 1959 as a lieutenant colonel, AUS. Currently Mr. Connor is Deputy Chief of the Organizational History Branch, OCMH.

Preface

The Army Organization Act of 1950 named *armor* as one of the basic branches of the Army and specified that it would be a continuation of *cavalry*. *Armor-Cavalry* thus deals with units of the armor branch and with the general development of that branch within the U.S. Army.

In effect, the Organization Act abolished *cavalry* as a basic arm, but it abolished neither the cavalry's missions nor the units that were a part of that arm. Nor did it require that cavalry units relinquish their traditional names. Current rolls of the Army thus contain both cavalry and armor units within the armor branch.

Except for the cavalry battalions of the 1st Cavalry Division (Airmobile), organized under modified infantry tables of organization, the organizations called cavalry still perform old cavalry missions of reconnaissance and security, for which they are now equipped with armored vehicles, light tanks, and helicopters. These units descend directly from the horse cavalry regiments, whose designations they still bear. They include five separate armored cavalry regiments—the only units in the Regular Army that have retained their regimental organization—and the cavalry squadrons and troops assigned to divisions and separate brigades. The squadrons and troops are elements of regiments whose regimental headquarters have been inoperational since the regiments were reorganized under the Combat Arms Regimental System (CARS) in the late 1950's.

While some armor units also have their origins in the old horse cavalry, today's armor organizations are in the main the descendants of the armored regiments and tank battalions that served in World War II. Like their predecessors, present-day armor units close with and destroy enemy forces by tactics of maneuver, firepower, and shock. They are equipped with medium or heavy tanks.

In the narrative portion of this volume, all three components of the Army—the Regular Army, the Army Reserve, and the Army National Guard—are discussed; however, the lineages include only units of the Regular Army and the Army Reserve. Because of a number of factors, including several recent major reorganizations, lineages of most Army

National Guard armor and cavalry units had yet to be completed at the time this volume was ready for the printer. These lineages will be included in a subsequent volume.

The lineages contained herein for regiments organized under the Combat Arms Regimental System include only those units that have been active at some time since CARS was instituted. Hence, the inactive elements for which lineages are provided should not be construed as being all of the inactive elements that exist; indeed, they represent only a small percentage of the total.

While the volume was in preparation, the conflict in Vietnam progressively involved more units. Changes in the lineage and honors of many units thus had to be made to bring them as near up to date as possible. Generally, a cut-off date of 30 June 1967 has been used. When the volume went to the printer, Department of the Army General Orders confirming Vietnam campaign participation credits had not been published, but the credits for armor and cavalry units as of the summer of 1968 were determined and are included. Also included are unit decorations reported up to that time.

Although preparation of the volume has been a collaborative effort, Mrs. Stubbs wrote the narrative from the beginning through the cavalry of World War I, and Mr. Connor wrote that portion dealing with the tanks of World War I to the end. The bulk of the unit lineages were prepared earlier by Mrs. Stubbs; updating and lineages for recent units have been added by Mr. Connor, Miss Janice E. McKenney, and Mr. John B. Wilson.

Those who have contributed freely of their time and knowledge to this endeavor are numerous, and to all we are grateful. Without their contributions and the co-operation and advice of many others—especially our associates in the Organization History Branch of OCMH—this publication would not have been possible.

The Institute of Heraldry, U.S. Army, furnished the art work for unit coats of arms and distinctive insignia as well as the heraldic material included with the lineage of each regiment. A prime source for the bibliographies was Charles E. Dornbusch, *Histories, Personal Narratives, United States Army,* Cornwallville, New York, Hope Farm Press 1967. Mr. Frederick P. Todd prepared a portion of the original draft for the early period, and a manuscript entitled "The Development of the Medium Tank of World War II" by Mr. Robert Ross Smith, together with his bibliography, was most helpful in a later phase of the narrative.

The review panel (Mr. Charles B. MacDonald, Deputy Chief Historian, OCMH, chairman; Brig. Gen. Paul M. Robinett, USA, Retired; Col. Raymond C. Ball, then Chief, Historical Services Division, OCMH; and Miss Mary Ann Bacon, Chief, Editorial Branch, OCMH) provided both written and oral comments that were of much assistance. General Jacob L. Devers, USA, Retired, read the narrative and commented constructively upon it. Additional comments on the draft and suggestions were furnished by Maj. Gen. Albert C. Smith, USA, Retired, a former Chief of Military History; Col. Ridgway P. Smith, Jr., USA, Retired; Col. Robert J. Icks, USAR, Retired; Lt. Col. William H. Zierdt, Jr., USAR, Retired; and Mr. John Wike, Mr. William G. Bell, and Mr. Detmar H. Finke of OCMH. Also, the many articles and books by Colonel Icks, a recognized authority on tanks and armor, were valuable sources. Although the authors are indeed grateful for the help they received, they are solely responsible for all sins of commission or omission.

From the beginning, Brig. Gen. Hal C. Pattison, Chief of Military History, himself an armor officer with broad experience, and Dr. Stetson Conn, Chief Historian, OCMH, provided valuable comments, suggestions, and continuous guidance for the entire project. We owe our thanks, too, to Mr. Joseph R. Friedman, Editor in Chief, OCMH, for many helpful suggestions and to Miss Bacon and Miss Barbara J. Harris for editorial work on the manuscript. The photographs were chosen by Miss Ruth A. Phillips. Without the long hours of typing draft after draft, most capably done by Miss Maxine L. Pressley and Mrs. Eunice V. Blue, this volume would still be only a bundle of largely illegible scribbled notes of little use to anyone.

Washington, D.C.   MARY LEE STUBBS
14 June 1968   STANLEY RUSSELL CONNOR

Contents

Chart

Illustrations

All illustrations are from the files of the Department of Defense.

ARMOR-CAVALRY:

REGULAR ARMY
AND
ARMY RESERVE

History of the Organization of the Armor and Cavalry

Revolutionary War

At the time of the American Revolution, the term *cavalry* was applied to that branch of the military service whose members served and fought on horseback; the word *horse* was used about as often and meant essentially the same thing. By the eighteenth century specialization had developed sufficiently in cavalry to bring forth three distinctive types of mounted commands, varying in mission, armament, and weight of horses: the heavy cavalry, used primarily for shock effect in battle; the light cavalry, designed for reconnaissance, screening missions, and messenger service; and the dragoons, trained to fight both on foot and on horse. In actual practice, these distinctions were far from precise, and they tended to decrease in importance in the nineteenth century. In North America, the traditional cavalryman has ever been the light dragoon—a soldier trained and equipped to fight mounted or dismounted, to perform screening and reconnaissance, and to act as a scout or messenger. True heavy and true light horse have been rare.

The Continental Army of the American Revolution was mainly composed of infantry, with very little artillery and cavalry. In 1774, on the eve of the Revolution, some colonies had volunteer mounted units of troop size, but these troops were as much social organizations as military commands. They had select memberships who elected their own officers, furnished their own horses, arms, and uniforms, and made their own regulations.

The Continental Army fought through 1775 and 1776 with a few of the mounted militia commands as its only cavalry. Outstanding among these organizations was the Light Horse of the City of Philadelphia, a troop organized in November 1774 and today still active in the Army National Guard as Troop A, 1st Squadron, 223d Cavalry (First Troop Philadelphia City Cavalry). That tiny organization served as General Washington's escort in 1775 and in the bitter days of Trenton and Princeton, displaying then, as later in the war, "a Spirit of Bravery which will ever do Honor to them and will ever be gratefully remembered by me," to quote their Commander in Chief. Another such troop

ENCOUNTER BETWEEN AN AMERICAN OFFICER AND A BRITISH DRAGOON
*near Philadelphia. (From a painting by James Peale, now in a private
collection.)*

was the Connecticut Light Horse commanded by Elisha Sheldon. It, too, had elicited Washington's praise for its service in the summer of 1776.

General Washington's experience with cavalry in the summer campaign of 1776 led him to recommend the establishment of one or more mounted units in the Continental Army, and Congress on 12 December 1776 constituted a regiment of light dragoons and appointed Elisha Sheldon of Connecticut as its commander. Congress also authorized Washington to appoint the other officers of the regiment, but he delegated the duty to Sheldon, reserving for himself the right to refuse any officer so appointed if he thought him unfit for cavalry service. Washington indicated that he expected Sheldon to appoint only gentlemen of "true spirits and good character" and observed that gentlemen of fortune and of reputable families generally made the most useful officers.

In accordance with General Washington's instructions, the new regiment was to have, besides Sheldon as its lieutenant colonel commandant, one other field officer, a major; a regimental staff of an adjutant, a surgeon, and a surgeon's mate; and 6 troops. Each troop was to consist of a captain, a lieutenant, a cornet,* a quartermaster, 2 sergeants, 2 corporals, a trumpeter, a farrier, and 34 privates.

On 27 December 1776, Congress authorized a total of 3,000 light horse. During the winter and the spring of 1777 the Army began organizing four regiments: the 1st Continental Light Dragoons (Bland's Horse), the 2d Continental Light Dragoons (Sheldon's Horse), the 3d Continental Light Dragoons (Baylor's Horse), and the 4th Continental Light Dragoons (Moylan's Horse).

In January 1777 Washington proposed a new plan of organization for the cavalry regiments. As approved by Congress on 14 March of the same year, the new organization called for a colonel, a lieutenant colonel, and a major as field officers; a chaplain, a regimental quartermaster, a surgeon, a surgeon's mate, a paymaster, a riding master, a saddler, a trumpeter major, an adjutant, and 4 supernumeraries on the staff; and a captain, a lieutenant, a cornet, a quartermaster sergeant, an orderly or drill sergeant, a trumpeter, a farrier, an armorer, 4 corporals, and 32 privates in each of the 6 troops.

Although Congress authorized an increase in the strength of the light dragoon regiments in 1778, constant difficulties in recruiting men, procuring horses, arms, and accouterments, and retaining the men once they enlisted kept the four regiments from ever reaching full strength. When Friedrich Wilhelm, Baron von Steuben, Inspector General of the Army, inspected the cavalry in 1780 he found only 1,000 men in all. In the same year Washington and Steuben therefore recommended that the four understrength cavalry regiments be converted to legions—organizations composed of both cavalry and infantry. To back up his recommendation, Washington cited the high cost of horses and forage and the need of mounted troops to work in conjunction with foot soldiers. Another factor influencing the organization of legions was the dragoons' limited firepower. The dragoons were armed with heavy sabers, flintlock pistols carried in saddle holsters, and, when they were available, carbines.** Because of the shortage of carbines, the dragoons lacked the protection of long-range firearms and thus were unable to defend their own camps during attacks. Infantrymen therefore had to be assigned to duty with the dragoons to protect them. Cavalry (and armor) throughout modern history have normally worked with infantry in battle. The legion as an organization thus seemed to be a logical solution to one of Washington's organizational problems.

Congress complied with Washington's recommendation on 21 October 1780, directing that a legion would consist of four troops of mounted dragoons and two companies of dismounted dragoons. The men of the dismounted companies were to be armed as light infantry.

*The rank of *cornet* was the lowest commissioned officer rank in the dragoons of the time. Cornet in the dragoons was the equivalent of ensign in the infantry. In 1799 both ranks were abolished in the Regular Army and replaced by that of second lieutenant. *Cornet,* as a rank, survives today in the First Troop Philadelphia City Cavalry of the National Guard.

**The carbine of that period was a short-barreled, smoothbore shoulder arm.

The legionary organization was retained to the end of the war. Outstanding leaders of the legions included Henry (Light Horse Harry) Lee, William Washington, Charles Armand (the Marquis de la Rouërie), and Count Casimir Pulaski. Pulaski, by virtue of his appointment as "Commander of the Horse" in September 1777, is often referred to as the first Chief of Cavalry of the United States Army.

By 1780 the center of the war had shifted to the southern states, but large British commands remained in the north. The four dragoon regiments were split between the areas. In the north, they never again saw service as regiments, but special commands drawn from them raided strongholds and supply lines in New York and Long Island. On 9 November 1782, the 1st and 3d Continental Light Dragoons, then in the south, were consolidated to form Baylor's Dragoons. And when the war ended the regiments that had served in the south together could muster less than two hundred men.

Other mounted organizations figured prominently in the war. In the south were the commands of Francis Marion, Thomas Sumter, and Andrew Pickens. These partisan units were small organizations that operated independently and usually fought on foot, using their horses chiefly for transportation. Mounted frontiersmen were especially effective in the Battles of King's Mountain (October 1780) and Cowpens (January 1781) in the Carolinas. In the Battle of Guilford's Court House in March of 1781, Washington's dragoons and those of Henry Lee's legion fought mounted, Lee's dragoons having the first encounter with the enemy.

When the American Revolution came to an end in 1783, the remaining fragments of the Continental Cavalry were discharged. During the next fifty years mounted organizations existed in the Regular Army only for brief periods and then only as a very small part of the Army. The first such unit, a squadron of dragoons added in 1792, was broken up even before it was organized. Its four companies were assigned one each to the four sublegions that comprised the Legion of the United States. When that organization was abandoned in 1796, the Army returned to a regimental-type organization and the mounted portion was reduced to two companies. Two years later, when American relationships with France became strained, Congress authorized six new dragoon companies for service during the period of the differences between the two countries. The six new companies, together with the old ones, were to have formed a regiment of light dragoons, but for reasons of economy the new companies were never organized. Although the company officers were appointed, no enlisted dragoons were enrolled and no horses provided. In 1800 the two old companies were dismounted and two years later they, too, were disbanded.

For six years thereafter the Regular Army had no cavalry. From 1783 on, however, volunteer troops of horse existed in all the states. All volunteer militia organizations were recognized by the Militia Act of 1792. At least one mounted troop was authorized for each "division" of common militia infantry, but numerically the total cavalry was not to exceed one-eleventh of the infantry.

Mounted Kentucky militiamen figured prominently in General Anthony Wayne's victory over the Indians at Fallen Timbers in August 1794. There they helped drive the Indians from cover behind the fallen trees and into the open prairie where the Indians were at the mercy of the mounted soldiers.

War of 1812 to Civil War

By 1808 war with England was again threatening, and Congress increased the Regular Army by eight regiments—one each of light dragoons, light artillery, and riflemen and five of infantry. The dragoon regiment of eight companies constituted the only cavalry in the Regular establishment until 1812, when a second regiment was authorized. The two regiments were the cavalry force of the Regular Army during the War of 1812, and at no time were they at full authorized strength. Detachments from the regiments took part in a number of actions during 1812 and 1813—at Mississineway River in the Indiana Territory in December 1812, at the siege of Fort Meigs at the mouth of the Maumee River in Ohio the next spring, and later in Canada.

Early in 1814 Congress enacted legislation to improve the structure of the Army. By an act of 30 March the two dragoon regiments were consolidated into an 8-troop command designated the Regiment of Light Dragoons. Although the consolidated regiment seldom operated as a single unit and a year later was disbanded, detachments saw action at Lundy's Lane, Fort Erie, and Bladensburg.

Mounted militia companies throughout this period were a familiar sight in all the frontier campaigns and, when called upon, gave good account of themselves. Johnson's Kentucky Mounted Volunteers, for example, were at the Battle of the Thames River in Canada in 1813, and General Coffee's mounted Tennessee militia fought under Andrew Jackson in Alabama in 1814.

The Regiment of Dragoons was disbanded on 15 June 1815, and for seventeen years the Regular establishment again had no cavalry. Despite the arguments in Army circles for a small mounted force, Congress stood firm in its dedication to economy and a minimum standing Army.

During these years the western frontier moved well beyond the Allegheny Mountains, across the Mississippi River, up the Missouri, Arkansas, and Red Rivers, and into the plains area where the Indian was at home on horseback. By 1830 seven Army posts—scattered for 800 miles from Fort Snelling on the upper Mississippi to Fort Gibson on the Arkansas and garrisoned by detachments of Regular infantry and artillery—formed the only bulwark against Indian attack.

On occasion, mounted militia were called out to reinforce the Regulars. Although these volunteers were called cavalrymen, their horses usually were the same ones with which they had plowed the field and dragged logs for the new cabin. Despite poor military organization, the mounted volunteers were generally effective and constituted the only semblance of a cavalry force, but the reports of money spent to equip and pay them were later used by the advocates of cavalry to argue that a Regular force would be less expensive.

In 1813 uprisings by the Menominees at Prairie du Chien in the Northwest Territory and by Black Hawk's band at Rock Island, Illinois, provided tangible evidence of the need for an Army capable of tracking down and pursuing the Indians beyond their usual haunts. Finally, in June 1832, Congress authorized the organization of a Battalion of Mounted Rangers for defense of the frontier. Some 600 hardy frontiersmen were brought together. Experience with this battalion proved the value of a mounted force, but it also indicated the importance of having the force properly trained and disciplined. As a result, on 2 March 1833 Congress authorized a regiment of dragoons in lieu of the Battalion of Mounted Rangers. The new organization, the Regiment of United States Dragoons, was an answer to advocates of a mounted force as well as to the economy minded. It would be mounted for speed, yet trained and equipped to fight both mounted and dismounted.

The regiment, made up of a field and staff (headquarters) and 10 companies, had 34 officers and 714 men, many of whom were formerly in the Battalion of Mounted Rangers. The Ranger commander, Maj. Henry Dodge, was promoted to colonel and given command of the new regiment. Among others on the commissioned staff were a number of experienced infantrymen who were to become famous as cavalrymen. Lt. Col. Stephen Watts Kearny entered from the 3d Infantry, Lt. Jefferson Davis from the 1st Infantry, and Lt. Philip St. George Cooke from the 6th Infantry. The combination of Regulars and Rangers gave to the new regiment some officers with a thorough knowledge of military principles and others well acquainted with the type of action that all were soon to experience. None, however, were schooled in cavalry tactics. The officers of the regiment themselves practiced drilling in squads in order to be able to teach the men.

The Army then in the field consisted of 4 regiments (36 companies) of artillery, 7 regiments (70 companies) of infantry, and a regiment (10 companies) of dragoons. The total of 4,282 actually in field service manned some 50 posts scattered over the country.

While most of the Eastern Department had been cleared of Indians, three major tribes (Seminole, Creek, and Cherokee) remained in the southeast. The most troublesome were the Seminoles in Florida, and in 1835 eleven companies of artillery and infantry were sent south to subdue them. Maj. Gen. Winfield Scott, who commanded the force, reported on 29 January 1836 that no mounted troops would be needed, but later wrote that horsemen would be essential to the campaign, adding that two mounted Regular companies would be worth twice that number of foot. Meanwhile, the states were called upon for mounted troops.

Congress on 23 May 1836 authorized the raising of 10,000 volunteers and a second regiment of dragoons. The volunteers could be either foot or mounted and the dragoon regiment was to be a duplicate of the regiment of dragoons already in the service. To get the organization of the new Regular regiment started, a detachment of the 1st Regiment of Dragoons, already in Florida, was reorganized as a company of the 2d Regiment of Dragoons and recruiting stations were opened at various places in the Eastern Department. In December 1836 five companies, organized in New York and South Carolina, sailed for Savannah where they left their ships, mounted the horses brought to Georgia for their use, and proceeded to Florida. The men of the remaining companies were more fortunate; they went to Jefferson Barracks, Missouri, where the regimental commander opened a school of instruction for them. In October 1837 the trained companies joined the others in Florida, traveling 1,200 miles overland in 55 days.

In the Florida war, the 2d Dragoons fought mounted less frequently than dismounted. The swamps, marshes, and rivers that separated the hummocks where the Indians had built their villages were almost impassable on foot, and the horse was often an encumbrance.

Besides the Regular cavalry, many mounted volunteers entered the Federal service during the Seminole War. In the first year, 152 companies, totaling 10,712 men, were accepted from the nearby states, and a regiment of friendly Creek Indians was organized. A South Carolina regiment, the Indian regiment, and 35 additional companies served in Florida. The others were employed in Creek and Cherokee country and on the southwestern frontier, mainly to discourage other tribes from helping the Seminoles.

At the end of the Seminole War, the Army was greatly reduced, and the dragoons were hit hard. First, the strength of the company was reduced by 10 privates; next, the number of horses in a company was cut to 40; finally, effective 4 March 1843, the 2d Dragoons were dismounted and reorganized as the Regiment of Riflemen. To turn dragoons into riflemen, only three major changes in the regimental organization actually took place: horses were eliminated, rifles replaced carbines, and the farriers and blacksmiths were discharged. Nevertheless, by this act the mounted force of the U.S. Army was again reduced to one regiment.

No sooner were the dragoons dismounted than agitation for remounting them began. It was argued that at least two mounted regiments should be stationed on the western frontier and maintained there in readiness for swift offensive action. If action were not needed, the mounted force should make a show of strength at least once a year by marching into the Indian country. In 1844, as a result of these arguments and pressure from the frontier states for a greater number of mounted Regulars in that area, Congress passed legislation to remount the riflemen and to restore to the regiment its original designation. Instead of moving to the western frontier, however, the 2d Dragoons joined Brig. Gen. Zachary Taylor in Texas in 1845.

In 1846, after war with Mexico had begun, the mounted force was further increased. Legislation passed in May of that year to strengthen the entire Army included provision for seven regiments of cavalry manned by 12-month volunteers, a Regular regiment designated the Regiment of Mounted Riflemen, and an increase in the number of privates in each cavalry company.

The Regiment of Mounted Riflemen was constituted to help establish a military road to the Oregon Territory. For a number of years the opening of the road, part of it through unexplored territory, had been discussed. Money was finally appropriated and a plan developed calling for forts from the Missouri to the Columbia. That there ought to be military protection for the project was evident, and for once a mounted force appeared to be the most economical solution.

Debates in Congress on organizing this new force brought out the point that mounted troops could be used to carry the mail, as messengers, and to guard settlers going west. One member of Congress said he would vote for raising the regiment just to restore a rifle regiment to the Army. Although the United States had once been the rifle country of the world, he contended, it had fallen behind the European nations. There was not one rifle regiment in the establishment. He further stated that the unit should be mounted because, he thought, it was idle to send infantry against Indians who would be on horseback.

Headquarters of the Regiment of Mounted Riflemen was established at Jefferson Barracks in October 1846. The companies, organized at Fort McHenry, Maryland, in Columbus, Ohio, and at Jefferson Barracks, were concentrated at the barracks by the end of the year. But, instead of going to Oregon as intended, the unit joined General Scott's force in Mexico. In crossing the Gulf of Mexico from New Orleans to Point Isabel, Texas, the horses were washed overboard during a storm and the regiment, except for two companies mounted on captured Mexican horses, had to fight as infantry.

The regiment was armed with the Model 1841 rifle and a flintlock pistol. Through the efforts of Capt. Samuel H. Walker of the regiment and inventor Samuel Colt, the War Department purchased 1,000 Colt single-action, 6-shot revolvers for the regiment. More than 200 of the revolvers reached Vera Cruz before the end of the war, but there is no record that the unit used them in the Mexican War campaigns.

As first organized, each company of the Regiment of Mounted Riflemen had 64 privates; in 1847 the number was increased to 70, equalizing that of the dragoons. At this time, too, the regiments of dragoons and riflemen were each authorized an additional major, to be promoted from among the captains.

When, because of the Mexican War, the Regular establishment was further increased by 10 new regiments in 1847, 9 were infantry, and the tenth was designated the 3d Regiment of Dragoons. Even though classed as Regular, these 10 units were formed only for the duration and were disbanded at the close of the war.

The Mexican War afforded U.S. mounted Regular troops the first opportunity since the Revolution to engage mounted troops of a foreign organized army, and American cavalrymen took part in all of the major campaigns of the war. The 2d Dragoons were in every battle from Palo Alto to Chapultepec. The Mounted Riflemen, fighting dismounted at Chapultepec, earned from General Winfield Scott, Commanding General of the Army, the compliment that became their motto: "Brave Rifles! Veterans! You have been baptized in fire and blood and have come out steel."

During the war the regiments were broken up and the companies scattered. As in the Seminole War they often fought as infantry, but their usual missions were reconnaissance and pursuit. Several small engagements, however, were decided by traditional cavalry charges—horses at the gallop, sabers slashing. A good example was the action at Morena Bridge, near Vera Cruz, on 25 March 1847, when Col. William S. Harney placed his dismounted dragoons and infantry on the right and left of the bridge, holding mounted dragoons in reserve. After a few rounds of artillery from two cannon, the foot soldiers attacked. Once they had made some headway against the enemy, the mounted men joined in and, with their sabers swinging, drove the Mexicans across the bridge. The Mexicans re-formed on the far side, but when the cavalry thundered over the bridge the enemy broke once again, and the dragoons pursued.

While Generals Scott and Taylor with most of the Regular Army and the Volunteers were winning battles in Mexico, the commands of Col. Stephen Watts Kearny and Capt. John C. Fremont were securing California and New Mexico for the United States. Colonel Kearny's force, principally mounted, consisted of his own 1st Regiment of Dragoons, the 1st Regiment of Missouri Volunteer Cavalry under Col. Alexander W. Doniphan, a mounted company from St. Louis known as the Laclede Rangers, two batteries of artillery, two small companies of volunteer infantry, and some Indian guides. Fremont had a very small command consisting principally of mounted frontiersmen.

When the war with Mexico came to an end and the usual postwar reductions of the Army began, the Regiment of Mounted Riflemen was retained as a part of the Regular establishment. All the other new regiments were mustered out, and the Volunteers were discharged and returned home.

The Regiment of Mounted Riflemen was at once ordered overland to Oregon, but many of its members took advantage of a wartime law that

AN AMERICAN CAVALRY CHARGE AT THE BATTLE OF RESACA DE LA PALMA

permitted Regulars to receive discharges at the conclusion of hostilities. As a result, the depleted regiment had to wait for recruits at Fort Leavenworth, Kansas. On 10 May 1849 it started its 2,000-mile trek westward, but still its organizational problems continued. After reaching the Oregon Territory the riflemen deserted in droves to go to California and join in the search for gold. In 1851 a mere skeleton of the regiment returned to Jefferson Barracks. It was again brought up to strength and then sent to the Department of Texas where, to implement the treaty of Guadalupe Hidalgo, it tried to keep the Indians of Mexico out of the United States and those of the United States in.

By 1853 the Army of 15 regiments—4 artillery, 8 infantry, and 3 cavalry— was thinly distributed over a greatly expanded country. Artillerymen garrisoned the forts of the eastern and southern coastal areas and along the Canadian border, while infantry and cavalrymen in companies and troops dotted the area westward from the Mississippi River. Seldom were more than two cavalry troops stationed together.

Although by that time the strength of the Army had been increased by some 3,000 to provide additional privates to companies then in the Indian country, arguments for further increases continued. The Secretary of War asked especially that more cavalry be organized for service in the Pacific Department and between the Rockies and the Sierra Nevada Range. In his report of 4 December 1854 he proposed that the horse regiments be brought under one arm:

The cavalry force of our army being all required for active service of the same kind, there appears no propriety in making a permanent distinction in the designation and armament of the several regiments; it is, therefore, proposed to place all the regiments of cavalry on the same footing in these respects, and to leave it in the power of the executive to arm and equip them in such manner as may be required by the nature of the service in which they may be employed.

In 1855 the mounted force grew by two regiments. This time the new organizations were called *cavalry*. The 1st and 2d Cavalry were constituted on 3 March 1855 not by an act expressly dealing with Army organization, but by an addition to an appropriations bill. The two regiments were organized in the same manner as existing horse regiments but, contrary to the Secretary's recommendation, General Orders prescribing their organization made them a distinct and separate arm. Thus, the mounted force consisted of dragoons, mounted riflemen, and cavalrymen.

The 1st and 2d Cavalry were provisionally armed and equipped with available weapons. A board composed of the field officers of the two commands met in Washington in early 1855 and recommended that parts of their regiments be furnished experimental arms and equipment for trial purposes. As a result, the companies received various types of carbines, including a Springfield that was muzzle-loading, and the Merrill and the Perry, both of which loaded at the breech. Their pistols were Navy-pattern Colt revolvers and their sabers the Prussian type used by the dragoons. The dragoons remained armed with their Mexican War weapons—the Hall carbines, sabers, and horse pistols. The mounted riflemen had their Colt revolvers and percussion rifles, but they were not issued sabers. Although the rifles could be fired from horseback, the riflemen were expected to do most of their fighting dismounted.

For the Army, the years between 1848 and 1860 were marked by a succession of marches, expeditions, and campaigns against the Indians. The Army also provided protection for the settlers' wagon trains, and it explored and surveyed the hostile Indian country. In this period, too, the slavery problem increased in intensity. When open warfare broke out in Kansas Territory between slavery and antislavery factions, nearly all the 1st Cavalry and the 2d Dragoons, together with some infantry companies, were sent there to keep the peace. They succeeded in stopping the fighting, but soon thereafter these companies and the rest of the Army were involved in a major conflict that lasted four long years.

Civil War

At the outbreak of the Civil War in 1861, the mounted forces in the Regular Army consisted of the five regiments mentioned, still bearing their different names—dragoons, riflemen, and cavalry—and still considered three distinct arms. Besides their different firearms and the number of privates per company, which varied from time to time, the regiments had uniforms that differed principally in the color of the trim, which in 1861 was orange for the dragoons, green for the riflemen, and yellow for the cavalry. The three arms also had distinctive insignia. The dragoons and cavalrymen wore crossed sabers and the riflemen "a trumpet perpendicular." In later years the trumpet perpendicular was incorporated in the coat of arms and distinctive insignia of the 3d Cavalry—now 3d Armored Cavalry—the descendant organization of the Regiment of Mounted Riflemen.***

Small as they were, the Regular mounted forces could have been of valuable service in the early days of the Civil War if they had been readily available, but they were not. When the war began the companies of the horse regiments were widely scattered over the country; most were in the west and southwest, too distant for ready concentration. In the Battle of Bull Run in July 1861 only seven companies of Regular cavalry were included in the Union Army of about 40,000 men.

So wide a distribution of the nation's mounted forces would in itself have been sufficient cause for concern to the Army in the opening battles. Other factors, however, were equally disruptive and hard to overcome. Many officers joined the Confederacy—four of the five colonels commanding the mounted regiments resigned from the Army. More important, however, was the fact that the military leaders of the day neither valued nor understood the potential of the horse regiments. Although the cavalrymen on the western Plains had learned through experience that the continuous, long-range fire of the new breech-loading rifles had destroyed the effectiveness of the saber charge against infantry, General Scott and others in Washington clung to that precept for the employment of cavalry. They did not visualize the effective employment of cavalry in broken, wooded areas. Believing that the war would be short, and noting the cost of arming, equipping, and training a mounted force, they agreed that the new improved firearms carried by the less expensive infantry rendered a more mobile force unnecessary. In January 1862 Maj. Gen. George B. McClellan urged the Secretary of War to authorize no more cavalry, to reduce the number of cavalry regiments then in the field, and to strengthen the regiments of this arm that were retained. Nevertheless, before the war ended, 272 regiments, plus 45 separate battalions, and 78 separate companies of cavalry saw service in the Union Army. Although no complete official roll of the organizations in the Confederate cavalry has been found, various estimates exist, and of

***For convenience, the word *cavalry,* unless otherwise indicated, will be understood to mean all three mounted forces.

SUTTER'S FORT, *a pre-Civil War Army post in California. (From a lithograph by William Endicott.)*

these the most reliable shows 137 regiments, 143 separate battalions, and 101 separate companies of cavalry.

Unlike the infantry regiments, which were first mustered in to serve three months, the volunteer cavalry commands were accepted first for one year and later for three. The expense involved in equipping the cavalry soldier was still considerably greater than that for the infantryman, and it also took longer to train the cavalryman and his mount. Many organizations were severely reduced long before the term of enlistment had expired, but, since no satisfactory replacement system was ever agreed upon by all of the states and the Federal Government, the earlier regiments were retained at skeletal strength while whole new organizations entered the conflict.

While a number of mounted regiments and smaller organizations of Volunteers were mustered in for service in the Union Army, only one mounted regiment was added to the Regular establishment during the entire four years of the war. The new Regular regiment, at first designated the 3d Cavalry, differed from the other horse regiments in that from its beginning it had 12 companies instead of 10. In it, 2 companies constituted a squadron, and 2 squadrons a battalion, which was commanded by a major. A company could have any number of privates up to 72. In contrast, the volunteer regiments were modeled after the pattern of the old Regular cavalry.

In August 1861 all six Regular horse regiments were redesignated cavalry and renumbered as the 1st through the 6th in order, according to their respective dates of organization. All were to be armed with the saber, revolver, and carbine. Although these regiments had been known by different names, all were light cavalry. Their members were mounted on light horses, they were trained to fight mounted or dismounted, and they depended on their firearms rather than shock action with sabers. Nevertheless, the dragoons and riflemen objected to giving up their distinctive names. One captain wrote that with the renaming of the old regiments the units lost the honor attached to the old names, and the change had a demoralizing effect on the troops. The dragoons and riflemen also resisted the changes in their distinctive uniform trim; now all were expected to wear the yellow trimmings of the cavalry. Fortunately, from the dragoon and riflemen point of view, under an economy measure that permitted the use of the old uniforms until they were worn out, much orange and green trim was in evidence for a long time.

In July 1862 the number of companies in the five oldest cavalry regiments was increased from ten to twelve, thus giving them the same number of companies as the new regiment. At that time, too, the fixed squadron and battalion organization was abandoned. In actual field service, however, usually four companies, but often fewer, operated as a squadron or battalion.

In 1863 the number of privates authorized in each cavalry company was increased to one hundred, but probably no company ever succeeded in having that many men present and equipped for duty. Recruiting for Regular Army units was extremely difficult in the face of state competition. Bounties offered by Federal officers were met and exceeded by the states. So attractive were their offers that many men enlisted in one unit, deserted, and enlisted in another just to collect the bounties.

During the first two years of the war, the rule of service in the Union Army was to assign one or more regiments of cavalry to each division of infantry for such duties as the division commander might order. The regiments were then broken down into small detachments for use as orderlies and escorts for general officers, guards for division wagon trains, and pickets to protect the front of infantry lines. Although the cavalry did some effective work in the field, its discipline and morale suffered for want of a responsible chief and of a compact organization. Some cavalry brigades were organized and attached to the various corps in the summer of 1862, but it was not until 1863 that the cavalry made more than an indifferent showing. By then, as the war entered what Maj. Gen. William T. Sherman called its professional stage, the Union cavalry had gained the experience, organization, weapons, and remount service it needed, and from that time on its superiority grew steadily.

GENERAL SHERIDAN

Soon after assuming command of the Army of the Potomac in January 1863, Maj. Gen. Joseph Hooker authorized the formation of a Cavalry Corps. The various regiments and brigades scattered through the Army were combined into divisions and placed in a separate command, a major step toward consolidation, but the idea still prevailed in the Army that the cavalry should be used for the infantry's protection and convenience.

Another cavalry improvement in 1863 was the establishment of a Cavalry Bureau, the chief of which was charged with responsibility for organizing and equipping the cavalry forces and providing their mounts and remounts. He was also responsible for establishing depots for the reception of cavalry recruits and for the collection and initial training of cavalry horses. The Giesboro Depot in the District of Columbia became the principal remount depot for the supply of the armies in the east; St. Louis and Nashville were the depots in the Mississippi Valley.

Cavalry in the Union Army became a really effective force in 1864. Maj. Gen. Philip H. Sheridan, who assumed command of the Cavalry Corps of the Army of the Potomac in April of that year, believed that the functions of a large body of cavalry attached to an active army were not limited to guarding wagon trains or serving as advance guards or flankers for infantry columns, and upon assuming his new command he demanded the right to use the corps independently. He proved that a large force of cavalry, properly organized and led and acting as a unit, could be successful against either cavalry or infantry.

Under Sheridan's leadership, the Union cavalry played a conspicuous part in numerous operations of 1864 and 1865. Some good examples are Sheridan's raid on Richmond, Maj. Gen. James H. Wilson's invasion of Alabama, and the flank attacks on Lee's army in the campaign that ended at Appomattox.

Whereas the Union leaders were slow to recognize the true value of and the need for a mounted force, the Confederate leaders seemed from the beginning to appraise cavalry and its functions at their true value. For the first two years of the war the Confederate cavalry was a strong, well-organized force, proving its efficiency on many occasions. Even before the Army of Northern Virginia was organized, separate mounted companies of the South demonstrated their effectiveness by destroying bridges along the Confederate first line of defense and gathering information about Union actions. Instead of being wasted in detail, the Confederate cavalry regiments and battalions, which had the same organization as those of the Union, were grouped into large forces capable of independent action and permitted to perform it.

The Confederate cavalry was the first to demonstrate the effectiveness of the cavalry raid, a distinct product of the American Civil War. By the end of 1862, Maj. Gen. J. E. B. Stuart and his cavalrymen had successfully accomplished two raids by which they not only gained information about the Union Army's strengths and dispositions but also obtained much needed supplies. Of equal importance, Stuart's raids greatly alarmed Federal leaders in Washington, causing them to draw off troops for the defense of that city.

The Confederate cavalry also included the partisan groups led by Brig. Gens. Turner Ashby, John H. Morgan, and Col. John Mosby. These very active commands were classified as cavalry because their men were excellent horsemen. Since the groups operated either wholly in Confederate territory or, as in the case of Morgan, in and out of friendly territory at their own dictates, they were usually able to keep themselves supplied with good mounts. They were also deserving of the name cavalry for the service they performed. The men were expert raiders who made sudden and successful attacks upon Union outposts and supply trains and disrupted lines of communications, brought in reliable information about strengths and movements, and sometimes fought delaying actions.

Unfortunately for the Confederacy, the effectiveness of its cavalry began to decline about the same time that that of the Union cavalry was on the increase. The Confederate decline was due partly to the increased efficiency of the Union horse units and partly to the fact that the South's sources of supply of both men and horses were diminishing.

Indian Wars Period

At the end of the Civil War the ranks of the Regular cavalry regiments were thin indeed, as were those of the other Regular regiments. Of the 448 companies of cavalry, infantry, and artillery authorized, 153 were not organized, and few,

5TH CAVALRY CHARGING AT GAINES MILL, VIRGINIA, 1864. (*From a painting by W. T. Trego.*)

if any, of those in being were at full strength. By July 1866 this shortage had eased since many of the members of the disbanded Volunteer outfits had by then enlisted as Regulars. By that time, however, it became apparent in Washington that the Army, even at full strength, was not large enough to perform all its duties. Consequently, on 28 July Congress authorized 4 additional cavalry regiments and enough infantry companies to reorganize the existing 19 regiments—then under two different internal organizations—into 45 regiments with 10 companies each. After this increase there were 10 regiments of cavalry, 5 of artillery, and 45 of infantry. Cavalry companies accounted for 20 percent of the total number of company-sized organizations. The Regular Army's authorized strength of approximately 57,000 officers and men was then more than double what it had been at the close of the war. The whole arrangement was remarkable because it was the first time in the nation's history that the Regular establishment had been increased substantially immediately after a war.

Recruiting for the increase began at once. Emphasis was placed upon securing veteran Volunteers before they left the service. The officers were selected from both Volunteers and Regulars; each candidate was required to have had at last two years of honorable service in the Civil War.

The new cavalry regiments, numbered 7th, 8th, 9th, and 10th, were organized under the same tables as the 6 already in existence. A regiment consisted of 12 companies formed into 3 squadrons of 4 companies each. Besides the commanding officer who was a colonel, the regimental staff included 7 officers, 6 enlisted men, a surgeon, and 2 assistant surgeons. Each company was authorized 4 officers, 15 noncommissioned officers, and 72 privates. A civilian veterinarian accompanied the regiment although he was not included in the table of organization.

The 9th and 10th Cavalry were composed of Negro enlisted men and white officers. Their organization differed from the others in that each had an assigned chaplain whose duties included instructing the enlisted men in fundamental school subjects. At that time and until 1901, chaplains were normally assigned to Army posts.

During the Civil War, some cavalry companies began to call themselves troops. For many years the smallest unit for administrative purposes in the cavalry was officially the company. The word *troop* had first officially been used in an act of 17 July 1862, which prescribed the organization of a "company or troop." The next step came when the revised regulations of 1873 omitted *company*. Yet for almost ten more years the U.S. Army had cavalry companies. By 1881 many units were using the newer term, and in 1883 all were directed to use it. Still later, however, it was not unusual for both terms to be used in the same regiment.

Another important provision of the act of 28 July 1866 was the authorization of a corps of Indian Scouts as an integral part of the Army. Before 1866, friendly Indians had often been employed as Army guides on the frontier, but they were not officially a part of the establishment. Under the new arrangement 1,000 Indians could be enlisted as scouts in the Indian country. They were apportioned to the various commands and continued to be used in varying numbers for about fifty years. They were last employed in the Punitive Expedition into Mexico in 1916. Most commanders found the scouts to be excellent light cavalrymen.

Among the peacetime problems the Army helped to solve, those occurring in the Great Plains and the Far West most needed the services of the mounted arm. By 1868 the bulk of the cavalry was in the west. Ninety-two companies were stationed among 59 posts within the vast area from the Canadian border to the Rio Grande and from Kansas to California. The Plains Indians who inhabited much of this area were splendid riders. They traveled and fought on horseback with a skill that gained the respect of the U.S. cavalrymen. They had mobility and speed, and since these features were characteristic of American cavalry, mounted soldiers were a more effective force than infantry in employment against them. The cavalrymen pursued marauding Indians on horseback,

INDIAN WARFARE. (*From a painting by Charles Schreyvogel.*)

and if the chase ended, as it usually did, in a dismounted fight, the cavalrymen were trained for that as well.

During the years immediately following the Civil War, the Army was indispensable to the opening of the Plains area. The numerous discoveries of precious metals, the availability of cheap land, and the construction of wagon roads and railroads brought more and more settlers to the new west. All needed military protection since the Indians resisted the encroachment of white society. The many posts established ahead of settlements, and abandoned when the frontier had moved beyond them, testify to the fact that the Army continuously cleared the way for civilization.

The fluid condition of the frontier caused most of the Army's work to be performed by small units. Usually a company of infantry and one of cavalry garrisoned a post, but often a single company constituted the only military protection for miles. One officer wrote that his men, few in number, kept horses saddled at all times to be ready for the danger, which was ever-present. In 1882 the troops of the 10 cavalry regiments were dispersed among 55 posts in the Indian country. The posts having the largest mounted forces were located in the Departments of Missouri and Texas. The 1st and 5th Cavalry were the most widely dispersed, troops of the 1st occupying 10 stations in Washington, Oregon, Idaho, Nevada, and California, and those of the 5th 7 posts in Wyoming and Nebraska.

Such fragmentation made serious training for a foreign war impossible. Even though the country was well insulated and did not seem to be threatened by foreign powers, the high command recognized as a dangerous liability the inability to concentrate and train its units. Maj. Gen. John M. Schofield, commander of the Division of the Pacific 1882–83 and of the Division of Missouri 1883–86, described the Army as a mere police force. Beginning in the 1880's, to offset the evils of fragmentation, schools were established to give intensive training. The first of these was the School of Application for Infantry and Cavalry founded at Fort Leavenworth, Kansas, in 1881. Here, graduates of West Point put to practical application the theories they had learned at the Academy. Here, also, came student officers detailed from the field to improve the knowledge of their profession. The school troops came from the four companies of infantry and four of cavalry, plus the one light battery of artillery, which garrisoned the post. Twenty years later the school was expanded into the General Service and Staff College and opened to officers of all branches; today it is the Command and General Staff College.

In 1887 Congress appropriated $200,000 for a school at Fort Riley, Kansas, to instruct enlisted men of cavalry and light artillery, but five years went by before the Cavalry and Light Artillery School was formally established. Once it opened its doors, however, complete regimental troops and batteries trained there, as did recruits before they joined a regiment. In the years that followed, the school changed names several times, in 1907 becoming the Mounted Service School; in 1919, the Cavalry School; on 1 November 1946, the Ground General School; and in 1950, the Army General School. The school was discontinued in May 1955.

When first established, the School of Application for Infantry and Cavalry and the Cavalry and Light Artillery School were simply military posts with a training responsibility added. The department commander could order the men at the post off to duty at any time, but while not otherwise employed the garrisons formed the basis for practical instruction that enabled the officers and men who participated to study the duties of the soldier in garrison, in camp, and on the march.

The U.S. cavalry did not fight against a formally organized foe during the period of 1866–91, but doctrine and drill did evolve for use should such an enemy appear. The foundation of all the rules was the basic thought that cavalrymen must be drilled as infantry and must at all times be prepared to fight on foot. Such a provision was no more than a natural extension of Civil War experience. Instructions for mounted cavalry charges were also included.

A rather startling alteration occurred when the cavalry in 1873 adapted the *Infantry Tactics,* accepted by the infantry in 1867, as its drill manual. This system, prepared by Maj. Gen. Emory Upton, altered previous teaching because it based troop evolutions upon movements by fours. These movements were suited to drill with horses since they allowed room for the mounts to maneuver where earlier ones had not. The cavalry continued to drill by the infantry system until late in 1891, when the War Department issued separate sets of drill regulations for the cavalry, infantry, and artillery. For the cavalry, the squadron consisted of not more than four and not less than two troops, and the troop in marching was divided into two, three, or four platoons, depending upon the number of fours.

Improvement in troop distribution came about very slowly. During the late 1880's subjugation of most of the Indians and completion of many miles of railroad made possible the concentration of larger forces at fewer posts. Unfortunately, cavalry did not profit to the same degree as infantry. Indeed, until the outbreak of the War with Spain in 1898, all the cavalry units except one squadron at Fort Myer, Virginia, and one at Fort Ethan Allen, Vermont, were still stationed in the west. In that area, 92 troops remained divided among 31 posts. In many instances, as before, one troop formed the entire garrison of a post; at others there were as many as four troops; the average was two.

From 1866 until 1901 no new cavalry regiments were added to the Regular Army. There were, however, some alterations in regimental organization. In the major reduction of the Army in 1869–70, the cavalry companies lost a few non-commissioned officers, but for six years thereafter the authorized strength and organization of the companies were unchanged. In the meantime, campaigns against the Indians continued and commanders clamored for more mounted troops. At the time cavalry still constituted about one-fifth of the entire Army, roughly the same ratio as in France and Germany.

In June 1876 the Sioux wiped out Col. George A. Custer and nearly half (5 companies) of the 7th Cavalry at the Little Big Horn. Partly as a result of this catastrophe, Congress voted a permanent increase in the mounted force. The new law actually cut 5,000 from the total number of enlisted men in the Army as a whole, but added 2,500 to the cavalry units employed against the Indians. Each company so employed could have 100 enlisted men, provided the total Army strength of 25,000, then authorized, was exceeded by no more than 2,500. The maximum 100-man cavalry company continued until 1890, but few units reached the authorized strength and fewer maintained it.

By 1890 the abatement of the Indian threat brought about the first reduction in cavalry since the Civil War Troops L and M of all regiments were disbanded and the number of privates in each of the other companies was reduced to 44, in effect a reduction of about 50 percent.

A Crow Indian Trooper, Troop L, 1st Cavalry, Fort Custer, Montana

The next year part of the cut was restored in an experiment that attempted to integrate Indian soldiers into Regular Army units. The primary object was to give employment to a considerable number of warriors from the most dangerous tribes. Troops L of the 1st through the 8th Cavalry were reactivated with Indian enlisted personnel drawn, as nearly as possible, from the area in which each regiment was serving. For example, Troop L, 1st Cavalry, in Montana was filled in a very short time by members of the Crow tribe. That fall (1891), the regimental commander reported that the new troopers possessed all the characteristics and traits essential to good light cavalry. Nevertheless, due partly to the language barrier and partly to the general attitude that existed between the two races, the experiment failed and the last unit of this type, Troop L, 7th Cavalry, was disbanded in 1897.

Changes in the arms, uniforms, and accouterments of cavalry were few and slow. The large supply of equipment on hand in 1865, sufficient to equip the regiments for a number of years, delayed readjustments. The Spencer repeater carbines, furnished the horseman during the war, were gradually replaced after 1873 by the converted single-shot Springfield rifle and carbines of the same pattern, both .45-caliber. In the category of hand guns, a few .45-caliber Colt revolvers, using metallic cartridges, were purchased in 1871–72 for testing. These revolvers became standard and remained so until replaced in 1894 by the smaller caliber .38.

Brig. Gen. George Crook, the Indian fighter and peacemaker, improved the logistics of the Indian Wars when he discarded wagon trains in favor of pack mules and thus could usually have supplies at hand. There was no waiting for the trains to catch up because the mules, each carrying about 200 pounds, were a part of the column.

Although at the beginning of the Civil War cavalry horses were scarce in the Union Army, the shortage was soon corrected and at the war's end the Army had a surplus of horses of all classes, including those for the cavalry. During the year following the close of the war, the Army sold more than 104,000 horses of all classes at public auction, and as of 30 June 1866 it still had at depots 4,645 surplus serviceable horses, of which 3,829 were for the cavalry. During the year 1866, only 150 more were purchased and they were for use in the Department of California where it was wiser to buy than to risk transporting from the east.

In 1883 the Army began to purchase horses in open market (from farmers, ranchers, and others) instead of by contract as had been the custom. This system appealed to cavalry officers and they fought for its retention when the contract method was resumed two years later. Their attitude can be understood, for in open-market procurement cavalry officers inspected and purchased horses for the cavalry, while under the contract method the Quartermaster General's Department procured and inspected all types of horses for the Army. Naturally cavalrymen, believing that only cavalrymen could select cavalry horses, objected to the change.

Cavalry officers also fought for the establishment of a remount station where all cavalry horses would be broken and trained before being shipped to the troops, and where better horses could be bred. General Crook's description of a shipment of forty horses received in his command in 1884 shows why the officers felt as they did. One of the forty bucked itself to death, another died of an obscure disease, a third gave out on the road, and sixteen were condemned by a board of officers of the regiment receiving them.

Giesboro and other depots that had made possible a ready supply of mounts during the Civil War were closed when the Cavalry Bureau was abolished on 4 October 1866. Then Carlisle, Pennsylvania, became the principal cavalry depot, but was important as a station for collecting recruits rather than for breaking and training horses. Even four years later in 1870 when the principal cavalry depot was established at St. Louis Arsenal in the midst of what was then the horse country, the depot was not important as a remount station. Thus, despite the arguments for a more effective remount service, no stations were established for this purpose until almost forty years later. In May of 1908

Congress authorized the establishment of a remount service, and the War Department turned over to the Quartermaster Department the Fort Reno reservation for use as a remount depot. Additional stations were opened in 1911 at Fort Keogh in Montana and at Front Royal, Virginia, and in 1916 at El Paso and Fort Sam Houston, Texas.

The cavalry fought its last Indian battle of any significance in the winter of 1890–91 when it engaged and subdued the Sioux at Wounded Knee Creek in southwestern South Dakota. Except for labor uprisings for which the Army sometimes was called out, the next few years were comparatively peaceful.

1892–1916

The years following the Indian Wars saw some improvements in the mounted arm. There were the new drill regulations, already mentioned, and the Army adopted a new shoulder arm—the Krag-Jörgensen. Manufactured as both a carbine and a rifle, the Krag-Jörgensen was a .30-caliber magazine weapon. It had a muzzle velocity of about 2,000 feet per second, and it used a cartridge containing smokeless powder. The new weapon was not in full supply by 1898 when the United States intervened in the trouble between Spain and her island possessions, but there were enough carbines to equip the Regular cavalry and one regiment of Volunteers.

Despite minor improvements, the U.S. cavalry of 1898 was not prepared for war. Enlisted cavalrymen numbered fewer than 6,000, and they were as scattered as at the opening of the Civil War, mainly through the western part of the country, though part of the 3d Cavalry was at Fort Ethan Allen, Vermont, and part of the 6th Cavalry was at Fort Myer, Virginia. Most of the troopers were garrisoning posts in Montana, Wyoming, Colorado, Kansas, and other western states. Again they were called in from great distances, some arriving on their mounts and others coming by rail.

Except for their wide dispersion, the Regular cavalry regiments of 1898 were in no worse condition than was the rest of the Army at the time. There were then only 27,000 enlisted men in the entire Army and therefore the Army had to be strengthened. For the Regular cavalry, an act of 26 April 1898 authorized the reactivation of 2 troops in each regiment—some of the reactivated troops had been inactive since 1890, and others were last filled with Indians—and added to each troop a lieutenant, a sergeant, 4 corporals, and 34 privates. A troop then aggregated 104 and a regiment 1,262 officers and men.

There was no further increase in the Regular mounted arm then, but the Regular force was augmented by Volunteer organizations mustered for short terms. They were of two classes: the Volunteer Army of the United States, consisting of State Organized Militia units; and the United States Volunteers, consisting of new units recruited at large. Of the first type, three regiments and nine separate troops of cavalry were mustered in from eight states. Illinois, Texas, and Ohio each furnished a regiment; Pennsylvania, three troops (Philadelphia City Troop, Governor's Troop, and Sheridan's Troop); Kentucky and New York, two troops each; and Nevada and Utah, one troop each. The Pennsylvanian and New York troops served in Puerto Rico and the Nevada troop in the Philippine Islands. The others did not leave the United States. Many of these units have since had continuous existence in their respective states. Now, having been converted and reorganized to be of present-day usefulness, they no longer bear the name cavalry, but each proudly remembers its origin and record in the old arm.

Acts of Congress approved on 22 and 23 April 1898 authorized the Secretary of War to organize from the nation at large Volunteer units having special qualifications. These units were to have federally appointed officers and were not to exceed a total of 3,000 men. Although Congress did not specify that the specially qualified units would be cavalry, the regiments organized under these acts were the First, Second, and Third United States Volunteer Cavalry. Of these, only one, the First United States Volunteer Cavalry, took part in the War with Spain. This regiment, better known as the "Rough Riders," had as its leaders Col. Leonard Wood and Lt. Col. Theodore Roosevelt. When organized in May 1898, the First United States Volunteer Cavalry mustered 47 officers and 994 enlisted men. It served dismounted in Cuba from 22 June until 8 August 1898 and was disbanded 15 September of the same year. The Second and Third United States Volunteer Cavalry were organized in May 1898 and disbanded in the fall of that year without having been outside the United States.

Antiquated militia laws, in effect since 1792, permitted the induction into Federal service of state organizations, poorly trained and equipped, and far below authorized strength. A look at the equipment these units brought in explains to some extent their lack of training. The firearms belonging to many of the units were worthless outmoded pieces that had to be replaced by the Federal Government. In exchange for their unserviceable arms, they received the single-shot Springfield .45-caliber rifles or carbines. These were of two models, 1896 and 1898, and the safety lock on the 1896 model worked exactly opposite to that on the 1898 model. This difference accounted for some of the objections raised by men who received the Springfields, but their complaints were partially adjusted when an effort was made to furnish only one model within a unit. Another objection to the Springfield was based upon a comparison of it with the newer smaller-caliber Krag-Jörgensen, adopted in 1892 as a standard arm for Regulars. The Krag-Jörgensen was in short supply, while the supply of Springfields was plentiful. Fortunately the Volunteers, after training with the Springfields, were almost convinced that its single-shot action, except in rapid-fire target practice, was as effective as the newer magazine-type carbine, and that the Springfield's larger bullet was more deadly.

Two large forces, one in the east and one in the west, assembled simultaneously. In preparation for service in two widely separated parts of the world, thousands of men and horses moved by way of Chickamauga, Georgia, to Tampa, Florida, for shipment to the West Indies and some 10,000 men in San Francisco awaited transportation to the Philippine Islands. Many ships were needed to move them and only a few were available. No cavalry was included in the first three shipments to the Philippines.

The Regular cavalrymen who moved east for service in the West Indies were little affected by the climate and inconveniences of the southern camps, but they were not prepared for the problems occasioned by the lack of shipping space. Because there was no room on the transports for them, about one-third of the men of each regiment and all of the horses, except those of the officers, were left behind when the expedition finally got under way. Once in combat, the troopers again demonstrated their ability to fight on foot as well as mounted.

In accordance with the act of 22 April 1898, the U.S. forces were organized into Army corps, divisions, and brigades. These were provisional commands, which ceased to exist after the war ended. Among the general officers chosen to head these larger organizations were many who had achieved prominence as cavalry leaders in the Civil and Indian Wars. Of particular interest is the fact that two former Confederate cavalrymen, for many years forbidden to serve in the United States Army, were among them—Maj. Gen. Joseph Wheeler and Maj. Gen. Fitzhugh Lee. General Wheeler commanded the cavalry division in the West Indies, and it was he who later asked for cavalrymen and their mounts in the Philippine Islands. General Lee commanded the Seventh Corps in Florida.

General Wheeler's dismounted cavalry division in Cuba consisted of about 3,000 troopers from the 1st, 3d, 6th, 9th, and 10th Cavalry and the Rough Riders. Armed with their carbines and revolvers—their sabers were left behind with the horses—and fighting as infantry, they won a victory at La Guasima on 24 June and about a week later joined the infantrymen in storming and capturing San Juan Hill and capturing the city of Santiago. In this action the Rough Riders, who in their eagerness dashed ahead of the Regulars and caught the first fire from the Spaniards' Mauser rifles, suffered heavy casualties.

There was also one mounted squadron in Cuba and one mounted troop in Puerto Rico. The squadron, composed of Troops A, C, D, and F of 2d Cavalry, mounted on local horses and commanded by Lt. Col. William A. Rafferty, formed part of an independent brigade under Brig. Gen. John C. Bates. In the dense undergrowth covering most of the country, the squadron was unable to perform some of the duties usually assigned to a mounted command, but in the Battle of El Caney its mounted detachments escorted batteries and trains to

COL. THEODORE ROOSEVELT AND A GROUP OF HIS ROUGH RIDERS

the front lines, and the individual troopers acted as couriers and litter bearers. The other mounted unit, in Puerto Rico, was Troop C, New York Volunteer Cavalry.

Although no cavalry units went to the Philippine Islands in 1898, one regiment, the 4th, arrived the next year and less than two years later eight Regular regiments were employed there. In the meantime, the term of service of the Volunteers mustered for the War with Spain having expired with the signing of the Treaty of Paris, Congress acted on 2 March 1899, to increase the military force. Among other measures, it authorized three additional cavalry units and an increase in the number of enlisted men in a cavalry troop to one hundred. Two new cavalry units were organized: one the 11th United States Volunteer Cavalry, composed mainly of Americans then in the Philippine Islands; the other a squadron of Filipinos. These units were organized from volunteers recruited in accordance with the provisions of the act of 2 March 1899, which permitted enlistments of volunteers from the country at large or from localities where their services were needed, and from the Volunteer organizations whose terms of service had expired. The act also provided that volunteers having special qualifications in horsemanship and marksmanship were to be assigned to cavalry for service either mounted or dismounted. Both Volunteer cavalry organizations were disbanded on 2 July 1901.

The service of the cavalry in the Philippine Islands after the capture of Aguinaldo, the leader of the Filipino independence movement, in March 1901 might well be described as daily and nightly patrols by small detachments commanded by junior officers. These little groups often encountered large bands of insurgents armed with bolos and U.S. rifles. A regimental report from the history of the 1st Cavalry is typical of the period:

On December 8, 1900, detachment Troop M engaged a force of two hundred insurgents on Boot Peninsula, Lake Taal, dispersing them in a running fight of two and one-half hours duration. Private Ernest Shrey, Troop M, killed. Four insurgents killed; captured three prisoners, their arms and ammunition.

On 5 May 1901, Lieutenant Hartman with Troop K engaged about two hundred and fifty insurgents at Mount Solo, drove them from three separate positions, killing one, capturing three, also six ponies, three rifles, and three bolos.

This type of warfare afforded little space for grand strategy and tactics, but the work performed by the enterprising and courageous junior officers won them promotions and helped prepare them for higher commands in World War I. Chief among the young American officers was John J. Pershing, Captain of Cavalry.

While some U.S. troops were thus occupied in the Philippine Islands, affairs in China drew others still farther away from home. The United States made a substantial contribution to the international army that went to China at the turn of the century to protect the various embassies from attack by the Chinese Boxers. A cavalryman commanded the American contingent in the international force and the greater part of one U.S. cavalry regiment formed a part of it. The American commander was Maj. Gen. Adna R. Chaffee, Sr., an experienced Indian fighter; the cavalry regiment was the 6th, the same organization in which General Chaffee had enlisted as a private in 1861. While the regimental headquarters and 1st Squadron, 6th Cavalry, guarded American interests in Tientsin, the 3d Squadron formed a part of the force that stormed the walls of "The Forbidden City" at Peking and became the first white troops to enter the city. In China, the American cavalrymen met and fought beside cavalrymen of other nations. Among them were the First Bengal Lancers, of whom officers of the 6th furnished most complimentary reports.

On 2 February 1901, when the 2-year enlistments of the Volunteers were about to expire and the end of occupation duties in the Philippines appeared to be nowhere in sight, Congress passed an act that provided for an increase in the cavalry and infantry and completely reorganized the artillery. The increase in cavalry included 5 new regiments, numbered the 11th through the 15th. Also, it added a captain, 3 second lieutenants, a commissary sergeant, and 2 color sergeants to each regiment, old and new, and by it all regiments got a regimental

A GROUP INCLUDING MEN OF TROOP L, 6TH CAVALRY, *on the Avenue of Statues near the Ming tombs, outside Peking.*

chaplain. The act also contained provisions for further increasing the enlisted strength of a troop from 100 to 164 at the discretion of the President. As a result, the number of enlisted men in a cavalry regiment varied. Units within the United States were reduced to the minimum, while those serving in the new island possessions were increased according to the duties being performed in each. Naturally, the greatest number were required in the Philippines, and for some years the cavalry regiments took turns serving there as well as in Hawaii, Panama, and various stations in this country, the last again mainly in the west.

From 1901 to 1916 the size of the Army varied from year to year. In 1901 Congress set the maximum strength at 100,000, and thereafter until 1916 the actual strength was regulated by annual appropriations. From 1902 to 1911 it averaged 65,616. The cavalry continued to comprise about one-fifth of the total. The Army's actual strength on 30 June 1915 was 105,993, including the Hospital Corps, the Philippine Scouts, and a regiment of Puerto Rican infantry. Of these, 15,424 were assigned to the cavalry. More than seven full regiments, or about one-half of all the cavalry, were serving on the Mexican border, two regiments were in the Philippine Islands, and one was in Hawaii.

During these years when greater interest in a more effective tactical organization of the Army was manifested, cavalry received special consideration. In 1908 the Army Chief of Staff and various department commanders recommended an increase in the infantry and artillery and a reorganization of the cavalry along "more modern" lines. For a time, it was believed that U.S.

cavalry regiments should be reorganized to conform to the pattern of European regiments of the same arm. New formations suggested were actually a revival of those prescribed in Scott and Poinsett's *Tactics* more than seventy-five years earlier and, so far as written instructions went, had been in force during the Civil War.

European armies still clung to the idea of heavy cavalry, trained almost exclusively for the charge in mass and relying on sabers and lances. On the other hand, U.S. cavalrymen were convinced that open order formations in which the pistol, or revolver, was the principal arm produced more decisive results in mounted combat, especially when accompanied by the element of surprise and employed against fugitives or inferior troops. From 1911 until 1916 the Army conducted various experiments in cavalry reorganization and employment.

In 1911 and 1912 the 12-troop regiment was temporarily reorganized into one of six troops by consolidating two troops into one. It was supposed that this action would result in a more compact unit and bring all men within the sound of the colonel's voice. Employment of cavalry versus cavalry in mounted action was contemplated. Experimental drill regulations prescribed double rank formations, as was the European custom, and field regulations stressed more mounted action. Horsemanship, improvement of mounts, and proficiency in the use of the saber were emphasized. At the same time, it was clearly stated that cavalry's efficiency with the rifle and in fighting dismounted must not be lessened.

In answer to several Congressional proposals to reduce the cavalry from fifteen to ten regiments, the Chief of Staff in 1912 opposed any reduction, pointing out that the small amount of cavalry in the Organized Militia made it most essential that the fifteen Regular mounted regiments "be maintained and maintained at the highest degree of efficiency." At the same time, the Chief of Staff called attention to the damaging effects upon regiments that resulted from detaching troops to police the National Parks. Since the opening of Yellowstone in 1872, cavalry troops had been detached from their regiments to police the National Park lands. With the management of the reservations now under the Department of Interior, the Army suggested that Interior should employ its own rangers. When this advice was followed a few years later, the Army agreed to discharge cavalry enlisted men volunteering for service as rangers.

In October 1914 experimental cavalry service regulations (based upon the experimental drill regulations) were issued to all cavalry regiments and were given an "extensive try out" in the border service of 1915 and 1916. Reports from cavalry commanders showed that 90 percent of the commanders preferred the old statutory organization of troop, squadron, and regiment employed in single rank. They believed that a mounted unit of any size from platoon through regiment, employed in successive lines each in single rank, was just as powerful as the same number of troopers in a double rank. They also contended that this system afforded much less danger of inversion and provided fresh reinforcements with proper timing, or distances, between the lines.

Consequently, new drill and service regulations issued in 1916 retained the former organization and instruction for single rank formations, but provided for movements in double rank when circumstances required. Also taken from the 1914 experimental regulations was the basic principle—leading. The new manual stated that mounted units must be habitually led by their commanders. The manual also treated in detail the training of the recruit and the new mount.

Plans for a more effective organization included better location of the cavalry. Upon their return from Cuba and the Philippine Islands, cavalry units had again been stationed at posts established during the Indian Wars, located far from centers of population and supply. Most of the posts were entirely too small, and many were in sections of the country where for several months in the year climatic conditions made outdoor work impracticable. As late as 1911, 49 posts in 24 states and territories were still in use, 16 of them by cavalry alone or by cavalry with infantry. Thirty-one posts had a capacity for less than a regiment, 6 could accommodate little more than a regiment, and only one could care for a brigade. The average number of companies at a post was 9, or about 650 men. Secretary of War Henry L. Stimson described the Army so distributed as "merely groups of local constabulary instead of a national organization."

In 1910–11 internal conditions in Mexico resulted in the overthrow of the government of that country and caused the United States to concentrate most of its Army strength in the southwest. Thus, for a while necessity solved the problem of a badly scattered Army. The greater part of the Regular Army moved to the border area in March 1911. While most of the cavalry patrolled the border from the mouth of the Rio Grande to San Diego, California, other units in the area were organized into one division and two independent brigades for maneuver purposes. One cavalry regiment, the 3d, formed a part of the division, and the 9th and 10th Cavalry plus a signal company made up the independent cavalry brigade. When the immediate danger subsided about five months later, the division and brigade organizations were broken up and the units comprising them returned to their former stations. One important result of the experiment was the decision to move cavalry to permanent stations in the southwest, and some outfits that had been employed there in mounted patrol duty remained in the area.

When counterrevolutions occurred in Mexico in 1913, back to the border area went a large part of the Regular Army. From then throughout World War I and many years afterward, except for the short time they were in Mexico as part of the Punitive Expedition, most U.S. cavalry regiments maintained border patrols from the Gulf of Mexico almost to California, a distance of approximately 1,700 miles. The duties of these patrols included protecting the border from incursions by individuals and small raiding parties; preventing violations of neutrality laws; and, in conjunction with civil authorities, barring passage of arms and ammunition from the United States into Mexico. In addition, U.S. soldiers gave medical aid to all wounded who were brought across the border. In general, the troopers performing border service lived a monotonous and unenviable life. In that desert area there was no natural protection from the burning sun of the day, and the tents in which they were housed provided little defense against the cold nights. In addition, many troopers were wounded because the Mexicans ignored repeated U.S. warnings not to fire in the direction of the border.

On the night of 8 March 1916 border events came to a head when Mexican bandits made a surprise attack on Columbus, New Mexico. As a result, U.S. soldiers crossed the border for the ostensible purpose of capturing the bandit leader, Francisco (Pancho) Villa. The Punitive Expedition into Mexico was principally a horse cavalry action, the last such in American history.

In many respects the service performed by the troopers in Mexico was comparable to that they experienced in tracking down the elusive Indians in the years following the Civil War. The hardships they endured were increased by the lack of co-operation on the part of the Mexican Government and the natives. Conflicting information as to the direction the bandits took after their forays more often than not sent the Americans on long circuitous routes, thus delaying their arrival at strategic points and giving the bandits plenty of time to escape. The rough, irregular terrain and the varied climate of Mexico added many discomforts.

It was after a forced march through the irregular terrain, during which the men were in their saddles for 17 hours out of 24, that U.S. troops fought the only battle of the expedition directly concerned with Villa. On 29 March 1916 Col. George A. Dodd and 400 men of the 7th Cavalry surprised and attacked 500 Villistas at Guerrero.

On 9 May 1916 National Guard units from Texas, New Mexico, and Arizona were called into Federal service for patrol duty along the Mexican border. About five weeks later, on 18 June 1916, most of the remainder of the National Guard was called in. In all, these included 3 regiments, 13 separate squadrons, and 22 separate troops of cavalry. There were 108 regiments and 7 battalions of infantry and 6 regiments, 12 battalions, and 17 batteries of field artillery. Cavalry constituted a very small portion of the National Guard since the states preferred to have infantry regiments—they were considerably less expensive—but by the National Defense Act of 1916, they were required to organize more auxiliary troops and fewer infantry. The states were in the midst of a reorganization program when National Guard units were ordered into Federal service. In spite of all the confusion, the National Guardsmen moved to the border area on schedule, and eventually better legislation corrected many of the weaknesses revealed during their tour there.

U.S. Cavalry in the Mexican Foothills During the Pursuit of Villa

Not since the Civil War had a sizable force been assembled for a sufficient period to train officers in the field grades. The numerous posts scattered over the vast area in which the Indian Wars were fought usually were garrisoned by a force comprised of a troop of cavalry and a company of infantry and led by company officers. Seldom were troops from several posts assembled in sufficient forces or for periods of time sufficient for officers to get practice in leading units larger than a company. In fact, during the Indian Wars many of the actions were fought by detachments commanded by lieutenants.

Even though the transportation and supply system tested during the Punitive Expedition into Mexico was found lacking in many respects, the trial gave hope of improvement over the established system. One of the innovations was the introduction of motor trucks as part of the logistics system, and many disappointments and inconveniences were occasioned by the mechanical failures of the trucks. Members of the expedition and others in Washington averse to change were not in the least surprised or disappointed that the new equipment had not yet proved that the gasoline engine would replace the horse. Yet there

4-WHEEL-DRIVE TRUCKS *of the Pershing expedition, near the Mexican border.*

were a farsighted few who believed in the gasoline engine and would not let their experiences discourage them in their plans for future developments.

During these years some changes were made in the composition of the cavalry regiments. In 1906 a machine gun platoon, commanded by a commissioned officer, was added to each regiment, and in 1912 a headquarters detachment and a supply detachment were added. By 1915 the machine gun platoon and the headquarters and supply detachments had become experimental troops, and the next year they became permanent. At that time, too, the experimental organization of a 6-troop regiment and the idea of reorganizing U.S. cavalry along European lines were abandoned.

Thus, the cavalry regiment of 1916 had a headquarters, a headquarters troop, a supply troop, a machine gun troop, and 12 lettered troops, the last organized into 3 squadrons of 4 troops each. All regiments had the usual complement of officers (a colonel, a lieutenant colonel, 3 majors, 15 captains, 16 first lieutenants, and 16 second lieutenants), but the number of enlisted men varied with the service required of the regiment. For example, the authorized enlisted strength of regiments serving within the continental United States was 70 men in a troop, while regiments in the Philippine Islands were permitted a total of 105 enlisted men in each lettered troop.

The National Defense Act approved on 3 June 1916 set the peace strength of the Regular Army at 220,000 officers and men and of the National Guard at 450,000. Increases to reach these strengths were to be spread over a period of five years. In units, additions to the Regular Army amounted to 10 regiments of cavalry, 33 of infantry, and 15 of field artillery; 13 battalions of engineers; 93 companies of coast artillery; and a number of signal, medical, and other auxiliary troops.

The act also provided for the organization of brigades and divisions, which previously had not been permanent—that is, they had been organized during an emergency and existed only so long as the specific emergency lasted. Civil War brigades and divisions, for example, were disbanded when the war ended, and new ones created for the War with Spain were not continued after the close of that struggle.

The new plan called for 2 cavalry and 7 infantry divisions. A cavalry division consisted of a headquarters, 3 brigades (each with 3 cavalry regiments), a horse field artillery regiment, a mounted engineer battalion, a mounted signal battalion, an aero squadron, and the necessary trains: ammunition, supply, engineer, and sanitary. The remaining 7 authorized cavalry regiments were assigned to the 7 infantry divisions, a regiment to each division, to provide a mobile force capable of performing reconnaissance, counterreconnaissance, and security missions for the division. Because of their mobility, the cavalry divisions were free for reconnaissance or other duties that took them considerable distances from the remainder of the Army. The regimental organization under the 1916 act remained unchanged, retaining its 12 lettered troops in 3 squadrons, a headquarters troop, a supply troop, and a machine gun troop. Enlisted strength of a line troop was fixed at 70 for peace and 105 for war.

As part of the 1916 plan for increase of the Army, two cavalry regiments were authorized in the first increment. Designated as the 16th and 17th, they were organized in July 1916 at Forts Sam Houston and Bliss, Texas, respectively. To enable the new organizations to become operational as soon as possible, experienced officers and men from existing cavalry regiments were transferred to the new ones, and by mid-July 1916 the 16th and 17th Cavalry were in fair shape. These were the last additions to the cavalry arm until after the declaration of war on Germany.

In the matter of arms and equipment during this period, it is important that in 1904 the new U.S. rifle Model 1903 replaced the Krag-Jörgensen as the standard arm of cavalry, as well as infantry, and remained so until the beginning of World War II. Cavalrymen readily accepted the new shoulder arm. It could be handled as well while mounted as on foot, and it had a range greater than that of the carbine.

A new side arm, the Colt automatic pistol caliber .45, was approved 29 March 1911, and by the time of the Punitive Expedition all troops in the United States were armed with it. Units going to the Philippine Islands, where there had been so much demand for an arm of this caliber, took it with them, but no special effort was made to supply those already there.

In 1914 the semaphore code, until that time used only by field artillery, was authorized for cavalry, infantry, and engineers. The fifty-six kits furnished for each cavalry regiment were distributed four to a troop.

World War I

Cavalry

The cavalry organization of seventeen regiments in effect when the United States entered the war against Germany was based upon the National Defense Act of 1916. In May 1917 emergency laws called for immediate increase to the full strength authorized by the National Defense Act, and organization of the remaining eight new cavalry regiments began at once. To speed up the process, certain old units in June 1917 transferred two-thirds of their men to the new regiments.

The new regiments were numbered the 18th through the 25th. But, one month after their organization was completed, all eight began training as field artillery. On 1 October 1917 Congress acted to make their conversion to field artillery legal, and on 1 November 1917 the 18th through the 25th Cavalry were redesignated as the 76th through the 83d Field Artillery. Although Congress specified that the units would reorganize as cavalry after the emergency, such action was never taken. Hence, the histories of the former 18th through 25th Cavalry are currently perpetuated in a number of artillery units.

An act of Congress on 18 May 1917 provided for twenty National Army (or temporary) cavalry regiments, which were designated 301st through 320th. Fifteen of them, the 301st through the 315th, were organized in early 1918 at various National Army camps, but in August of that year they, too, were converted to field artillery. Thirty field artillery regiments, the 44th through the 72d, and nine trench mortar batteries, the 15th through the 23d, were organized from them. None of those units served outside the United States and all were demobilized in January–February of 1919. The 316th through the 320th Cavalry were not activated during the war years.

By the time the United States entered World War I, the machine gun, together with improved artillery, barbed wire, and elaborate field fortifications, had produced a stalemate on the European Western Front. The Allies and the Germans, with their opposing armies anchored on the sea in the west and on the mountains in the east, repeatedly used waves of infantrymen and heavy artillery barrages in vain efforts to break the deadlock. Their critical need was for mobility and shock action, both traditional roles of horse cavalry, but static trench warfare and the machine gun had made use of the horse impractical.

Four regiments of U.S. cavalry—the 2d, 3d, 6th, and 15th—nevertheless formed a part of the American Expeditionary Forces, and engaged chiefly in remount duty. That they would have been used otherwise during the latter part of the war, had they been available, was implied by General Pershing in 1920. He stated that, once the forces were in the open, cavalry would have been of great value on several occasions, and Allied cavalry trained in American tactics would have been most effective in the pursuit of the enemy northward toward the Meuse.

Since U.S. cavalrymen had been trained to fight dismounted as well as mounted, many of them did see action as foot soldiers. Again, as in earlier wars, many individual awards for gallantry were earned by the dismounted troopers who fought in other arms and services.

Only a very small portion of the U.S. cavalry saw any mounted service in France. In late August 1918, just before the St. Mihiel offensive, a provisional squadron was formed from Troops, B, D, F, and H of the 2d Cavalry. Fourteen officers and 404 enlisted men from those troops with convalescent horses furnished from the veterinary hospital moved to old Camp Jeanne d'Arc, near Neufchâteau, for training in mounted action. Lt. Col. Oliver P. M. Hazzard commanded the squadron. Among the troop commanders was Capt. Ernest N. Harmon who, during World War II, was to command the 2d Armored Division and then the XXII Corps.

After about ten days of training, one troop of the Provisional Squadron was detached and marched to Menil-la-Tour, where it reported for courier duty with the 1st, 42d, and 89th Divisions. The remainder of the squadron reported to the 1st Division on the night of 11 September 1918, and by a few minutes past noon of the next day U.S. cavalrymen, mounted, were at Nonsard, about five miles behind the original front line of the enemy. Sent out on reconnaissance duty beyond their capabilities, the cavalrymen met the enemy in considerable force and were routed. Later, in the Meuse-Argonne action, the squadron with three troops maintained liaison between flank divisions and those on the front lines. Among the trenches, which made movement of a whole troop impracticable, small patrols, sometimes riding and sometimes walking, acted as military police and couriers. By mid-October, when withdrawn from the front, the squadron had only 150 mounted effectives, largely because of the evacuation of sick and wounded horses.

After the armistice, Headquarters, Band, and six troops of the 2d Cavalry acted as advance guard for the Army movement into Germany, and afterward were stationed along the Rhine with the American Army of Occupation.

Although few U.S. cavalry regiments went to Europe during World War I, all were well represented there by individual cavalrymen. For example, between May and September 1917, one regiment alone—the new 16th Cavalry—lost most of its original officers by promotion in the National Army, and from May 1917 until November 1918 more than a hundred enlisted members of that regiment received commissions in the National Army. Many of these men saw service in France. After the armistice twenty-six of them returned and reenlisted as noncommissioned officers.

Vacancies in cavalry units created by promotion and reassignment were filled by new personnel, and the regiments were moved to the Mexican border, an area well known to the older cavalrymen. Germany's efforts to rekindle trouble between the United States and Mexico were met by the concentration of a cavalry force in the southwest. In December 1917 the 15th Cavalry Division—three brigades of three regiments each—was organized in Texas. There were no other cavalry divisions in the Army then, but no explanation for designating this one the 15th has been found. Like the divisions organized during previous emergencies, the life of the 15th was short. Actually, a full division organization was not completed, and it was discontinued in May 1918. The brigade headquarters lasted until July 1919 when they, too, were disbanded.

Tanks

Few recognized during World War I that the means for returning mobility and shock action to combat was already present in a device destined to revolutionize warfare on the ground and in the air. This was the internal combustion engine, which had made possible the development of the tank and eventually would lead to the mechanized forces that were to assume the old roles of horse cavalry and to loosen the grip of the machine gun on the battlefield. With increased firepower and protection, these mechanized forces would, only some twenty years later, become the armor of World War II. When the armored artillery, the armored personnel carrier, the wheeled cargo vehicle, and supporting aviation—all with adequate communications—were added to constitute the combined arms team of the modern armored division, commanders regained the capability of maneuver in most of the land areas of the world.

In the early stages of World War I, neither the Allies nor the Germans foresaw the ultimate value of the tank. In late 1914 after observing a small American-made caterpillar tractor in France, Lt. Col. Ernest D. Swinton, an English officer, recommended to the British Committee of Imperial Defence that caterpillar tractors be armored and armed for use in combat. Although his proposal was not immediately accepted by the committee, it gained strong support of one of its members, Winston S. Churchill, then First Lord of the Admiralty. The Royal Navy, largely at Churchill's urging, sponsored experiments and tests of the vehicle as a type of "land ship" during 1915, and the tank at last became a reality. In an effort to keep secret the real purpose of the early models when they were being shipped to France, the English labeled them *tanks*—for use as water tanks by Russia. Thus originated the name of tank for the new weapon. The naval background of the tank's development also explains such nautical tank terms as hatch, hull, bow, and ports.

A Small British Tank Near Chaudin, France, *July 1918. The soldiers are French.*

The first test of the tank in action came when the British, on 15 September 1916, used forty-nine 30-ton Mark I's in the Somme area. The results were encouraging. More spectacular was their success over a year later, when on 20 November 1917 around 400 tanks penetrated almost six miles on a 7-mile front in an attack at Cambrai. This was the first large-scale employment of tanks in combat. Unfortunately, success was not complete because the infantry failed to exploit and secure the tanks' gains. The massed tank attack was proved feasible, nonetheless, and allayed American fears as to the tank's value; it gave renewed impetus to the United States' tank plans, and agreement was soon reached with Great Britain and France for co-ordination of all tank programs.

The British scored another victory the following year, on 18 August 1918, with 600 tanks in the Amiens salient. General Eric von Ludendorff referred to that date as the "Black Day" of the German Army, since for the first time entire German units collapsed.

The French launched their first tank attack on 16 April 1917, seven months after the initial British tank action. Of the 194 tanks used in this unsuccessful French attempt to break through the German lines, the Germans reported that 66 were destroyed. A second French tank attack, on 5 May 1917, met with considerable success, prompting a German declaration that "tanks were able, for the first time, to show their full worth without heavy losses." The most suc-

A French Tank Near Gutrey, France, 18 July 1918

cessful French employment of tanks during the war was their use of 350 tanks in the Aisne-Marne offensive, beginning on 18 July 1918.

Numerous mechanical failures and the inability of the British and French to mount any sustained tank drives in the early tank actions had cast doubt on the usefulness of tanks. But tank operations and training methods in the British and French sectors had been studied carefully by United States observers, and their reports and conclusions prompted Maj. Gen. John J. Pershing, Commander in Chief, American Expeditionary Forces (AEF), to request in September 1917 that 600 heavy and 1,200 light tanks be produced in the United States.

The resulting American-produced heavy tank was the 43.5-ton Mark VIII, patterned after a British model. Armed with two 6-pounder and five .30-caliber machine guns, it was operated by an 11-man crew, had a maximum speed of 6.5 miles per hour, and a range of 50 miles. The American-built 6½-ton M1917 light tank was a copy of the French Renault. It had a maximum speed of 5.5 miles per hour and could travel 30 miles on its 30-gallon fuel capacity. The U.S. program was augmented in the summer of 1918 by the development of a 3-ton, 2-man tank, originated by the Ford Motor Company. This third tank to be mass-produced during 1918 was powered by two Ford Model T, 4-cylinder engines, armed with a .30-caliber machine gun, and had a maximum speed of 8 miles per hour.

COLONEL ROCKENBACH, *after his promotion to brigadier general.*

During the fall of 1917, General Pershing approved plans for an overseas tank corps, based upon an army to be composed of 20 combat divisions. As originally planned, the tank corps was to consist of a headquarters and 5 heavy and 20 light tank battalions. Later plans increased the heavy battalions to 10. On 22 December 1917 Col. Samuel D. Rockenbach was appointed Chief of the Tank Corps, AEF. Plans developed for this organization called for a general headquarters, 3 tank centers (for training and replacement of personnel), 2 army tank headquarters, and 10 brigades. Assembly of the Tank Corps, with an authorized strength of 14,827, began on 26 January 1918, and Colonel Rockenbach was soon placed on the staff of the Commander in Chief, AEF, as an adviser on all tank matters.

In the organization of the Tank Corps, AEF, all tank units were assigned to the General Headquarters, Tank Corps. For specific combat missions, they were attached to armies or to subordinate elements and reverted to general headquarters control as directed. An army tank headquarters, designed to function with an army headquarters, consisted of a headquarters and a heavy artillery mobile ordnance repair shop.

Tables of organization and equipment (TOE) for other Tank Corps organizations were developed in 1918, although shortages of personnel and equipment for their full use prevented conclusive tests during combat. The tables provided for a light battalion of 72 light tanks and a heavy battalion of 69 heavy tanks. Both types of battalions had three companies of three platoons each and a battalion headquarters. All platoons were equipped with 5 tanks. The tank brigade, with a combined total of 225 tanks, consisted of 2 light battalions, a heavy battalion, a repair and salvage company, and a brigade headquarters. Almost identical to the brigade headquarters was the headquarters of a light or a heavy tank center.

In the United States developments were also under way for a tank organization similar to that overseas. The War Department, on 18 February 1918, authorized a Tank Service, National Army, under the Chief of Engineers, and the 65th Engineers was reorganized into tank units. The Tank Service, with an authorized strength of 914 officers and 14,746 men, became a separate branch on 5 March. Col. Ira C. Welborn was named its first director and charged with organizing, arming, equipping, and training tank units. Among Welborn's duties were the supervision of all tank activities in the United States, including procurement of officers and enlisted men, and the establishment and maintenance of tank camps. The primary tank training camp was Camp Colt, Pennsylvania, which was commanded for almost seven months of 1918 by Capt., Maj., and then Lt. Col. Dwight D. Eisenhower. On 22 March 1918 the Tank Service became the Tank Corps. Neither the Tank Service nor the Tank Corps in the United States had any direct command relationship with the Tank Corps, AEF.

Units of the Tank Corps, AEF, and the Tank Corps, National Army, were organized in three separate areas during 1918—in the United States, in England, and in France. Some repetition of numerical designations resulted, and redesignations were required to eliminate the duplications. Tank units of all types were finally numbered in the 300 series.

The first tank units were organized in February 1918 as elements of the 65th Engineers. The 1st Separate Battalion, Heavy Tank Service, 65th Engineers, and the 1st and 2d Battalions, Light Tank Service, 65th Engineers, were at Camp Upton, New York, while Company D, 2d Battalion, Heavy Tank Service, 65th Engineers, was at Camp Meade, Maryland. These elements were redesignated during the war as separate battalions, numbered in the 300 series. All tank battalions were numbered 301–346, but those from 309 through 325 were not organized.

Four tank brigades were formed. Originally organized as the 1st, 2d, 3d, and 4th Provisional Tank Brigades, they were redesignated in late 1918 as the 304th through the 307th Tank Brigades, respectively.

The tank centers were also in the 300 series—being numbered from 301 through 314, although the 305th through the 308th and the 312th and 313th were never organized. The first tank centers, established overseas in February and March 1918, were initially designated as the 1st Light Tank Center and the 2d Heavy Tank Center. They, too, were redesignated into the 300 series.

There were no National Guard tank units during World War I. However, since the lineage of National Guard units is determined on a geographical basis, a tank unit currently in the National Guard may descend from a World War I National Guard unit, or an even earlier organization.

Despite concentrated efforts to organize and equip tank units as soon as possible, by June 1918 only 700 men were in the AEF Tank Corps and about 5,000 in the continental U.S. organization. By late July 1918 the combat tank units overseas were: 2 heavy battalion headquarters, 3 heavy companies, 2 light battalion headquarters, and 6 light companies. In the United States there were: a heavy battalion headquarters, 12 heavy companies, a light battalion head-quarters, and 24 light companies. As late as mid-August 1918 no combat tanks, either American- or foreign-made, had been assigned to any unit of either Tank Corps. By the fall of 1918, nevertheless, American tank units, using British and French tanks, were in combat. Three battalions of light tanks fought with the U.S. First Army and a battalion of heavies was with the U.S. 27th and 30th Divisions.

American tank units first entered combat on 12 September 1918 against the St. Mihiel salient with the First Army. They belonged to the 344th and 345th Light Tank Battalions, elements of the 304th Tank Brigade, commanded by Lt. Col. George S. Patton, Jr., under whom they had trained at the tank center in Bourg, France. Forty-five of the 2-man French Renault light tanks, probably the most popular type among Americans, had been issued to each battalion only about two weeks before the action. Weighing a little over 7 tons, the Renault had a maximum speed of 6 miles per hour and was armed with either a 37-mm. gun or a machine gun.

For the attack, initially, the 344th was assigned to the 1st Division and the 345th to the 42d Division, with 16 tanks from the 344th and 25 from the 345th composing the brigade reserve. Muddy conditions, caused by heavy rain the night before the offensive, resulted in a much greater consumption of gasoline than anticipated. Although the mud, lack of gas, and mechanical failure caused many tanks to stall in the German trenches, the attack succeeded and much valuable experience was gained. In most actions tanks supported the infantry, but at times they executed normal cavalry reconnaissance missions.

In early October the tactical situation was ideal for tank employment since the Germans were short of artillery and relying heavily on their machine guns. On the other hand, the U.S. light tank battalions had been in almost continuous action during the Meuse-Argonne Campaign and numerous rear area moves and were too weak to furnish effective support. General Pershing sent the chief of the AEF Tank Corps to Paris with instructions to "give anything in the A.E.F. for 500 tanks," but only forty-eight could be obtained locally.

The third U.S. light tank battalion, the 331st, joined the AEF in the final phase of the war. Located at Varennes, France, during early November 1918, it was also credited with participation in the Meuse-Argonne Campaign.

MEMBERS OF THE 327TH BATTAL-
ION, *Tank Corps, ready to go into
action near Varennes, France,
1 October 1918.*

In the heavy tank category, the 301st Heavy Tank Battalion trained at the
British Tank School at Wareham, England, from April until August 1918. It
was to remain with the British Tank Corps until American tanks became available, but when the battalion arrived in France in late August 1918 and could
not be supplied with American tanks, it was equipped with 47 British Mark
V and Mark V Star tanks and assigned to the U.S. 27th Division. Both the
Mark V and the Mark V Star had 8-man crews and a maximum speed of approximately 4 miles per hour. The Mark V Star, weighing 36 or 37 tons, depending upon armament, was about 5 tons heavier than the Mark V. Both
were armed with either 2 6-pounder guns or an additional 2 machine guns,
which were added to the Mark V's usual 4 machine guns or the Star's usual 5.

The 301st was first committed on 29 September at the Battle of Le Catelet-
Bony, in support of a British offensive. For that engagement, its tanks were
divided among three U.S. infantry regiments of the 27th Division and the
Australian Corps Reserve. Although the attack reached its objective, it was
several hours late and considered as unsuccessful. Heavy mist and haze made
visibility extremely poor, but the failure was attributed mainly to lack of combined tank and infantry training before the operation and a consequent lack
of co-ordination between the two as the attack progressed. Thus, the value of
tank-infantry training and co-operation was recognized from the beginning of

COLONEL PATTON

the development of tactical doctrine involving the use of tanks and has continued to be given emphasis.

In the 301st's next action, on 8 October at Brancourt with the 30th Division, tank-infantry co-operation was excellent, and the tanks earned a large share of the credit for the successful advance. The 301st's tanks were again parceled out for the Battle of the Selle on 17 October, this time being split between the 27th and 30th Divisions. By 23 October the battalion could muster only a composite company of twelve tanks to support the British at Marmol Forest, but the attack reached its objective.

By the armistice of 11 November 1918, the AEF was critically short of tanks; no American-made tanks were completed in time for use in combat. The new weapon was a very complex item, not only requiring extensive technical training for its crew but a long lead time for production as well.

At the end of the war, the strength of the AEF Tank Corps and the Tank Corps, National Army, had reached a total of 1,090 officers and 14,780 men,

53 percent being in the United States and the remainder either overseas or en route.

After the war, General von Ludendorff of the German High Command praised the Allied tanks as being a principal factor in Germany's defeat. The Germans had been too late in recognizing the value of tanks to consider them in their own plans. Even if their already hard-pressed industry could have produced tanks in quantity, fuel was in very short supply. Of the total of ninety tanks fielded by the Germans during 1918, seventy-five had been captured from the Allies.

At the war's end, the main role of the tank was considered to be that of close support for the infantry. The U.S. tank units fought so briefly and were so fragmentized during the war, and the number of tanks available to them was so limited, that there was practically no opportunity to develop tactics for the large-scale employment of tanks. Nonetheless, the work of the tanks was sufficiently impressive to imbue at least a few military leaders with the idea that the use of tanks in mass was the most likely principal role of armor in the future.

Highlights of U.S. Army appraisal for the development and use of tanks, developed from combat experience, were: (1) the need for a tank with more power, fewer mechanical failures, heavier armor, longer operating range, and better ventilation; (2) the need for combined training of tanks with other combat arms, especially the infantry; (3) the need for improved means of communication and of methods for determining and maintaining directions; and (4) the need for an improved supply system, especially for gasoline and ammunition.

Between the World Wars

Tanks

Although the tank of World War I was slow, clumsy, unwieldy, difficult to control, and mechanically unreliable, its value as a combat weapon had been clearly proven. But, despite the lessons of World War I, the combat arms were most reluctant to accept a separate and independent role for armor and continued to struggle among themselves over the proper use of tanks. At the outset, thought of the tank as an auxiliary to and a part of the infantry was the predominant opinion, although a few leaders contended that an independent tank arm should be retained. After World War I came the usual American clamor for demobilization. The resulting sudden decrease in Tank Corps personnel, especially within the United States, was in sharp contrast with the rapid increase in the number of tanks on hand—and full production was just beginning. In mid-1919 the U.S. Army had 863 tanks and after deliveries on outstanding contracts were complete, 1,163. Had the war in Europe continued, there would have been five fully trained and equipped tank brigades ready for action in the spring of 1919, one for each army corps. As it turned out, the production for World War I became the mainstay of the Army's tank pool for almost two decades.

In August 1919 the General Headquarters, Tank Corps, AEF, returned to the United States, and its chief, Brig. Gen. Samuel D. Rockenbach, became the new Chief of the Tank Corps, U.S. Army, a position he held until it was eliminated in 1920.

The Tank Corps requirements of the reorganized Regular Army after World War I were set by the General Staff in late 1918 at a general headquarters and 5 tank brigades, based upon an army of 5 corps, each with 4 divisions. As in World War I, the brigade was to consist of 3 battalions, 2 light and 1 heavy, and a repair and salvage company. Also the organization of elements within the brigade remained essentially the same as those of World War I.

Tables of organization for all units immediately following the war were of two types—one for war, the other for peace. The one for peace called for approximately two-thirds of the personnel and equipment authorized under the war table.

For the light tank regiment, the peacetime table included 162 tanks and 1,266 men. Three battalions were in a regiment, each battalion being further subdivided into three companies and a battalion headquarters and headquarters company. The light tank company within the regiment was almost identical in organization and equipment to the separate tank company of the division. Both had a company headquarters and 3 light tank platoons; each platoon had 5 tanks and an authorized strength of 13 men.

For the heavy tank regiment, the peacetime table authorized 90 tanks and 1,771 men. The heavy tank platoon had 3 tanks and 33 men; otherwise, organization and equipment within the heavy and light regiments were essentially the same.

In addition to the light and heavy categories of American-produced tanks of World War I, a third classification, the medium, began receiving attention in 1919. It was hoped that this in-between type would incorporate the best features of the 6½-ton light and the Mark VIII heavy and would replace both. The meaning of the terms *light, medium,* and *heavy* tanks changed between the wars. During World War I and immediately thereafter, the light tank was considered to be up to 10 tons, the medium (produced by the British) was roughly between 10 and 25 tons, and the heavy was over 25 tons. For World War II, increased weights resulted in the light tank being over 20 tons, the medium over 30, and the heavy, developed toward the end of the war, over 60 tons. During the period between the world wars, the weights of the classifications varied generally within these extremes.

The National Defense Act of 1920 attempted, among other things, to settle the tank into its proper place within the Army, based upon World War I experiences. Under the act's comprehensive provisions, the Tank Corps was abolished, and tank units were assigned to infantry, becoming known as "Infantry (Tanks)." Moreover, the act's stipulation that "hereafter all tank units shall form a part of the Infantry" left little doubt as to the tank role for the immediate future.

Between 1918 and 1922 an official War Department position on tanks was sought repeatedly by the Chief of Ordnance, the Chief of the Tank Corps, and the latter's successor, the Chief of Infantry. The War Department policy statement, which finally came in April 1922, was a serious blow to tank development. Reflecting prevailing opinion, it stated that the tank's primary mission was "to facilitate the uninterrupted advance of the riflemen in the attack." The War Department considered that two types of tanks, the light and the medium, should fulfill all missions. The light tank was to be truck transportable and not exceed 5 tons gross weight. For the medium, restrictions were even more stringent; its weight was not to exceed 15 tons, so as to bring it within the weight capacity of railroad flatcars, the average existing highway bridge, and, most significantly, available Engineer Corps ponton bridges. Although an experimental 15-ton tank, the M1924, reached the mock-up stage, this and other attempts to satisfy War Department and infantry specifications proved to be unsatisfactory. In reality it was simply impossible to build a 15-ton vehicle meeting both War Department and infantry requirements.

In 1926 the General Staff reluctantly consented to the development of a 23-ton tank, although it made clear that efforts were to continue toward the production of a satisfactory 15-ton vehicle. The infantry—its new branch chief overriding the protests of some of his tankmen who wanted a more heavily armed and armored medium—decided, too, that a light tank, transportable by truck, best met infantry requirements. The net effect of the infantry's preoccupation with light tanks and the limited funds available for tank development in general was to slow the development of heavier vehicles and, ultimately, to contribute to the serious shortage of mediums at the outbreak of World War II.

Extensive tests were also made between the world wars on another type of tank, a model designed and developed by a private manufacturer, J. Walter Christie. The Christie tank embodied the ability to operate both on tracks and on large, solid-rubber-tired bogie wheels. The tracks were removable to permit operation on wheels over moderate terrain. Also featured was a suspension system of independently sprung wheels. The Christie had many advantages, including the amazing ability, by 1929, to attain speeds of 69 miles per hour on wheels and 42 miles per hour on tracks, although at these speeds the tank could not carry full equipment. To the infantry and cavalry the Christie was the best answer to their need for a fast, lightweight tank, and they were enthusiastic about its convertibility. On the other hand, the Ordnance Department, while recognizing the usefulness of the Christie, was of the opinion that it was mechanically unreliable and that such dual-purpose equipment generally violated good engineering practice. The controversy over the advantages and drawbacks of Christie tanks raged for more than twenty years, with the convertible principle being abandoned in 1938. But the Christie ideas had great impact upon tank tactics and unit organization in many countries and, finally, upon the U.S. Army as well.

Actually, between the world wars there was much theoretical but little tangible progress in tank production and tank tactics in the United States. Production was limited to a few hand-tooled test models, only thirty-five of which were built between 1920 and 1935. Regarding the use of tanks with infantry, the official doctrine of 1939 largely reiterated that of 1923. It maintained that "As a rule, tanks are employed to assist the advance of infantry foot troops, either preceding or accompanying the infantry assault echelon."

Upon adoption of the National Defense Act of 1920—which created the Army of the United States, to consist of the Regular Army, Organized Reserves, and National Guard—tank units allocated to the Regular Army were based primarily upon assignment of a tank company to each infantry and cavalry division. This meant thirteen separate companies, numbered the 1st through the 13th, but only ten were organized. Also provided were five tank battalions, the 15th through the 19th—although only three were ever activated—and the Headquarters, 1st Tank Group. Most of these units traced their origins to Tank Corps organizations of World War I. In 1929 the five battalions and the group headquarters were used to form the 1st and 2d Tank Regiments, which in 1932 became the 66th Infantry (Light Tanks) and the 67th Infantry (Medium Tanks), respectively. Two new light tank regiments, the 68th and 69th, were constituted in 1933. The 68th was organized in early 1940 by consolidating some of the former divisional tank companies; the 69th was disbanded without being activated. Also in early 1940 the 66th, 67th, and 68th Infantry (Tanks) were used to form the Provisional Tank Brigade at Fort Benning, Georgia. Later the same year when all infantry tank units were transferred to a newly organized Armored Force, the 66th, 67th, and 68th Infantry were redesignated the 66th, 67th, and 68th Armored Regiments, and all were assigned to the 2d Armored Division. A new 69th Armored Regiment was organized in the 1st Armored Division.

Units of the new Organized Reserves of post-World War I were organized exceedingly understrength. By the outbreak of World War II, most of them had only officer cadres and did not enter active Federal service as organized units. As in the Regular Army, each infantry and cavalry division of the Organized Reserves had its tank company, their designations being 76th through 91st, 94th through 104th, and 461st through 466th. Also organized were the 301st through the 324th Tank Battalions and the headquarters of the 6th through the

12th Tank Groups. Several of these units were descendants of the former Tank Corps, but the majority had no prior history. Except for the 301st, 306th, and 314th, all of which had been disbanded in 1928, the tank battalions of the Organized Reserves were reorganized in 1929 as elements of the 306th through the 312th Tank Regiments. In 1932 these regiments were redesignated as the 420th through the 426th Infantry (Tanks). The following year another regiment, the 427th, was organized.

Meanwhile, in the National Guard after World War I, twenty-two tank companies were provided initially for its infantry and cavalry divisions. They were numbered as the 22d through the 45th, except that the 25th and the 39th were omitted. There were no other National Guard tank units, although a few tank companies of infantry divisions were used, after being called into Federal service for World War II, to form four tank battalions, the 191st through the 194th.

Cavalry

Between the wars the cavalry was slow in adopting mechanization. A factor bearing on the reluctance was that tanks were legally the responsibility of infantry. Although use of the tank by cavalry, as a supplement to achieve the utmost in mobility, had some support, cavalry clung to the horse as being indispensable to its type missions. Immediately after the war, the tank's slow speed was no minor consideration in the cavalry's reluctance to accept it. A few light mechanized vehicles were being used in cavalry units by the late 1920's, however, and the mechanized cavalry regiment, equipped with combat cars, came into being in the early 1930's. Actually the combat cars were modified infantry tanks, but were called *combat cars* to distinguish them from the tanks of infantry.

Staunch cavalrymen contended that the stalemate on the Western Front in World War I was the exception, not the rule, and that cavalry, with its essential characteristics of mobility and firepower, would have an important place in future warfare. They believed, however, that the very distant reconnaissance missions performed by cavalry in its strategical role would, for the most part, be taken over by the airplane.

After World War I, the AEF Cavalry Board concluded that "the role of cavalry, in general, has changed but little when considering war of movement." Although small units up to squadron size would "still have opportunities for mounted action . . .," the AEF Board continued, "the mounted combat of large bodies of cavalry is probably a thing of the past." The board's recommendation that cavalry units not be assigned as organic elements of infantry divisions, but that they be attached for operations, as needed, was accepted.

The Office of the Chief of Cavalry was established by the 1920 National Defense Act, and Maj. Gen. Willard A. Holbrook was appointed as the first chief. The total personnel authorization for cavalry was set at 950 officers and 20,000 enlisted men; its actual strength on 30 June 1920 was 965 officers and 15,812 men. In numbers of units, cavalry was little affected by the immediate reduction in the Regular Army at the war's end, since the mounted arm already had been fixed at 17 regiments.

In addition to the established regiments, squadrons, and troops, the larger units of cavalry divisions and brigades were provided by the 1920 act. Two cavalry divisions, the 1st and the 2d, were added to the Regular Army, the 1st being active and the 2d inactive. Each division contained two cavalry brigades, and each brigade had two regiments, a machine gun squadron, and a headquarters troop. Other divisional elements were a horse artillery battalion with 75-mm. guns, a mounted engineer battalion, an ambulance company, the division trains, and the special troops (headquarters, signal, ordnance, and veterinary).

The reorganization of the cavalry under the 1920 act took place in 1921. By then, lack of funds and reduced personnel authorization for the Army had cut the mounted arm to less than half of its former strength. Except for a regiment of Philippine Scouts—the 26th Cavalry, which was organized in 1922—the number of cavalry regiments was pared from seventeen to fourteen by inactivation of the 15th, 16th, and 17th. The remaining regiments were reconstructed to consist of a headquarters, a headquarters troop, a service troop (redesignated from the former supply troop), and only six lettered troops. The troops, designated as A through F, were grouped into two squadrons of three troops each. The regimental machine gun troop was eliminated, since its pack animals were believed to reduce the regiment's mobility. Machine gun troops and other surplus elements of the regiment were either redesignated into newly organized units or disbanded. Among those newly organized were machine gun squadrons, separate machine gun troops, training center squadrons, and the headquarters troops of two cavalry divisions and four cavalry brigades. All in all, the mounted arm lost three whole regiments and ninety-eight troops, some of the troops having been in continuous existence for almost a hundred years. By mid-1923 the assigned strength of cavalry had dropped to 721 officers and 8,887 men, which is approximately where it stood until the late 1930's.

The unit organizations effected in 1921 lasted seven years, major changes not coming until February 1928. At that time, lettered troops of the regiments were decreased from six to four. Troops A and B of each regiment formed the 1st Squadron, and E and F formed the 2d Squadron. Also, separate machine gun squadrons and troops were eliminated, and the machine gun troop was returned to the regiment.

This new regimental organization was designed to reduce overhead, increase firepower, and retain mobility. It provided for easy expansion to war strength and retained for the regiment, if required to take the field at peacetime strength, the capability of delivering powerful and flexible firepower. This firepower had been increased not only by the return of the machine gun troop to the regiment, but by doubling the machine guns in that troop from four to eight. Reduction in wagons and pack animals in the new regiment was offset by the addition of three 1½-ton trucks and three stripped, modified automobiles, called light cross-country cars.

Many famous old cavalry units were dangerously near being lost to the Army because of these organizational changes. But the policy of retaining surplus units on the rolls of the Army in an inactive status was established, permitting units to be preserved for future use rather than being disbanded or redesignated. As a result, most former cavalry troops have been restored to their original regiments.

The strength and composition of cavalry regiments of 1928–39 were principally governed by the total strength of the Army, the number of regiments kept active, and the desire for a troop large enough to be an effective fighting unit, even at peacetime strength. For that period each regiment had an approximate average of 690 men: headquarters troop, 78; band, 28; 4 rifle troops, 119 each; and a machine gun troop, 108. Each rifle troop had a troop headquarters, 3 rifle platoons of 3 squads each, and a machine rifle platoon, also of 3 squads.

The real beginning of the Armored Force was in 1928, twelve years before it was officially established, when Secretary of War Dwight F. Davis directed that a tank force be developed in the Army. Earlier that year he had been much impressed, as an observer of maneuvers in England, by a British Experimental Armored Force. Actually the idea was not new. A small group of dedicated officers in the cavalry and the infantry had been hard at work since World War I on theories for such a force. The continued progress in the design of armor, armament, engines, and vehicles was gradually swinging the trend toward more mechanization, and the military value of the horse declined. Proponents of mechanization and motorization pointed to advances in the motor vehicle industry and to the corresponding decrease in the use of horses and mules. Furthermore, abundant oil resources gave the United States an enviable position of independence in fuel requirements for the machines. Although the horse was not yet claimed to be obsolete, his competition was gaining rapidly, and realistic cavalrymen, sensing possible extinction, looked to at least partial substitution of the faster machines for horses in cavalry units. As late as 1938, on the other hand, the Chief of Cavalry, Maj. Gen. John K. Herr, proclaimed, "We must not be misled to our own detriment to assume that the untried machine can displace the proved and tried horse." He favored a balanced force made up of both horse and mechanized cavalry.

Secretary Davis' 1928 directive for the development of a tank force resulted in the assembly and encampment of an experimental mechanized force at Camp Meade, Maryland, from 1 July to 20 September 1928. The combined arms team consisted of elements furnished by Infantry (including tanks), Cavalry, Field Artillery, the Air Corps, Engineer Corps, Ordnance Department, Chemical Warfare Service, and Medical Corps. An effort to continue the experiment in 1929 was defeated by insufficient funds and obsolete equipment, but the 1928 exercise did bear fruit, for the War Department Mechanization Board, appointed to study results of the experiment, recommended the permanent establishment of a mechanized force.

The Army Chief of Staff, General Charles P. Summerall, was convinced that the tank must be included in the artillery-infantry-machine-gun team, although he had reported in 1928 that the Renault tank had "demonstrated that it was too slow to operate with Cavalry." Just before leaving office in October 1930, General Summerall directed: "Assemble that mechanized force now, station it at Fort Eustis, Virginia. Make it permanent, not temporary."

Within a few weeks the Mechanized Force was organized at Fort Eustis, with Col. Daniel Van Voorhis commanding. Through his leadership in the early development of mechanization, Van Voorhis earned the title of "Grandfather of the Armored Force."

When cavalrymen began to think in terms of a balanced mechanized force in 1931, they, like infantrymen, also preferred the light tank for use in the traditional role of light cavalry. For all practical purposes, therefore, the early 1930's found both the cavalry and the infantry, though internally divided over tactical doctrine, firmly committed to the light tank.

The separate Mechanized Force at Fort Eustis was short-lived, for the War Department, under a new Army Chief of Staff, General Douglas MacArthur, decided in late 1931 to dissolve the organization. In its place, all arms and services were directed to adopt mechanization and motorization, "as far as is practicable and desirable," and were permitted to conduct research and to experiment as necessary. Cavalry was given the task of developing combat vehicles that would "enhance its power in roles of reconnaissance, counterreconnaissance, flank action, pursuit, and similar operations." One of its regiments was to be equipped exclusively with such vehicles. Infantry was to give attention to machines intended to increase its striking power against strongly held positions. Although General MacArthur further decreed that "no separate corps will be established in the vain hope that through a utilization of machines it can absorb the missions, and duplicate the capabilities of all others," increased emphasis was placed upon mechanization.

Two years later General MacArthur set the stage for the coming complete mechanization of the cavalry, declaring, "The horse has no higher degree of mobility today than he had a thousand years ago. The time has therefore arrived when the Cavalry arm must either replace or assist the horse as a means of transportation, or else pass into the limbo of discarded military formations. But," he went on, "there is no possibility of eliminating the need for certain units capable of performing more distant missions than can be efficiently carried out by the mass of the Army. The elements assigned to these tasks will be the cavalry of the future, but manifestly the horse alone will not meet its requirements in transportation."

The organizational structure planned for the new mechanized cavalry regiment in 1932 was similar to the horse regiment. With an authorized strength of 42 officers and 610 enlisted men, the mechanized regiment was divided into a covering squadron, a combat car squadron, a machine gun troop, and a headquarters troop. Like the horse regiment, it had four lettered troops but was equipped with combat vehicles instead of horses. Its covering squadron was divided into an armored car troop and a scout troop, while the combat car squadron had two combat car troops. The mechanized regiment had thirty-five combat cars (light, fast tanks), which were about equally divided among the troops of the combat car squadron and the scout troop of the covering squadron.

Great mobility, armor protection, and firepower were the distinctive characteristics of mechanized cavalry. Its principal role was "in employment on distant missions covering a wide area," but it was not expected to hold objectives for prolonged periods without support of artillery and infantry or horse cavalry.

The cavalry division, in which other arms were combined with cavalry, also underwent organizational changes designed to take advantage of the speed and striking power of modern machines. In the new division three types of units were added—an armored car troop, a tank company, and an air observation squadron. The division retained its 2 horse brigades and had an aggregate war strength of 465 officers and 8,840 men.

Cavalry selected Fort Knox, Kentucky, as its site to develop and test combat vehicles; personnel and equipment from the Fort Eustis force formed the nucleus of the command. In early 1933 the 1st Cavalry arrived from Marfa, Texas, and the process of replacing horses with machines in the regiment began. Thus did the first American mechanized cavalry organization come into being. During the next four years other units, including a battalion of field artillery, a quartermaster company, and another cavalry regiment, the 13th, were moved to Fort Knox and mechanized. The War Department in 1938 modified its 1931 directive for all arms and services to adopt mechanization and motorization. Thereafter, development of mechanization was to be accomplished by two of the combat arms only—the cavalry and the infantry.

In early 1938 the two cavalry regiments and other Fort Knox units were used to form the 7th Cavalry Brigade, with the then Brig. Gen. Daniel Van Voorhis in command. Later that year he was succeeded by Col. Adna R. Chaffee. Formerly second-in-command of the Mechanized Force at Fort

GENERAL CHAFFEE

Eustis, Colonel Chaffee was already a well-known pioneer in, and strong advocate of, mechanization. Recognized as the "Father of the Armored Force," he dedicated his career to the development of armor not only through his service at Fort Knox but also on the War Department General Staff.

The shockingly quick success of the German blitzkrieg into Poland in September 1939 profoundly affected military tactics and doctrine around the world, but perhaps nowhere was the impact greater than upon the cavalry of the U.S. Army. Tank enthusiasts at Fort Knox now began to advocate publicly what they had been considering privately—the formation of true armored divisions, including tanks, motorized infantry, and other arms and services.

Although mechanized cavalrymen had no initial success in their attempts to form armored divisions, a motorized infantry regiment, the 6th, was added to the Fort Knox brigade for the 1940 Louisiana maneuvers. An improvised armored division, formed with the 7th Cavalry Brigade (Mechanized) and the Provisional Tank Brigade from Fort Benning, proved successful—the mechanized troops, in effect, dominated the maneuvers.

Besides the 7th Cavalry Brigade, composed of the 1st and 13th Cavalry (Mechanized), the Regular Army cavalry in 1940 had 12 regiments, 2 of which were horse-mechanized, and the 26th Cavalry of the Philippine Scouts (Regular Army officers with Filipino enlisted men). In addition, 18 cavalry regiments were in the National Guard and 24 in the Organized Reserves.

World War II

Armored Force

At the end of the twenty years between World Wars I and II, an Armored Force finally emerged, but it did not evolve easily. Ardent supporters of armor had advocated even more than mechanized regiments or brigades. They urged divisions, at the least, and some recommended mechanized corps and armies. From the beginning of the 7th Cavalry Brigade's organization in the 1930's, almost continuous efforts had been made to expand it into a division. And while the Chiefs of Infantry and Cavalry had generally supported these attempts, both were opposed to the conversion of any of their existing units to accomplish the expansion. To them this would have resulted in the loss of units, as well as the loss of personnel, at the expense of their authorized branch strengths. Actually, the goal of armor advocates was the organization of a mechanized force that would be completely free from the control of other arms.

At the start of World War II Germany's rapid conquest of Poland in September 1939 demonstrated the power and speed of German armor. In the spring of 1940, panzer units of the German war machine were on the move again, this time rolling westward through the Low Countries and France. Also, during the U.S. Army maneuvers of 1939–40, it had been evident to armor enthusiasts that development of mechanization under cavalry and infantry was not being given enough consideration. The German successes and the Army maneuvers helped armor leaders to convince the War Department of the value of armor and the urgency of establishing similar units in the U.S. Army. On 10 July 1940 the Armored Force was created with Chaffee, promoted now to brigadier general, as its first chief. Since there was no Congressional authorization for a separate armored branch, it was established technically "for purposes of service test."

Authorized 530 officers and 9,329 enlisted men, the new organization was built around the 7th Cavalry Brigade (Mechanized) and the 6th Infantry (Armored) at Fort Knox, and the approximately seven infantry tank battalions in the three infantry (tank) regiments of the Provisional Tank Brigade at Fort Benning. From these units the Armored Force was assembled, and by mid-1942 its assigned strength reached 148,192. Also under command of General Chaffee was the I Armored Corps, activated on 15 July 1940 and consisting of the 1st Armored Division (successor to the 7th Cavalry Brigade) at Fort Knox and the 2d Armored Division (organized from the Provisional Tank Brigade) at Fort Benning. Other elements of the Armored Force were the 70th Tank Battalion at Fort Meade, the Armored Force Board, and an Armored Force School and Replacement Training Center.

Inheriting fewer than 1,000 mostly obsolete tanks and other vehicles, the Armored Force was hampered from the beginning in its efforts to equip its units. One armored division alone, to be fully equipped, required 3,243 vehicles, of which 1,140 were of the combat type. To speed manufacture of new vehicles of all types, current designs were placed in mass production, but it was not until 1943 that the equipment shortage began to ease.

As Chief of the Armored Force, General Chaffee, initially functioning directly under the War Department, was given control over all existing tank units in both infantry and cavalry, as well as certain field artillery and service units. Although not technically the head of an arm, he, in effect, ranked equally with the branch chiefs. As they were activated, all armored corps, armored divisions, and other tank units were to be included in the new organization. Soon responsibility for the development of tactics and techniques for all of its units was also added to the Armored Force's functions.

The illness and then the death of General Chaffee in August 1941 deprived the Armored Force of its first chief. He was succeeded on 1 August 1941 by Maj. Gen. Jacob L. Devers, an artilleryman. The third chief, Maj. Gen. Alvan C. Gillem, Jr., an infantryman, took over from General Devers on 11 May 1943. Each of these chiefs made significant contributions to the development of armored vehicles and weapons and to the organization and training of armored units.

On 7 December 1941 the Japanese bombed Pearl Harbor, and the United States entered the war. The establishment of the Army Ground Forces in March 1942 brought several policy changes. In time the chiefs of arms were eliminated, but the Armored Force was retained as an independent command. Armored divisions and corps, on the other hand, were placed under the commanders of combined arms—those commanding standard corps and armies. Also, as armored units began more advanced phases of training with larger units of other branches, they were detached from the Armored Force. As units were deployed overseas, they were released from the control of the Armored Force. Hence, as the war progressed, the number of units directly controlled by the Armored Force greatly declined, and its attention became centered upon the training of replacement personnel, development of armor tactics and doctrine, and test and procurement of equipment—all functions requiring close and continuous coordination with armored units in combat overseas.

The Armored Force was redesignated twice during the war, becoming the Armored Command on 2 July 1943 and the Armored Center on 20 February 1944. These changes in name better described its changing functions as the war continued.

Four armored corps were activated under the Armored Force, based upon the then American tactical doctrine for employment of armored divisions and larger organizations under armored corps and armies. Under this plan two armored divisions and one motorized infantry division were to form an armored corps. But by late 1943 the War Department decided that armored divisions could be employed properly by standard corps, and it directed that the II, III, and IV Armored Corps be redesignated as the XVIII, XIX, and XX Corps, respectively. The I Armored Corps had already been inactivated overseas and its personnel used in the organization of Seventh Army headquarters.

The basic element of the Armored Force was the armored division—a complete, self-sufficient, combined arms team, whose components, strength, and equipment varied during the war. The first concept saw the division composed of five principal elements: (1) command, (2) reconnaissance, (3) striking, (4) support, and (5) service. Among these, its prime strength was in the striking force, an armored brigade, bristling with 368 tanks and made up of two light armored regiments, a medium armored regiment, and a field artillery regiment. For reconnaissance, the division had a reconnaissance battalion and an attached aviation observation squadron. The division support element had an armored infantry regiment, a field artillery battalion, and an engineer battalion. In the service element were quartermaster, ordnance, and medical battalions and a signal company.

Armor planners designed the armored division as a powerful striking force to be used in rapid offensive action against vital rear area installations. Those objectives were to be reached by penetrating weak points or enveloping open flanks, not by attacking enemy strongpoints. The division's ability for sustained combat was a most important ingredient. Its main characteristics were high mobility, protected firepower, and shock.

Based primarily upon combat experiences, the armored division as originally planned underwent five separate reorganizations. Only two were of much consequence, the one of 1 March 1942 and the other of 15 September 1943.

The 1942 reorganization left the division with 2 armored regiments (one less than previously), or a total of 6 tank battalions, 2 light and 4 medium. Another major change was the elimination of the armored brigade setup and the addition of two combat command headquarters that became popularly known as Combat Commands "A" and "B." These new type organizations provided great flexibility in that they could be composed of any combination of divisional units for as long as the division commander desired. The reorganized artillery called for three identical battalions and a division artillery commander, whose functions closely paralleled those of the infantry division artillery commander. Tanks in the division totaled 390, an increase of nine, with the proportion of mediums to lights being almost two to one, reversing the 1940 ratio of over two to one in favor of the lights. The aggregate strength of the original 1942 division, including attached chaplain and medical personnel, increased the division from 12,697 to 14,620.

The 1943 reorganization, in effect, eliminated another armored regiment from the division, for it replaced the 2 regiments with 3 tank battalions, thereby matching the division's 3 infantry and 3 artillery battalions. Within the new tank battalion, there was an increase from 3 tank companies to 4, 3 being equipped with medium tanks and the fourth with light tanks. In addition to the two combat commands (CCA and CCB) another major headquarters was added to the division, the reserve command (known as CCR or CCC), which was intended for control of the division reserve on the march rather than in combat. The reorganization also changed the armored reconnaissance battalion to a cavalry reconnaissance squadron, a title more in consonance with its cavalry mission. The 1943 division lost about one-third of its tanks, ending up with 263, with the proportion of mediums to lights remaining the same, about two to one. A similar substantial reduction in personnel brought the division strength down to 10,937, or a drop of almost 4,000.

Armored divisions organized under both the 1942 and the 1943 tables of organization participated in combat. The 1st, 2d, and 3d Armored Divisions were in action while under the 1942 tables. The 1st, "Old Ironsides," was later reorganized in Italy under the 1943 tables, but the 2d, "Hell on Wheels," and the 3d, "Spearhead," remained under the 1942 tables throughout the war. All other armored divisions were organized under the 1943 or later tables.

The 1942 organizations were known as "heavy" divisions, while those of 1943 and later were known as "light" divisions. Both types proved to be successful in combat, although each had weaknesses. The heavy division was capable of more sustained action, even though it was very weak in infantry. The light division helped correct the infantry imbalance, but it still needed at least an additional rifle company to form tank-infantry teams on a balanced basis.

In the 1943 division's reserve command, personnel authorizations proved to be inadequate and armored group headquarters and headquarters companies were attached to several divisions to alleviate the deficiency. Not until after the war did new tables of organization and equipment finally rectify this situation.

Near the end of the war the War Department already had under study a proposed structure for the postwar armored division. Recommendations of experienced commanders indicated a trend toward more armored infantry and a total divisional strength of about 15,000, an increase of 4,000. Tank elements appeared headed for little change, although many leaders favored either the light or the heavy type of division. Most commanders agreed that one, perhaps two, tank battalions should be organic to the infantry division. Hence, combat had taught and these proposals would seem to indicate that in the armored division, infantrymen are needed to support tanks, whereas in the infantry division, tanks are needed to support the infantry.

The number of armored divisions increased rapidly from only two in early 1941 to fourteen in late 1942. By the end of the war, sixteen had been activated and all saw service in the war against the European Axis Powers. They were designated as the 1st through the 14th and the 16th and 20th Armored Divisions.

Each of the several reorganizations of armored divisions during the war period usually resulted in numerous redesignations, including numerical changes, for the organic elements, and involved both the armored and the armored infantry regiments. The regiments within most divisions were broken up into separate battalions and other regiments were eliminated. The numerical designations of the resulting battalions had no appearance of any sequence or pattern. Separate armored groups were also formed from the headquarters portion of many of the split-up regiments. Only the 2d and 3d Armored Divisions kept their regiments intact, the 2d retained the 41st Armored Infantry and the 66th and 67th Armored Regiments, and the 3d retained the 36th Armored Infantry and the 32d and 33d Armored Regiments.

Although armor enthusiasts at the beginning of the war insisted upon the mass employment doctrine for armored divisions, and even for armored corps and armies, they also foresaw the continued need for close support of infantry by tanks. They suspected, too, that this infantry need would be satisfied by stripping armored divisions of some of their organic tank battalions to form tank-infantry teams. To prevent the weakening of the armored divisions, separate tank battalions, especially designed for attachment to infantry divisions, were organized concurrently with armored divisions.

When the Armored Force was established in 1940, the 70th Tank Battalion was its only separate or nondivisional tank battalion. By early 1941 four additional separate tank battalions, the 191st through the 194th, were organized from eighteen scattered National Guard divisional tank companies that had been inducted into Federal service. The 192d and the 194th went immediately to the Pacific, where they were assigned to the Provisional Tank Group and fought in the early Philippine Islands Campaign.

At first the structure of the separate tank battalion conformed closely to that of the former infantry tank battalion, but it was later revised to permit the separate battalion to be interchangeable with the tank battalion of the armored division. The 1943 tables of organization eliminated the light and medium battalions and called for a single type of tank battalion composed of one light tank company, three medium tank companies, and headquarters and service companies. This distribution gave the battalion a striking force in its medium companies and a reconnoitering, exploiting, and covering force in its light company. The dual capability of the separate battalion and the battalion of the armored division greatly simplified the functions of the Armored Force in training, supply, administrative, and personnel matters.

To help control the separate battalions, tank group headquarters were organized. With as many as five battalions under the group originally, experience soon proved that number to be too large and a maximum of three was set, a figure that generally prevailed for the remainder of the war. The tank group was primarily charged with supervision of training, but it was also used for specific combat missions. A few tank groups were later expanded to include armored infantry battalions and became armored groups. Their composition closely resembled that usually found in the combat commands of armored divisions.

Additional Regular Army separate (or nondivisional) tank battalions were constituted in 1941 as the 71st through the 80th Tank Battalions, but were shortly redesignated the 751st through the 760th and activated. Most of the separate battalions that followed during World War II were also numbered in the 700 series. By the end of 1944 a peak of 65 such active tank battalions was reached, which was slightly higher than the total of 54 that were elements of the armored divisions.

Tank Design and Production

The devastating firepower and speed of the U.S. Army's armored divisions of World War II was largely the result of the genius of American industry. When Germany invaded western Europe in 1940, the U.S. Army had only 28 new tanks—18 medium and 10 light—and these were soon to become obsolete, along with some 900 older models on hand. The Army had no heavy tanks and no immediate plans for any. Even more serious than the shortage of tanks was industry's lack of experience in tank manufacture and limited production facilities. Furthermore, the United States was committed to helping supply its allies. By 1942 American tank production had soared to just under 25,000, almost doubling the combined British and German output for that year. And in 1943, the peak tank production year, the total was 29,497. All in all, from 1940 through 1945, U.S. tank production totaled 88,410.

Tank designs of World War II were based upon many complex considerations, but the principal factors were those thought to be best supported by combat experience. Among these, early combat proved that a bigger tank was not necessarily a better tank. The development goal came to be a tank combining all the proven characteristics in proper balance, to which weight and size were only incidentally related. Top priority went to mechanical reliability and firepower. Almost as important were maneuverability, speed, and good flotation (low ground pressure). Armor protection for the crew was perhaps less important, although it remained a highly desirable characteristic. The problem here was that only a slight addition to the thickness of armor plate greatly increased the total weight of the tank, thereby requiring a more powerful and heavier engine. This, in turn, resulted in a larger and heavier transmission and suspension system. All of these pyramiding increases tended to make the tank less maneuverable, slower, and a larger and easier target. Thicker armor plate beyond a certain point, therefore, actually meant less protection for the crew. Determining the point at which the optimum thickness of armor was reached, in balance with other factors, presented a challenge that resulted in numerous proposed solutions and much disagreement.

According to Lt. Gen. Lesley J. McNair, Chief of Staff of GHQ, and later Commanding General, Army Ground Forces, the answer to bigger enemy tanks was more powerful guns instead of increased size. And, in his high positions, General McNair understandably exerted much influence upon the development of tanks, as well as antitank guns.

Since emphasis of the using arms was upon light tanks during 1940 and 1941, their production at first was almost two to one over the mediums. But in 1943, as the demand grew for more powerful tanks, the lights fell behind, and by 1945 the number of light tanks produced was less than half the number of mediums.

In early October 1939 the first tank order of the World War II period called for over 300 light (11½ tons) M2A4 tanks. The following year a much improved light tank, the M3, known in England as the General Stuart, was adopted. Although very similar to the M2A4, the M3 was 3½ tons heavier, mounted a 37-mm. gun, and had a maximum speed of 35 miles per hour. Several design changes resulted in a new model, the M4, but its number was soon changed to the M5 to avoid confusion with the M4 medium tank. The M5's weight was increased to 16 tons and its top speed to 40 miles per hour. With the trend toward heavier tanks and more powerful guns, the M5 was replaced in 1944 by the M24 light tank, mounting a 75-mm. gun and weighing 20 tons.

In the medium tank class, improvements in the M2A1 resulted in a completely redesigned tank, known as the M3 medium. As originally produced, it weighed 31 tons and had a top speed of about 25 miles per hour. A 75-mm. gun was mounted in the right sponson and the 37-mm. gun remained in the turret. As furnished to the British under lend-lease, this first model of the M3 medium was known as the General Lee, which is sometimes confused with the later General Grant. The Grant was essentially the same vehicle except for its lower silhouette, achieved by removing the cupola from its turret.

A much improved M3 medium was standardized in 1941 as the M4, better known throughout the war by its British designation, the General Sherman. It weighed around 33 tons and had a maximum speed of about 26 miles per hour. Built on the M3 chassis, the M4 mounted a 75-mm. gun that was, for the first time, in a fully rotating turret. By 1943, numerous redesigns of the M4 medium resulted in modified models mounting 76-mm. or 105-mm. guns, but through all of the changes the basic medium of the U.S. Army remained the M4 mounting the 75-mm. gun. Although it was no match for German heavy tanks in firepower and armor protection, the M4 medium, with its superior mechanical reliability and capacity for traversing rough terrain, especially in mountainous areas, was the workhorse of the war. Employed in practically every conceivable way that a tank could be used, it performed the infantry-accom-

An M3 Medium, or "General Grant," Tank *of the 1st Armored Division in North Africa.*

panying role, it operated as light cavalry, it spearheaded armored attacks, it played an antitank role, and it functioned as auxiliary artillery.

Although emphasis had been placed first upon the development of the light and then upon the medium tank during the early 1940's, there were those who favored a heavier tank. They were willing to sacrifice some speed and maneuverability for the additional shock and firepower primarily needed to overcome heavy fortifications in the direct support of infantry attacks. Several variations of a heavy tank were developed, the M6 being standardized in early 1943. Weighing about 63 tons, it mounted a 3-inch high-velocity gun. Test results achieved by the vehicle did not justify its tremendous weight and, also, since medium tanks were adequately proving themselves in combat in North Africa, the War Department decided to provide for only one heavy tank company.

Continued experiments toward the development of a more reliable heavy tank were largely inspired by the appearance in 1943 of German heavy Panther (47-ton) and Tiger (63-ton) tanks. Great technical strides were made not only in more powerful guns, better armor, and more powerful engines, but also in the transmission and suspension mechanisms. Furthermore, the search was continuous for more effective ammunition and less weight in all components. Finally, a successful heavy tank, the M26 or General Pershing, was developed in

SHERMAN TANKS, MOUNTING 76-MM. GUNS, *move toward the firing line near Bavigne, Luxembourg.*

time for a few to be used in Europe late in the war. Mounting a 90-mm. gun, it weighed approximately 46 tons and had a maximum speed of 25 miles per hour. Although their engagements were limited, the new M26 heavies were very popular with the U.S. Army units with which they fought.

There were several other types of World War II tanks that can be classified as special purpose. In organizations generally of battalion size, they were usually modifications or adaptations of standard tanks and were designed for the specific type of missions intimated by their unit designations. They included amphibious (DD, or duplex-drive, and LVT, or landing vehicle, tank), airborne, searchlight, mine exploders, earth movers (tankdozer and "Rhino," or "Hedgerow Buster," very successfully used in hedgerows of Normandy), flamethrowers, and rocket launchers. Also, a tank for battlefield illumination that projected a light beam through a 2-by-24-inch slit from a searchlight mounted in the turret instead of a 37-mm. gun. Developed behind a tight curtain of secrecy and known simply as the CDL (canal defense light) tank, it was described as a high-powered searchlight for the defense of the Suez Canal. Its combat use was limited to the Rhine River crossings in early 1945.

Tank Destroyers

A paramount reaction in the United States to the German blitzkrieg in Europe, which appeared to be irresistible in 1940, was the demand for some

A CONVOY OF GENERAL PERSHING TANKS NEAR WESEL, GERMANY

means of stopping German armor. The German successes were adversely affecting morale of combat troops, and there was an urgent need for new, effective weapons to calm their fears and prove the vulnerability of the tank.

The main question was whether the job could be done better by tanks or by guns. The American answer was high-velocity guns that were eventually called tank destroyers, although many leaders still favored tanks. Among the most aggressive proponents of mobile antitank guns were General McNair and Lt. Col. Andrew D. Bruce, the latter becoming the first commander of the Tank Destroyer Center.

Other antitank questions that arose involved whether or not the guns should be self-propelled and the size of their caliber. The answers to these and related questions depended principally upon the tactical doctrine to be adopted for antitank units, which, in time, was to be based upon combat experience.

Following experiments in the maneuvers of 1940, the War Department adopted the doctrine of mass employment of high-velocity guns by fast-moving antitank units against tanks. The doctrine called for a minimum of antitank guns

SELF-PROPELLED TANK DESTROYER, *painted white to blend in with the snow. Luxembourg.*

to be placed in fixed initial positions and a maximum to be held in mobile reserve. Choosing the motto "Seek, Strike, and Destroy," tank destroyers were to be aggressive in reconnaissance—seeking out the enemy main armored attack formations and to be prepared for them, but not to chase them. To help dispel the passive connotation of their mission, the antitank battalions were redesignated in late 1941 as tank destroyer battalions.

Antitank companies, equipped with towed 37-mm. guns, first appeared in infantry regiments in the fall of 1940 and augmented the infantry division artillery's 37-mm. antitank guns. Later equipped with 57-mm. guns, the antitank company remained in the infantry regiment for the duration of the war. The divisional artillery antitank units were mostly absorbed by the larger antitank battalions organized in 1941.

When antitank units were first formed, many National Guard divisions were already in Federal service. Consequently, several National Guard units or their personnel were used in the formation of these and later tank destroyer organizations.

The Tank Destroyer Center was temporarily established at Fort Meade, Maryland, then moved to the new Camp Hood, Texas, in February 1942. Later that year, having virtually become a new arm, tank destroyer strength reached almost 100,000. It had 80 active battalions, with 64 more planned. By early 1943, 106 battalions were active, the maximum for the war, only 13 short of the total number of tank battalions. The numerical designations of most tank destroyer battalions were in the 600, 700, and 800 series.

By early 1944 a combination of two principal factors resulted in the inactivation of 28 tank destroyer battalions. First, massed armored forces had not been used against American forces during 1943, and thus fewer tank destroyer units were required. Second, divisions in combat had serious strength shortages, and personnel from tank destroyer units were used as replacements. The rapid decrease left only 78 active tank destroyer battalions, and by the end of March 1945 an additional 10 battalions had been inactivated.

Although there was little need for the concentration of tank destroyer battalions during combat, thirteen tank destroyer groups and a tank destroyer brigade saw action in World War II campaigns, but not as complete organizations. The groups were the 1st through the 9th and the 12th, 16th, 20th, and 23d. The brigade was designated as the 1st. Two brigade headquarters had been organized, but the 2d Tank Destroyer Brigade was inactivated in early 1944.

On the question of self-propelled versus towed guns, combat commanders wavered until the decision was finally made in November 1943 that half the battalions would be self-propelled and half would be towed. Generally the towed gun delivered more accurate fire and was easier to conceal, while the self-propelled one was more mobile and more easily positioned for action. The self-propelled gun, like the tank, was often employed in close support of infantry, although the tank destroyer was not designed or intended for an offensive role.

With a strength of a little less than 800 men, the tank destroyer battalion of 1944 was largely self-sufficient and included strong reconnaissance and antiaircraft elements. It had a total of thirty-six 3-inch or 76-mm. guns (towed or self-propelled), which, in addition to performing their primary antitank missions, were frequently used in a general role of supporting artillery. Various other uses included destroying antitank guns, covering withdrawals, helping to clear minefields, and reinforcing artillery fires. In combat, tank destroyer battalions were usually attached to divisions or other separate organizations.

In general, antitank developments confirmed that tanks could be stopped by guns, and even the psychological influence of tank destroyers upon friendly troops was very effective. Tank destroyers had become a quasi-arm, operating independently, and had successfully resisted all attempts to be absorbed by the old arms and the Armored Force. Battlefield experience, however, showed that a superior tank was a better antitank weapon than the very thinly protected tank destroyer and, with the end of the war, tank destroyers went out of existence. Tank destroyer units were either redesignated, inactivated, or disbanded, and many became tank units.

Cavalry

With the approach of World War II and the creation of the Armored Force in 1940, one of the most perplexing problems confronting the U.S. Army was the form of organization and tactical doctrine for its cavalry. During the years of peace when economy had been the keynote for U.S. military forces, it had been easy to shunt this problem aside; but now, with danger to the free world increasing and partial mobilization already under way, the Army had to face up to how to organize and equip its cavalry.

At the heart of the question, of course, was the military value of the horse. And cavalrymen themselves were far from being united, thus making any solution even more difficult. Many cavalrymen favored complete mechanization, others supported a combination of horses and machines, and still a third group continued to prefer only horses. The last Chief of Cavalry, Maj. Gen. John K. Herr, in testimony before a Congressional committee in 1939 maintained that horse cavalry had "stood the acid test of war," whereas the motor elements advocated by some to replace it had not. Pointing to this country's more than 12,000,000 horses and over 4,500,000 mules at that time, as well as its predominant motor industry, he held that the United States was in a most favorable position to develop the best cavalry forces in the world, both mechanized and horse. On the role of cavalry General Herr declared that those "who wish to reduce cavalry to a purely reconnaissance arm, are entirely wrong, unless reconnaissance is the only mission which cavalry can perform." To Herr, reconnaissance was important to cavalry, but was not its primary mission. "While cavalry must fight in carrying out its mission of reconnaissance, pursuit and covering," he reasoned, "it must also fight in cooperation with the other ground arms to further the accomplishment of the main mission." On types of cavalry his view was that, "although in some cavalry missions it may be better to use horse cavalry alone or mechanized cavalry alone, on the whole the best results can be accomplished by using them together."

This horse-mechanized principle had been applied to two cavalry regiments, the 4th and the 6th. In those units large vans were used for transporting horses to keep pace with the mechanical elements. The horses could be unloaded quickly and employed in mounted actions to supplement operations of the mechanized cavalry. With the 4th and 6th Cavalry already partially mechanized and the 1st and 13th Cavalry under the Armored Force, ten horse cavalry regiments remained. Of these, the 5th, 7th, 8th, and 12th were organic elements of the 1st Cavalry Division, and by late 1941 the 2d, 9th, 10th, and 14th were in the 2d Cavalry Division. Only the 3d and 11th Cavalry were nondivisional mounted regiments.

The Office of the Chief of Cavalry was eliminated in March 1942, along with those of the other combat arms chiefs. His functions were transferred to the newly formed Army Ground Forces and the trend toward mechanization quickened. Nondivisional regiments and squadrons were completely mechanized in the same manner as were the cavalry components of infantry and armored divisions. Several cavalry regiments were used in forming new armored divisions.

Upon the activation of the 9th and 10th Armored Divisions in 1942, initial War Department directives converted and redesignated the 2d, 3d, 11th, and 14th Cavalry as the 2d, 3d, 11th, and 14th Armored Regiments. After transfer of personnel and equipment to the new organizations was almost complete, the directives were changed to inactivate the old cavalry regiments and to activate the armored ones as newly constituted units. During 1943 all four of the old cavalry regiments were reactivated as mechanized cavalry units. Later, in 1951, the descendants of these 4 armored and 4 cavalry regiments were consolidated and reorganized to form 4 armored cavalry regiments.

All nondivisional mechanized cavalry regiments were broken up in 1943 to form separate groups and squadrons. The reorganization coincided with a new War Department principle governing the employment of mechanized cavalry: the units were "organized, equipped, and trained to perform reconnaissance missions employing infiltration tactics, fire, and maneuver." The directive also specified that the units were to engage in combat only to the extent necessary to accomplish their missions. Except for the cavalry divisions, therefore, the official cavalry mission, in general, was reconnaissance, a doctrine that held for the remainder of the war.

Of the two cavalry divisions active during World War II, only the 1st Cavalry Division fought as a unit. It fought dismounted in four major campaigns in the Southwest Pacific and performed occupational duties in Japan following the war. The 2d Cavalry Division was partially inactivated in July 1942, its 4th Cavalry Brigade (including the 9th and 10th Cavalry regiments) remaining active. The division was fully reactivated in February 1943, then completely inactivated between February and May 1944 in North Africa, its personnel being transferred to service units.

Neither of the two cavalry divisions took horses overseas, the explanation being that transportation of horses was too costly in ship tonnage and feeding and upkeep too complex for a motorized army. Whether or not this explanation was valid, it was clear that horses were being banished from the last cavalry unit and, for all practical purposes, from the Army.

The 1st Cavalry Division fought as infantry under special tables of organization and equipment that increased its strength to approximately 11,000 men, around 4,000 less than an infantry division; it retained the basic square or 4-regiment, 2-brigade formation of the cavalry division. Special allowances of heavy weapons and other infantry-type equipment were supplied to the 1st Cavalry Division to compensate for its lack of a 155-mm. howitzer field artillery battalion.

The National Guard, before any of its units were inducted into Federal service during 1940–41, had 4 cavalry divisions, the 21st through the 24th. All 4 were broken up and none entered Federal service, although many of their elements did. Also, conversions and reorganizations of 17 National Guard cavalry regiments before induction resulted in the organization of 7 horse-mechanized cavalry regiments, as well as several field artillery regiments, coast artillery regiments and separate battalions, and an antitank battalion. Thus, after the reshuffling, 7 partially mechanized regiments and a brigade of 2 horse cavalry regiments entered Federal service. The horse-mechanized regiments were the 101st (New York), 102d (New Jersey), 104th (Pennsylvania), 106th (Illinois), 107th (Ohio), 113th (Iowa), and the 115th (Wyoming); the horse brigade was the 56th (Texas), consisting of the 112th and 124th Cavalry (Texas). While in Federal service, all of the horse-mechanized regiments were completely mechanized and split up to form groups and separate squadrons, similarly to those of the Regular Army. The horse regiments, the 112th and 124th, were dismounted, withdrawn from the 56th Cavalry Brigade, and re-organized as infantry with much the same composition as regiments of the 1st Cavalry Division. Finally, in mid-1944, the Headquarters and Headquarters Troop, 56th Cavalry Brigade, became the 56th Reconnaissance Troop, Mechanized.

Seventy-three nondivisional cavalry units were active in the Army during the war. In general, they were squadrons and groups, many of which had been formed by breaking up nondivisional cavalry regiments. Each mechanized cavalry group was composed of a headquarters and headquarters troop and two or more attached mechanized cavalry reconnaissance squadrons. Groups were assigned to armies and further attached to corps, most of the attachments, in practice, being permanent. Corps frequently attached the groups to divisions—usually infantry divisions—for operations only.

Divisional cavalry units included a mechanized cavalry reconnaissance squadron for each light armored division, an armored reconnaissance battalion for each heavy armored division, and a cavalry reconnaissance troop for each infantry division.

The last horse cavalry unit of the Army to fight mounted was the 26th Cavalry regiment of the Philippine Scouts, which, in early 1942 after withdrawal to Bataan, was forced to destroy its horses and fight on foot. The fall of the Philippines did not bring the military use of horses to an end. Although no U.S. unit while overseas was fully organized under tables of organization and equipment providing for horses, there were several instances of their use by provisionally organized units. For operations in jungles and mountains, horses proved to be especially suitable as pack animals. For example, during a 700-mile march through the jungles of India and Burma, the 5307th Composite Unit (Provisional), a task force under Brig. Gen. Frank D. Merrill and nicknamed

"Merrill's Marauders," had approximately 340 horses as well as 360 mules. In another action the 3d Infantry Division, while in Sicily, organized the 3d Provisional Reconnaissance Troop, Mounted, which was employed for several months during the invasion of Italy and the subsequent fighting in its mountainous terrain. In September 1943 the troop had 143 horses; 349 mules were also in its attached pack train.

Between mid-1940 and mid-1941 the cavalry strength of the active army more than quadrupled, from slightly under 13,000 to over 53,000. By 31 May 1945 it reached 91,948, its peak strength during the war.

Most of the mechanized cavalry units fought in Europe, where, notwithstanding their prescribed general reconnaissance role, the types of missions assigned and the approximate percentages of their frequency of occurrence were: (1) defensive combat, including defense, delaying action, and holding of key terrain until the arrival of main forces, 33 percent; (2) special operations, including acting as a mobile reserve, providing for security and control of rear areas, and operating as an army information service, 29 percent; (3) security for other arms, including blocking, screening, protecting flanks, maintaining contact between larger units, and filling gaps, 25 percent; (4) offensive combat, including attack, pursuit, and exploitation, 10 percent; and (5) reconnaissance, 3 percent. Hence, purely reconnaissance missions for mechanized cavalry were rare, and defensive missions were common. For offensive, defensive, and security missions, the mechanized cavalry group was normally reinforced by a battalion of field artillery, a battalion of tank destroyers, and a company of combat engineers.

Mechanized cavalry units operated dismounted during combat almost twice as frequently as they did mounted. But this was no surprise to cavalry leaders, whose general mood was that such units in the future should be trained and organized for considerable dismounted action.

A unique role was spectacularly performed by the 6th Cavalry Group, assigned to the Third Army, in Europe. Taking advantage of the power of its communications equipment and the speed of its vehicles, the army commander, Lt. Gen. George S. Patton, Jr., used the group to maintain contact with his far-flung forces, elements of which were often as much as a hundred miles away from his army command post. Patton actually renamed the group the Army Information Service; it became more popularly known as Patton's "Household Cavalry."

Many cavalrymen were of the opinion that mechanized cavalry had been either generally improperly employed or inadequately organized for the several types of missions it had been called upon to perform during the war. In fact, a group of combat-experienced senior officers and mechanized unit commanders concluded that "the mission which was assigned to mechanized cavalry, reconnaissance with minimum of fighting, was unsound . . . ," and that its mission "should be combat." They believed that "the future role of mechanized cavalry should be the traditional cavalry role of a highly mobile, heavily armed and lightly equipped combat force, and that the capability of mechanized cavalry, particularly that normally operating under the corps, to perform that role, should be exploited."

Post-World War II

Armor, as the ground arm of mobility, emerged from World War II with a lion's share of the credit for the Allied victory. Indeed, armor enthusiasts at that time regarded the tank as being the main weapon of the land army. But demobilization quickly followed the end of hostilities and, in essence, the armor strength was destroyed. By mid-1948 the Regular Army divisions of all types were reduced to ten; the 2d Armored Division remained as the lone division organized as armored until 1951, when the 1st Armored Division was again activated. Furthermore the Armored Center at Fort Knox was inactivated on 30 October 1945, and most of its functions were assumed by the Armored School.

Even after the end of World War II, however, there was unusual need for mechanized organizations in the requirements of the occupational forces in Europe. Highly mobile security forces with flexible organizations and a minimum of personnel were needed, and armor and cavalry units were more readily adaptable to the task than infantry. Consequently, the U.S. Constabulary in Europe absorbed most of the elements of the 1st and 4th Armored Divisions. These units were gradually reorganized and redesignated as constabulary organizations, the U.S. Constabulary becoming fully operational on 1 July 1946.

In addition to its headquarters and special troops, the Constabulary consisted of the 1st, 2d, and 3d Constabulary Brigades and the 1st, 2d, 3d, 4th, 5th, 6th, 10th, 11th, 14th, and 15th Constabulary Regiments. Most regiments had the usual three squadrons. Each regiment, to carry out its peculiar peacetime duties, had a light tank troop, a motorcycle platoon (25 motorcycles), and a horse platoon (30 horses).

By early 1947 the Constabulary strength reached nearly 35,000, but continuing turnover in personnel was one of its major problems. On 24 November 1950, Headquarters and Headquarters Company, U.S. Constabulary, was inactivated; most of its units were assigned to the newly activated Seventh Army. The last of the units, the 2d Constabulary Brigade and the 15th and 24th Constabulary Squadrons, continued to operate until inactivated on 15 December 1952.

Since the Armored Force had been created as a temporary measure for World War II, armor was not a permanent arm to which officers could be assigned. The officers retained their basic branch while serving with armored (tank) units. To prevent the loss of identity of armored officers, the War Department began action in early 1947 to assign them to the cavalry. At the same time, announcement was made of expected eventual statutory approval of an armored cavalry arm to replace cavalry. Pending that action, all qualified armored (tank) officers were to be detailed in cavalry, unless they objected. Cavalry officers not qualified in and not desiring to serve with armor could be transferred to or detailed to other arms and services.

As late as August 1949, official publications listed armored cavalry, instead of cavalry, as a branch of the Army. Described as "an arm of mobility, armor-protected firepower, and shock action," armored cavalry was to engage in all types of combat actions in co-ordination with other arms and services. Reconnaissance types of missions were usually to be performed by light armored cavalry units, which were to avoid sustained offensive or defensive combat.

Use of the term *armored cavalry* was a compromise between those who wanted the word *armor* in the new branch name and those who were as reluctant to discard the term *cavalry* as they had been to part with their horses. To others, especially those who had not served with horse cavalry, armor was a new medium, and that term best described the branch. On the other hand, proponents for the continued use of the term *cavalry* contended that armor, or whatever it might be called, still was the mounted branch—regardless of its mode of transportation—teaching the same principles of mobility, firepower, and shock action. The combination term, *armored cavalry,* was not popular with either group, but the matter was finally resolved, at least legally, when Congress, in its Army Organization Act of 1950, designated *armor* as the new branch name and further provided that it would be "a continuation of the cavalry."

The armored division after World War II was larger and heavier than it had been during the war. Its authorized personnel strength was increased in 1948 from 10,670 to 15,973; its tank strength was increased from 272 to 373, most of the additional tanks being in the medium and heavy classes. The reserve command received additional officers, men, and equipment, placing it on a par with the two combat commands and enabling it to function as a third combat command when needed. Also added to the division were a battalion of heavy tanks, a battalion of heavy artillery, and a battalion of infantry; infantry companies were increase from 3 to 4 in the battalions, boosting the total infantry companies for the division from 9 to 16.

The 1st Cavalry Division, which continued to be the only division bearing the cavalry designation, was reorganized as infantry in 1945, its units retaining their cavalry designations. In the 1949 reorganization, however, only the division and its cavalry regiments survived the change to infantry designations, the squadrons becoming battalions and the troops becoming companies. The 1949 reorganization deleted one cavalry regiment, leaving the division with three, the 5th, 7th, and 8th; the 12th was inactivated and withdrawn.

Except for the cavalry units in the U.S. Constabulary and those in the 1st Cavalry Division, there were no other active cavalry regiments in the Regular Army until the 3d Armored Cavalry was organized in 1948. Later that year three other armored cavalry regiments, the 2d, 6th, and 14th, were organized, their elements consisting of converted and redesignated units of the U.S. Constabulary.

The armored cavalry regiment of late 1948, with three reconnaissance battalions as its principal elements, had an authorized strength of 2,883 and was equipped with 72 light and 69 medium tanks.

One of the most difficult problems facing the National Guard after World War II was preservation of the historical continuity of its units. While in Federal service during the war, most National Guard units had undergone many redesignations, reorganizations, and inactivations. After the war the types of units allotted to the National Guard often varied considerably from the types inducted during the war. To keep from losing the histories of units traditional to certain geographical areas, the Department of the Army permitted the postwar units to retain the histories of the prewar units. Thus, in most instances, units allotted after the war perpetuated histories of prewar units.

Heading the post-World War II list of National Guard armor and cavalry units were the 49th and 50th Armored Divisions of Texas and New Jersey, respectively. Nondivisional units included 5 armored groups, 3 cavalry groups, 31 tank battalions, and 15 cavalry reconnaissance squadrons. Each of the 25 National Guard infantry divisions had a mechanized cavalry reconnaissance troop and a tank battalion, and each infantry regiment had a tank company. The National Guard had no horse cavalry units.

In the Organized Reserves, cavalry and tank units activated in late 1946 were the 19th Armored Division, the 301st through the 304th Cavalry Groups, the 75th Amphibian Tank Battalion, the 782d Tank Battalion, the 314th and 315th Cavalry Reconnaissance Battalions, and the 83d Reconnaissance Troop. In early 1948 the Organized Reserves became the Organized Reserve Corps, and in 1952 this component became the Army Reserve.

With swift advances during the postwar period in the development of atomic and recoilless weapons, rockets, and guided missiles, the tank appeared to many to be obsolete. Although emphasis upon armor did decline, efforts continued toward development of a tank with greater firepower and armor protection without losing mobility. But costs were increasing sharply. For example, the initial price of equipping an armored division rose from 30 million dollars in 1944 to about 200 million in 1950. A single light tank costing $27,000 in 1939 increased to about $225,000 in 1950.

Because of rising costs and the trend toward atomic weapons and missiles, the modern Army's requirement for tanks was not sufficient to command all the funds for the tank development many advocated. Some progress, however, was made. In late 1948 the M46 Patton was introduced. Named for General Patton, the M46 was a modified version of the M26 of late World War II. Still mounting a 90-mm. gun, but with increased power and speed, the M46 was capable of 30 miles per hour. The Army was also modifying the M24 light tank into the T37 and T41, mounting 76-mm. guns.

Korean War

When North Korea suddenly attacked the Republic of Korea on 25 June 1950, the U.S. Army was weak in tanks, and its units initially entered combat in Korea without them. The 7th, 24th, and 25th Infantry Divisions and the 1st Cavalry Division (organized as infantry), all on occupational duty in Japan, had assigned to them the 77th, 78th, 79th, and 71st Tank Battalions, respectively. But only one company (A) of each battalion had been organized, and those companies had only M24 light tanks. Heavier tanks, it was feared, would damage Japanese roads and bridges.

Although the rugged terrain in Korea had been considered generally unsuitable for tank employment, Russian-made T34's were used with success by the North Koreans during the early days of the war. American tanks were rushed to the scene in support of the United Nations and engaged in their first combat on 10 July. For several weeks they were outnumbered, and it was not until late August that the tank balance in Korea was tipped in favor of the United Nations. By then more than 500 U.S. tanks were in the Pusan Perimeter, outnumbering the enemy's there by over five to one. For the remainder of the war, tank units of battalion size and smaller were in most combat actions.

Tank battalions in the early Korean fighting of July and August 1950 were the 6th, 70th, 72d, 73d, and 89th, averaging 69 tanks each. The 6th was equipped with M46 Pattons; the other battalions were about equally divided between M26 Pershings and M4A3 Shermans. The 64th Tank Battalion entered the war in early November 1950 with the 3d Infantry Division.

No armored divisions were sent to Korea, although six armored divisions, the 1st, 2d, 3d, 5th, 6th, and 7th, were soon active. Actually only two, the 1st and 2d, were organized as armored, the others being principally training organizations, and only the 2d went overseas, going to Germany in 1951.

The armored division strength and organization were little changed by a TOE of late 1952, but its tanks, totaling 343, mounted more powerful guns. One battalion was authorized 69 heavy tanks (T43's, which later became M103's) with 120-mm. guns, the heaviest weapon yet carried by an American tank. Weighing approximately sixty tons and carrying a crew of five, the T43

MEN OF COMPANY B, 7TH CAVALRY, IN AN M4A3 TANK NEAR CHIPYONG,
KOREA

was the largest and most powerful tank that had been produced by the United
States. Three battalions of the division each had 72 mediums (M47's) with
90-mm. guns, and the reconnaissance battalion had 30 light tanks (T41E1's)
mounting 76-mm. guns. The new model light tank was a modified version of
the T41, and was christened the "Walker Bulldog" in early 1951 in honor
of Lt. Gen. Walton H. Walker, killed in the Korean War. An additional 28
light tanks were dispersed within the division—3 to each combat command
and to the division headquarters company and 2 to each tank and armored
infantry battalion.

In mid-1952 a new medium tank, the M48, also named the Patton, was
introduced. With an improved fire control system, it was proclaimed to be
capable of more first round hits than any other American tank yet built.
Weighing 45 to 50 tons and armed with a high-velocity 90-mm. gun, the new
medium had a crew of four—one less than its preceding model.

The activation in 1951 of the 11th Armored Cavalry brought the total
active regiments of this type to five for the Korean War period, but none

served in the Far East. The other four active regiments were the 2d, 3d, 6th, and 14th. The primary role of the armored cavalry regiment was described in 1951 as being "to engage in security, light combat, and reconnaissance missions. The regiment is not designed to engage in combat with hostile armor or strongly organized defenses."

Many Army National Guard units went into Federal service during the Korean War. Eight N.G. infantry divisions were called in, and organic to each were a tank battalion and a reconnaissance company. The 40th Infantry Division (California) and 45th (Oklahoma) fought in Korea; the 28th (Pennsylvania) and 43d (Connecticut, Rhode Island, and Vermont) went to Germany; and the 31st (Alabama and Mississippi), 37th (Ohio), 44th (Illinois), and 47th (Minnesota and North Dakota) became training organizations for individual replacements for the Army. Other National Guard units entering Federal service brought N.G. units mobilized to approximately one-fourth of the total number organized and federally recognized.

Early in the war the period of service was set at 21 months; later it was extended to 24 months. In August 1952 when it became obvious that two years would not see the end of the war, Congress—disturbed that many areas of the country had sent most of their Guard units into service and had few at home stations—passed legislation to provide for the organization of corresponding National Guard units. These units would bear the same designations as those in the service, with the addition of "(NGUS)" after their designations. This arrangement permitted the states and territories to organize units, and to assign men returning from duty with a unit in Federal service to its counterpart in the National Guard. Maximum Federal service for Guard units (not personnel) was fixed at five years, and as the units reverted to state or territory control, the corresponding NGUS units were dropped.

Generally the system worked as planned, but in a few instances it did not. The NGUS units in some states or territories were not organized in the same geographical areas as their counterparts and hence were not historical continuations of them. Other units, upon release from active military service, were not relocated in their former areas. In both instances, significant factors were the continuing changes in Department of the Army mobilization requirements for National Guard units and changes in the organizational structure for Regular Army units that were also applied to the National Guard.

Although the Korean Armistice Agreement of 27 July 1953 ended large-scale combat in Korea, military forces were still required in positions of readiness.

Post-Korean War

The decade following the Korean armistice was marked by two major reorganizations of U.S. Army divisions, both of which influenced the structure of armor units. First came the pentomic (or pentana) plan of 1957–59, then the Reorganization Objective Army Divisions (ROAD) plan of 1962–64. Underlying these reorganizations were developments in nuclear weapons that made wide dispersion, high mobility, and great flexibility—without loss of massed firepower—mandatory characteristics for military forces. Combat areas of future nuclear wars were viewed as much broader and deeper than battle-fields of the past, requiring small, self-contained, fast-moving units. Speed was imperative not only in the concentration of forces for attack but also in dispersion for defense. On the other hand, the Army had to retain its ability to fight limited or nonnuclear wars, where the requirements for mobility or dispersion were not as important.

Tests of new division organizational concepts for atomic warfare, begun in early 1955, culminated in late 1956 in the pentomic organization, and by mid-1958 the new scheme had been applied to all armored divisions. Since combat commands already provided much of the flexibility that was sought, little change was made in the basic structure of the armored division. The greatest change was in firepower, the division artillery being given an atomic capability. The division still had its four tank battalions, and all were authorized 90-mm.-gun tanks (one battalion had previously been authorized 120-mm.-gun tanks). Armored infantry and field artillery battalions also remained at four each. A small increase in tanks brought the full-strength total to 360— 306 mounting 90-mm. guns and 54 mounting 76-mm's. Strength of the new division stood at 14,617, only 34 fewer than its former number.

From 1951 to 1955 the Regular Army had two active armored divisions— the 1st and the 2d. In 1955 the 3d and 4th were added. Three continued as active divisions for the remainder of the 1953–68 period; the 1st Armored Division was reduced to a single combat command from 1957 to 1962.

By late 1955 the Army National Guard armored divisions had been increased from 2 to 6 by converting 4 infantry divisions—the 27th, 30th (that portion in Tennessee), 40th, and 48th. The North Carolina portion of the 30th Infantry Division became a full infantry division and retained "30th" also as its numerical designation. As of mid-1967, Army National Guard had the following armor units: 6 armored divisions, 2 armored brigades (separate), 7 armored cavalry regiments, an armored cavalry squadron, and 16 separate tank battalions. Also, the 17 infantry divisions of the National Guard had 34 tank battalions and 17 cavalry squadrons.

The second major reorganization of Army divisions, known as ROAD, was completed in 1964. Under this plan the Army was to have four types of divisions —airborne, infantry, armored, and mechanized—the base upon which each was built, being essentially the same. All had their usual types of organic reconnaissance, artillery, and support units. The main differences came in the maneuver elements—tank and infantry battalions—which varied with mission and other factors. All had three brigade headquarters, which, in the armored division, corresponded to its former combat commands. Thus while the organization of all divisions became more flexible, the change in the armored division was less than in other types.

For example, a ROAD armored division with a composition of 6 tank and 5 mechanized infantry battalions would have a full-strength total of 15,966. Since each tank battalion was equipped with 2 light- and 54 medium-gun tanks and each mechanized infantry battalion had 2 light-gun tanks, this combination of maneuver battalions gave an armored division 40 light- and 324 medium-gun tanks, including the 18 light tanks of its armored cavalry squadron.

Concurrent with the division reorganizations, another major change having far-reaching effect upon the organization of most combat-type units was the Combat Arms Regimental System, or CARS. Arrival of the atomic era with its new weapons and tactical doctrine had rendered the regiment, the traditional fighting unit of the Army, obsolete—it was too large.

Even during World War II armored regiments, except those of the 2d and 3d Armored Divisions, were broken up to form separate battalions, and many old cavalry regiments had been dismembered to form new units. With approval of the CARS plan early in 1957, the old cavalry and armored regiments could be revived, at least in name, to continue their regimental histories.

As illustrated in Chart No. 1, the plan provided an average of approximately fifteen battalions that could be organized to perpetuate the lineage and honors of a single regiment. The regimental headquarters was placed under Department of the Army control, and the other regimental elements were used to form separate battalions or squadrons as needed. Within these battalions and squadrons the organic elements were new.

Parent regiments for use under CARS were carefully selected. Except for the 2d, 3d, 6th, 11th, and 14th Armored Cavalry regiments, the 1st through the 17th Cavalry regiments were included. Armor parent regiments were the 32d through the 35th, the 37th, 40th, 63d, 64th, the 66th through the 70th, and the 72d, 73d, 77th, and 81st. A subsequent decision by the Department of the Army that CARS cavalry regiments would contain reconnaissance-type units instead of tank battalions caused the redesignation of three cavalry regiments—the 13th, 15th, and 16th—as the 13th, 15th, and 16th Armor. Not affected by this decision were those elements of the 5th, 7th, and 8th Cavalry, assigned to the 1st Cavalry Division, which remained organized as infantry. When the CARS reorganization was completed, cavalry had 9 regiments and armor had 20. Elements of these parent regiments were organized in both the Regular Army and the Army Reserve. Army National Guard parent regiments were selected from National Guard units.

The 2d, 3d, 6th, 11th, and 14th Armored Cavalry, which were not reorganized under CARS, retained their regimental structure. Four armored cavalry

ARMOR OR CAVALRY REGIMENTS
Under Combat Arms Regimental System

(Organic elements vary in number and designations)

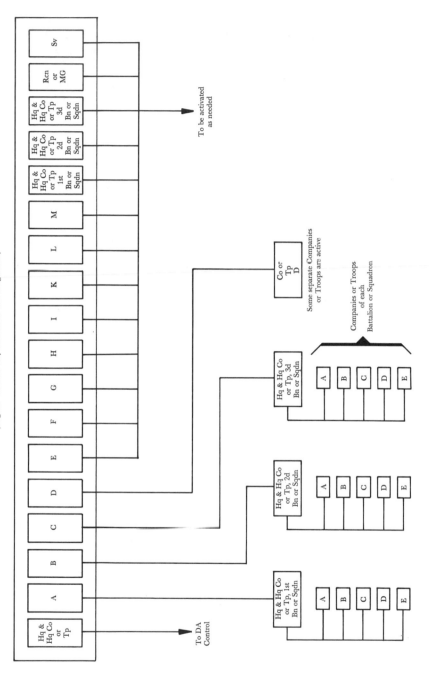

regiments remained active in the Regular Army, the 6th being inactivated in May 1961 and reactivated in March 1967.

Under the 1963 reorganization of the armored cavalry regiment, its organic elements reverted to the traditional cavalry designations of squadrons and troops and an aviation company was added. There was little change in the personnel or tank totals for the regiment. Under the 1965 tables, the regiment's full strength rose to 3,349, an increase of 550, and an air cavalry troop replaced the aviation company. The 1965 regiment had 48 helicopters, while its tanks numbered 132, an increase of 10.

In an era abundant with new weapons and organizations for the modern Army, yet another new military concept dawned in the mid-1950's when air vehicles were included in cavalry units. As part of a training maneuver, Operation SAGEBRUSH, during the winter of 1955-56, tests were made of an organization, called "Sky Cav," that had light tanks, reinforced infantry, and helicopters. Among its special equipment were electronic, photographic, and other devices for detecting an enemy at night as well as during the day. Initially the idea stemmed from a broadening of the term *communications* to cover "not only the transmission of information within Army units but also the acquisition and relay of combat intelligence on enemy activities, including observation and reconnaissance." It was in the nature of this reconnaissance phase of communications that "Sky Cav," combining both air and ground elements in the same unit, was born. First to be authorized a unit of this type was the airborne division, its airborne reconnaissance troop of 1956 being authorized 12 helicopters—10 light cargo and 2 observation. In 1957, with the advent of CARS, Troop B, 17th Cavalry, was organized in the 101st Airborne Division and was soon followed by Troop A, 17th Cavalry, in the 82d Airborne Division.

By late 1957 the feasibility of armed helicopters had been accepted by the Department of the Army, and a third dimension was added to the Army battlefield. In September 1959 a provisional unit, called an aerial reconnaissance and security troop, was organized for test purposes within the 2d Infantry Division. It was equipped with 27 helicopters, 17 of which were armed.

When the divisions were reorganized under ROAD, the 1963 tables of organization and equipment provided for an air cavalry troop in the armored cavalry squadron in all types of divisions. The mission of the air cavalry troop was described as being the extension, by aerial means, of the squadron's reconnaissance and security capabilities. The troop's principal elements were an aero scout platoon, an aero rifle platoon, a service platoon, a flight operations section, and an aero weapons section. At full strength, it was equipped with 26 helicopters. In the airborne division, the air cavalry troop had greater firepower and a few more men.

When the 120-mm.-gun tank was eliminated in late 1955, more emphasis had been placed upon the medium-gun tank as the Army's main battle tank.

LAUNCHING A SHILLELAGH *from the General Sheridan armored reconnaissance airborne assault vehicle.*

By mid-1959 the first of the new M60 series, in the medium tank class, was placed in production. Mounting a 105-mm. gun and having a diesel engine, the M60 had more firepower and greater operational range than its predecessor, the M48. It also had improved crew protection and slightly less over-all weight.

The development of an entirely new weapons system, known as the Shillelagh, to provide a direct fire, surface-to-surface, guided missile that could be vehicle mounted, was hailed in 1961 as the initiation of a program to produce a "radical, new main battle tank." Four years later the Shillelagh system was installed on a revolutionary new tank, the XM551 General Sheridan, and for the first time a guided missile became part of a combat vehicle's main armament. Its 152-mm.-gun launcher had the dual capability of firing conventional rounds and launching missiles; the conventional ammunition represented another first with its fully combustible cartridge case. Also, with aluminum armor, the new tank weighed only about 16.5 tons combat loaded and had a maximum speed of over 40 miles per hour. The General Sheridan not only had greater firepower and ground mobility than any other current U.S. Army tank but also had both amphibious and airdrop capabilities. Moreover, its Shillelagh missile system was

MEN OF TROOP B, 1ST RECONNAISSANCE SQUADRON, 9TH CAVALRY *jumping from a helicopter near Dic Pho, Vietnam.*

adaptable for installation on existing tanks in the M60 series. Changes in tactics and doctrine were in process to keep pace with the combat potential of the remarkable new tank and weapons system. Despite these giant strides in the development of armor vehicles and weapons, a program for yet another new main battle tank for the 1970 Army was already under way in a co-operative effort of the United States and West Germany. After three years of development, the first prototype of this joint undertaking—the MBT–70, described as the most advanced military tracklaying combat vehicle in existence—was unveiled in October 1967.

During the summer of 1965 the 1st Cavalry Division was reorganized as still another type of division, called airmobile, and was dispatched to the Republic of Vietnam when the U.S. Army began deploying major combat forces to help that country in its struggle for independence. The airmobile principle emphasized the use of Army aircraft to increase the division's battlefield mobility.

The airmobile scheme appears to have an even more far-reaching potential than this divisional concept—that of providing the long-sought capability of vertical envelopment by armor. Almost continuous experiments during World War II and since have still not resulted in a successful airborne tank. So far, a tank light enough to be airborne has not been rugged enough for survival in modern warfare. But progress in weight reducing—such as aluminum armor—and in air transportability—such as the air supertransport—is rapidly narrowing the gap separating armor and airborne, and another major breakthrough could be in the offing.

The Army's arm of mobility spans nearly all of the 200 years of U.S. Army history. From the horse cavalry of the American Revolution to the armor and air cavalry of the Vietnam conflict, continuous improvements have been made in organization and techniques to take advantage of the constant advances in weaponry and equipment.

A few modern cavalry units can trace their lineages as far back as 1833, but the cavalry as an arm did not come into real prominence in the U.S. Army until the Civil War. Although some units existed from the American Revolution through the War of 1812, there were no organized cavalry units at all from 1815 to 1833. Then, as the country moved westward, horse cavalry in the Indian Wars—both before and after the Civil War—indelibly etched its place in U.S. Army history.

After the coming of the internal combustion engine in the early 1900's, warfare entered upon a new phase during World War I. Tanks emerged and horses were used little. Between World Wars I and II, both tanks (as a part of infantry) and cavalry continued. Cavalry gradually became partially mechanized, some of its mechanized elements joining with tanks to form the Armored Force for World War II. The remaining cavalry units were either mechanized or dismounted before entering combat. Following World War II, after much controversy, the mechanized cavalry and armored units were finally welded together in 1950 into a single armor branch. Now, with airmobile units becoming prominent, another transition may be in the making. First, the mounted arm had the horse, next the tank, and then the helicopter as its means of mobility. Currently airborne armored units are being seriously discussed, and the types of future organizations and their tactics appear to be limitless. The only reasonable prediction that can be made is that change and progress will continue. With that background, no conclusion for this narrative has more appeal than a quotation from General Chaffee, made at the start of World War II, that rings as true today as it did then:

It is often said, and it may be true in the abstract, that the *principles* of war do not change. It is, nevertheless, absolutely true that *methods* do change and are constantly changing. We may study the great captains of the past to learn of their principles and, above all, of their character, but do not let us be tied too much to their methods. For methods change with every change of armament and equipment.

HERALDIC ITEMS

Heraldic items for Army organizations reflect history, tradition, ideals, and accomplishments. Coats of arms, historic badges, and distinctive insignia have been so designed that each is distinctive to the organization for which approved. They serve as identifying devices and as an inspiration and an incentive for unity of purpose.

A coat of arms or a historic badge and a distinctive insignia are authorized for each regiment. The designs of these items are based on the lineages and battle honors of the organizations.

While the custom of bearing various symbols on shields, helmets, and flags existed in antiquity, heraldry was not introduced until the Middle Ages. The use of heraldic devices became more prevalent with the increased use of armor and the requirements for insignia to assist in distinguishing friend from foe on the battlefield. The symbols selected for use on these devices were commemorative of incidents of valor, mythological beasts, and, later, other symbols to which specific symbolism was ascribed. These heraldic bearings were placed on a surcoat worn over the armor, from which the term *coat of arms* was derived. Gradually a formal system of heraldry evolved, complete with rules for design, use, and display. These rules or principles were for the purpose of facilitating designs that would be distinctive and easily recognized. Present-day heraldic devices stem from this heraldic system which was established during the twelfth and thirteenth centuries.

A complete coat of arms consists of a shield, a crest, and a motto. The shield, the most important portion of the arms, contains the field or ground on which the charges are placed. The crest as originally used was placed upon the top of the helmet of the chief or leader to enable his followers to distinguish him during battle. The crest is placed upon a wreath of six skeins or twists composed of the principal metal and principal color of the shield, alternately, in the order named. This wreath (or torse) represents the piece of cloth which the knight twisted around the top of his helmet, and by means of which the actual crest was attached. Mottoes have been in use longer than coats of arms, many of the older ones having originated from war cries. They usually are of an idealistic nature and sometimes allude to a well-known event in the history of the organization.

Some organizations are authorized historic badges of a symbolic composition in lieu of coats of arms. These badges are not shield-shaped, but they include mottoes.

The elements of the coat of arms or the badge, as applicable, are embroidered on the organizational flag—the central element of which is the American eagle. The shield of the coat of arms is on the eagle's breast; a scroll bearing the motto is held in his beak; and the crest is placed above his head. On flags of those organizations which have historic badges in lieu of coats of arms, the badge is placed above the eagle's head and the scroll bearing the motto is in his beak.

Distinctive insignia, manufactured in metal and enamel and worn on the uniform by all personnel of the regiment, usually are based on elements of the design of the coat of arms or historic badge. Thus the organizational flag (color) and the distinctive insignia include the same design elements.

Heraldic items today, as in the past, serve to distinguish specific organizations and their members.

1st Cavalry

2d Armored Cavalry

3d Armored Cavalry

4th Cavalry

5th Cavalry

6th Armored Cavalry

7th Cavalry

8th Cavalry

9th Cavalry

10th Cavalry

11th Armored Cavalry

12th Cavalry

13th Cavalry

14th Armored Cavalry

15th Cavalry

16th Armor

17th Cavalry

32d Armor

33d Armor

34th Armor

35th Armor

37th Armor

40th Armor

63d Armor

64th Armor

66th Armor

67th Armor

68th Armor

69th Armor

70th Armor

72d Armor

73d Armor

77th Armor

81st Armor

LINEAGES AND HERALDIC DATA

Asterisks

Asterisks (*) appearing in the lists of honors for units under the Combat Arms Regimental System (CARS) indicate the honors for which a particular unit is the *earning unit*. This means that either the unit itself, or a unit from which it has directly descended, earned the honor.

Honors for CARS Units

Campaigns and decorations for each battalion and squadron under CARS include all honors of the parent regiment. For troop-sized elements (those that have not been used to form squadrons or battalions), only the honors for which those troops are the *earning units* are listed. In the latter instances, asterisks are unnecessary and are not used, since all of the honors shown for these troops are *earned*.

Authorities for Decorations

Authorities announcing decorations are shown parenthetically in lineages for regiments and for those decorations of their component elements for which the elements are the *earning units*.

89

314-902 O - 69 - 8

1st CAVALRY
(1st Regiment of Dragoons)

HERALDIC ITEMS

COAT OF ARMS

Shield: Tenné (Dragoon yellow), a dragon passant or. (And for informal use the escutcheon encircled with a sword belt sable buckled at base with the belt plate of the Dragoons of 1836 proper bearing the regimental motto in base and "First Cavalry" in chief between two eight-pointed mullets of rays one on dexter side, the other on sinister, all or.)

Crest: On a wreath of the colors, or and tenné, a hawk rising with wings addorsed and elevated sable, langued and membered gules.

Motto: *Animo et fide* (Courageous and Faithful).

Symbolism: The regiment was organized in 1833 as the Regiment of United States Dragoons. Many of its officers and men came from the Battalion of Mounted Rangers that had taken part in the Black Hawk War, shown by the crest.

The color of the Dragoons was orange, shown by the color of the shield, and the dragon is an allusion to the name *Dragoon.* The gold eight-pointed star on the encircling belt was the insignia of the Dragoons until 1851.

DISTINCTIVE INSIGNIA

The distinctive insignia is the crest of the regiment charged upon an eight-pointed orange star surrounded by a black sword belt bearing the motto *Animo et Fide* with the old dragoon belt plate.

LINEAGE AND HONORS

LINEAGE

Constituted 2 March 1833 in the Regular Army as the United States Regiment of Dragoons. Organized 4 March 1833 at Jefferson Barracks, Missouri. Redesignated 15 May 1836 as 1st Regiment of Dragoons. Redesignated 3 August 1861 as 1st Cavalry.

Assigned to 15th Cavalry Division December 1917–May 1918. Assigned to 1st Cavalry Division 20 August 1921–3 January 1933. Reorganized and redesignated 16 January 1933 as 1st Cavalry, Mechanized.

Redesignated 15 July 1940 as 1st Armored Regiment, Light, and assigned to 1st Armored Division. Regiment (less 2d Battalion) reorganized and redesignated 20 July 1944 as 1st Tank Battalion and remained assigned to 1st Armored Division; 2d Battalion concurrently disbanded.

1st Tank Battalion converted and redesignated 1 May 1946 as 1st Constabulary Squadron; concurrently, relieved from assignment to 1st Armored Division and assigned to 15th Constabulary Regiment. Inactivated 20 December 1948 in Germany; concurrently, relieved from assignment to 15th Constabulary Regiment, converted and redesignated as 1st Medium Tank Battalion and assigned to 1st Armored Division. Activated 7 March 1951 at Fort Hood, Texas. Redesignated 20 May 1953 as 1st Tank Battalion. Inactivated (less Company A) 15 February 1957 at Fort Polk, Louisiana, and relieved from assignment to 1st Armored Division. (Company A concurrently reorganized and redesignated as Headquarters and Headquarters Company, 1st Medium Tank Battalion, 1st Cavalry.)

2d Battalion, 1st Armored Regiment, reconstituted 27 February 1951 in the Regular Army, redesignated as 100th Tank Battalion, and assigned to 1st Armored Division. Activated 7 March 1951 at Fort Hood, Texas. Inactivated 15 February 1957 at Fort Polk, Louisiana, and relieved from assignment to 1st Armored Division.

1st and 100th Tank Battalions consolidated and redesignated 15 February 1957 as 1st Cavalry, a parent regiment under the Combat Arms Regimental System (Headquarters and Headquarters Company, 1st Tank Battalion, redesignated as Headquarters and Headquarters Troop, 1st Cavalry).

CAMPAIGN PARTICIPATION CREDIT

Mexican War
Buena Vista
Coahuila 1846
New Mexico 1846
New Mexico 1847
Chihuahua 1848

Indian Wars
Modocs
Apaches
Nez Perces
Bannocks
Pine Ridge
California 1846
California 1852
California 1860
California 1868
New Mexico 1849
New Mexico 1850
New Mexico 1851
New Mexico 1854
New Mexico 1855
New Mexico 1856
Oregon 1851
Oregon 1853
Oregon 1855
Oregon 1856
Oregon 1860
Oregon 1866
Oregon 1867
Oregon 1868
Colorado 1855
Arizona 1857
Arizona 1859
Arizona 1866
Arizona 1868
Arizona 1869
Arizona 1870
Arizona 1871
Arizona 1872
Arizona 1881
Washington 1858
Idaho 1879
Montana 1887

Civil War
Peninsula
Antietam
Fredericksburg
Chancellorsville
Gettysburg
Wilderness
Spotsylvania
Cold Harbor
Petersburg
Shenandoah
Appomattox
New Mexico 1862
Virginia 1862
Virginia 1863
Virginia 1864
Virginia 1865
Maryland 1863

War With Spain
Santiago

Philippine Insurrection
Luzon 1901
Luzon 1902

World War II
Algeria-French Morocco
(with arrowhead)
Tunisia
Naples-Foggia
Anzio
Rome-Arno
North Apennines
Po Valley

Vietnam
Counteroffensive, Phase III
Tet Counteroffensive

DECORATIONS
None.

1st SQUADRON, 1st CAVALRY

(1st Regiment of Dragoons)

RA

(1st Armored Division)

LINEAGE

Constituted 2 March 1833 in the Regular Army as Company A, the United States Regiment of Dragoons. Organized 12 August 1833 at Nashville, Tennessee; joined Regiment 28 August 1833 at Jefferson Barracks, Missouri. Redesignated 15 May 1836 as Company A, 1st Regiment of Dragoons. Redesignated 3 August 1861 as Company A, 1st Cavalry. (Cavalry companies officially designated as troops in 1883.) (1st Cavalry assigned to 15th Cavalry Division December 1917–May 1918; assigned to 1st Cavalry Division 20 August 1921– 3 January 1933.) Reorganized and redesignated 16 January 1933 as Company A, 1st Cavalry, Mechanized.

Reorganized and redesignated 15 July 1940 as Company A, 1st Armored Regiment, an element of the 1st Armored Division. Reorganized and redesignated 20 July 1944 as Company A, 1st Tank Battalion, with personnel from Company G, 1st Armored Regiment.

Converted and redesignated 1 May 1946 as Troop A, 1st Constabulary Squadron; concurrently, relieved from assignment to 1st Armored Division and assigned to 15th Constabulary Regiment. Inactivated 20 December 1948 in Germany; concurrently, converted and redesignated as Company A, 1st Medium Tank Battalion, relieved from assignment to 15th Constabulary Regiment and assigned to 1st Armored Division. Activated 7 March 1951 at Fort Hood, Texas. Redesignated 20 May 1953 as Company A, 1st Tank Battalion.

Reorganized and redesignated 15 February 1957 as Headquarters and Headquarters Company, 1st Medium Tank Battalion (Patton), 1st Cavalry, and assigned to 1st Armored Division (organic elements concurrently constituted and activated). Reorganized and redesignated 3 February 1962 as 1st Squadron, 1st Cavalry.

94

CAMPAIGN PARTICIPATION CREDIT

Mexican War
  *Buena Vista
  *Coahuila 1846
  New Mexico 1846
  New Mexico 1847
  Chihuahua 1848

Indian Wars
  *Modocs
  *Apaches
  Nez Perces
  *Bannocks
  *Pine Ridge
  California 1846
  *California 1852
  California 1860
  *California 1868
  New Mexico 1849
  New Mexico 1850
  New Mexico 1851
  New Mexico 1854
  New Mexico 1855
  New Mexico 1856
  *Oregon 1851
  *Oregon 1853
  Oregon 1855
  Oregon 1856
  Oregon 1860
  Oregon 1866
  *Oregon 1867
  Oregon 1868
  Colorado 1855
  Arizona 1857
  Arizona 1859
  Arizona 1866
  Arizona 1868
  Arizona 1869
  Arizona 1870
  Arizona 1871
  Arizona 1872
  Arizona 1881
  Washington 1858

  Idaho 1879
  *Montana 1887

Civil War
  *Peninsula
  *Antietam
  *Fredericksburg
  *Chancellorsville
  *Gettysburg
  *Wilderness
  *Spotsylvania
  *Cold Harbor
  *Petersburg
  *Shenandoah
  *Appomattox
  New Mexico 1862
  *Virginia 1862
  *Virginia 1863
  *Virginia 1864
  *Virginia 1865
  *Maryland 1863

War With Spain
  *Santiago

Philippine Insurrection
  Luzon 1901
  Luzon 1902

World War II
  *Algeria-French Morocco
    (with arrowhead)
  *Tunisia
  *Naples-Foggia
  *Anzio
  *Rome-Arno
  *North Apennines
  *Po Valley

Vietnam
  *Counteroffensive, Phase III
  *Tet Counteroffensive

DECORATIONS

  None.

2d SQUADRON, 1st CAVALRY

(1st Regiment of Dragoons)

RA

(2d Armored Division)

LINEAGE

Constituted 2 March 1833 in the Regular Army as Company B, the United States Regiment of Dragoons. Organized 29 July 1833 at Sacketts Harbor, New York; joined Regiment 6 September 1833 at Jefferson Barracks, Missouri. Redesignated 15 May 1836 as Company B, 1st Regiment of Dragoons. Redesignated 3 August 1861 as Company B, 1st Cavalry. (Cavalry companies officially designated as troops in 1833.) (1st Cavalry assigned to 15th Cavalry Division December 1917–May 1918; assigned to 1st Cavalry Division 20 August 1921–3 January 1933.) Reorganized and redesignated 16 January 1933 as Company B, 1st Cavalry, Mechanized.

Reorganized and redesignated 15 July 1940 as Company B, 1st Armored Regiment, an element of the 1st Armored Division. Reorganized and redesignated 20 July 1944 as Company B, 1st Tank Battalion.

Converted and redesignated 1 May 1946 as Troop B, 1st Constabulary Squadron; concurrently, relieved from assignment to 1st Armored Division and assigned to 15th Constabulary Regiment. Inactivated 20 December 1948 in Germany; concurrently, converted and redesignated as Company B, 1st Medium Tank Battalion, relieved from assignment to 15th Constabulary Regiment and assigned to 1st Armored Division. Activated 7 March 1951 at Fort Hood, Texas. Redesignated 20 May 1953 as Company B, 1st Tank Battalion. Inactivated 15 February 1957 at Fort Polk, Louisiana, and relieved from assignment to 1st Armored Division.

Redesignated 1 October 1957 as Headquarters and Headquarters Company, 2d Medium Tank Battalion (Patton), 1st Cavalry; concurrently, assigned to 3d Armored Division and activated in Europe (organic elements concurrently constituted and activated). Redesignated 1 July 1963 as 2d Squadron, 1st Cavalry; concurrently, relieved from assignment to 3d Armored Division, transferred (less personnel and equipment) from United States Army, Europe, to Fort Hood, Texas, assigned to 2d Armored Division and reorganized.

96

CAMPAIGN PARTICIPATION CREDIT

Mexican War
  Buena Vista
  Coahuila 1846
  *New Mexico 1846
  *New Mexico 1847
  *Chihuahua 1848

Indian Wars
  *Modocs
  Apaches
  *Nez Perces
  *Bannocks
  *Pine Ridge
  California 1846
  California 1852
  *California 1860
  California 1868
  New Mexico 1849
  New Mexico 1850
  New Mexico 1851
  New Mexico 1854
  *New Mexico 1855
  New Mexico 1856
  Oregon 1851
  Oregon 1853
  Oregon 1855
  Oregon 1856
  *Oregon 1860
  Oregon 1866
  Oregon 1867
  Oregon 1868
  Colorado 1855
  *Arizona 1857
  Arizona 1859
  Arizona 1866
  Arizona 1868
  Arizona 1869
  Arizona 1870
  Arizona 1871
  Arizona 1872
  Arizona 1881
  Washington 1858
  Idaho 1879

  *Montana 1887
  *Kansas 1847
  *Nebraska 1849

Civil War
  *Peninsula
  *Antietam
  *Fredericksburg
  *Chancellorsville
  *Gettysburg
  *Wilderness
  *Spotsylvania
  *Cold Harbor
  *Petersburg
  *Shenandoah
  *Appomattox
  New Mexico 1862
  *Virginia 1862
  *Virginia 1863
  *Virginia 1864
  *Virginia 1865
  *Maryland 1863

War With Spain
  *Santiago

Philippine Insurrection
  Luzon 1901
  Luzon 1902

World War II
  *Algeria-French Morocco
    (with arrowhead)
  *Tunisia
  *Naples-Foggia
  *Anzio
  *Rome-Arno
  *North Apennines
  *Po Valley

Vietnam
  *Counteroffensive, Phase III
  *Tet Counteroffensive

DECORATIONS

None.

3d SQUADRON, 1st CAVALRY

(1st Regiment of Dragoons)

RA

(1st Armored Division)

LINEAGE

Constituted 2 March 1833 in the Regular Army as Company C, the United States Regiment of Dragoons. Organized in June 1833 at Louisville, Kentucky; joined Regiment 3 July 1833 at Jefferson Barracks, Missouri. Redesignated 15 May 1836 as Company C, 1st Regiment of Dragoons. Redesignated 3 August 1861 as Company C, 1st Cavalry. (Cavalry companies officially designated as troops in 1883.) (1st Cavalry assigned to 15th Cavalry Division December 1917–May 1918; assigned to 1st Cavalry Division 20 August 1921–3 January 1933.) Reorganized and redesignated 16 January 1933 as Company C, 1st Cavalry, Mechanized.

Reorganized and redesignated 15 July 1940 as Company C, 1st Armored Regiment, an element of the 1st Armored Division. Reorganized and redesignated 20 July 1944 as Company C, 1st Tank Battalion.

Converted and redesignated 1 May 1946 as Troop D, 1st Constabulary Squadron; concurrently, relieved from assignment to 1st Armored Division and assigned to 15th Constabulary Regiment. Inactivated 20 December 1948 in Germany; concurrently, converted and redesignated as Company D, 1st Medium Tank Battalion, relieved from assignment to 15th Constabulary Regiment and assigned to 1st Armored Division. Activated 7 March 1951 at Fort Hood, Texas. Redesignated 20 May 1953 as Company D, 1st Tank Battalion. Inactivated 15 February 1957 at Fort Polk, Louisiana, and relieved from assignment to 1st Armored Division.

Redesignated 22 November 1965 as Headquarters and Headquarters Troop, 3d Squadron, 1st Cavalry. Assigned 16 June 1967 to 1st Armored Division and activated at Fort Hood, Texas (organic elements concurrently constituted and activated).

98

Campaign Participation Credit

Mexican War
Buena Vista
Coahuila 1846
*New Mexico 1846
New Mexico 1847
*California 1847
Chihuahua 1848

Indian Wars
Modocs
*Apaches
*Nez Perces
*Bannocks
*Pine Ridge
*California 1846
*California 1850
*California 1852
California 1860
California 1868
New Mexico 1849
New Mexico 1850
New Mexico 1851
New Mexico 1854
New Mexico 1855
New Mexico 1856
*Oregon 1851
*Oregon 1853
*Oregon 1855
*Oregon 1856
*Oregon 1860
Oregon 1866
Oregon 1867
Oregon 1868
Colorado 1855
Arizona 1857
Arizona 1859
*Arizona 1866
*Arizona 1868
*Arizona 1869
*Arizona 1870
Arizona 1871

Arizona 1872
Arizona 1881
*Washington 1858
Idaho 1879
Montana 1887

Civil War
*Peninsula
*Antietam
*Fredericksburg
*Chancellorsville
*Gettysburg
*Wilderness
*Spotsylvania
*Cold Harbor
*Petersburg
*Shenandoah
*Appomattox
New Mexico 1862
*Virginia 1862
*Virginia 1863
*Virginia 1864
*Virginia 1865
*Maryland 1863

War With Spain
*Santiago

Philippine Insurrection
*Luzon 1901
*Luzon 1902

World War II
*Algeria-French Morocco
(with arrowhead)
*Tunisia
*Naples-Foggia
*Anzio
*Rome-Arno
*North Apennines
*Po Valley

Decorations
None.

4th SQUADRON, 1st CAVALRY

(1st Regiment of Dragoons)

RA

(United States Military Academy)

LINEAGE

Constituted 2 March 1833 in the Regular Army as Company D, the United States Regiment of Dragoons. Organized 25 July 1833 at Cincinnati, Ohio; joined Regiment 3 August 1833 at Jefferson Barracks, Missouri. Redesignated 15 May 1836 as Company D, 1st Regiment of Dragoons. Resdesignated 3 August 1861 as Company D, 1st Cavalry. (Cavalry companies officially designated as troops in 1883.) (1st Cavalry assigned to 15th Cavalry Division December 1917–May 1918; assigned to 1st Cavalry Division 20 August 1921–3 January 1933.)

Reorganized and redesignated 7 September 1921 as Headquarters Detachment, 1st Machine Gun Squadron. Inactivated 1 February 1928 at Marfa, Texas. Activated 15 July 1940 as Company D, 1st Armored Regiment, an element of the 1st Armored Division at Fort Knox, Kentucky. Disbanded 20 July 1944 at Bolgheri, Italy.

Reconstituted 27 February 1951 in the Regular Army and redesignated as Company A, 100th Tank Battalion, an element of the 1st Armored Division. Activated 7 February 1951 at Fort Hood, Texas. Inactivated 15 February 1957 at Fort Polk, Louisiana, and relieved from assignment to 1st Armored Division.

Redesignated 15 May 1958 as Headquarters and Headquarters Company, 4th Medium Tank Battalion (Patton), 1st Cavalry; concurrently, assigned to the United States Military Academy and activated at West Point, New York (organic elements concurrently constituted and activated). Redesignated 1 May 1966 as 4th Battalion, 1st Cavalry. Redesignated 29 December 1966 as 4th Squadron, 1st Cavalry.

100

CAMPAIGN PARTICIPATION CREDIT

Mexican War
Buena Vista
Coahuila 1846
New Mexico 1846
New Mexico 1847
Chihuahua 1848

Indian Wars
Modocs
*Apaches
*Nez Perces
*Bannocks
*Pine Ridge
California 1846
California 1852
California 1860
California 1868
New Mexico 1849
New Mexico 1850
New Mexico 1851
New Mexico 1854
*New Mexico 1855
*New Mexico 1856
Oregon 1851
Oregon 1853
Oregon 1855
Oregon 1856
Oregon 1860
Oregon 1866
Oregon 1867
Oregon 1868
*Colorado 1855
Arizona 1857
*Arizona 1859
Arizona 1866
Arizona 1868
Arizona 1869
Arizona 1870
Arizona 1871
Arizona 1872

Arizona 1881
Washington 1858
*Idaho 1879
*Montana 1887

Civil War
Peninsula
Antietam
Fredericksburg
Chancellorsville
Gettysburg
*Wilderness
*Spotsylvania
*Cold Harbor
*Petersburg
*Shenandoah
*Appomattox
*New Mexico 1862
Virginia 1862
*Virginia 1863
*Virginia 1864
*Virginia 1865
Maryland 1863

War With Spain
*Santiago

Philippine Insurrection
Luzon 1901
Luzon 1902

World War II
*Algeria-French Morocco
    (with arrowhead)
*Tunisia
*Naples-Foggia
*Anzio
*Rome-Arno
North Apennines
Po Valley

DECORATIONS

None.

TROOP E, 1st CAVALRY

(1st Regiment of Dragoons)

RA
(11th Infantry Brigade)

LINEAGE

Constituted 2 March 1833 in the Regular Army as Company E, the United States Regiment of Dragoons. Organized 29 June 1833 at New York, New York; joined Regiment 4 August 1833 Jefferson Barracks, Missouri. Redesignated 15 May 1836 as Company E, 1st Regiment of Dragoons. Redesignated 3 August 1861 as Company E, 1st Cavalry. (Cavalry companies officially designated as troops in 1883.) (1st Cavalry assigned to 15th Cavalry Division December 1917–May 1918; assigned to 1st Cavalry Division 20 August 1921–3 January 1933.) Reorganized and redesignated 16 January 1933 as Company E, 1st Cavalry, Mechanized.

Reorganized and redesignated 15 July 1940 as Company E, 1st Armored Regiment, an element of the 1st Armored Division. Disbanded 20 July 1944 at Bolgheri, Italy.

Reconstituted 27 February 1951 in the Regular Army and redesignated as Company B, 100th Tank Battalion, an element of the 1st Armored Division. Activated 7 March 1951 at Fort Hood, Texas. Inactivated 15 February 1957 at Fort Polk, Louisiana, and relieved from assignment to 1st Armored Division.

Redesignated 15 April 1966 as Troop E, 1st Cavalry, and assigned to 11th Infantry Brigade. Activated 1 July 1966 in Hawaii.

CAMPAIGN PARTICIPATION CREDIT

Mexican War
  Buena Vista
  Coahuila 1846

Indian Wars
  Apaches
  Nez Perces
  Bannocks
  Pine Ridge
  California 1852
  Oregon 1851
  Oregon 1853
  Oregon 1855
  Oregon 1856
  Oregon 1860
  Arizona 1866
  Arizona 1867
  Arizona 1868
  Arizona 1869
  Arizona 1870
  Washington 1858
  Montana 1887

Civil War
  Peninsula
  Fredericksburg
  Chancellorsville

Gettysburg
Wilderness
Spotsylvania
Cold Harbor
Petersburg
Shenandoah
Appomattox
Virginia 1862
Virginia 1863
Virginia 1864
Virginia 1865
Maryland 1863

War With Spain
  Santiago

World War II–EAME
  Algeria-French Morocco
    (with arrowhead)
  Tunisia
  Naples-Foggia
  Anzio
  Rome-Arno

Vietnam
  Counteroffensive, Phase III
  Tet Counteroffensive

DECORATIONS

None.

6th SQUADRON, 1st CAVALRY

(1st Regiment of Dragoons)

RA

(2d Armored Division)

LINEAGE

Constituted 2 March 1833 in the Regular Army as Company F, the United States Regiment of Dragoons. Organized 5 December 1833 at Jefferson Barracks, Missouri. Redesignated 15 March 1836 as Company F, 1st Regiment of Dragoons. Redesignated 3 August 1861 as Company F, 1st Cavalry. (Cavalry companies officially designated as troops in 1883.) (1st Cavalry assigned to 15th Cavalry Division December 1917–May 1918; assigned to 1st Cavalry Division 20 August 1921–3 January 1933.) Reorganized and redesignated 16 January 1933 as Company F, 1st Cavalry, Mechanized.

Reorganized and redesignated 15 July 1940 as Company F, 1st Armored Regiment, an element of the 1st Armored Division. Disbanded 20 July 1944 near Bolgheri, Italy.

Reconstituted 27 February 1951 in the Regular Army and redesignated as Company C, 100th Tank Battalion, an element of the 1st Armored Division. Activated 7 March 1951 at Fort Hood, Texas. Inactivated 15 February 1957 at Fort Polk, Louisiana, and relieved from assignment to 1st Armored Division.

Redesignated 19 June 1967 as Headquarters and Headquarters Troop, 6th Squadron, 1st Cavalry, assigned to 2d Armored Division, and activated at Fort Hood, Texas (organic elements concurrently constituted and activated).

104

Campaign Participation Credit

Mexican War
Buena Vista
*Vera Cruz
*Cerro Gordo
*Contreras
*Molino del Rey
*Chapultepec
Coahuila 1846
New Mexico 1846
New Mexico 1847
Chihuahua 1848

Indian Wars
*Modocs
Apaches
*Nez Perces
*Bannocks
*Pine Ridge
California 1846
California 1852
California 1860
California 1868
New Mexico 1849
New Mexico 1850
*New Mexico 1851
*New Mexico 1854
*New Mexico 1855
*New Mexico 1856
Oregon 1851
Oregon 1853
Oregon 1855
Oregon 1856
Oregon 1860
*Oregon 1866
*Oregon 1867
*Oregon 1868
*Colorado 1855
Arizona 1857
Arizona 1859
Arizona 1866
Arizona 1868
Arizona 1869
Arizona 1870

Arizona 1871
Arizona 1872
Arizona 1881
Washington 1858
*Idaho 1866
Idaho 1879
Montana 1887

Civil War
*Peninsula
Antietam
*Fredericksburg
*Chancellorsville
*Gettysburg
*Wilderness
*Spotsylvania
*Cold Harbor
*Petersburg
*Shenandoah
*Appomattox
New Mexico 1862
*Virginia 1862
*Virginia 1863
*Virginia 1864
*Virginia 1865
*Maryland 1863

War With Spain
Santiago

Philippine Insurrection
Luzon 1901
Luzon 1902

World War II
*Algeria-French Morocco
(with arrowhead)
*Tunisia
*Naples-Foggia
*Anzio
*Rome-Arno
North Apennines
Po Valley

Decorations

None.

7th SQUADRON, 1st CAVALRY

(1st Regiment of Dragoons)

RA
(nondivisional)

LINEAGE

Constituted 2 March 1833 in the Regular Army as Company G, the United States Regiment of Dragoons. Organized 16 January 1834 at Jefferson Barracks, Missouri. Redesignated 15 May 1836 as Company G, 1st Regiment of Dragoons. Redesignated 3 August 1861 as Company G, 1st Cavalry. (Cavalry companies officially designated as troops in 1883.) (1st Cavalry assigned to 15th Cavalry Division December 1917–May 1918; assigned to 1st Cavalry Division 20 August 1921–3 January 1933.) Reorganized and redesignated 16 January 1933 as Company G, 1st Cavalry, Mechanized.

Reorganized and redesignated 15 July 1940 as Company G, 1st Armored Regiment, an element of the 1st Armored Division. Disbanded 20 July 1944 in Italy.

Reconstituted 28 March 1967 in the Regular Army and redesignated as Headquarters and Headquarters Troop, 7th Squadron, 1st Cavalry (organic elements concurrently constituted). Activated 25 April 1967 at Fort Knox, Kentucky.

106

CAMPAIGN PARTICIPATION CREDIT

Mexican War
  Buena Vista
  Coahuila 1846
  *New Mexico 1846
  *New Mexico 1847
  *Chihuahua 1848

Indian Wars
  *Modocs
  Apaches
  *Nez Perces
  *Bannocks
  *Pine Ridge
  California 1846
  California 1852
  California 1860
  California 1868
  *New Mexico 1849
  *New Mexico 1850
  *New Mexico 1851
  *New Mexico 1854
  *New Mexico 1855
  *New Mexico 1856
  Oregon 1851
  Oregon 1853
  Oregon 1855
  Oregon 1856
  Oregon 1860
  Oregon 1866
  Oregon 1867
  Oregon 1868
  Colorado 1855
  *Arizona 1857
  *Arizona 1859
  *Arizona 1866
  *Arizona 1868
  *Arizona 1869
  *Arizona 1870
  Arizona 1871
  Arizona 1872
  *Arizona 1881
  Washington 1858

  *Idaho 1879
  *Montana 1887

Civil War
  Peninsula
  Antietam
  Fredericksburg
  Chancellorsville
  Gettysburg
  *Wilderness
  *Spotsylvania
  *Cold Harbor
  *Petersburg
  *Shenandoah
  *Appomattox
  *New Mexico 1862
  Virginia 1862
  *Virginia 1863
  *Virginia 1864
  *Virginia 1865
  Maryland 1863

War With Spain
  *Santiago

Philippine Insurrection
  Luzon 1901
  Luzon 1902

World War II
  *Algeria-French Morocco
    (with arrowhead)
  *Tunisia
  *Naples-Foggia
  *Anzio
  *Rome-Arno
  North Apennines
  Po Valley

Vietnam
  *Tet Counteroffensive

DECORATIONS

None.

8th SQUADRON, 1st CAVALRY

RA
(nondivisional)

LINEAGE

Constituted 2 March 1833 in the Regular Army as Company H, the United States Regiment of Dragoons. Organized 2 March 1834 at Jefferson Barracks, Missouri. Redesignated 15 May 1836 as Company H, 1st Regiment of Dragoons. Redesignated 3 August 1861 as Company H, 1st Cavalry. (Cavalry companies officially designated as troops in 1883.) (1st Cavalry assigned to 15th Cavalry Division December 1917–May 1918.)

Reorganized and redesignated 20 August 1921 as Headquarters Troop, 1st Cavalry Brigade, and assigned to 1st Cavalry Division. Inactivated 25 March 1949 in Japan and relieved from assignment to 1st Cavalry Division.

Converted and redesignated 20 May 1949 as Headquarters Troop, 1st Constabulary Brigade, and activated at Dotzheim, Germany. Inactivated 15 August 1951 in Germany. Disbanded 5 December 1951.

Reconstituted 10 May 1967 in the Regular Army and redesignated as Headquarters and Headquarters Troop, 8th Squadron, 1st Cavalry (organic elements concurrently constituted). Activated 25 August 1967 at Fort Knox, Kentucky.

CAMPAIGN PARTICIPATION CREDIT

Mexican War
Buena Vista
Coahuila 1846
New Mexico 1846
New Mexico 1847
Chihuahua 1848

Indian Wars
*Modocs
Apaches
*Nez Perces
*Bannocks
Pine Ridge
California 1846
California 1852
California 1860
*California 1867
California 1868
*New Mexico 1849
New Mexico 1850
*New Mexico 1851
*New Mexico 1854
*New Mexico 1855
New Mexico 1856
Oregon 1851
Oregon 1853
Oregon 1855
Oregon 1856
Oregon 1860
Oregon 1866
Oregon 1867
*Oregon 1868
Colorado 1855
Arizona 1857
Arizona 1859
Arizona 1866
Arizona 1868
Arizona 1869
Arizona 1870
Arizona 1871
Arizona 1872
Arizona 1881
*Washington 1858

Idaho 1879
Montana 1887

Civil War
*Peninsula
Antietam
Fredericksburg
*Chancellorsville
*Gettysburg
*Wilderness
*Spotsylvania
*Cold Harbor
*Petersburg
*Shenandoah
*Appomattox
New Mexico 1862
Virginia 1862
*Virginia 1863
*Virginia 1864
Virginia 1865
*Maryland 1863

War With Spain
Santiago

Philippine Insurrection
Luzon 1901
Luzon 1902

World War II
Algeria-French Morocco (with
  arrowhead)
Tunisia
Naples-Foggia
Anzio
Rome-Arno
North Apennines
Po Valley
*New Guinea
*Bismarck Archipelago
  (with arrowhead)
*Leyte (with arrowhead)
*Luzon

DECORATIONS

*Presidential Unit Citation (Army), Streamer embroidered LUZON (Headquarters Troop, 1st Cavalry Brigade, cited; DA GO 33, 1948)

*Philippine Presidential Unit Citation, Streamer embroidered 17 OCTOBER 1944 TO 4 JULY 1945 (Headquarters Troop, 1st Cavalry Brigade, cited; DA GO 47, 1950)

Bibliography, 1st Cavalry

Barry, Louise, editor. "With the First U.S. Cavalry in Indian Country, 1859–1861," *Kansas Historical Quarterly,* XXIV (1958).

Beers, Henry Putney. *The Western Military Frontier, 1815–1846.* Philadelphia: 1935.

Bennett, James Augustus. *Forts and Forays . . . A Dragoon in New Mexico 1850–1856.* Albuquerque: 1948. Edited by Clinton E. Brooks and Frank D. Reeve.

Brackett, Albert G. *History of the United States Cavalry, From the Formation of the Federal Government to the 1st of June 1863.* New York: 1865.

Catlin, George. *Letters and Notes on the Manners, Customs, and Condition of the North American Indians . . . 1832–1839,* Vol. II. Edinburgh: 1841. Also about 12 editions 1841–1926, various titles and publishers.

Cooke, Philip St. George. *Scenes and Adventures in the Army.* Philadelphia: 1857.

————. *The Conquest of New Mexico and California: A History and Personal Narrative.* New York: 1878.

Department of the Army. AMERICAN FORCES IN ACTION series.
   To Bizerte With the II Corps. 1943.
   Anzio Beachhead. 1947.

Dodge, Henry. *Col Dodge's Journal. Expeditions of the Dragoons to the Rocky Mountains, during the Summer of 1835 . . . .* Washington: circa 1836.

Emory, W. H. *Notes of a Military Reconnaissance from Fort Leavenworth, in Missouri, to San Diego, in California . . . Made in 1846–7 with the Advanced Guard of the "Army of the West."* Washington: 1848. "Report of Lieut. Col. P. St. George Cooke of his march from Santa Fe, New Mexico, to San Diego, Upper California," and "Journal of Captain A. R. Johnston, First Dragoons."

Hildreth, James. *Dragoon Campaigns to the Rocky Mountains; being a History of the Enlistment, Organization, and First Campaigns of the Regiment of United States Dragoons, together with the Incidents of a Soldier's Life, and Sketches of Scenery and Indian Character.* New York: 1836.

Howe, George F. *The Battle History of the 1st Armored Division.* Washington: 1954.

Irving, Washington. *A Tour of the Prairie.* New York: 1835.

Lowe, Percival G. *Five Years a Dragoon ('49 to '54) and Other Adventures on the Great Plains.* Kansas City, Mo.: 1906.

Pelzer, Louis. *Henry Dodge.* Iowa City: 1911.

————. *Marches of the Dragoons in the Mississippi Valley.* Iowa City: 1917.

Rhodes, Charles D. *History of the Cavalry of the Army of the Potomac.* Kansas City, Mo.: 1900.

Rodenbough, Theo. F., and William L. Haskin, eds. *The Army of the United States.* New York: 1896. R. P. P. Wainwright, "The First Regiment of Cavalry." 1896.

Unit Members. *A History and Photographic Record of the 1st U.S. Cavalry, Animo et Fide* . . . . San Antonio, Tex.: 1920.

———. *Field, Staff and Officers of the First Regiment of Cavalry From March 4, 1833 to June 1, 1900. Campaigns, Battles and Engagements in which the First Regiment of Cavalry has Taken Part.* Fort Meade, S.D.: 1900.

———. *Historical and Pictorial Review, 1st Armored Regiment (L), 1st Armored Division of the U.S. Army, Fort Knox, Kentucky.* Baton Rouge, La.: 1941.

———. *History of 1st United States Cavalry, 1833–1927.* Camp Marfa, Tex.: 1927.

———. "Unit History, 1833–1956. 1st Medium Tank Battalion (Patton), 1st Cavalry, Fort Polk, Louisiana." Fort Polk: 1956.

UNITED STATES ARMY IN WORLD WAR II

Howe, George F. *Northwest Africa: Seizing the Initiative in the West.* 1957.

Wainwright, R. P. P., and Charles A. Kraus. *History of the First U.S. Cavalry, 1833–1906.* Fort Clark, Tex.: 1906.

2d ARMORED CAVALRY
(Second Dragoons)

HERALDIC ITEMS

COAT OF ARMS

Shield: Tenné, a dragoon in the uniform of the Mexican War mounted on a white horse brandishing a sabre and charging a Mexican field gun defended by a gunner armed with a rammer all proper, in chief two eight-pointed mullets or.

Crest: On a wreath of the colors (or and tenné) the head dress of the dragoons of 1836 proper.

Motto: *Toujours Prêt* (Always Ready).

Symbolism: The color of the facings of the old dragoon regiment was orange, which is used for the field of the shield; the insignia was an eight-pointed star of gold, two of them (conforming with the numerical designation) are placed on the shield. The traditional episode in the regiment is the charge of Captain May's squadron on the Mexican artillery at Resaca de la Palma, which is commemorated by the principal charge on the shield. The crest is self-explanatory.

DISTINCTIVE INSIGNIA

The distinctive insignia is a gold eight-pointed star of rays surmounted by a green palmetto leaf charged with a silver fleur-de-lis, on a green ribbon scroll forming the base of the device, the regimental motto *Toujours Prêt* in gold letters.

LINEAGE AND HONORS

LINEAGE

Constituted 23 May 1836 in the Regular Army as 2d Regiment of Dragoons and organized with Headquarters at Jefferson Barracks, Missouri. Redesignated 5 March 1843 as 2d Regiment of Riflemen and concurrently dismounted. Remounted and redesignated 4 April 1844 as 2d Regiment of Dragoons. Redesignated 3 August 1861 as 2d Cavalry.

113

Assigned to 2d Cavalry Division 15 August 1927–15 July 1942. Inactivated 15 July 1942 at Fort Riley, Kansas; personnel and equipment transferred to 2d Armored Regiment (see ANNEX). Redesignated 15 January 1943 and activated as 2d Cavalry, Mechanized, at Fort Jackson, South Carolina.

Regiment broken up 22 December 1943 and its elements reorganized and redesignated as Headquarters and Headquarters Troop, 2d Cavalry Group, Mechanized, and 2d and 42d Cavalry Reconnaissance Squadrons, Mechanized. These units converted and redesignated 1 May 1946 as Headquarters and Headquarters Troop, 2d Constabulary Regiment, and 2d and 42d Constabulary Squadrons, respectively. These units converted and redesignated by elements 16 November 1948 as elements of the 2d Armored Cavalry (Headquarters and Headquarters and Service Troop, 2d Constabulary Regiment, redesignated as Headquarters and Headquarters Troop, 2d Armored Cavalry).

2d, 776th, and 19th Tank Battalions (see ANNEX) consolidated 8 January 1951 with 2d Armored Cavalry. (Battalions and companies redesignated 23 May 1960 as squadrons and troops.)

ANNEX

2d Armored Regiment constituted 11 July 1942 in the Army of the United States and assigned to 9th Armored Division. Activated 15 July 1942 at Fort Riley, Kansas, with personnel and equipment from 2d Cavalry.

Regiment broken up 9 October 1943 and its elements reorganized and redesignated as follows: 2d Armored Regiment (less 1st and 3d Battalions, Band, and Maintenance, Service, and Reconnaissance Companies) as 2d Tank Battalion; 1st Battalion as 776th Tank Battalion and relieved from assignment to 9th Armored Division; 3d Battalion as 19th Tank Battalion; Reconnaissance Company as Troop D, 89th Cavalry Reconnaissance Squadron, Mechanized (separate lineage); Band and Maintenance and Service Companies disbanded.

2d Tank Battalion inactivated 7 October 1945 at Camp Patrick Henry, Virginia. Relieved 9 January 1951 from assignment to 9th Armored Division.

776th Tank Battalion reorganized and redesignated 28 January 1944 as 776th Amphibian Tank Battalion. Inactivated 21 January 1946 at Camp Anza, California.

19th Tank Battalion inactivated 9 October 1945 at Camp Patrick Henry, Virginia. Relieved 8 January 1951 from assignment to 9th Armored Division.

2d, 776th, and 19th Tank Battalions consolidated 8 January 1951 with 2d Armored Cavalry.

CAMPAIGN PARTICIPATION CREDIT

Mexican War
    Palo Alto
    Resaca de la Palma
    Monterey
    Buena Vista
    Vera Cruz
    Cerro Gordo
    Contreras
    Churubusco
    Molino del Rey
    Chapultepec
    Nuevo Leon
    Tamaulipas 1846
    Texas 1846
    Vera Cruz 1847

Civil War
    Peninsula
    Manassas
    Antietam
    Fredericksburg
    Chancellorsville
    Gettysburg
    Wilderness
    Spotsylvania
    Cold Harbor
    Petersburg
    Shenandoah
    Virginia 1863
    Virginia 1864
    Maryland 1863

Indian Wars
    Seminoles
    Little Big Horn
    Nez Perces
    Bannocks
    Cheyennes
    New Mexico 1852
    New Mexico 1854
    Wyoming 1866
    Wyoming 1867
    Kansas 1869
    Montana 1870
    Montana 1872
    Montana 1879
    Montana 1880

War With Spain
    Santiago

World War I
    Aisne-Marne
    St. Mihiel
    Meuse-Argonne

World War II
    Normandy
    Northern France
    Rhineland
    Ardennes-Alsace
    Central Europe
    Leyte (with arrowhead)
    Ryukyus

Troops additionally entitled to Campaign Participation Credit as follows:

Troop A:
Indian Wars
    Apaches
    Wyoming 1870
World War II–AP
    Western Pacific (with arrowhead)

Troop B:
Indian Wars
    Oklahoma 1854
    Wyoming 1872
    Wyoming 1874

Troop C:
Civil War
    Henry and Donelson
    Shiloh
    Missouri 1861
    Tennessee 1862

Troop E:
Indian Wars
    Wyoming 1869

Troop F:
Indian Wars
    Nebraska 1855
    Nebraska 1870

Troop K:
Indian Wars
    Montana 1881

Troop L:
Indian Wars
    New Mexico 1860
World War I
    Oise-Aisne
    Champagne 1918

DECORATIONS

Presidential Unit Citation (Army), Streamer embroidered BASTOGNE (2d Tank Battalion cited; WD GO 17, 1945)

Belgian Croix de Guerre 1940 with Palm, Streamer embroidered BASTOGNE; cited in the Order of the Day of the Belgian Army for action at BASTOGNE (2d Tank Battalion cited; DA GO 43, 1950 and DA GO 27, 1959)

Headquarters Troop, 1st Squadron, and Troops A, B, and C each additionally entitled to: Philippine Presidential Unit Citation, Streamer embroidered 17 OCTOBER 1944 TO 4 JULY 1945 (776th Amphibian Tank Battalion cited; DA GO 47, 1950)

BIBLIOGRAPHY, 2D ARMORED CAVALRY

Allen, Robert S. *Lucky Forward*. New York: 1947.

Bates, Alfred E. and Edward J. McClernand. "The Second Regiment of Cavalry," *Journal, Military Service Institute* (May 1892).

Beers, Henry Putney. *The Western Military Frontier, 1815–1846*. Philadelphia: 1935.

Brackett, Albert G. *History of the United States Cavalry From the Formation of the Federal Government to the 1st of June 1863*. New York: 1865.

———. "The Story of a Regiment," *American Historical Record*, I (1877), pp. 488–494, 538–543.

Cooke, Philip St. George. *The Conquest of New Mexico and California: A History and Personal Narrative*. New York: 1878.

DuBois, John Van Deusen. *Campaigning in the West, 1856–1861*. Edited by George P. Hammond. Tucson: 1949.

Dyer, George. *XII Corps, Spearhead of Patton's Third Army*. Baton Rouge: 1947.

"Expedition Through the Everglades by one who was with Col. Harney," *The Pathetic and Lamentable Narrative of Miss Perine, on the Massacre and Destruction of Indian Key Village in August, 1840*. Philadelphia: 1841.

Fleming, David L. *From Everglades to Canon with the Second Dragoons, May 23rd, 1836–May 23rd, 1911: 75th Anniversary*. Jolo, P.I.: 23 May 1911.

Johnson, R. W. *A Soldier's Reminiscences in Peace and War*. Philadelphia: 1886.

Lambert, Arthur Lawson and B. Layton. *The Ghosts of Patton's Third Army . . . A History of the Second US Cavalry*. Munich, Ger.: 1945.

Lambert, Joseph I. *One Hundred Years with the Second Cavalry*. Topeka, Kans.: 1939.

May, Charles A. *A Card*—defense of his conduct at Buena Vista. N.p. 1848.

Perry, Redding F. "The 2d Cavalry in France," *The Cavalry Journal,* Vol. 37, No. 150 (January 1928).

Reavis, L. U. *The Life and Military Services of General William Selby Harney.* St. Louis: 1878.

Roberts, Thomas D. "Resaca de la Palma: A Traditional Episode in the History of the Second Cavalry," *Journal of the American History Foundation* (Fall 1937).

Rodenbough, Theo. F., compiler. *From Everglade to Canon with the Second Dragoons . . . 1836–1875.* New York: 1875.

Rodenbough, Theo. F., and William L. Haskin, eds. *The Army of the United States.* New York: 1896. Alfred E. Bates and Edward J. McClernand, "The Second Regiment of Cavalry."

Rodney, Dorsey R., compiler. *Centennial, Second United States Cavalry— Toujours Pret—1836–1936.* Fort Riley, Kans.: 1936.

"Rosters of Officers and Non-commissioned Officers Second U.S. Cavalry, Fort Ethan Allen, Vermont, January 1, 1915." Fort Ethan Allen: 1915.

"Roster of Commissioned Officers of the Second Regiment of U.S. Cavalry, Commanded by Colonel Eli L. Huggins." Headquarters, Fort Myer, Va.: July 1, 1902.

Schmoekel, Wolf W., and David Roe. *The Dragoon Story, A History of the 2d Armored Cavalry Regiment.* Washington: 1958.

Sherrill, Stephen H. "The Experiences of the First Troop of Cavalry to Get into Action in the World War," *Cavalry Journal* (April 1923).

Stevens, Lt. "Sketch of the Line of March of the 2nd U.S. Dragoons Commanded by Col. D. E. Twiggs from Fort Jesup, La., to Corpus Christi, Texas, between the 25th of July and 27 Aug. 1845," *Journal of the Military Service Institution,* Vol. 40 (1907).

Terrall, Edgar A. Jr., comp. *The Training and Combat History of Company "D" 19th Tank Battalion, from May 1943 to July 1945.* Charlotte, N.C.: 1945.

Unit Members. *Always Ready; 116th Anniversary of the 2d Armored Cavalry.* Darmstadt, Ger.: 1952.

———. *Always Ready; 117th Anniversary of the 2d Armored Cavalry.* Darmstadt, Ger.: 1953.

———. *Always Ready; 118th Anniversary of the 2d Armored Cavalry.* Darmstadt, Ger.: 1954.

———. *119th Anniversary . . . 2d Armored Cavalry.* Darmstadt, Ger.: 1955.

———. *2d Armored Cavalry Regiment, 122d Anniversary, 1836–1958.* Nurnberg, Ger.: 1958.

————. *Historical and Pictorial Review, 2d Cavalry Regiment, Second Cavalry Division, Camp Funston, Kansas, 1941.* Baton Rouge, La.: 1941.

————. *The 19th Tank Battalion, A History* . . . . Hof Saale, Ger.: 1945.

UNITED STATES ARMY IN WORLD WAR II

Blumenson, Martin. *Breakout and Pursuit.* 1961.

Cole, Hugh M. *The Ardennes: Battle of the Bulge.* 1965.

————. *The Lorraine Campaign.* 1952.

3d ARMORED CAVALRY
(Brave Rifles)

HERALDIC ITEMS

COAT OF ARMS

Shield: Vert, on a cross argent, a tower of the field; on a chief or a bend gules.

Crest: On a wreath of the colors a trumpet palewise or.

Motto: "Brave Rifles! Veterans! You have been baptized in fire and blood and have come out steel."

Symbolism: The regiment's original green facings on the uniform and its gold trumpet insignia are shown by the color of the shield and by the crest. The unit's first engagement was the capture of Vera Cruz, and it continued with especially distinguished service throughout the campaign of 1847 to the capture of Mexico City. Upon entering the city, it hoisted the Stars and Stripes over the national palace and displayed the regimental standard from the palace balcony, which drew from General Scott the statement, "Brave Rifles! Veterans! You have been baptized in fire and blood and have come out steel." The campaign is shown by the cross for Vera Cruz and the tower in green (the Mexican color) for fortified Mexico City, the first and last engagements thereof. The chief, taken from the arms of Lorraine, commemorates the regiment's World War I service.

DISTINCTIVE INSIGNIA

The distinctive insignia is a gold trumpet with a cord paleways with mouthpiece up. Below the trumpet a green ribbon scroll with the words *Brave Rifles* and the numeral *3* in gold; the scroll to be in three loops, "Brave" on the left, "3" below the trumpet and "Rifles" on the right.

119

LINEAGE AND HONORS

LINEAGE

Constituted 19 May 1846 in the Regular Army as the Regiment of Mounted Riflemen. Organized 12 October 1846 at Jefferson Barracks, Missouri. Redesignated 3 August 1861 as 3d Cavalry.

Inactivated 15 July 1942 at Fort Benning, Georgia; personnel and equipment transferred to 3d Armored Regiment (see ANNEX). Redesignated 18 January 1943 as 3d Cavalry, Mechanized. Activated 15 March 1943 at Camp Gordon, Georgia.

Regiment broken up 3 November 1943 and its elements reorganized and redesignated as Headquarters and Headquarters Troop, 3d Cavalry Group, Mechanized, and 3d and 43d Cavalry Reconnaissance Squadrons, Mechanized.

Headquarters and Headquarters Troop, 3d Cavalry Group, Mechanized, inactivated 22 December 1945 at Camp Kilmer, New Jersey. Activated 26 February 1946 at Fort George G. Meade, Maryland. Redesignated 5 November 1948 as Headquarters and Headquarters Company, 3d Armored Cavalry; organization of the remainder of 3d Armored Cavalry completed 3 November 1948 by redesignation of elements of the 3d and 43d Cavalry Reconnaissance Squadrons, Mechanized (both active), and by reconstitution, redesignation, and activation of certain other elements of the 3d Cavalry which had been inactivated or demobilized during 1921–1928.

3d, 777th, and 21st Tank Battalions (see ANNEX) consolidated 8 January 1951 with 3d Armored Cavalry. (Battalions and companies redesignated 1 June 1960 as squadrons and troops.)

ANNEX

3d Armored Regiment constituted 11 July 1942 in the Army of the United States and assigned to 10th Armored Division. Activated 15 July 1942 at Fort Benning, Georgia, with personnel and equipment from 3d Cavalry.

Regiment broken up 20 September 1943 and its elements reorganized and redesignated as follows: 3d Armored Regiment (less 1st and 3d Battalions, Band, and Maintenance, Service, and Reconnaissance Companies) as 3d Tank Battalion; 1st Battalion as 777th Tank Battalion and relieved from assignment to 10th Armored Division; 3d Battalion as 21st Tank Battalion; Reconnaissance Company as Troop D, 90th Cavalry Reconnaissance Squadron, Mechanized (separate lineage); Band and Maintenance and Service Companies disbanded.

Above battalions inactivated as follows: 3d Tank Battalion 13 October 1945 at Camp Patrick Henry, Virginia. 777th Tank Battalion 24 October 1945 at Camp San Luis Obispo, California. 21st Tank Battalion 19 October 1945 at Camp Myles Standish, Massachusetts.

3d, 777th, and 21st Tank Battalions consolidated 8 January 1951 with 3d Armored Cavalry; concurrently, 3d and 21st Tank Battalions relieved from assignment to 10th Armored Division.

CAMPAIGN PARTICIPATION CREDIT

Mexican War
  Vera Cruz
  Cerro Gordo
  Contreras
  Churubusco
  Chapultepec
  Vera Cruz 1847

Indian Wars
  Comanches
  Little Big Horn
  Cheyennes
  Utes
  Texas 1856
  New Mexico 1857
  New Mexico 1858
  New Mexico 1860
  New Mexico 1861
  New Mexico 1867
  New Mexico 1869
  Oklahoma 1868
  Arizona 1870
  Arizona 1871
  Arizona 1882

Civil War
  Chattanooga
  New Mexico 1861
  New Mexico 1862
  Alabama 1863
  Tennessee 1863
  Arkansas 1864

War With Spain
  Santiago

Philippine Insurrection
  San Isidro
  Luzon 1899
  Luzon 1900

World War I
  Without inscription

World War II
  Northern France
  Rhineland
  Ardennes-Alsace
  Central Europe

Troops additionally entitled to Campaign Participation Credit as follows:

Troop A:
Indian Wars
  Texas 1855
  New Mexico 1859
Philippine Insurrection
  Luzon 1901

Troop B:
Indian Wars
  Nebraska 1872

Troop C:
Indian Wars
  South Dakota 1877

Troop F:
Indian Wars
  Texas 1869

Troop I:
Mexican War
  Molino del Rey

DECORATIONS

Presidential Unit Citation (Army), Streamer embroidered BASTOGNE (3d Tank Battalion [less Company C] and Company C, 21st Tank Battalion, cited; WD GO 17, 1945)

Belgian Croix de Guerre 1940 with Palm, Streamer embroidered BASTOGNE; Cited in the Order of the Day of the Belgian Army for action at BASTOGNE (3d Tank Battalion [less Company C] and Company C, 21st Tank Battalion, cited; DA GO 43, 1950 and DA GO 27, 1959)

Troop G additionally entitled to: French Croix de Guerre with Silver-Gilt Star, World War II, Streamer embroidered MOSELLE (Troop B, 43d Cavalry Reconnaissance Squadron, cited; DA GO 43, 1950)

Troop L additionally entitled to: French Croix de Guerre with Palm, World War II, Streamer embroidered LORRAINE (Troop C, 3d Cavalry Reconnaissance Squadron, cited; DA GO 43, 1950)

BIBLIOGRAPHY, 3D ARMORED CAVALRY

Brackett, Albert G. *History of the United States Cavalry from the Formation of the Federal Government to the 1st of June 1863*. New York: 1865.

Clark, Louise M. "The Regiment of Mounted Rifles, Their Problems and Their Chaplain," *Clark County History*, Vol. V, 1964. Vancouver, Washington.

Davis, Richard Harding. *The West Through a Car Window*. New York: 1892.

Deibert, Ralph C. *A History of the Third United States Cavalry*. Harrisburg, Pennsylvania: 1933.

Hammond, George P. *Campaigns in the West 1856–1861; the Journals . . . Colonel John Van Deusen DuBois . . . of Joseph Heger*. Tucson, Arizona: 1949.

Lane, Lydia S. *I Married a Soldier or Old Days in the Old Army*. Philadelphia: 1893.

Maury, Dabney H. *Recollections of a Virginian in the Mexican, Indian, and Civil Wars*. New York: 1894.

Remington, Frederic. "A Sergeant of the Orphan Troop," *Harper's New Monthly Magazine* (August 1897).

Rodenbough, Theo. F., and William L. Haskin, eds. *The Army of the United States*. New York: 1896. Charles Morton, "The Third Regiment of Cavalry."

Settle, Raymond W., ed. *The March of the Mounted Riflemen, First United States Military Expedition . . . from Fort Leavenworth to Fort Vancouver . . . Journals of Major Osborne Cross and George Gibbs . . . official report of Colonel Loring*.

Unit Members. *The Ghost Corps Thru Hell and Highwater*. Europe: 1945.

———. *The Story of the 3d Armored Cavalry Regiment*. Philadelphia: 1949.

———. *The 3d Cavalry Reconnaissance Squadron (Mecz.) in World War II, 9 August 1944 to 9 May 1945*. San Angelo, Texas: 1945.

———. *Basic Training, Training Battalion, Third Cavalry Group, Fort George G. Meade, Maryland*. Fort George G. Meade: 1948.

———. "History, Customs, and Traditions, 1846–1861." Fort George G. Meade: 1861.

————. *XX Corps Operational Report*, 6 Volumes: 1 Aug–1 Sep 1944, 1 Sep–6 Dec 1944, 15 Dec 1944–12 Mar 1945, 13 Mar–25 Mar 1945, 27 Mar–17 Apr 1945, 18 Apr–8 May 1945.

UNITED STATES ARMY IN WORLD WAR II

Cole, Hugh M. *The Lorraine Campaign*. 1950.

Wilcox, Cadmus M. *History of the Mexican War*. Washington: 1892.

4th CAVALRY

HERALDIC ITEMS

COAT OF ARMS

Shield: Or, on a pale embattled azure pierced by a sabre gules a cannon reversed of the field and thereon a sabre and a bayonet saltirewise and an arrow palewise all points down of the third.

Crest: On a wreath of the colors a cratered mount vert bearing a sabre bendwise or and in the crater a kris reversed gules.

Motto: *Paratus et Fidelis* (Prepared and Loyal).

Symbolism: The shield is yellow for cavalry. The attack on the intrenchments at Selma is symbolized by the embattled blue pale and red bayonet. The capture of Hood's artillery is shown by the reversed cannon, the rout of the enemy's cavalry at Murfreesborough by the reversed sabre, and the successful Indian campaigns by the reversed arrow. The Bud Dajo campaign is indicated by the conventionalized volcano of the crest, and the defeat of the Moros by the reversed kris in the crater. On both shield and crest is the regiment's triumphant sabre at the charge.

DISTINCTIVE INSIGNIA

The distinctive insignia is the shield of the coat of arms.

LINEAGE AND HONORS

LINEAGE

Constituted 3 March 1855 in the Regular Army as 1st Cavalry. Organized 26 March 1855 at Jefferson Barracks, Missouri. Redesignated 3 August 1861 as 4th Cavalry.

Reorganized and redesignated 16 April 1942 as 4th Cavalry, Mechanized. Regiment broken up 21 December 1943 and its elements reorganized and redesignated as Headquarters and Headquarters Troop, 4th Cavalry Group, Mechanized, and 4th and 24th Cavalry Reconnaissance Squadrons, Mechanized.

Headquarters and Headquarters Troop, 4th Cavalry Group, Mechanized, converted and redesignated 1 May 1946 as Headquarters and Headquarters Troop, 4th Constabulary Regiment. Reorganized and redesignated 10 February 1948 as Headquarters and Headquarters and Service Troop, 4th Constabulary Regiment. Inactivated 1 May 1949 at Salzburg, Austria. Redesignated 20 August 1953 as Headquarters and Headquarters Company, 4th Armored Cavalry.

4th Cavalry Reconnaissance Squadron, Mechanized, converted and redesignated 1 May 1946 as 4th Constabulary Squadron; assigned 17 June 1946 to 4th Constabulary Regiment. Reorganized and redesignated 1 April 1949 as 4th Reconnaissance Battalion; concurrently, relieved from assignment to 4th Constabulary Regiment. Reorganized and redesignated 1 December 1951 as 4th Armored Cavalry Reconnaissance Battalion. Headquarters and Headquarters Company, 4th Armored Cavalry Reconnaissance Battalion redesignated 1 July 1955 as Headquarters and Headquarters Company, 4th Armor Group (4th Armored Cavalry Reconnaissance Battalion [less Headquarters and Headquarters Company] concurrently inactivated at Camp McCaulcy, Austria).

24th Cavalry Reconnaissance Squadron, Mechanized, converted and redesignated 1 May 1946 as 24th Constabulary Squadron; assigned 17 June 1946 to 4th Constabulary Regiment. Relieved 1 May 1949 from assignment to 4th Constabulary Regiment and assigned to the United States Constabulary. Inactivated 15 December 1952 at Hersfeld, Germany. Redesignated 21 April 1953 as 524th Reconnaissance Battalion.

Headquarters and Headquarters Company, 4th Armored Cavalry; 524th Reconnaissance Battalion; and 4th Armored Cavalry Reconnaissance Battalion (less former Headquarters and Headquarters Company, then designated as Headquarters and Headquarters Company, 4th Armor Group) consolidated, reorganized, and redesignated 15 February 1957 as 4th Cavalry, a parent regiment under the Combat Arms Regimental System (Headquarters and Headquarters Company, 4th Armored Cavalry; concurrently, redesignated as Headquarters and Headquarters Troop, 4th Cavalry). (Headquarters and Headquarters Company, 4th Armor Group inactivated 1 April 1963 in Germany; concurrently, redesignated as Headquarters and Headquarters Troop, 14th Squadron, 4th Cavalry.)

CAMPAIGN PARTICIPATION CREDIT

Indian Wars
  Comanches
  Apaches
  Little Big Horn
  Cheyennes
  Kansas 1857
  Kansas 1860
  Mexico 1873
  New Mexico 1882

Civil War
  Bull Run
  Mississippi River
  Peninsula
  Antietam
  Fredericksburg
  Murfreesborough
  Chickamauga
  Atlanta
  Franklin
  Nashville
  Missouri 1861
  Kentucky 1862
  Mississippi 1862
  Mississippi 1864
  Tennessee 1863
  Tennessee 1864
  Alabama 1864
  Alabama 1865

Georgia 1864
Georgia 1865

Philippine Insurrection
  Manila
  Malolos
  Laguna de Bay
  San Isidro
  Cavite
  Tarlac
  Jolo
  Luzon 1899
  Luzon 1900
  Luzon 1901

World War II
  Normandy (with arrowhead)
  Northern France
  Rhineland
  Ardennes-Alsace
  Central Europe

Vietnam
  Defense
  Counteroffensive
  Counteroffensive, Phase II
  Counteroffensive, Phase III
  Tet Counteroffensive

DECORATIONS

Presidential Unit Citation (Army), Streamer embroidered BOGHEIM, GERMANY (4th Cavalry Reconnaissance Squadron cited; WD GO 109, 1945)

Presidential Unit Citation (Army), Streamer embroidered BING LONG PROVINCE (1st Squadron, 4th Cavalry, cited; DA GO 31, 1967)

French Croix de Guerre with Silver Star, World War II, Streamer embroidered NORMANDY (4th [less Troop B] and 24th Cavalry Reconnaissance Squadrons cited; DA GO 43, 1950)

Cited in the Order of the Day of the Belgian Army for action in the ARDENNES (4th Cavalry Group, 4th and 24th Cavalry Reconnaissance Squadrons cited; DA GO 43, 1950)

1st SQUADRON, 4th CAVALRY

RA

(1ST INFANTRY DIVISION)

LINEAGE

Constituted 3 March 1855 in the Regular Army as Company A, 1st Cavalry. Organized in June 1855 at Fort Columbus, New York; joined the Regiment 11 June 1855 at Jefferson Barracks, Missouri. Redesignated 3 August 1861 as Company A, 4th Cavalry. (Cavalry companies officially designated as troops in 1883).

Reorganized and redesignated 16 April 1942 as Troop E, 4th Cavalry, Mechanized. Reorganized and redesignated 21 December 1943 as Company F, 4th Cavalry Reconnaissance Squadron, Mechanized. Converted and redesignated 1 May 1946 as Troop E, 4th Constabulary Squadron. Converted and redesignated 1 April 1949 as Company D, 4th Reconnaissance Battalion. Reorganized and redesignated 1 December 1951 as Medium Tank Company, 4th Armored Cavalry Reconnaissance Battalion. Inactivated 1 July 1955 at Camp McCauley, Austria.

Consolidated 15 February 1957 with 1st Reconnaissance Company (see AN-NEX) and redesignated as Headquarters and Headquarters Troop, 1st Reconnaissance Squadron, 4th Cavalry; concurrently, activated at Fort Riley, Kansas, and assigned to 1st Infantry Division (organic elements concurrently constituted and activated). Reorganized and redesignated 2 January 1964 as 1st Squadron, 4th Cavalry.

ANNEX

1st Reconnaissance Troop constituted 1 August 1940 in the Regular Army and activated at Fort Devens, Massachusetts, and assigned to 1st Infantry Division. Reorganized and redesignated 1 March 1943 as 1st Reconnaissance Troop, Mechanized. Inactivated 30 November 1946 in Germany. Converted and redesignated 10 October 1948 as 1st Reconnaissance Company and activated in Germany.

128

CAMPAIGN PARTICIPATION CREDIT

Indian Wars
  *Comanches
  *Apaches
  Little Big Horn
  Cheyennes
  *Kansas 1857
  *Kansas 1860
  *Mexico 1873
  New Mexico 1882

Civil War
  *Bull Run
  Mississippi River
  *Peninsula
  *Antietam
  Fredericksburg
  Murfreesborough
  *Chickamauga
  *Atlanta
  *Franklin
  *Nashville
  Missouri 1861
  Kentucky 1862
  Mississippi 1862
  *Mississippi 1864
  *Tennessee 1863
  Tennessee 1864
  *Alabama 1864
  *Alabama 1865
  *Georgia 1864
  *Georgia 1865

Philippine Insurrection
  Manila
  *Malolos
  Laguna de Bay
  *San Isidro
  *Cavite
  *Tarlac
  Jolo
  *Luzon 1899
  *Luzon 1900
  *Luzon 1901

World War II
  *Algeria-French Morocco
    (with arrowhead)
  *Tunisia
  *Sicily (with arrowhead)
  *Normandy (with arrowhead)
  *Northern France
  *Rhineland
  *Ardennes-Alsace
  *Central Europe

Vietnam
  *Defense
  *Counteroffensive
  *Counteroffensive, Phase II
  *Counteroffensive, Phase III
  *Tet Counteroffensive

DECORATIONS

*Presidential Unit Citation (Army), Streamer embroidered BOGHEIM, GERMANY (4th Cavalry Reconnaissance Squadron cited; WD GO 109, 1945)

*Presidential Unit Citation (Army), Streamer embroidered BING LONG PROVINCE (1st Squadron, 4th Cavalry, cited; DA GO 31, 1967)

*French Croix de Guerre with Palm, World War II, Streamer embroidered KASSERINE (1st Reconnaissance Troop cited; DA GO 43, 1950)

*French Croix de Guerre with Palm, World War II, Streamer embroidered NORMANDY (1st Reconnaissance Troop cited; DA GO 43, 1950)

*French Croix de Guerre with Silver Star, World War II, Streamer embroidered NORMANDY (4th [less Troop B] and 24th Cavalry Reconnaissance Squadrons cited; DA GO 43, 1950)

*French Croix de Guerre Fourragère, World War II (1st Reconnaissance Troop cited; DA GO 43, 1950)

*Belgian Fourragère 1940 (1st Reconnaissance Troop cited; DA GO 43, 1950)

*Cited in the Order of the Day of the Belgian Army for action at MONS (1st Reconnaissance Troop cited; DA GO 43, 1950)

*Cited in the Order of the Day of the Belgian Army for action at EUPEN-MALMEDY (1st Reconnaissance Troop cited; DA GO 43, 1950)

*Cited in the Order of the Day of the Belgian Army for action in the ARDENNES (4th Cavalry Group, 4th and 24th Cavalry Reconnaissance Squadrons cited; DA GO 43, 1950)

Troop A additionally entitled to: Valorous Unit Award, Streamer embroidered AP BAU BANG (Troop A, 1st Squadron, 4th Cavalry, cited; DA GO 20, 1967)

2d SQUADRON, 4th CAVALRY

RA

(4th Armored Division)

Constituted 3 March 1855 in the Regular Army as Company B, 1st Cavalry. Organized in September 1855 at Rome, New York; joined the Regiment 20 September 1855 at Fort Leavenworth, Kansas. Redesignated 3 August 1861 as Company B, 4th Cavalry. (Cavalry companies officially designated as troops in 1883.)

Reorganized and redesignated 16 April 1942 as Troop F, 4th Cavalry, Mechanized. Reorganized and redesignated 21 December 1943 as Company F, 24th Cavalry Reconnaissance Squadron, Mechanized. Converted and redesignated 1 May 1946 as Troop E, 24th Constabulary Squadron. Inactivated 15 December 1952 in Germany. Converted and redesignated 21 April 1953 as Company D, 524th Reconnaissance Battalion.

Redesignated 15 October 1957 as Troop B, 4th Cavalry. Redesignated 1 December 1957 as Headquarters and Headquarters Company, 2d Battle Group, 4th Cavalry; concurrently, assigned to 1st Cavalry Division and activated in Korea (organic elements concurrently constituted and activated. Reorganized and redesignated 1 August 1963 as 2d Squadron, 4th Cavalry; concurrently, relieved from assignment to 1st Cavalry Division, transferred (less personnel and equipment) from United States Army, Pacific, to United States Army, Europe, and assigned to 4th Armored Division.

CAMPAIGN PARTICIPATION CREDIT

Indian Wars
*Comanches
*Apaches
*Little Big Horn
Cheyennes
*Kansas 1857
*Kansas 1860
*Mexico 1873
New Mexico 1882

Civil War
Bull Run
*Mississippi River
Peninsula
Antietam
Fredericksburg
*Murfreesborough
*Chickamauga
*Atlanta
*Franklin
*Nashville
*Missouri 1861
*Kentucky 1862
*Mississippi 1864
*Tennessee 1863

Tennessee 1864
*Alabama 1864
*Alabama 1865
*Georgia 1864
*Georgia 1865

Philippine Insurrection
Manila
Malolos
Laguna de Bay
*San Isidro
*Cavite
*Tarlac
Jolo
*Luzon 1899
*Luzon 1900
Luzon 1901

World War II
*Normandy (with arrowhead)
*Northern France
*Rhineland
*Ardennes-Alsace
*Central Europe

DECORATIONS

Presidential Unit Citation (Army), Streamer embroidered BOGHEIM, GERMANY

*French Croix de Guerre with Silver Star, World War II, Streamer embroidered NORMANDY (4th [less Troop B] and 24th Cavalry Reconnaissance Squadrons cited; DA GO 43, 1950)

*Cited in the Order of the Day of the Belgian Army for action in the ARDENNES (4th Cavalry Group, 4th and 24th Cavalry Reconnaissance Squadrons cited; DA GO 43, 1950)

3d SQUADRON, 4th CAVALRY

RA

(25th Infantry Division)

Constituted 3 March 1855 in the Regular Army as Company C, 1st Cavalry. Organized 17 June 1855 at Jefferson Barracks, Missouri. Redesignated 3 August 1861 as Company C, 4th Cavalry. (Cavalry companies officially designated as troops in 1883.)

Reorganized and redesignated 1 February 1928 as Machine Gun Troop, 4th Cavalry. Reorganized and redesignated 1 February 1940 as Service Troop, 4th Cavalry. Reorganized and redesignated 16 April 1942 as Service Troop, 4th Cavalry, Mechanized.

Consolidated 21 December 1943 with Headquarters Troop, 4th Cavalry, and redesignated as Headquarters Troop, 4th Cavalry Group, Mechanized. Converted and redesignated 1 May 1946 as Headquarters Troop, 4th Constabulary Regiment. Reorgainzed and redesignated 10 February 1948 as Headquarters and Service Troop, 4th Constabulary Regiment. Inactivated 1 May 1949 in Austria. Redesignated 20 August 1953 as Headquarters Company, 4th Armored Cavalry.

Former Troop C (organized 1855) withdrawn 15 February 1957; concurrently, consolidated with Troop C, 4th Cavalry (see ANNEX 1) and 25th Reconnaissance Company (active) (see ANNEX 2), redesignated as Headquarters and Headquarters Troop, 3d Reconnaissance Squadron, 4th Cavalry, assigned to 25th Infantry Division, and activated in Hawaii (organic elements concurrently constituted and activated). Reorganized and redesignated 29 July 1963 as 3d Squadron, 4th Cavalry.

ANNEX 1

Troop C, 4th Cavalry, constituted 1 February 1940 in the Regular Army. Activated 1 January 1941 at Fort Meade, South Dakota. Reorganized and redesignated 16 April 1942 as Troop C, 4th Cavalry, Mechanized. Reorganized and redesignated 21 December 1943 as Troop C, 24th Cavalry Reconnaissance Squadron, Mechanized. Reorganized and redesignated 1 May 1946 as Troop C, 24th Constabulary Squadron. Inactivated 15 December 1952 in Germany. Redesignated 21 April 1953 as Company C, 524th Reconnaissance Battalion. Redesignated 1 February 1957 as Troop C, 4th Cavalry.

ANNEX 2

25th Reconnaissance Troop constituted 28 October 1942 in the Regular Army and assigned to 25th Infantry Division. Activated 3 November 1942 at Schofield Barracks, Hawaii. Reorganized and redesignated 1 January 1944 as 25th Cavalry Reconnaissance Troop, Mechanized. Redesignated 10 October 1945 as 25th Mechanized Cavalry Reconnaissance Troop. Redesignated 20 March 1949 as 25th Reconnaissance Company.

CAMPAIGN PARTICIPATION CREDIT

Indian Wars
 *Comanches
 *Apaches
 Little Big Horn
 Cheyennes
 Kansas 1857
 *Kansas 1860
 *Mexico 1873
 *New Mexico 1882

Civil War
 Bull Run
 *Mississippi River
 Peninsula
 Antietam
 Fredericksburg
 *Murfreesborough
 *Chickamauga
 *Atlanta
 *Franklin
 *Nashville
 *Missouri 1861
 *Kentucky 1862
 *Mississippi 1862
 *Mississippi 1864
 *Tennessee 1863
 Tennessee 1864
 *Alabama 1864
 *Alabama 1865
 *Georgia 1864
 *Georgia 1865

Philippine Insurrection
 *Manila
 *Malolos
 *Laguna de Bay

*San Isidro
*Cavite
*Tarlac
Jolo
*Luzon 1899
*Luzon 1900
Luzon 1901

World War II
 *Normandy (with arrowhead)
 *Northern France
 *Rhineland
 *Ardennes-Alsace
 *Central Europe
 *Guadalcanal
 *Northern Solomons (with arrowhead)
 *Luzon

Korean War
 *UN defensive
 *UN offensive
 *CCF intervention
 *First UN counteroffensive
 *CCF spring offensive
 *UN summer-fall offensive
 *Second Korean winter
 *Korea, summer-fall 1952
 *Third Korean winter
 *Korea, summer 1953

Vietnam
 *Counteroffensive
 *Counteroffensive, Phase II
 *Counteroffensive, Phase III
 *Tet Counteroffensive

DECORATIONS

Presidential Unit Citation (Army), Streamer embroidered BOGHEIM, GERMANY

*Presidential Unit Citation (Army), Streamer embroidered GUADALCANAL (25th Reconnaissance Troop cited; DA GO 36, 1951)

*Philippine Presidential Unit Citation, Streamer embroidered 17 OCTOBER 1944 TO 4 JULY 1945 (25th Reconnaissance Troop cited; DA GO 47, 1950)

*Republic of Korea Presidential Unit Citation, Streamer embroidered MASAN-CHINJU (25th Reconnaissance Company cited; DA GO 35, 1951)

*Republic of Korea Presidential Unit Citation, Streamer embroidered MUNSAN-NI (25th Reconnaissance Company cited; DA GO 19, 1955)

*Cited in the Order of the Day of the Belgian Army for action in the ARDENNES (4th Cavalry Group, 4th and 24th Cavalry Reconnaissance Squadrons cited; DA GO 43, 1950)

Troop A additionally entitled to: Valorous Unit Award, Streamer embroidered CU CHI DISTRICT (Troop A, 3d Squadron, 4th Cavalry, cited; DA GO 20, 1967)

4th SQUADRON, 4th CAVALRY

AR
(inactive)

LINEAGE

Constituted 3 March 1855 in the Regular Army as Company D, 1st Cavalry. Organized 3 June 1855 at Jefferson Barracks, Missouri. Redesignated 3 August 1861 as Company D, 4th Cavalry. (Cavalry companies officially designated as troops in 1883.)

Inactivated 10 September 1921 at Brownsville, Texas; concurrently, redesignated as Headquarters Troop, 2d Cavalry Divison.

Activated 1 April 1941 at Fort Riley, Kansas. Inactivated 15 July 1942 at Fort Riley, Kansas. Activated 25 February 1943 at Fort Clark, Texas. Inactivated 10 May 1944 in North Africa.

Redesignated 11 May 1959 as Headquarters and Headquarters Troop, 4th Reconnaissance Squadron, 4th Cavalry; withdrawn from Regular Army, allotted to the Army Reserve, and assigned to 102d Infantry Division (organic elements concurrently constituted). Activated 1 June 1959 with Headquarters at Kansas City, Missouri. Reorganized and redesignated 1 April 1963 as 4th Squadron, 4th Cavalry. Inactivated 31 December 1965 at Kansas City, Missouri, and relieved from assignment to 102d Infantry Division.

136

Campaign Participation Credit

Indian Wars
  *Comanches
  *Apaches
  *Little Big Horn
  Cheyennes
  *Kansas 1857
  *Kansas 1860
  Mexico 1873
  New Mexico 1882

Civil War
  Bull Run
  *Mississippi River
  Peninsula
  Antietam
  Fredericksburg
  *Murfreesborough
  *Chickamauga
  *Atlanta
  *Franklin
  *Nashville
  *Missouri 1861
  *Kentucky 1862
  *Mississippi 1862
  *Mississippi 1864

  *Tennessee 1863
  *Tennessee 1864
  *Alabama 1864
  *Alabama 1865
  *Georgia 1864
  *Georgia 1865

Philippine Insurrection
  Manila
  Malolos
  Laguna de Bay
  *San Isidro
  *Cavite
  *Tarlac
  Jolo
  *Luzon 1899
  *Luzon 1900
  *Luzon 1901

World War II
  Normandy (with arrowhead)
  Northern France
  Rhineland
  Ardennes-Alsace
  Central Europe

Decorations

Presidential Unit Citation (Army), Streamer embroidered BOGHEIM, GERMANY

TROOP E, 4th CAVALRY

LINEAGE

Constituted 3 March 1855 in the Regular Army as Company E, 1st Cavalry. Organized July–October 1855 at Harrisburg, Pennsylvania; joined the Regiment 18 November 1855 at Fort Leavenworth, Kansas. Redesignated 3 August 1861 as Company E, 4th Cavalry. (Cavalry companies officially designated as troops in 1883.)

Reorganized and redesignated 16 April 1942 as Troop A, 4th Cavalry, Mechanized. Reorganized and redesignated 21 December 1943 as Troop A, 4th Cavalry Reconnaissance Squadron, Mechanized. Converted and redesignated 1 May 1946 as Troop A, 4th Constabulary Squadron. Converted and redesignated 1 April 1949 as Company A, 4th Reconnaissance Battalion. Redesignated 1 December 1951 as Company A, 4th Armored Cavalry Reconnaissance Battalion. Inactivated 1 July 1955 at Camp McCauley, Austria.

Redesignated 20 April 1959 as Headquarters and Headquarters Troop, 5th Reconnaissance Squadron, 4th Cavalry; concurrently, withdrawn from the Regular Army, allotted to the Army Reserve and assigned to 103d Infantry Division (organic elements concurrently constituted). Activated 18 May 1959 with Headquarters at Ottumwa, Iowa. Inactivated 15 March 1963 at Ottumwa, Iowa, and relieved from assignment to 103d Infantry Division. Headquarters and Headquarters Troop, 5th Reconnaissance Squadron, 4th Cavalry, redesignated 3 December 1963 as Troop E, 4th Cavalry, and assigned to 205th Infantry Brigade. Activated 15 January 1964 at Madison, Wisconsin.

138

Home Area: Fifth United States Army.

CAMPAIGN PARTICIPATION CREDIT

Indian Wars
  Comanches
  Little Big Horn
  Kansas 1857
  Kansas 1860
  Mexico 1873

Civil War
  Bull Run
  Peninsula
  Antietam
  Chickamauga
  Atlanta
  Franklin
  Nashville
  Mississippi 1864
  Tennessee 1863

Alabama 1864
Alabama 1865
Georgia 1864
Georgia 1865

Philippine Insurrection
  Manila
  Malolos
  Tarlac
  Luzon 1899

World War II–EAME
  Normandy (with arrowhead)
  Northern France
  Rhineland
  Ardennes-Alsace
  Central Europe

DECORATIONS

Presidential Unit Citation (Army), Streamer embroidered BOGHEIM, GERMANY (4th Cavalry Reconnaissance Squadron cited; WD GO 109, 1945)

French Croix de Guerre with Silver Star, World War II, Streamer embroidered NORMANDY (4th Cavalry Reconnaissance Squadron [less Troop B] cited; DA GO 43, 1950)

    Cited in the Order of the Day of the Belgian Army for action in the ARDENNES (4th Cavalry Reconnaissance Squadron cited; DA GO 43, 1956)

BIBLIOGRAPHY, 4TH CAVALRY

Brackett, Albert G. *History of the United States Cavalry From the Formation of the Federal Government to the 1st of June 1863.* New York: 1865.

Carter, Robert G. *On the Border with Mackenzie: or, Winning West Texas from the Comanches.* Washington: 1935.

————. *On the Trail of Deserters: a Phenomenal Capture . . . .* Washington: 1920.

Department of the Army. AMERICAN FORCES IN ACTION series. *Utah Beach to Cherbourg.* 1947.

Epps, Ernest E. *The History of the Fourth Cavalry Reconnaissance Squadron, European Theater of Operations.* Germany: 1945.

Forsyth, George A. *Thrilling Days in Army Life.* New York and London: 1900.

Herr, John K., and Edward S. Wallace. *The Story of the U.S. Cavalry.* Boston: 1953.

Larson, James. *Sergeant Larson, 4th Cavalry.* San Antonio, Texas: 1935.

Rodenbough, Theo. F., and William L. Haskin, eds. *The Army of the United States.* New York: 1896. "The Fourth Regiment of Cavalry."

Unit Members. *Fourth Cavalry, U.S. Army, 1855–1930.* Fort Meade, South Dakota: 1930.

———. *Roster of Commanding Officers of the Fourth U.S. Cavalry, Colonel Edgar Z. Steever, Commanding, Fort Meade, South Dakota.* Fort Meade, South Dakota: 1909.

———. *History of the 4th Cavalry.* Fort Riley: 1957.

———. *"Organization Day, 2d Battle Group, 4th Cavalry, Korea."* Korea: 1961.

UNITED STATES ARMY IN WORLD WAR II

Blumenson, Martin. *Breakout and Pursuit.* 1961.

Cole, Hugh M. *The Ardennes: Battle of the Bulge.* 1965.

MacDonald, Charles B. *The Siegfried Line Campaign.* 1963.

5th CAVALRY
(Black Knights)

HERALDIC ITEMS

COAT OF ARMS

Shield: Or a cross moline sable, on a chief embattled of the last a maltese cross argent.

Crest: On a wreath of the colors (or and sable) a bundle of five arrows sable armed and flitted gules, tied with a rattlesnake skin having five rattles proper.

Motto: Loyalty and Courage.

Symbolism: The shield is yellow for cavalry. The cross moline symbolizes the charge of the regiment on Longstreet's troops at Gaines Mill in 1862, a charge that saved the Union artillery and that is characterized by the regimental historian as "its most distinguished service." The cross moline represents the iron pieces of a millstone (moulin, the French word for mill). The black chief of the shield with the maltese cross is for the Puerto Rican Expedition of 1898. (It symbolizes the original name of the island, San Juan, named for the old knights of St. John who wore a white maltese cross on a black habit.) The partition line is embattled to suggest the castle on the Spanish arms.

The crest is for the Indian campaigns. The number of arrows corresponds to the numerical designation of the regiment.

DISTINCTIVE INSIGNIA

The distinctive insignia is the shield, crest, and motto of the coat of arms.

LINEAGE AND HONORS

LINEAGE

Constituted 3 March 1855 in the Regular Army as 2d Cavalry. Organized 28 May 1855 at Louisville, Kentucky. Redesignated 3 August 1861 as 5th

Cavalry. Assigned to 15th Cavalry Division December 1917–May 1918. Assigned 18 December 1922 to 1st Cavalry Division.

Dismounted 28 February 1943 and reorganized 4 December 1943 partly under cavalry and partly under infantry tables of organization and equipment. Reorganized wholly as infantry 20 July 1945 but retained cavalry designations. Reorganized 25 March 1949 with troops redesignated as companies. Relieved 15 October 1957 from assignment to 1st Cavalry Division.

Reorganized 15 November 1957 as a parent regiment under the Combat Arms Regimental System.

CAMPAIGN PARTICIPATION CREDIT

Indian Wars
  Comanches
  Apaches
  Little Big Horn
  Nez Perces
  Bannocks
  Cheyennes
  Utes
  Texas 1856
  Texas 1860
  Oklahoma 1858
  Oklahoma 1859
  Arizona 1872
  Arizona 1874

Civil War
  Bull Run
  Peninsula
  Antietam
  Fredericksburg
  Chancellorsville
  Gettysburg
  Wilderness
  Spotsylvania
  Cold Harbor
  Petersburg
  Shenandoah
  Appomattox
  Virginia 1861
  Virginia 1862
  Virginia 1863

  Virginia 1864
  Maryland 1863

Philippine Insurrection
  Without inscription

Mexican Expedition
  Mexico 1916–1917

World War II
  New Guinea
  Bismarck Archipelago
    (with arrowhead)
  Leyte (with arrowhead)
  Luzon

Korean War
  UN defensive
  UN offensive
  CCF intervention
  First UN counteroffensive
  CCF spring offensive
  UN summer-fall offensive
  Second Korean winter
  Third Korean winter

Vietnam
  Defense
  Counteroffensive
  Counteroffensive, Phase II
  Counteroffensive, Phase III
  Tet Counteroffensive

DECORATIONS

Presidential Unit Citation (Army), Streamer embroidered LOS NEGROS ISLAND (5th Cavalry cited; DA GO 16, 1949)

Presidential Unit Citation (Army), Streamer embroidered PLEIKU PROVINCE (1st and 2d Battalions, 5th Cavalry, cited; DA GO 40, 1967)

Philippine Presidential Unit Citation, Streamer embroidered 17 OCTOBER 1944 TO 4 JULY 1945 (5th Cavalry cited; DA GO 47, 1950)

Republic of Korea Presidential Unit Citation, Streamer embroidered WAEGWAN-TAEGU (5th Cavalry cited; DA GO 35, 1951)

Republic of Korea Presidential Unit Citation, Streamer embroidered KOREA (5th Cavalry cited; DA GO 24, 1954)

Chryssoun Aristion Andrias (Bravery Gold Medal of Greece), Streamer embroidered KOREA (5th Cavalry cited; DA GO 2, 1956)

1st BATTALION, 5th CAVALRY

(Black Knights)

RA

(1st Cavalry Division)

LINEAGE

Constituted 3 March 1855 in the Regular Army as Company A, 2d Cavalry. Organized May–June 1855 at Jefferson Barracks, Missouri. Redesignated 3 August 1861 as Company A, 5th Cavalry. (Cavalry companies officially designated as troops in 1883.) (5th Cavalry assigned to 15th Cavalry Division December 1917–May 1918; assigned 18 December 1922 to 1st Cavalry Division. Dismounted 28 February 1943 and reorganized 4 December 1943 partly under cavalry and partly under infantry tables of organization. Reorganized wholly as infantry 20 July 1945 but retained cavalry designations.) Redesignated 25 March 1949 as Company A, 5th Cavalry.

Reorganized and redesignated 15 November 1957 as Headquarters and Headquarters Company, 1st Battle Group, 5th Cavalry, and remained assigned to 1st Cavalry Division (organic elements concurrently constituted and activated in Korea). Reorganized and redesignated 1 September 1963 as 1st Battalion, 5th Cavalry. Transferred (less personnel and equipment) 1 July 1965 from Korea to Fort Benning, Georgia, and reorganized.

144

CAMPAIGN PARTICIPATION CREDIT

Indian Wars
  *Comanches
  *Apaches
  *Little Big Horn
  *Nez Perces
  Bannocks
  *Cheyennes
  *Utes
  *Texas 1856
  *Texas 1860
  *Oklahoma 1858
  *Oklahoma 1859
  Arizona 1872
  Arizona 1874

Civil War
  Bull Run
  *Peninsula
  *Antietam
  *Fredericksburg
  *Chancellorsville
  *Gettysburg
  Wilderness
  Spotsylvania
  Cold Harbor
  *Petersburg
  *Shenandoah
  *Appomattox
  *Virginia 1861
  *Virginia 1862
  *Virginia 1863
  *Virginia 1864
  *Maryland 1863

War With Spain
  *Puerto Rico

Philippine Insurrection
  *Without inscription

Mexican Expedition
  *Mexico 1916–1917

World War II
  *New Guinea
  *Bismarck Archipelago
    (with arrowhead)
  *Leyte (with arrowhead)
  *Luzon

Korean War
  *UN defensive
  *UN offensive
  *CCF intervention
  *First UN counteroffensive
  *CCF spring offensive
  *UN summer-fall offensive
  *Second Korean winter
  *Third Korean winter

Vietnam
  *Defense
  *Counteroffensive
  *Counteroffensive, Phase II
  *Counteroffensive, Phase III
  *Tet Counteroffensive

DECORATIONS

*Presidential Unit Citation (Army), Streamer embroidered LOS NEGROS ISLAND (5th Cavalry cited; DA GO 16, 1959)

*Presidential Unit Citation (Army), Streamer embroidered LEYTE (Troop A, 5th Cavalry, cited; WD GO 47, 1945)

*Presidential Unit Citation (Army), Streamer embroidered KAMYANGJANG-NI (Companies A and B, 5th Cavalry, cited; DA GO 36, 1951)

*Presidential Unit Citation (Army), Streamer embroidered PLEIKU PROVINCE (1st Battalion, 5th Cavalry, cited; DA GO 40, 1967)

*Philippine Presidential Unit Citation, Streamer embroidered 17 OCTOBER 1944 TO 4 JULY 1945 (5th Cavalry cited; DA GO 47, 1950)

*Republic of Korea Presidential Unit Citation, Streamer embroidered WAEGWAN-TAEGU (5th Cavalry cited; DA GO 35, 1951)

*Republic of Korea Presidential Unit Citation, Streamer embroidered KOREA (5th Cavalry cited; DA GO 24, 1954)

*Chryssoun Aristion Andrias (Bravery Gold Medal of Greece), Streamer embroidered KOREA (5th Cavalry cited; DA GO 2, 1956)

2d BATTALION, 5th CAVALRY

(Black Knights)

RA

(1st Cavalry Division)

LINEAGE

Constituted 3 March 1855 in the Regular Army as Company B, 2d Cavalry. Organized June–July 1855 at Jefferson Barracks, Missouri. Redesignated 3 August 1861 as Company B, 5th Cavalry. (Cavalry companies officially designated as troops in 1883.) (5th Cavalry assigned to 15th Cavalry Division December 1917–May 1918; assigned 18 December 1922 to 1st Cavalry Division. Dismounted 28 February 1943 and reorganized 4 December 1943 partly under cavalry and partly under infantry tables of organization. Reorganized wholly as infantry 20 July 1945 but retained cavalry designations.) Redesignated 25 March 1949 as Company B, 5th Cavalry.

Inactivated 15 November 1957 in Japan and relieved from assignment to 1st Cavalry Division; concurrently, redesignated as Headquarters and Headquarters Troop, 2d Reconnaissance Squadron, 5th Cavalry. Redesignated 19 June 1963 as Headquarters and Headquarters Company, 2d Battalion, 5th Cavalry (organic elements concurrently constituted). Activated 1 August 1963 in Korea and assigned to 1st Cavalry Division. Transferred (less personnel and equipment) 1 July 1965 from Korea to Fort Benning, Georgia, and reorganized.

146

CAMPAIGN PARTICIPATION CREDIT

Indian Wars
 *Comanches
 *Apaches
 *Little Big Horn
 *Nez Perces
 *Bannocks
 *Cheyennes
 *Utes
 Texas 1856
 *Texas 1860
 Oklahoma 1858
 *Oklahoma 1859
 *Arizona 1872
 *Arizona 1874

Civil War
 *Bull Run
 *Peninsula
 *Antietam
 *Fredericksburg
 *Chancellorsville
 *Gettysburg
 Wilderness
 *Spotsylvania
 Cold Harbor
 *Petersburg
 *Shenandoah
 *Appomattox
 *Virginia 1861
 *Virginia 1862
 *Virginia 1863

 *Virginia 1864
 *Maryland 1863

Philippine Insurrection
 *Without inscription

Mexican Expedition
 *Mexico 1916–1917

World War II
 *New Guinea
 *Bismarck Archipelago
 (with arrowhead)
 *Leyte (with arrowhead)
 *Luzon

Korean War
 *UN defensive
 *UN offensive
 *CCF intervention
 *First UN counteroffensive
 *CCF spring offensive
 *UN summer-fall offensive
 *Second Korean winter
 *Third Korean winter

Vietnam
 *Defense
 *Counteroffensive
 *Counteroffensive, Phase II
 *Counteroffensive, Phase III
 *Tet Counteroffensive

DECORATIONS

*Presidential Unit Citation (Army), Streamer embroidered LOS NEGROS ISLAND (5th Cavalry cited; DA GO 16, 1949)

*Presidential Unit Citation (Army), Streamer embroidered KAMYANGJANG-NI (Companies A and B, 5th Cavalry, cited; DA GO 36, 1951)

*Presidential Unit Citation (Army), Streamer embroidered PLEIKU PROVINCE (2d Battalion, 5th Cavalry, cited; DA GO 40, 1967)

*Philippine Presidential Unit Citation, Streamer embroidered 17 OCTOBER 1944 TO 4 JULY 1945 (5th Cavalry cited; DA GO 47, 1950)

*Republic of Korea Presidential Unit Citation, Streamer embroidered WAEGWAN TAEGU (5th Cavalry cited; DA GO 35, 1951)

*Republic of Korea Presidential Unit Citation, Streamer embroidered KOREA (5th Cavalry cited; DA GO 24, 1954)

*Chryssoun Aristion Andrias (Bravery Gold Medal of Greece), Streamer embroidered KOREA (5th Cavalry cited; DA GO 2, 1956)

3d SQUADRON, 5th CAVALRY

(Black Knights)

(9th Infantry Division)

Constituted 3 March 1855 in the Regular Army as Company C, 2d Cavalry. Organized May–June 1855 at Pittsburgh, Pennsylvania. Redesignated 3 August 1861 as Company C, 5th Cavalry. (Cavalry companies officially designated troops in 1883.) (5th Cavalry assigned to 15th Cavalry Division December 1917–May 1918; assigned 18 December 1922 to 1st Cavalry Division. Dismounted 28 February 1943 and reorganized 4 December 1943 partly under cavalry and partly under infantry tables of organization. Reorganized wholly as infantry 20 July 1945 but retained cavalry designations.) Redesignated 25 March 1949 as Company C, 5th Cavalry. Inactivated 15 November 1957 in Japan and relieved from assignment to 1st Cavalry Division.

Redesignated 15 April 1958 as Headquarters and Headquarters Troop, 3d Reconnaissance Squadron, 5th Cavalry (organic elements concurrently constituted). Activated 1 July 1958 and assigned to 9th Infantry Division at Fort Carson, Colorado. Inactivated 31 January 1962 at Fort Carson, Colorado. Redesignated 1 February 1966 as 3d Squadron, 5th Cavalry, and activated at Fort Riley, Kansas.

CAMPAIGN PARTICIPATION CREDIT

Indian Wars
*Comanches
*Apaches
*Little Big Horn
Nez Perces
Bannocks
Cheyennes
Utes
*Texas 1856
Texas 1860
Oklahoma 1858
*Oklahoma 1859
*Arizona 1872
Arizona 1874

Civil War
Bull Run
*Peninsula
*Antietam
*Fredericksburg
*Chancellorsville
*Gettysburg
*Wilderness
*Spotsylvania
*Cold Harbor
*Petersburg
*Shenandoah
*Appomattox
*Virginia 1861
*Virginia 1862
*Virginia 1863

*Virginia 1864
*Maryland 1863

Philippine Insurrection
*Without inscription

Mexican Expedition
Mexico 1916–1917

World War II
*New Guinea
*Bismarck Archipelago
  (with arrowhead)
*Leyte (with arrowhead)
*Luzon

Korean War
*UN defensive
*UN offensive
*CCF intervention
*First UN counteroffensive
*CCF spring offensive
*UN summer-fall offensive
*Second Korean winter
*Third Korean winter

Vietnam
*Counteroffensive, Phase II
*Counteroffensive, Phase III
*Tet Counteroffensive

DECORATIONS

*Presidential Unit Citation (Army), Streamer embroidered LOS NEGROS ISLAND (5th Cavalry cited; DA GO 16, 1949)

*Philippine Presidential Unit Citation, Streamer embroidered 17 OCTOBER 1944 TO 4 JULY 1945 (5th Cavalry cited; DA GO 47, 1950)

*Republic of Korea Presidential Unit Citation, Streamer embroidered WAEGWAN-TAEGU (5th Cavalry cited; DA GO 35, 1951)

*Republic of Korea Presidential Unit Citation, Streamer embroidered KOREA (5th Cavalry cited; DA GO 24, 1954)

*Chryssoun Aristion Andrias (Bravery Gold Medal of Greece), Streamer embroidered KOREA (5th Cavalry cited; DA GO 2, 1956)

TROOP D, 5th CAVALRY

(Black Knights)

AR

(187th Infantry Brigade)

LINEAGE

Constituted 3 March 1855 in the Regular Army as Company D, 2d Cavalry. Organized April–June 1855. Redesignated 3 August 1861 as Company D, 5th Cavalry. (Cavalry companies officially designated as troops in 1883.) (5th Cavalry assigned to 15th Cavalry Division December 1917–May 1918; assigned 18 December 1922 to 1st Cavalry Division.) Troop D, 5th Cavalry, disbanded 1 September 1921.

Reconstituted 16 November 1943 in the Regular Army. Activated 4 December 1943 at Brisbane, Australia. (5th Cavalry dismounted 28 February 1943 and reorganized 4 December 1943 partly under cavalry and partly under infantry tables of organization. Reorganized wholly as infantry 20 July 1945 but retained cavalry designations.) Redesignated 25 March 1949 as Company D, 5th Cavalry. Inactivated 15 November 1957 in Japan and relieved from assignment to 1st Cavalry Division.

Redesignated 6 April 1959 as Headquarters and Headquarters Troop, 4th Reconnaissance Squadron, 5th Cavalry; concurrently, withdrawn from Regular Army, allotted to the Army Reserve, and assigned to 94th Infantry Division (organic elements concurrently constituted). Activated 1 May 1959 at Boston, Massachusetts. Inactivated 1 March 1963 at Boston, Massachusetts, and relieved from assignment to 94th Infantry Division.

Headquarters and Headquarters Troop, 4th Reconnaissance Squadron, 5th Cavalry, redesignated 3 December 1963 as Troop D, 5th Cavalry, and assigned to 187th Infantry Brigade. Activated 21 January 1964 at New Bedford, Massachusetts. Location changed 31 January 1966 to Roslindale, Massachusetts.

150

Home Area: First United States Army.

Campaign Participation Credit

Indian Wars
  Comanches
  Little Big Horn
  Bannocks
  Cheyennes
  Utes
  Texas 1856

Civil War
  Peninsula
  Antietam
  Fredericksburg
  Chancellorsville
  Gettysburg
  Petersburg
  Shenandoah
  Appomattox
  Virginia 1861
  Virginia 1862
  Virginia 1863
  Virginia 1864
  Maryland 1863

Mexican Expedition
  Mexico 1916–1917

World War II–AP
  New Guinea
  Bismarck Archipelago
    (with arrowhead)
  Leyte (with arrowhead)
  Luzon

Korean War
  UN defensive
  UN offensive
  CCF intervention
  First UN counteroffensive
  CCF spring offensive
  UN summer-fall offensive
  Second Korean winter
  Third Korean winter

Decorations

Presidential Unit Citation (Army), Streamer embroidered LOS NEGROS ISLAND (5th Cavalry cited; DA GO 16, 1949)

Philippine Presidential Unit Citation, Streamer embroidered 17 OCTOBER 1944 TO 4 JULY 1945 (5th Cavalry cited; DA GO 47, 1950)

Republic of Korea Presidential Unit Citation, Streamer embroidered WAEGWAN-TAEGU (5th Cavalry cited; DA GO 35, 1951)

Republic of Korea Presidential Unit Citation, Streamer embroidered KOREA (5th Cavalry cited; DA GO 24, 1954)

Chryssoun Aristion Andrias (Bravery Gold Medal of Greece), Streamer embroidered KOREA (5th Cavalry cited; DA GO 2, 1956)

5th SQUADRON, 5th CAVALRY

(Black Knights)

AR
(inactive)

LINEAGE

Constituted 3 March 1855 in the Regular Army as Company E, 2d Cavalry. Organized 28 May 1855 at Louisville, Kentucky. Redesignated 3 August 1861 as Company E, 5th Cavalry. (Cavalry companies officially designated as troops in 1883.) (5th Cavalry assigned to 15th Cavalry Division December 1917–May 1918; assigned 18 December 1922 to 1st Cavalry Division. Dismounted 28 February 1943 and reorganized 4 December 1943 partly under cavalry and partly under infantry tables of organization. Reorganized wholly as infantry 20 July 1945 but retained cavalry designations.) Redesignated 25 March 1949 as Company E, 5th Cavalry.

Inactivated 15 November 1957 in Japan; concurrently, redesignated as Headquarters and Headquarters Troop, 5th Reconnaissance Squadron, 5th Cavalry, and relieved from assignment to 1st Cavalry Division.

Redesignated 26 March 1963 as Headquarters and Headquarters Troop, 5th Squadron, 5th Cavalry; concurrently, withdrawn from the Regular Army, allotted to the Army Reserve, and assigned to 81st Infantry Division (organic elements concurrently constituted). Activated 1 April 1963 with Headquarters at Atlanta, Georgia. Inactivated 31 December 1965 at Atlanta, Georgia, and relieved from assignment to the 81st Infantry Division.

CAMPAIGN PARTICIPATION CREDIT

Indian Wars
  *Comanches
  *Apaches
  *Little Big Horn
  *Nez Perces
  *Bannocks
  *Cheyennes
  *Utes
  *Texas 1856
  *Texas 1860
  *Oklahoma 1858
  *Oklahoma 1859
  *Arizona 1872
  *Arizona 1874

Civil War
  *Bull Run
  *Peninsula
  *Antietam
  *Fredericksburg
  *Chancellorsville
  *Gettysburg
  *Wilderness
  *Spotsylvania
  *Cold Harbor
  *Petersburg
  *Shenandoah
  *Appomattox

  *Virginia 1861
  *Virginia 1862
  *Virginia 1863
  *Virginia 1864
  *Maryland 1863

Philippine Insurrection
  *Without inscription

Mexican Expedition
  *Mexico 1916–1917

World War II
  *New Guinea
  *Bismarck Archipelago
    (with arrowhead)
  *Leyte (with arrowhead)
  *Luzon

Korean War
  *UN defensive
  *UN offensive
  *CCF intervention
  *First UN counteroffensive
  *CCF spring offensive
  *UN summer-fall offensive
  *Second Korean winter
  *Third Korean winter

DECORATIONS

*Presidential Unit Citation (Army), Streamer embroidered LOS NEGROS ISLAND (5th Cavalry cited; DA GO 16, 1949)

*Philippine Presidential Unit Citation, Streamer embroidered 17 OCTOBER 1944 TO 4 JULY 1945 (5th Cavalry cited; DA GO 47, 1950)

*Republic of Korea Presidential Unit Citation, Streamer embroidered WAEGWAN-TAEGU (5th Cavalry cited; DA GO 35, 1951)

*Republic of Korea Presidential Unit Citation, Streamer embroidered KOREA (5th Cavalry cited; DA GO 24, 1954)

*Chryssoun Aristion Andrias (Bravery Gold Medal of Greece), Streamer embroidered KOREA (5th Cavalry cited; DA GO 2, 1956)

TROOP F, 5th CAVALRY

(Black Knights)

RA
(inactive)

LINEAGE

Constituted 3 March 1855 in the Regular Army as Company F, 2d Cavalry. Organized 28 May 1855 at Louisville, Kentucky. Redesignated 3 August 1861 as Company F, 5th Cavalry. (Cavalry companies officially designated as troops in 1883.) (5th Cavalry assigned to 15th Cavalry Division December 1917–May 1918; assigned 18 December 1922 to 1st Cavalry Division. Dismounted 28 February 1943 and reorganized 4 December 1943 partly under cavalry and partly under infantry tables of organization. Reorganized wholly as infantry 20 July 1943 but retained cavalry designations.) Redesignated 25 March 1949 as Company F, 5th Cavalry. Inactivated 15 November 1957 in Japan and relieved from assignment to 1st Cavalry Division.

Redesignated 12 February 1958 as Troop F, 5th Cavalry. Activated 15 February 1958 at Fort Devens, Massachusetts, and assigned to 2d Infantry Brigade. Inactivated 13 April 1962 at Fort Carson, Colorado, and relieved from assignment to 2d Infantry Brigade.

CAMPAIGN PARTICIPATION CREDIT

Indian Wars
  Comanches
  Apaches
  Little Big Horn
  Bannocks
  Cheyennes
  Utes
  Texas 1856
  Texas 1860
  Oklahoma 1858
  Oklahoma 1859

Civil War
  Peninsula
  Antietam
  Fredericksburg
  Chancellorsville
  Gettysburg
  Spotsylvania
  Petersburg
  Appomattox
  Virginia 1861
  Virginia 1862

Virginia 1863
Virginia 1864
Maryland 1863

Mexican Expedition
  Mexico 1916–1917

World War II–AP
  New Guinea
  Bismarck Archipelago
    (with arrowhead)
  Leyte (with arrowhead)
  Luzon

Korean War
  UN defensive
  UN offensive
  CCF intervention
  First UN counteroffensive
  CCF spring offensive
  UN summer-fall offensive
  Second Korean winter
  Third Korean winter

DECORATIONS

Presidential Unit Citation (Army), Streamer embroidered LOS NEGROS ISLAND (5th Cavalry cited; DA GO 16, 1949)

Philippine Presidential Unit Citation, Streamer embroidered 17 OCTOBER 1944 TO 4 JULY 1945 (5th Cavalry cited; DA GO 47, 1950)

Republic of Korea Presidential Unit Citation, Streamer embroidered WAEGWAN-TAEGU (5th Cavalry cited; DA GO 35, 1951)

Republic of Korea Presidential Unit Citation, Streamer embroidered KOREA (5th Cavalry cited; DA GO 24, 1954)

Chryssoun Aristion Andrias (Bravery Gold Medal of Greece), Streamer embroidered KOREA (5th Cavalry cited; DA GO 2, 1956)

BIBLIOGRAPHY, 5TH CAVALRY

Babcock, Conrad S. "Overland with the Cavalry," *St. Nicholas,* October 1936.

Brackett, Albert G. *History of the United States Cavalry From The Formation of the Federal Government to the 1st of June 1863.* New York: 1865.

Department of the Army
  Korea, 1950. Washington: 1952.

Department of the Army. AMERICAN FORCES IN ACTION series.
  The Admiralties: Operations of the 1st Cavalry Division. Washington: 1945.

Gugeler, Russell A. *Combat Actions in Korea.* Washington: 1954.

Herr, John K., and Edward S. Wallace. *The Story of the U.S. Cavalry.* Boston: 1953.

Johnson, Richard W. *A Soldier's Reminiscences.* Philadelphia: 1886.

Johnston, William P. *The Life of Albert Sidney Johnston, Embracing His Services in the Armies of the United States.* New York: 1878.

King, Charles. *Campaigning with Crook.* New York: 1880.

———. *The Fifth Cavalry in the Sioux War, 1876; Campaigning with Crook, and Stories of Army Life.* New York: 1890.

Mahr, Warren C., compiler. *1st Cavalry Division 1952–1954.* Atlanta, Georgia: 1954.

Middagh, S. H. "Extracts from a Regimental Scrap Book," *The Cavalry Journal,* October 1915 and January 1916.

Miller, John, jr., O. J. Carroll, and M. E. Tackley. *Korea 1951–1953.* Washington: 1956.

Oliver, William H., Jr., *Roughing it with the Regulars, by Wm. H. Oliver, Jr., late Troop "A", Fifth U.S. Regular Cavalry.* New York: 1901.

Price, George F. *Across the Continent with the Fifth Cavalry.* New York: 1883.

Reed, Louis A. *Illustrated Historical Review of the United States Army in Oahu, T.H.* Honolulu, Hawaii: 1911.

Rhodes, Charles D. *History of the Cavalry of the Army of the Potomac.* Kansas City, Missouri: 1900.

Rodenbough, Theo. F., and William L. Haskin, eds. *The Army of the United States.* New York: 1896. Eben Swift, "The Fifth United States Cavalry Regiment."

Unit Members. *History of the 5th United States Cavalry from 1855 to 1927.* Fort Clark: 1927.

———. *History Outline, 5th Cavalry Regiment 1855–1957.* N.p.: 1957.

———. *1st Cavalry Division "The First Team".* Japan: 1959.

———. *The First Team: The First Cavalry Division 18 July 1950– 18 January 1952.* Atlanta, Georgia: circa 1952.

———. *5th U.S. Cavalry, Fort Bliss, Texas.* Los Angeles: 1941.

———. *5th Cavalry Regiment History Outline, 1855–1955.* Japan: 1955.

UNITED STATES ARMY IN THE KOREAN WAR

Appleman, Roy E. *South to the Naktong, North to the Yalu.* 1961.

Hermes, Walter G. *Truce Tent and Fighting Front.* 1966.

UNITED STATES ARMY IN WORLD WAR II

Cannon, M. Hamlin. *Leyte: The Return to the Philippines.* 1954.

Miller, John, jr. *CARTWHEEL: The Reduction of Rabaul.* 1959.

Smith, Robert R. *The Approach to the Philippines.* 1953.

———. *Triumph in the Philippines.* 1963.

Wheeler, Homer W. *Buffalo Days.* Indianapolis: 1925.

Wright, B. C., compiler. *The 1st Cavalry Division in World War II.* Japan: 1947.

6th ARMORED CAVALRY
(The Fighting Sixth)

HERALDIC ITEMS

COAT OF ARMS

Shield: Azure, a unicorn rampant or.

Crest: On a wreath of the colors an imperial Chinese dragon rampant or lined azure, grasping in its dexter claw four arrows sable, armed and feathered gules.

Motto: *Ducit Amor Patriae* (Led by Love of Country).

Symbolism: The regiment took part in the eastern campaigns of the Civil War, its outstanding feats being at Williamsburg, Virginia, 1862, when it assaulted intrenched works, and at Fairfield, Pennsylvania, 1863. At Fairfield the unit engaged two enemy brigades of cavalry, completely neutralizing them and saving the supply trains of the Army, but in the process was literally cut to pieces. This is symbolized by the unicorn, held to represent the knightly virtues and, in the rampant position, a symbol of fighting aggressiveness, combined with speed and activity. The shield is blue, the color of the Federal uniform in the Civil War. The Chinese dragon represents the regiment's entrance into the Forbidden City in Peking in 1900. The arrows symbolize service in the Indian Wars.

DISTINCTIVE INSIGNIA

The distinctive insignia is the shield of the coat of arms.

LINEAGE AND HONORS

LINEAGE

Constituted 5 May 1861 in the Regular Army as 3d Cavalry. Organized 18 June 1861 at Pittsburgh, Pennsylvania. Redesignated 3 August 1861 as 6th Cavalry. Assigned to 3d Cavalry Division 15 August 1927–1 December 1939. Reorganized and redesignated 21 July 1942 as 6th Cavalry, Mechanized.

157

Regiment broken up 1 January 1944 and elements reorganized and re-designated as Headquarters and Headquarters Troop, 6th Cavalry Group, Mechanized, and 6th and 28th Cavalry Reconnaissance Squadrons, Mechanized. These units converted and redesignated 1 May 1946 as Headquarters and Headquarters Troop, 6th Constabulary Regiment, and 6th and 28th Constabulary Squadrons, respectively. These units converted and redesignated by elements 20 December 1948 as elements of the 6th Armored Cavalry (Headquarters and Headquarters and Service Troop, 6th Constabulary Regiment, as Headquarters and Headquarters Company, 6th Armored Cavalry). (Battalions and companies redesignated 24 June 1960 as squadrons and troops.)

Inactivated 24 October 1963 at Fort Knox, Kentucky. Activated 23 March 1967 at Fort George G. Meade, Maryland.

CAMPAIGN PARTICIPATION CREDIT

Civil War	Arizona 1882
Peninsula	New Mexico 1882
Antietam	Colorado 1884
Fredericksburg	
Chancellorsville	*War With Spain*
Gettysburg	Santiago
Wilderness	
Spotsylvania	*China Relief Expedition*
Cold Harbor	Without inscription
Petersburg	
Shenandoah	*Philippine Insurrection*
Appomattox	Without inscription
Virginia 1862	
Virginia 1863	*Mexican Expedition*
Virginia 1864	Mexico 1916–1917
Virginia 1865	
Maryland 1863	*World War I*
	Without inscription
Indian Wars	
Comanches	*World War II*
Apaches	Normandy
Pine Ridge	Northern France
Texas 1874	Rhineland
Oklahoma 1874	Ardennes-Alsace
Arizona 1876	Central Europe
Arizona 1881	

Troops additionally entitled to Campaign Participation Credit as follows:

Troop G:	*War With Spain*
Indian Wars	Puerto Rico
Texas 1867	
	Company M:
Troop K:	*China Relief Expedition*
Indian Wars	Peking
Arizona 1877	

DECORATIONS

Presidential Unit Citation (Army), Streamer embroidered HARLANGE POCKET (6th Cavalry Group cited; WDGO 40, 1946)

BIBLIOGRAPHY, 6TH ARMORED CAVALRY

Brackett, Albert G. *History of the United States Cavalry From The Formation of the Federal Government to the 1st of June 1863.* New York: 1865.

Brown, W. C. "The Charge of the Wagon Train," *Winners of the West* (newspaper). August 1932. Joplin, Missouri.

Carter, William H. *From Yorktown to Santiago with the Sixth U.S. Cavalry.* Baltimore: 1900.

————. *The Life of Lieutenant General Adna R. Chaffee.* Chicago: 1917.

Cogswell, Floyd. *History of the Sixth Cavalry Regiment: Sixth Cavalry Group at Home and Abroad.* Europe: 1947.

Herr, John K., and Edward S. Wallace. *The Story of the U.S. Cavalry.* Boston: 1953.

Historical and Pictorial Review, Sixth Cavalry, 28th Ordnance Company, C.A.S.C., Fort Oglethorpe, Georgia, of the United States Army. Baton Rouge, Louisiana: 1941.

Unit Members. *A Brief History of the Sixth Cavalry Regiment 1861–1950.* N.p.: 1950.

————. *Short History of the Sixth U.S. Cavalry.* Fort Oglethorpe, Georgia: 1920.

————. *6th Armored Cavalry—This is Your Regiment: A Brief History of the Regiment 1861–1958.* Fort Knox, Kentucky: 1958.

UNITED STATES ARMY IN WORLD WAR II

    Blumenson, Martin. *Breakout and Pursuit.* 1961.

    Cole, Hugh M. *The Lorraine Campaign.* 1950.

War Department, The Adjutant General, Military Information Division. *Report of Operations in South Africa and China.* Washington: 1901.

7th CAVALRY
(Garry Owen)

HERALDIC ITEMS

COAT OF ARMS

Shield: Or, on a chevron azure, between a phoenix rising from its ashes in dexter chief, the head of a North American Indian in war bonnet couped at the neck in sinister chief, all proper, and a yucca plant vert in base, seven horseshoes heels upward of the field.

Crest: On a wreath of the colors (or and azure) a dexter arm embowed vested azure, the hand in buckskin gauntlet proper, grasping an old-style U.S. Army sabre argent, hilted or.

Motto: The Seventh First.

Symbolism: The field is yellow, the cavalry color. The principal charge is a chevron whose origin tradition ascribes to the spur, which was formerly of that shape without rowel. The number of horseshoes corresponds to the numerical designation of the regiment. The phoenix symbolizes the resurrection of the regiment after its virtual extermination in the Battle of Little Big Horn in 1876. The Indian head and yucca commemorate Indian campaigns and the Punitive Expedition of 1916, respectively. The crest shows the position of "Raise Sabre" taken at the command "Charge" as prescribed in 1873, the arm being habited in the uniform of the period.

DISTINCTIVE INSIGNIA

Within a gold horseshoe showing seven nail holes, heels upward and the opening between the heels closed with a blue ribbon bearing the words *Garry Owen* in yellow letters, the crest of the regiment.

LINEAGE AND HONORS

LINEAGE

Constituted 28 July 1866 in the Regular Army as 7th Cavalry. Organized 21 September 1866 at Fort Riley, Kansas. Assigned to 15th Cavalry Division December 1917–May 1918. Assigned 13 September 1921 to 1st Cavalry Division.

161

Dismounted 28 February 1943 and reorganized 4 December 1943 partly under cavalry and partly under infantry tables of organization and equipment. Reorganized wholly as infantry 20 July 1945 but retained cavalry designations. Reorganized 25 March 1949 with troops redesignated as companies. Relieved 15 October 1957 from assignment to 1st Cavalry Division.

Reorganized 1 November 1957 as a parent regiment under the Combat Arms Regimental System.

CAMPAIGN PARTICIPATION CREDIT

Indian Wars
   Comanches
   Little Big Horn
   Nez Perces
   Pine Ridge
   Montana 1873
   Dakota 1874

Mexican Expedition
   Mexico 1916–1917

World War II
   New Guinea
   Bismarck Archipelago (with arrowhead)
   Leyte (with arrowhead)
   Luzon

Korean War
   UN defensive
   UN offensive
   CCF intervention
   First UN counteroffensive
   CCF spring offensive
   UN summer-fall offensive
   Second Korean winter
   Third Korean winter

Vietnam
   Defense
   Counteroffensive
   Counteroffensive, Phase II
   Counteroffensive, Phase III
   Tet Counteroffensive

DECORATIONS

Presidential Unit Citation (Army), Streamer embroidered ANTIPOLO, LUZON (2d Squadron, reinforced, cited; WD GO 36, 1946)

Presidential Unit Citation (Army), Streamer embroidered YONCHON, KOREA (1st Battalion and attached units cited; DA GO 74, 1952)

Presidential Unit Citation (Army), Streamer embroidered TAEGU, KOREA (3d Battalion cited; DA GO 33, 1952)

Presidential Unit Citation (Army), Streamer embroidered PUSAN, KOREA (3d Battalion and attached units cited; DA GO 35, 1952)

Presidential Unit Citation (Army), Streamer embroidered PLEIKU PROVINCE (1st and 2d Battalions cited; DA GO 40, 1967)

Philippine Presidential Unit Citation, Streamer embroidered 17 OCTOBER 1944 TO 4 JULY 1945 (7th Cavalry cited; DA GO 47, 1950)

Republic of Korea Presidential Unit Citation, Streamer embroidered WAEGWAN-TAEGU (7th Cavalry cited; DA GO 35, 1951)

Republic of Korea Presidential Unit Citation, Streamer embroidered KOREA (7th Cavalry and attached units cited; DA GO 24, 1954)

Chryssoun Aristion Andrias (Bravery Gold Medal of Greece), Streamer embroidered KOREA (7th Cavalry cited; DA GO 2, 1956)

1st BATTALION, 7th CAVALRY

RA

(1st Cavalry Division)

LINEAGE

Constituted 28 July 1866 in the Regular Army as Company A, 7th Cavalry. Organized 10 September 1866 at Fort Riley, Kansas. (Cavalry companies officially designated as troops in 1883.) (7th Cavalry assigned to 15th Cavalry Division December 1917–May 1918; assigned 13 September 1921 to 1st Cavalry Division. Dismounted 28 February 1943 and reorganized 4 December 1943 partly under cavalry and partly under infantry tables of organization. Reorganized wholly as infantry 20 July 1943 but retained cavalry designations.) Troop A, 7th Cavalry, redesignated 25 March 1949 as Company A, 7th Cavalry.

Reorganized and redesignated 1 November 1957 as Headquarters and Headquarters Company, 1st Battle Group, 7th Cavalry, and remained assigned to 1st Cavalry Division (organic elements concurrently constituted and activated in Korea). Reorganized and redesignated 1 September 1963 as 1st Battalion, 7th Cavalry. Transferred (less personnel and equipment) 1 July 1965 from Korea to Fort Benning, Georgia, and reorganized.

CAMPAIGN PARTICIPATION CREDIT

Indian Wars
  *Comanches
  *Little Big Horn
  *Nez Perces
  *Pine Ridge
  *Montana 1873
  *Dakota 1874

Mexican Expedition
  *Mexico 1916–1917

World War II
  *New Guinea
  *Bismarck Archipelago
    (with arrowhead)
  *Leyte (with arrowhead)
  *Luzon

Korean War
  *UN defensive
  *UN offensive
  *CCF intervention
  *First UN counteroffensive
  *CCF spring offensive
  *UN summer-fall offensive
  *Second Korean winter
  *Third Korean winter

Vietnam
  *Defense
  *Counteroffensive
  *Counteroffensive, Phase II
  *Counteroffensive, Phase III
  *Tet Counteroffensive

163

DECORATIONS

Presidential Unit Citation (Army), Streamer embroidered ANTIPOLO, LUZON

*Presidential Unit Citation (Army), Streamer embroidered YONCHON, KOREA (1st Battalion and attached units cited; DA GO 74, 1952)

Presidential Unit Citation (Army), Streamer embroidered TAEGU, KOREA

Presidential Unit Citation (Army), Streamer embroidered PUSAN, KOREA

*Presidential Unit Citation (Army), Streamer embroidered PLEIKU PROVINCE (1st Battalion cited, DA GO 40, 1967)

*Philippine Presidential Unit Citation, Streamer embroidered 17 OCTOBER 1944 TO 4 JULY 1945 (7th Cavalry cited; DA GO 47, 1950)

*Republic of Korea Presidential Unit Citation, Streamer embroidered KOREA (7th Cavalry and attached units cited; DA GO 24, 1954)

*Chryssoun Aristion Andrias (Bravery Gold Medal of Greece), Streamer embroidered KOREA (7th Cavalry cited; DA GO 2, 1956)

2d BATTALION, 7th CAVALRY

RA

(1st Cavalry Division)

LINEAGE

Constituted 28 July 1866 in the Regular Army as Company B, 7th Cavalry. Organized 10 September 1866 at Fort Riley, Kansas. (Cavalry companies officially designated as troops in 1883.) (7th Cavalry assigned to 15th Cavalry Division December 1917–May 1918; assigned 13 September 1921 to 1st Cavalry Division. Dismounted 28 February 1943 and reorganized 4 December 1943 partly under cavalry and partly under infantry tables of organization. Reorganized wholly as infantry 20 July 1943 but retained cavalry designations.) Troop B, 7th Cavalry, redesignated 25 March 1949 as Company B, 7th Cavalry.

Redesignated 1 July 1957 as Headquarters and Headquarters Troop, 2d Reconnaissance Squadron, 7th Cavalry; concurrently, consolidated with 3d Reconnaissance Company (see ANNEX), transferred (less personnel and equipment) from Japan to Fort Benning, Georgia, relieved from assignment to 1st Cavalry Division, assigned to 3d Infantry Division, and reorganized (organic elements concurrently constituted and activated). Redesignated 5 June 1963 as 2d Battalion, 7th Cavalry; concurrently, transferred (less personnel and equipment) from United States Army, Europe, to United States Army, Pacific, relieved from assignment to 3d Infantry Division, and assigned to 1st Cavalry Division; reorganized 1 September 1963 in Korea. Transferred (less personnel and equipment) 1 July 1965 from Korea to Fort Benning, Georgia, and reorganized.

ANNEX

3d Reconnaissance Troop constituted 1 August 1940 in the Regular Army and assigned to 3d Infantry Division. Activated 5 August 1940 at Fort Lewis, Washington. Redesignated 1 April 1941 as 3d Cavalry Reconnaissance Troop. Reorganized and redesignated 16 June 1944 as 3d Reconnaissance Troop, Mechanized. Reorganized and redesignated 15 August 1945 as 3d Mechanized Reconnaissance Troop. Reorganized and redesignated 10 January 1949 as 3d Reconnaissance Company.

165

CAMPAIGN PARTICIPATION CREDIT

Indian Wars
  *Comanches
  *Little Big Horn
  Nez Perces
  *Pine Ridge
  *Montana 1873
  *Dakota 1874

Mexican Expedition
  *Mexico 1916–1917

World War II
  *New Guinea
  *Bismarck Archipelago
    (with arrowhead)
  *Leyte (with arrowhead)
  *Luzon
  *Algeria-French Morocco
  *Tunisia
  *Sicily (with arrowhead)
  *Naples-Foggia
  *Anzio (with arrowhead)

  *Southern France (with arrowhead)
  *Rhineland
  *Ardennes-Alsace
  *Central Europe

Korean War
  *UN defensive
  *UN offensive
  *CCF intervention
  *First UN counteroffensive
  *CCF spring offensive
  *UN summer-fall offensive
  *Second Korean winter
  *Third Korean winter

Vietnam
  *Defense
  *Counteroffensive
  *Counteroffensive, Phase II
  *Counteroffensive, Phase III
  *Tet Counteroffensive

DECORATIONS

*Presidential Unit Citation (Army), Streamer embroidered COLMAR (3d Reconnaissance Troop cited; WD GO 44, 1945)

*Presidential Unit Citation (Army), Streamer embroidered YONCHON, KOREA (1st Battalion and attached units cited; DA GO 74, 1952)

Presidential Unit Citation (Army), Streamer embroidered TAEGU, KOREA

Presidential Unit Citation (Army), Streamer embroidered PUSAN, KOREA

*Presidential Unit Citation (Army), Streamer embroidered PLEIKU PROVINCE (1st and 2d Battalions, 7th Cavalry, cited; DA GO 40, 1967)

*French Croix de Guerre with Palm, World War II, Streamer embroidered COLMAR (3d Reconnaissance Troop cited; DA GO 43, 1950)

*French Croix de Guerre, World War II, Fourragère (3d Reconnaissance Troop cited; DA GO 43, 1950)

*Philippine Presidential Unit Citation, Streamer embroidered 17 OCTOBER 1944 TO 4 JULY 1945 (7th Cavalry cited; DA GO 47, 1950)

*Republic of Korea Presidential Unit Citation, Streamer embroidered WAEGWAN-TAEGU (7th Cavalry cited; DA GO 35, 1951)

*Republic of Korea Presidential Unit Citation, Streamer embroidered KOREA (7th Cavalry cited; DA GO 24, 1954)

*Chryssoun Aristion Andrias (Bravery Gold Medal of Greece), Streamer embroidered KOREA (7th Cavalry cited; DA GO 2, 1956)

3d SQUADRON, 7th CAVALRY

RA

(3d Infantry Division)

LINEAGE

Constituted 28 July 1866 in the Regular Army as Company C, 7th Cavalry. Organized 10 September 1866 at Fort Riley, Kansas. (Cavalry companies officially designated troops in 1883.) (7th Cavalry assigned to 15th Cavalry Division December 1917–May 1918; assigned 13 September 1921 to 1st Cavalry Division.) Inactivated 1 February 1928 as Troop C, 7th Cavalry. Activated 1 August 1940 at Fort Bliss, Texas. (7th Cavalry dismounted 28 February 1943 and reorganized 4 December 1943 partly under cavalry and partly under infantry tables of organization. Reorganized wholly as infantry 20 July 1943 but retained cavalry designations.) Redesignated 25 March 1949 as Company C, 7th Cavalry.

Transferred (less personnel and equipment) from Japan to Germany 1 July 1957; concurrently, consolidated with 10th Reconnaissance Company (see ANNEX), reorganized and redesignated as Headquarters and Headquarters Troop, 3d Reconnaissance Squadron, 7th Cavalry, relieved from assignment to 1st Cavalry Division, and assigned to 10th Infantry Division (organic elements concurrently constituted and activated). Relieved from assignment to 10th Infantry Division 14 June 1958 and assigned to 2d Infantry Division; reorganized at Fort Benning, Georgia. Redesignated 25 January 1963 as 3d Squadron, 7th Cavalry. Inactivated 20 February 1963 at Fort Benning, Georgia; concurrently, relieved from assignment to 2d Infantry Division. Assigned 18 April 1963 to 3d Infantry Division. Activated 5 June 1963 in Germany.

ANNEX

10th Mountain Cavalry Reconnaissance Troop constituted 1 November 1944 in the Army of the United States and assigned to 10th Mountain Division. Activated 6 November 1944 at Camp Swift, Texas. Inactivated 20 October 1945 at Camp Carson, Colorado. Redesignated 18 June 1948 as 10th Reconnaissance Company (10th Mountain Division concurrently redesignated as 10th Infantry Division). Allotted 25 June 1948 to the Regular Army. Activated 1 July 1948 at Fort Riley, Kansas.

Campaign Participation Credit

Indian Wars
*Comanches
*Little Big Horn
Nez Perces
*Pine Ridge
Montana 1873
Dakota 1874

Mexican Expedition
*Mexico 1916–1917

World War II
*New Guinea
*Bismarck Archipelago
(with arrowhead)

*Leyte (with arrowhead)
*Luzon
*North Apennines
*Po Valley

Korean War
*UN defensive
*UN offensive
*CCF intervention
*First UN counteroffensive
*CCF spring offensive
*UN summer-fall offensive
*Second Korean winter
*Third Korean winter

Decorations

Presidential Unit Citation (Army), Streamer embroidered ANTIPOLO, LUZON

*Presidential Unit Citation (Army), Streamer embroidered YONCHON, KOREA (1st Battalion and attached units cited; DA GO 74, 1952)

Presidential Unit Citation (Army), Streamer embroidered TAEGU, KOREA

Presidential Unit Citation (Army), Streamer embroidered PUSAN, KOREA

*Philippine Presidential Unit Citation, Streamer embroidered 17 OCTOBER 1944 TO 4 JULY 1945 (7th Cavalry cited; DA GO 47, 1950)

*Republic of Korea Presidential Unit Citation, Streamer embroidered WAEGWAN-TAEGU (7th Cavalry cited; DA GO 35, 1951)

*Republic of Korea Presidential Unit Citation, Streamer embroidered KOREA (7th Cavalry cited; DA GO 24, 1954)

*Chryssoun Aristion Andrias (Bravery Gold Medal of Greece), Streamer embroidered KOREA (7th Cavalry cited; DA GO 2, 1956)

4th SQUADRON, 7th CAVALRY

RA

(2d Infantry Division)

LINEAGE

Constituted 28 July 1866 in the Regular Army as Company D, 7th Cavalry. Organized 21 September 1866 at Fort Riley, Kansas. (Cavalry companies officially designated as troops in 1883.) (7th Cavalry assigned to 15th Cavalry Division December 1917–May 1918.) Reorganized and redesignated 13 September 1921 as Headquarters Troop, 1st Cavalry Division. Dismounted 28 February 1943. Redesignated 4 December 1943 as Headquarters Troop, 1st Cavalry Division, Special, and reorganized partly under cavalry and partly under infantry tables of organization. Reorganized wholly as infantry 20 July 1945 but retained cavalry designation. Reorganized and redesignated 25 March 1949 as Headquarters Company, 1st Cavalry Division. Disbanded 1 July 1960 in Korea.

Reconstituted 2 July 1960 and consolidated with Headquarters and Headquarters Troop, 4th Reconnaissance Squadron, 7th Cavalry (see ANNEX); consolidated unit designated Headquarters and Headquarters Troop, 4th Reconnaissance Squadron, 7th Cavalry. Redesignated 25 January 1963 as Headquarters and Headquarters Troop, 4th Squadron, 7th Cavalry, and assigned to 2d Infantry Division (organic elements concurrently constituted). Activated 20 February 1963 at Fort Benning, Georgia. Transferred (less personnel and equipment) 1 July 1965 from Fort Benning, Georgia, to Korea and reorganized.

ANNEX

Troop D, 7th Cavalry, constituted 13 November 1943 in the Regular Army and assigned to 1st Cavalry Division. Activated 4 December 1943 at Brisbane, Australia, partly under cavalry and partly under infantry tables of organization. Reorganized wholly as infantry 20 July 1945 but retained cavalry designation. Reorganized and redesignated 25 March 1949 as Company D, 7th Cavalry. Relieved 15 October 1957 from assignment to 1st Cavalry Division. Inactivated 1 November 1957 in Korea; concurrently, redesignated as Headquarters and Headquarters Troop, 4th Reconnaissance Squadron, 7th Cavalry.

169

Campaign Participation Credit

Indian Wars
*Comanches
*Little Big Horn
*Nez Perces
*Pine Ridge
*Montana 1873
*Dakota 1874

Mexican Expedition
*Mexico 1916–1917

World War II
*New Guinea

*Bismarck Archipelago
 (with arrowhead)
*Leyte (with arrowhead)
*Luzon

Korean War
*UN defensive
*UN offensive
*CCF intervention
*First UN counteroffensive
*CCF spring offensive
*UN summer-fall offensive
*Second Korean winter
*Third Korean winter

Decorations

Presidential Unit Citation (Army), Streamer embroidered ANTIPOLO, LUZON

*Presidential Unit Citation (Army), Streamer embroidered YONCHON, KOREA (1st Battalion and attached units cited; DA GO 74, 1952)

Presidential Unit Citation (Army), Streamer embroidered TAEGU, KOREA

Presidential Unit Citation (Army), Streamer embroidered PUSAN, KOREA

*Philippine Presidential Unit Citation, Streamer embroidered 17 OCTOBER 1944 TO 4 JULY 1945 (7th Cavalry cited; DA GO 47, 1950)

*Republic of Korea Presidential Unit Citation, Streamer embroidered WAEGWAN-TAEGU (7th Cavalry cited; DA GO 35, 1951)

*Republic of Korea Presidential Unit Citation, Streamer embroidered KOREA (7th Cavalry cited; DA GO 24, 1954)

*Chryssoun Aristion Andrias (Bravery Gold Medal of Greece), Streamer embroidered KOREA (7th Cavalry cited; DA GO 2, 1956)

5th BATTALION, 7th CAVALRY

RA

(1st Cavalry Division)

LINEAGE

Constituted 28 July 1866 in the Regular Army as Company E, 7th Cavalry. Organized 22 December 1866 at Fort Riley, Kansas. (Cavalry companies officially designated as troops in 1883.) (7th Cavalry assigned to 15th Cavalry Division December 1917–May 1918; assigned 13 September 1921 to 1st Cavalry Division. Dismounted 28 February 1943 and reorganized 4 December 1943 partly under cavalry and partly under infantry tables of organization. Reorganized wholly as infantry 20 July 1945 but retained cavalry designations.) Troop E, 7th Cavalry, redesignated 25 March 1949 as Company E, 7th Cavalry.

Inactivated 1 November 1957 in Japan; concurrently, redesignated as Headquarters and Headquarters Troop, 5th Reconnaissance Squadron, 7th Cavalry, and relieved from assignment to 1st Cavalry Division. Redesignated 26 March 1966 as 5th Battalion, 7th Cavalry, and assigned to 1st Cavalry Division (organic elements concurrently constituted). Activated 1 April 1966 at Fort Carson, Colorado.

CAMPAIGN PARTICIPATION CREDIT

Indian Wars
  *Comanches
  *Little Big Horn
  Nez Perces
  *Pine Ridge
  *Montana 1873
  *Dakota 1874

Mexican Expedition
  *Mexico 1916–1917

World War II
  *New Guinea
  *Bismarck Archipelago (with arrowhead)
  *Leyte (with arrowhead)
  *Luzon

Korean War
  *UN defensive
  *UN offensive
  *CCF intervention
  *First UN counteroffensive
  *CCF spring offensive
  *UN summer-fall offensive
  *Second Korean winter
  *Third Korean winter

Vietnam
  *Counteroffensive, Phase II
  *Counteroffensive, Phase III
  *Tet Counteroffensive

171

DECORATIONS

*Presidential Unit Citation (Army), Streamer embroidered ANTIPOLO, LUZON (2d Squadron, reinforced, cited; WD GO 36, 1946)

Presidential Unit Citation (Army), Streamer embroidered YONCHON, KOREA

Presidential Unit Citation (Army), Streamer embroidered TAEGU, KOREA

Presidential Unit Citation (Army), Streamer embroidered PUSAN, KOREA

*Philippine Presidential Unit Citation, Streamer embroidered 17 OCTOBER 1944 TO 4 JULY 1945 (7th Cavalry cited; DA GO 47, 1950)

*Republic of Korea Presidential Unit Citation, Streamer embroidered WAEGWAN-TAEGU (7th Cavalry cited; DA GO 35, 1951)

*Republic of Korea Presidential Unit Citation, Streamer embroidered KOREA (7th Cavalry and attached units cited; DA GO 24, 1954)

*Chryssoun Aristion Andrias (Bravery Gold Medal of Greece), Streamer embroidered KOREA (7th Cavalry cited; DA GO 2, 1956)

BIBLIOGRAPHY, 7TH CAVALRY

Adams, Jacob. *A Story of the Custer Massacre.* Carey, Ohio: 1965.

Abstract of the Official Record of Proceedings of the Reno Court of Inquiry, Convened . . . 13 January 1879 . . . Upon the Request of Major Marcus A. Reno, 7th Cavalry to Investigate His Conduct at the Battle of Little Big Horn. . . . Harrisburg: 1954.

Brininstool, E. A. *The Custer Fight, Captain Benteen's Story of the Battle of the Little Big Horn.* Hollywood, California: 1933.

———. *A Trooper with Custer.* Columbus, Ohio: 1925.

———. *Major Reno Vindicated, An Interesting Analysis Justifying His Conduct . . . During the Battle of the Little Big Horn . . .* From a letter written in 1925 by Colonel William Alexander Graham. Hollywood, California: 1935.

Chandler, Melbourne C. *Of Garry Owen in Glory; The History of the Seventh United States Cavalry Regiment.* Annandale, Virginia: 1960.

Custer, Elizabeth B. *Boots and Saddles.* New York: 1885.

———. *Following the Guidon.* New York: 1890.

Custer, George A. *My Life on the Plains.* N.p.: 1874.

Department of the Army
    Korea, 1950. Washington: 1952.

Department of the Army. AMERICAN FORCES IN ACTION series.
    The Admiralties: Operations of the 1st Cavalry Division. Washington: 1945.

Dustin, Fred. *The Custer Tragedy.* Ann Arbor, Michigan: 1939.

Fougera, Katherine G. *With Custer's Cavalry.* Caldwell, Idaho: 1940.

Garlington, E. A. *Chronological Sketch of Troop I, Seventh U.S. Cavalry.* N.p.: 1894.

Godfrey, Edward S. *Some Reminiscences, Including the Washita Battle November 27, 1868.* Washington: 1928.

Graham, W. A. *The Story of the Little Big Horn.* New York: 1926.

———. *The Custer Myth.* Harrisburg: 1953.

———. *The Colors of the Seventh at the Little Big Horn.* Harrisburg: circa 1955.

Gugeler, Russell A. *Combat Actions in Korea.* Washington: 1954.

Hanson, Joseph M. *The Conquest of the Missouri.* Chicago: 1909.

Herr, John K., and Edward S. Wallace. *The Story of the U.S. Cavalry.* Boston: 1953.

Hunt, Frazier and Robert. *I Fought with Custer; The Story of Sergeant Windolph . . . .* New York: 1947.

Kuhlman, Charles. *Legend Into History.* Harrisburg: 1951.

———. *Did Custer Disobey Orders at the Battle of the Little Big Horn?* Harrisburg: 1957.

Luce, Edward S. *Keogh, Comanche, and Custer.* Dedham, Massachusetts: 1939.

Mahr, Warren C., compiler. *1st Cavalry Division 1952–1954.* Atlanta, Georgia: 1954.

Marquis, Thomas Bailey. *Sketch Story of the Custer Battle.* Hardin, Montana: 1933.

———. *A Warrior Who Fought Custer.* Minneapolis: 1931.

———. *Two Days After the Custer Battle.* Hardin, Montana: 1935.

Miller, John, jr., O. J. Carroll, and M. E. Tackley. *Korea 1951–1953.* Washington: 1956.

Mulford, Ami Frank. *Fighting Indians in the 7th U.S. Cavalry, Custer's Favorite Regiment.* 2d ed. Corning, New York: 1879.

Parsons, John E., and John S. DuMont. *Firearms in the Custer Battle.* Harrisburg: 1953.

"Report of Reno to Chief of Ordnance," *Army and Navy Journal,* Vol. 14 (19 August 1876).

Rodenbough, Theo. F., and William L. Haskin, editors. *The Army of the United States.* New York: 1896. E. A. Garlington, "The Seventh Regiment of Cavalry."

Stewart, Edgar I. *Custer's Luck!* Norman, Oklahoma: 1955.

Unit Members. *1st Cavalry Division "The First Team."* Japan: 1959.

———. *Christmas 1917.* A History of Troop F, 7th Cavalry. El Paso: 1917.

———. *Illustrated Review of the Seventh United States Cavalry.* Denver: 1910.

Unit Members. *Occupation Diary, First Cavalry Division 1945–1950.*
Japan: 1950.

————. *The First Team: The First Cavalry Division 18 July 1950–18 January 1952.* Atlanta, Georgia: circa 1952.

UNITED STATES ARMY IN THE KOREAN WAR

Appleman, Roy E. *South to the Naktong, North to the Yalu.* 1961.

Hermes, Walter G. *Truce Tent and Fighting Front.* 1966.

UNITED STATES ARMY IN WORLD WAR II

Cannon, Hamlin M. *Leyte: The Return to the Philippines.* 1954.

Miller, John, jr. *CARTWHEEL: The Reduction of Rabaul.* 1959.

Smith, Robert R. *The Approach to the Philippines.* 1953.

————. *Triumph in the Philippines.* 1963.

Van de Water, Frederic F. *Glory Hunter.* Indianapolis: 1934.

Vestal, Stanley. *Sitting Bull, Champion of the Sioux.* Boston: 1932.

Wright, B. C., compiler. *The 1st Cavalry Division in World War II.* Japan:
1947.

8th CAVALRY

Heraldic Items

Coat of Arms

Shield: Azure on a fess or eight mullets pierced of the field, a demi-horse rampant issuant argent.

Crest: On a wreath of the colors (or and azure), a grizzly bear passant sable.

Motto: Honor and Courage.

Symbolism: The blue and gold of the shield were the unofficial colors of the regiment for about ten years before the approval of this coat of arms. The eight mullets show the regimental number and cavalry tradition ascribing the origin of the pierced mullet to the rowel of a spur. This is further indicated by the horse. The bear is the emblem of California, where the regiment was organized in 1866.

Distinctive Insignia

The distinctive insignia consists of the principal charges and motto of the coat of arms. It is a demihorse issuant rampant argent from a band fessways or charged with eight mullets azure pierced of the second, surmounting a ribbon scroll sable with the regimental motto—*Honor and Courage*—of the second.

Lineage and Honors

Lineage

Constituted 28 July 1866 in the Regular Army as 8th Cavalry. Organized 21 September 1866 at Angel Island, California. Assigned to 15th Cavalry Division December 1917–May 1918. Assigned 13 September 1921 to 1st Cavalry Division.

Dismounted 28 February 1943 and reorganized 4 December 1943 partly under cavalry and partly under infantry tables of organization and equipment. Reorganized wholly as infantry 20 July 1945 but retained cavalry designations. Reorganized 25 March 1949 with troops redesignated as companies.

Reorganized 15 October 1957 as a parent regiment under the Combat Arms Regimental System; concurrently, relieved from assignment to 1st Cavalry Division.

Campaign Participation Credit

Indian Wars
  Comanches
  Apaches
  Pine Ridge
  Arizona 1867
  Arizona 1868
  Arizona 1869
  Oregon 1868
  Mexico 1877

World War II
  New Guinea
  Bismarck Archipelago
    (with arrowhead)
  Leyte
  Luzon

Korean War
  UN defensive
  UN offensive
  CCF intervention
  First UN counteroffensive
  CCF spring offensive
  UN summer-fall offensive
  Second Korean winter
  Korea, summer-fall 1952
  Third Korean winter

Vietnam
  Defense
  Counteroffensive
  Counteroffensive, Phase II
  Counteroffensive, Phase III
  Tet Counteroffensive

Decorations

Presidential Unit Citation (Army), Streamer embroidered LUZON (2d Squadron, reinforced, cited; WD GO 38, 1946)

Presidential Unit Citation (Army), Streamer embroidered TAEGU (2d Battalion, reinforced, cited; DA GO 38, 1952)

Presidential Unit Citation (Army), Streamer embroidered PLEIKU PROVINCE (1st and 2d Battalions cited; DA GO 40, 1967)

Philippine Presidential Unit Citation, Streamer embroidered 17 OCTOBER 1944 TO 4 JULY 1945 (8th Cavalry cited; DA GO 47, 1950)

Republic of Korea Presidential Unit Citation, Streamer embroidered WAEGWAN-TAEGU (8th Cavalry cited; DA GO 35, 1951)

Republic of Korea Presidential Unit Citation, Streamer embroidered KOREA (8th Cavalry cited; DA GO 24, 1954)

Chryssoun Aristion Andrias (Bravery Gold Medal of Greece), Streamer embroidered KOREA (8th Cavalry cited; DA GO 2, 1956)

1st BATTALION, 8th CAVALRY

RA

(1st Cavalry Division)

LINEAGE

Constituted 28 July 1866 in the Regular Army as Company A, 8th Cavalry. Organized 20 September 1866 at Presidio of San Francisco, California. (Cavalry companies officially designated as troops in 1883.) (8th Cavalry assigned to 15th Cavalry Division December 1917–May 1918; assigned 13 September 1921 to 1st Cavalry Division. Dismounted 28 February 1943 and reorganized 4 December 1943 partly under cavalry and partly under infantry tables of organization and equipment. Reorganized wholly as infantry 20 July 1945 but retained cavalry designations.) Troop A, 8th Cavalry, redesignated 25 March 1949 as Company A, 8th Cavalry.

Reorganized and redesignated 1 December 1957 as Headquarters and Headquarters Company, 1st Battle Group, 8th Cavalry, and remained assigned to 1st Cavalry Division (organic elements constituted 15 October 1957 and activated 1 December 1957 in Korea). Reorganized and redesignated 1 September 1963 as 1st Battalion, 8th Cavalry. Transferred (less personnel and equipment) 1 July 1965 from Korea to Fort Benning, Georgia, and reorganized.

CAMPAIGN PARTICIPATION CREDIT

Indian Wars
    Comanches
    Apaches
    Pine Ridge
    Arizona 1867
    Arizona 1868
    *Arizona 1869
    Oregon 1868
    *Mexico 1877

World War II
    *New Guinea
    *Bismarck Archipelago
        (with arrowhead)
    *Leyte
    *Luzon

Korean War
    *UN defensive
    *UN offensive
    *CCF intervention
    *First UN counteroffensive
    *CCF spring offensive
    *UN summer-fall offensive
    *Second Korean winter
    *Korea, summer-fall 1952
    *Third Korean winter

Vietnam
    *Defense
    *Counteroffensive
    *Counteroffensive, Phase II
    *Counteroffensive, Phase III
    *Tet Counteroffensive

177

DECORATIONS

Presidential Unit Citation (Army), Streamer embroidered LUZON

Presidential Unit Citation (Army), Streamer embroidered TAEGU

*Presidential Unit Citation (Army), Streamer embroidered MANUS ISLAND (Troop A, 8th Cavalry, cited; WD GO 57, 1944)

*Presidential Unit Citation (Army), Streamer embroidered PLEIKU PROV-INCE (1st Battalion cited; DA GO 40, 1967)

*Philippine Presidential Unit Citation, Streamer embroidered 17 OCTOBER 1944 TO 4 JULY 1945 (8th Cavalry cited; DA GO 47, 1950)

*Republic of Korea Presidential Unit Citation, Streamer embroidered WAEGWAN-TAEGU (8th Cavalry cited; DA GO 35, 1951)

*Republic of Korea Presidential Unit Citation, Streamer embroidered KOREA (8th Cavalry cited; DA GO 24, 1954)

*Chryssoun Aristion Andrias (Bravery Gold Medal of Greece), Streamer embroidered KOREA (8th Cavalry cited; DA GO 2, 1956)

2d BATTALION, 8th CAVALRY

RA

(1st Cavalry Division)

LINEAGE

Constituted 28 July 1866 in the Regular Army as Company B, 8th Cavalry. Organized 23 October 1866 at Presidio of San Francisco, California. (Cavalry companies officially designated as troops in 1883.) (8th Cavalry assigned to 15th Cavalry Division December 1917–May 1918; assigned 13 September 1921 to 1st Cavalry Division. Dismounted 28 February 1943 and reorganized 4 December 1943 partly under cavalry and partly under infantry tables of organization and equipment. Reorganized wholly as infantry 20 July 1945 but retained cavalry designations.) Troop B, 8th Cavalry, redesignated 25 March 1949 as Company B, 8th Cavalry.

Reorganized and redesignated 1 April 1957 as Headquarters and Headquarters Troop, 2d Reconnaissance Squadron, 8th Cavalry; concurrently, consolidated with 4th Reconnaissance Company (see ANNEX); transferred (less personnel and equipment) from Japan to Fort Lewis, Washington; relieved from assignment to 1st Cavalry Division and assigned to 4th Infantry Division (organic elements concurrently constituted and activated at Fort Lewis, Washington). Reorganized and redesignated 1 September 1963 as 2d Battalion, 8th Cavalry; concurrently, transferred (less personnel and equipment) from Fort Lewis, Washington, to United States Army, Pacific, relieved from assignment to 4th Infantry Division and assigned to 1st Cavalry Division. Transferred (less personnel and equipment) 1 July 1965 from Korea to Fort Benning, Georgia, and reorganized.

ANNEX

4th Reconnaissance Troop constituted 20 July 1940 in the Regular Army and assigned to 4th Infantry Division. Activated 1 August 1940 at Fort Benning, Georgia. Reorganized and redesignated 10 June 1942 as 4th Reconnaissance Squadron.

Reorganized and redesignated 4 August 1943 as follows: Troop A, 4th Reconnaissance Squadron, as 4th Reconnaissance Troop, Mechanized, remained assigned to 4th Infantry Division; 4th Reconnaissance Squadron (less Troop

179

A) as 34th Reconnaissance Squadron, and relieved from assignment to 4th Infantry Division (hereafter separate lineage). 4th Reconnaissance Troop, Mechanized, redesignated 30 July 1945 as 4th Mechanized Cavalry Reconnaissance Troop. Inactivated 12 March 1946 at Camp Butner, North Carolina. Redesignated 6 July 1948 as 4th Reconnaissance Company and activated at Fort Ord, California.

CAMPAIGN PARTICIPATION CREDIT

Indian Wars
  Comanches
  Apaches
  Pine Ridge
  *Arizona 1867
  *Arizona 1868
  *Arizona 1869
  Oregon 1868
  Mexico 1877

World War II
  *New Guinea
  *Bismarck Archipelago
    (with arrowhead)
  *Leyte
  *Luzon
  *Normandy (with arrowhead)
  *Rhineland
  *Ardennes-Alsace
  *Central Europe

Korean War
  *UN defensive
  *UN offensive
  *CCF intervention
  *First UN counteroffensive
  *CCF spring offensive
  *UN summer-fall offensive
  *Second Korean winter
  *Korea, summer-fall 1952
  *Third Korean winter

Vietnam
  *Defense
  *Counteroffensive
  *Counteroffensive, Phase II
  *Counteroffensive, Phase III
  *Tet Counteroffensive

DECORATIONS

Presidential Unit Citation (Army), Streamer embroidered LUZON

Presidential Unit Citation (Army), Streamer embroidered TAEGU

*Presidential Unit Citation (Army), Streamer embroidered PLEIKU PROVINCE (2d Battalion cited; DA GO 40, 1967)

*Philippine Presidential Unit Citation, Streamer embroidered 17 OCTOBER 1944 TO 4 JULY 1945 (8th Cavalry cited; DA GO 47, 1950)

*Belgian Fourragère 1940 (4th Reconnaissance Troop cited; DA GO 43, 1950)

　　　*Cited in the Order of the Day of the Belgian Army for action in BELGIUM (4th Reconnaissance Troop cited; DA GO 43, 1950)

　　　*Cited in the Order of the Day of the Belgian Army for action in the ARDENNES (4th Reconnaissance Troop cited; DA GO 43, 1950)

*Republic of Korea Presidential Unit Citation, Streamer embroidered WAEGWAN-TAEGU (8th Cavalry cited; DA GO 35, 1951)

Republic of Korea Presidential Unit Citation, Streamer embroidered KOREA (8th Cavalry cited; DA GO 24, 1954)

*Chryssoun Aristion Andrias (Bravery Gold Medal of Greece), Streamer embroidered KOREA (8th Cavalry cited; DA GO 2, 1956)

Company B additionally entitled to: Valorous Unit Award, Streamer embroidered BINH DINH PROVINCE (Company B, 2d Battalion, cited; GO 3527 U.S. Army, Vietnam, 13 July 1967)

3d SQUADRON, 8th CAVALRY

RA
(8th Infantry Division)

LINEAGE

Constituted 28 July 1866 in the Regular Army as Company C, 8th Cavalry. Organized 27 October 1866 at Angel Island, California. (Cavalry companies officially designated as troops in 1883.) (8th Cavalry assigned to 15th Cavalry Division December 1917–May 1918; assigned 13 September 1921 to 1st Cavalry Division.) Troop C, 8th Cavalry, disbanded 1 February 1928 at Fort Bliss, Texas.

Reconstituted and activated 1 August 1940 at Fort Bliss, Texas, as an element of the 1st Cavalry Division. (8th Cavalry dismounted 28 February 1943 and reorganized 4 December 1943 partly under cavalry and partly under infantry tables of organization and equipment. Reorganized wholly as infantry 20 July 1945 but retained cavalry designations.) Redesignated 25 March 1949 as Company C, 8th Cavalry.

Reorganized and redesignated 1 August 1957 as Headquarters and Headquarters Troop, 3d Reconnaissance Squadron, 8th Cavalry; concurrently, consolidated with 8th Reconnaissance Company (see ANNEX), relieved from assignment to 1st Cavalry Division, transferred (less personnel and equipment) from Japan to Germany, and assigned to 8th Infantry Division (organic elements concurrently constituted and activated). Reorganized and redesignated 1 April 1963 as 3d Squadron, 8th Cavalry.

ANNEX

8th Cavalry Reconnaissance Troop constituted 7 May 1943 in the Army of the United States and assigned to 8th Infantry Division. Activated 15 May 1943 at Camp Young, California. Reorganized and redesignated 27 August 1943 as 8th Cavalry Reconnaissance Troop, Mechanized. Inactivated 1 November 1945 at Fort Leonard Wood, Missouri. Redesignated 10 August 1950 as 8th Reconnaissance Company. Activated 17 August 1950 at Fort Jackson, South Carolina, as an element of the 8th Infantry Division.

CAMPAIGN PARTICIPATION CREDIT

Indian Wars
  *Comanches
  *Apaches
  Pine Ridge
  Arizona 1867
  Arizona 1868
  *Arizona 1869
  *Oregon 1868
  Mexico 1877

World War II
  *New Guinea
  *Bismarck Archipelago
    (with arrowhead)
  *Leyte

*Luzon
*Normandy
*Northern France
*Rhineland
*Central Europe

Korean War
  *UN defensive
  *UN offensive
  *CCF intervention
  *First UN counteroffensive
  *CCF spring offensive
  *UN summer-fall offensive
  *Second Korean winter
  *Korea, summer-fall 1952
  *Third Korean winter

DECORATIONS

Presidential Unit Citation (Army), Streamer embroidered LUZON

Presidential Unit Citation (Army), Streamer embroidered TAEGU

*Philippine Presidential Unit Citation, Streamer embroidered 17 OCTOBER 1944 TO 4 JULY 1945 (8th Cavalry cited; DA GO 47, 1950)

*Republic of Korea Presidential Unit Citation, Streamer embroidered WAEGWAN-TAEGU (8th Cavalry cited; DA GO 35, 1951)

*Republic of Korea Presidential Unit Citation, Streamer embroidered KOREA (8th Cavalry cited; DA GO 24, 1954)

*Chryssoun Aristion Andrias (Bravery Gold Medal of Greece), Streamer embroidered KOREA (8th Cavalry cited; DA GO 2, 1956)

TROOP D, 8th CAVALRY

AR

LINEAGE

Constituted 28 July 1866 in the Regular Army as Company D, 8th Cavalry. Organized 27 October 1866 at Angel Island, California. (Cavalry companies officially designated as troops in 1883.) (8th Cavalry assigned to 15th Cavalry Division December 1917–May 1918; assigned 13 September 1921 to 1st Cavalry Division.) Troop D, 8th Cavalry, inactivated 15 September 1921 at Fort Bliss, Texas, and redesignated as Troop C, 3d Machine Gun Squadron. Disbanded 1 February 1928.

Reconstituted 16 November 1943 in the Regular Army and redesignated as Troop D, 8th Cavalry. Activated 4 December 1943 in Australia and reorganized under infantry tables of organization. Redesignated 25 March 1949 as Company D, 8th Cavalry. Inactivated 1 December 1957 in Japan and relieved from assignment to 1st Cavalry Division.

Redesignated 29 April 1959 as Headquarters and Headquarters Troop, 4th Reconnaissance Squadron, 8th Cavalry; concurrently, withdrawn from the Regular Army, allotted to the Army Reserve, and assigned to 96th Infantry Division (organic elements concurrently constituted). Activated 1 June 1959 at Salt Lake City, Utah. Inactivated 15 March 1963 at Salt Lake City, Utah, and relieved from assignment to 96th Infantry Division.

Headquarters and Headquarters Troop, 4th Reconnaissance Squadron, 8th Cavalry, redesignated 3 December 1963 as Troop D, 8th Cavalry, and assigned to 191st Infantry Brigade. Activated 1 September 1964 at Ogden, Utah.

Home Area: Sixth United States Army.

CAMPAIGN PARTICIPATION CREDIT

Indian Wars
  Arizona 1868
  Arizona 1869

World War II–AP
  New Guinea
  Bismarck Archipelago
    (with arrowhead)
  Leyte
  Luzon

Korean War
  UN defensive
  UN offensive
  CCF intervention
  First UN counteroffensive
  CCF spring offensive
  UN summer-fall offensive
  Second Korean winter
  Korea, summer-fall 1952
  Third Korean winter

184

DECORATIONS

Philippine Presidential Unit Citation, Streamer embroidered 17 OCTOBER 1944 TO 4 JULY 1945 (8th Cavalry cited; DA GO 47, 1950)

Republic of Korea Presidential Unit Citation, Streamer embroidered WAEGWAN-TAEGU (8th Cavalry cited; DA GO 35, 1951)

Republic of Korea Presidential Unit Citation, Streamer embroidered KOREA (8th Cavalry cited; DA GO 24, 1954)

Chryssoun Aristion Andrias (Bravery Gold Medal of Greece), Streamer embroidered KOREA (8th Cavalry cited; DA GO 2, 1956)

5th SQUADRON, 8th CAVALRY

AR
(inactive)

LINEAGE

Constituted 28 July 1866 in the Regular Army as Company E, 8th Cavalry. Organized 27 October 1866 at Angel Island, California. (Cavalry companies officially designated as troops in 1883.) (8th Cavalry assigned to 15th Cavalry Division December 1917–May 1918; assigned 13 September 1921 to 1st Cavalry Division. Dismounted 28 February 1943 and reorganized 4 December 1943 partly under cavalry and partly under infantry tables of organization and equipment. Reorganized wholly as infantry 20 July 1945 but retained cavalry designations.) Troop E, 8th Cavalry, redesignated 25 March 1949 as Company E, 8th Cavalry. Inactivated 1 December 1957 in Japan and relieved from assignment to 1st Cavalry Division.

Redesignated 31 March 1959 as Headquarters and Headquarters Troop, 5th Reconnaissance Squadron, 8th Cavalry; concurrently, withdrawn from the Regular Army, allotted to the Army Reserve, and assigned to 63d Infantry Division (organic elements concurrently constituted). Activated 1 May 1959 at San Diego, California. Reorganized and redesignated 1 October 1963 as 5th Squadron, 8th Cavalry. Inactivated 31 December 1965 at San Diego, California, and relieved from assignment to 63d Infantry Division.

Home Area: Sixth United States Army.

CAMPAIGN PARTICIPATION CREDIT

Indian Wars
*Comanches
Apaches
Pine Ridge
Arizona 1867
*Arizona 1868
*Arizona 1869
Oregon 1868
Mexico 1877

World War II
*New Guinea
*Bismarck Archipelago
(with arrowhead)

*Leyte
*Luzon

Korean War
*UN defensive
*UN offensive
*CCF intervention
*First UN counteroffensive
*CCF spring offensive
*UN summer-fall offensive
*Second Korean winter
*Korea, summer-fall 1952
*Third Korean winter

DECORATIONS

*Presidential Unit Citation (Army), Streamer embroidered LUZON (2d Squadron, reinforced, cited; WD GO 38, 1946)

*Presidential Unit Citation (Army), Streamer embroidered TAEGU (2d Battalion, reinforced, cited; DA GO 38, 1952)

*Philippine Presidential Unit Citation, Streamer embroidered 17 OCTOBER 1944 TO 4 JULY 1945 (8th Cavalry cited; DA GO 47, 1950)

*Republic of Korea Presidential Unit Citation, Streamer embroidered WAEGWAN-TAEGU (8th Cavalry cited; DA GO 35, 1951)

*Republic of Korea Presidential Unit Citation, Streamer embroidered KOREA (8th Cavalry cited; DA GO 24, 1954)

*Chryssoun Aristion Andrias (Bravery Gold Medal of Greece), Streamer embroidered KOREA (8th Cavalry cited; DA GO 2, 1956)

TROOP F, 8th CAVALRY

LINEAGE

Constituted 28 July 1866 in the Regular Army as Company F, 8th Cavalry. Organized 27 October 1866 at Angel Island, California. (Cavalry companies officially designated as troops in 1883.) (8th Cavalry assigned to 15th Cavalry Division December 1917–May 1918; assigned 13 September 1921 to 1st Cavalry Division. Dismounted 28 February 1943 and reorganized 4 December 1943 partly under cavalry and partly under infantry tables of organization. Reorganized wholly as infantry 20 July 1945 but retained cavalry designations.) Redesignated 25 March 1949 as Company F, 8th Cavalry. Inactivated 1 December 1957 in Japan and relieved from assignment to 1st Cavalry Division.

Redesignated 1 April 1968 as Troop F, 8th Cavalry, assigned to 23d Infantry Division and activated in Vietnam.

CAMPAIGN PARTICIPATION CREDIT

Indian Wars
  Arizona 1869
  New Mexico 1871

World War II–AP
  New Guinea
  Bismarck Archipelago
    (with arrowhead)
  Leyte
  Luzon

Korean War
  UN defensive
  UN offensive
  CCF intervention
  First UN counteroffensive
  CCF spring offensive
  UN summer-fall offensive
  Second Korean winter
  Korea, summer-fall 1952
  Third Korean winter

Vietnam
  *Tet Counteroffensive

DECORATIONS

Presidential Unit Citation (Army), Streamer embroidered LUZON (2d Squadron, reinforced, cited; WD GO 38, 1946)

Presidential Unit Citation (Army), Streamer embroidered TAEGU (2d Battalion, reinforced, cited; DA GO 38, 1952)

Philippine Presidential Unit Citation, Streamer embroidered 17 OCTOBER 1944 TO 4 JULY 1945 (8th Cavalry cited; DA GO 47, 1950)

Republic of Korea Presidential Unit Citation, Streamer embroidered WAEGWAN-TAEGU (8th Cavalry cited; DA GO 35, 1951)

Republic of Korea Presidential Unit Citation, Streamer embroidered KOREA (8th Cavalry cited; DA GO 24, 1954)

Chryssoun Aristion Andrias (Bravery Gold Medal of Greece), Streamer embroidered KOREA (8th Cavalry cited; DA GO 2, 1956)

BIBLIOGRAPHY, 8TH CAVALRY

Department of the Army
   Korea, 1950. Washington: 1952.
Department of the Army. AMERICAN FORCES IN ACTION series.
   The Admiralties: Operations of the 1st Cavalry Division. Washington: 1945.
Herr, John K., and Edward S. Wallace. *The Story of the U.S. Cavalry.* Boston: 1953.
Mahr, Warren C., compiler. *1st Cavalry Division 1952–1954.* Atlanta, Georgia: 1954.
Miller, John, jr., O. J. Carroll, and M. E. Tackley. *Korea 1951–1953.* Washington: 1956.
Richards, Frank S. *A Brief History of the 8th Cavalry Regiment and 2d Reconnaissance Squadron, 8th Cavalry Regiment after 1 April 1957.* Fort Lewis, Washington: 1961.
Rodenbough, Theo. F., and William L. Haskins, editors. *The Army of the United States.* New York: 1896. Charles M. O'Connor, "The Eighth Regiment of Cavalry," pp. 268–279.
Sydenham, Alvin H. "The Daily Journal of Alvin H. Sydenham." *Bulletin of the New York Public Library.* Appeared in serial form beginning February 1940.
Unit Members. *1st Cavalry Division "The First Team."* Japan: 1959.
   ———. *8th Cavalry: Honor and Courage.* Japan: circa 1952.
   ———. *Occupation Diary, First Cavalry Division 1945–1950.* Japan: 1950.
   ———. *The First Team: The First Cavalry Division 18 July 1950–18 January 1952.* Atlanta, Georgia: circa 1952.
UNITED STATES ARMY IN THE KOREAN WAR
   Appleman, Roy E. *South to the Naktong, North to the Yalu.* 1961.
   Hermes, Walter G. *Truce Tent and Fighting Front.* 1966.
UNITED STATES ARMY IN WORLD WAR II
   Cannon, M. Hamlin. *Leyte: The Return to the Philippines.* 1954.
   Miller, John, jr. *CARTWHEEL: The Reduction of Rabaul.* 1959.
   Smith, Robert R. *The Approach to the Philippines.* 1953.

Smith, Robert R. *Triumph in the Philippines.* 1963.
Westover, John G. *Combat Support in Korea.* Washington: 1955.
Wright, B. C., comp. *The 1st Cavalry Division in World War II.* Japan: 1947.

9th CAVALRY

HERALDIC ITEMS

COAT OF ARMS

Shield: Or, on a pile azure in chief a sun of eight points of rays between three five-pointed mullets two and one of the field, in base over all the blockhouse of San Juan Hill, Santiago, Cuba, proper.

Crest: On a wreath of the colors a horseshoe with nine nail holes heels down argent winged purpure debruised by two arrows in saltire sable armed and flitted gules.

Motto: We Can, We Will.

Symbolism: The field is yellow for the cavalry and the blue triangle with the sun and three five-pointed stars are from the old flag of the Philippine Insurrection with a change of color. The three stars also represent the three tours of duty in the islands. The blockhouse is the old pride of the regiment, a representation of the actual one taken at San Juan Hill in 1898. The wedge is blue and recalls the fact that the 9th split the Spanish line at Santiago with the capture of the blockhouse when it charged dismounted as infantry. The crest is the well-known Scotch device signifying the alertness of the mounted man, and the arrows are for the Indian campaigns of the regiment.

DISTINCTIVE INSIGNIA

The distinctive insignia is an Indian in breech clout and war bonnet, mounted on a galloping pony, brandishing a rifle in his right hand and holding a single rein in his left hand, all in gold, displayed upon a five-bastioned fort in blue edged with gold.

The five-bastioned fort was the badge of the Fifth Army Corps in Cuba, of which the Ninth Cavalry was a part. The yellow outline is for the Cavalry, and the blue for active service in the Spanish-American War. The mounted Indian represents the Indian campaigns of the regiment.

LINEAGE AND HONORS

LINEAGE

Constituted 28 July 1866 in the Regular Army as 9th Cavalry. Organized 21 September 1866 at Greenville, Louisiana. Assigned 1 March 1933 to 3d Cavalry Division. Relieved 10 October 1940 from assignment to 3d Cavalry Division and assigned to 2d Cavalry Division. Inactivated 7 March 1944 in North Africa.

Redesignated 20 October 1950 as 509th Tank Battalion and relieved from assignment to 2d Cavalry Division. Activated 1 November 1950 at Camp Polk, Louisiana. Inactivated 10 April 1956 at Fort Knox, Kentucky.

Reorganized and redesignated 1 December 1957 as 9th Cavalry, a parent regiment under the Combat Arms Regimental System.

CAMPAIGN PARTICIPATION CREDIT

Indian Wars	*Philippine Insurrection*
Comanches	Without inscription
Utes	
Pine Ridge	*World War II*
New Mexico 1877	European-African-Middle Eastern
New Mexico 1878	Theater without inscription
New Mexico 1879	
New Mexico 1880	*Vietnam*
New Mexico 1881	Defense
Montana 1887	Counteroffensive
	Counteroffensive, Phase II
War With Spain	Counteroffensive, Phase III
Santiago	Tet Counteroffensive

DECORATIONS

Presidential Unit Citation (Army), Streamer embroidered PLEIKU PROVINCE (1st Squadron cited; DA GO 40, 1967)

1st SQUADRON, 9th CAVALRY

RA
(1st Cavalry Division)

LINEAGE

Constituted 28 July 1866 in the Regular Army as Company A, 9th Cavalry. Organized in October 1866 at Greenville, Louisiana. (Cavalry companies officially designated as troops in 1883.) (9th Cavalry assigned 1 March 1933 to 3d Cavalry Division; relieved from assignment to 3d Cavalry Division 10 October 1940 and assigned to 2d Cavalry Division.) Inactivated 7 March 1944 in North Africa.

Converted and redesignated 20 October 1950 as Company A, 509th Tank Battalion (9th Cavalry concurrently relieved from assignment to 2d Cavalry Division). Activated 1 November 1950 at Camp Polk, Louisiana. Inactivated 10 April 1956 at Fort Knox, Kentucky. Redesignated 15 October 1957 as Troop A, 9th Cavalry.

Redesignated 1 November 1957 as Headquarters and Headquarters Troop, 1st Reconnaissance Squadron, 9th Cavalry; concurrently, consolidated with 16th Reconnaissance Company (see ANNEX), assigned to 1st Cavalry Division, and activated in Korea (organic elements constituted 15 October 1957 and activated 1 November 1957). Reorganized and redesignated 1 September 1963 as 1st Squadron, 9th Cavalry. Transferred (less personnel and equipment) 1 July 1965 from Korea to Fort Benning, Georgia, and reorganized.

ANNEX

302d Cavalry Reconnaissance Troop, Mechanized, constituted 13 November 1943 in the Army of the United States. Activated 4 December 1943 in Australia and assigned to 1st Cavalry Division. Redesignated 15 October 1945 as 302d Mechanized Cavalry Reconnaissance Troop. Redesignated 25 March 1949 as 16th Reconnaissance Company.

193

CAMPAIGN PARTICIPATION CREDIT

Indian Wars
    Comanches
    Utes
    Pine Ridge
    New Mexico 1877
    New Mexico 1878
    *New Mexico 1879
    *New Mexico 1880
    New Mexico 1881
    Montana 1887

War With Spain
    *Santiago

Philippine Insurrection
    *Without inscription

World War II
    *European-African-Middle Eastern
      Theater without inscription

*New Guinea
*Bismarck Archipelago
*Leyte (with arrowhead)
*Luzon

Korean War
    *UN defensive
    *UN offensive
    *CCF intervention
    *First UN counteroffensive
    *CCF spring offensive
    *UN summer-fall offensive
    *Second Korean winter

Vietnam
    *Defense
    *Counteroffensive
    *Counteroffensive, Phase II
    *Counteroffensive, Phase III
    *Tet Counteroffensive

DECORATIONS

*Presidential Unit Citation (Army), Streamer embroidered TAEGU (16th Reconnaissance Company cited; DA GO 38, 1952)

*Presidential Unit Citation (Army), Streamer embroidered PLEIKU PROVINCE (1st Squadron cited; DA GO 40, 1967)

*Philippines Presidential Unit Citation, Streamer embroidered 17 OCTOBER 1944 TO 4 JULY 1945 (302d Cavalry Reconnaissance Troop cited; DA GO 47, 1950)

*Republic of Korea Presidential Unit Citation, Streamer embroidered WAEGWAN-TAEGU (16th Reconnaissance Company cited; DA GO 35, 1951)

*Chryssoun Aristion Andrias (Bravery Gold Medal of Greece), Streamer embroidered KOREA (16th Reconnaissance Company cited; DA GO 2, 1956)

Troop B additionally entitled to: Valorous Unit Award, Streamer embroidered PLEI ME (Troop B, 1st Squadron, cited; GO 4692, U.S. Army, Vietnam, 1967)

2d SQUADRON, 9th CAVALRY

RA

(24th Infantry Division)

LINEAGE

Constituted 28 July 1866 in the Regular Army as Company B, 9th Cavalry. Organized in October 1866 at Greenville, Louisiana. (Cavalry companies officially designated troops in 1883.) (9th Cavalry assigned 1 March 1933 to 3d Cavalry Division; relieved from assignment to 3d Cavalry Division 10 October 1940 and assigned to 2d Cavalry Division.) Inactivated 7 March 1944 in North Africa.

Converted and redesignated 20 October 1950 as Company B, 509th Tank Battalion (9th Cavalry concurrently relieved from assignment to 2d Cavalry Division). Activated 1 November 1950 at Camp Polk, Louisiana. Inactivated 10 April 1956 at Fort Knox, Kentucky.

Redesignated 1 December 1957 as Headquarters and Headquarters Troop, 2d Reconnaissance Squadron, 9th Cavalry; concurrently, consolidated with 9th Reconnaissance Company (see ANNEX), assigned to 9th Infantry Division, and activated at Fort Carson, Colorado (organic elements concurrently constituted and activated). 2d Reconnaissance Squadron, 9th Cavalry, relieved from assignment to 9th Infantry Division 1 July 1958, assigned to 24th Infantry Division, and reorganized in Europe. Reorganized and redesignated 28 January 1963 as 2d Squadron, 9th Cavalry.

ANNEX

9th Reconnaissance Troop constituted 1 August 1940 in the Regular Army and assigned to 9th Infantry Division. Activated 10 August 1940 at Fort Bragg, North Carolina. Redesignated 20 August 1943 as 9th Cavalry Reconnaissance Troop, Mechanized. Redesignated 8 September 1945 as 9th Mechanized Cavalry Reconnaissance Troop. Inactivated 30 November 1946 in Europe. Redesignated 12 July 1948 as 9th Reconnaissance Company and activated at Fort Dix, New Jersey.

CAMPAIGN PARTICIPATION CREDIT

Indian Wars
  *Comanches
  Utes
  Pine Ridge
  New Mexico 1877
  New Mexico 1878
  *New Mexico 1879
  *New Mexico 1880
  New Mexico 1881
  Montana 1887

War With Spain
  *Santiago

Philippine Insurrection
  *Without inscription

World War II
  *Tunisia
  *Sicily
  *Normandy
  *Northern France
  *Rhineland
  *Ardennes-Alsace
  *Central Europe

DECORATIONS

*Belgian Fourragère 1940 (9th Cavalry Reconnaissance Troop cited; DA GO 43, 1950)

*Cited in the Order of the Day of the Belgian Army for action at MEUSE RIVER (9th Cavalry Reconnaissance Troop cited; DA GO 43, 1950)

*Cited in the Order of the Day of the Belgian Army for action in the ARDENNES (9th Reconnaissance Troop cited; DA GO 43, 1950)

TROOP C, 9th CAVALRY

AR
(157th Infantry Brigade)

LINEAGE

Constituted 28 July 1866 in the Regular Army as Company C, 9th Cavalry. Organized during September and October 1866 at New Orleans, Louisiana. (Cavalry companies officially designated as troops in 1883.) (9th Cavalry assigned 1 March 1933 to 3d Cavalry Division.) Inactivated 1 April 1939 at Fort Riley, Kansas. (9th Cavalry relieved from assignment to 3d Cavalry Division 10 October 1940 and assigned to 2d Cavalry Division.) Activated 15 January 1941 at Fort Riley, Kansas. Inactivated 7 March 1944 in North Africa.

Converted and redesignated 20 October 1950 as Company C, 509th Tank Battalion. (9th Cavalry concurrently relieved from assignment to 2d Cavalry Division.) Activated 1 November 1950 at Camp Polk, Louisiana. Inactivated 10 April 1956 at Fort Knox, Kentucky.

Redesignated 17 March 1959 as Headquarters and Headquarters Troop, 3d Reconnaissance Squadron, 9th Cavalry; concurrently, withdrawn from the Regular Army, allotted to the Army Reserve, and assigned to 79th Infantry Division (organic elements concurrently constituted). Activated 6 April 1959 at Philadelphia, Pennsylvania. Inactivated 28 February 1963 at Philadelphia, Pennsylvania, and relieved from assignment to 79th Infantry Division.

Headquarters and Headquarters Troop, 3d Reconnaissance Squadron, 9th Cavalry, redesignated 3 December 1963 as Troop C, 9th Cavalry, and assigned to 157th Infantry Brigade. Activated 1 February 1964 at Bristol, Pennsylvania. Location changed 31 January 1966 to Wilkes-Barre, Pennsylvania.
Home Area: First United States Army.

CAMPAIGN PARTICIPATION CREDIT

Indian Wars
New Mexico 1879
New Mexico 1880

War With Spain
Santiago

DECORATIONS
None.

197

4th SQUADRON, 9th CAVALRY

RA

(6th Infantry Division)

LINEAGE

Constituted 28 July 1866 in the Regular Army as Company D, 9th Cavalry. Organized during September and October 1866 at New Orleans, Louisiana. (Cavalry companies officially designated as troops in 1883.) Demobilized 1 December 1921 in the Philippine Islands.

Reconstituted 19 March 1959 and redesignated as Headquarters and Headquarters Troop, 4th Reconnaissance Squadron, 9th Cavalry; concurrently, withdrawn from the Regular Army, allotted to the Army Reserve, and assigned to 83d Infantry Division (organic elements concurrently constituted). Activated 20 March 1959 at Mansfield, Ohio. Reorganized and redesignated 15 April 1963 as 4th Squadron, 9th Cavalry. Inactivated 31 December 1965 at Mansfield, Ohio.

Withdrawn 24 November 1967 from the Army Reserve and allotted to the Regular Army; concurrently, relieved from assignment to 83d Infantry Division, assigned to 6th Infantry Division, and activated at Fort Campbell, Kentucky.

CAMPAIGN PARTICIPATION CREDIT

Indian Wars
  Comanches
  *Utes
  *Pine Ridge
  New Mexico 1877
  New Mexico 1878
  New Mexico 1879
  *New Mexico 1880
  New Mexico 1881
  *Montana 1887

War With Spain
  *Santiago

Philippine Insurrection
  *Without inscription

World War II
  European-African-Middle
    Eastern Theater without
    inscription

DECORATIONS

None.

TROOP E, 9th CAVALRY

RA
(nondivisional)

LINEAGE

Constituted 28 July 1866 in the Regular Army as Company E, 9th Cavalry. Organized in 1866 in Louisiana. (Cavalry companies officially designated as troops in 1883.) (9th Cavalry assigned 1 March 1933 to 3d Cavalry Division; relieved 10 October 1940 from assignment to 3d Cavalry Division and assigned to 2d Cavalry Division.) Inactivated 7 March 1944 in North Africa. Disbanded 20 October 1950.

Reconstituted 1 December 1957 in the Regular Army and redesignated as Headquarters and Headquarters Troop, 5th Reconnaissance Squadron, 9th Cavalry. Redesignated 2 October 1962 as Headquarters and Headquarters Troop, 5th Squadron, 9th Cavalry, and assigned to 194th Armored Brigade (organic elements concurrently constituted). Activated 21 December 1962 at Fort Ord, California.

Inactivated 4 January 1968 at Fort Ord, California, and relieved from assignment to 194th Armored Brigade; concurrently, Headquarters and Headquarters Troop, 5th Squadron, 9th Cavalry, redesignated as Troop E, 9th Cavalry, and activated at Fort Ord, California.

CAMPAIGN PARTICIPATION CREDIT

Indian Wars
  Comanches
  Pine Ridge
  New Mexico 1879

War With Spain
  Santiago

DECORATIONS

None.

BIBLIOGRAPHY, 9TH CAVALRY

Cashin, Hershel V., *et al. Under Fire with the Tenth Cavalry . . . Review of the Negro's Participation in the Wars of the United States . . . the Ninth and Tenth Cavalries . . . Indlian Campaigns.* New York: 1899.

Downey, Fairfax. *Indian Fighting Army.* New York: 1941.

Herr, John K., and Edward S. Wallace. *The Story of the U.S. Cavalry.* Boston: 1953.

Hutcheson, Grote. "A Register of the Commissioned Officers Belonging to the Ninth U.S. Cavalry, From its Organization, July 28, 1866, to July 28, 1893 . . ." Fort Robinson: 1893.

Leckie, William H. *The Buffalo Soldiers, A Narrative of the Negro Cavalry in the West*. Norman, Oklahoma: 1967.

Rodenbough, Theo. F., and William L. Haskin, editors. *The Army of the United States*. New York: 1896. Grote Hutcheson, "The Ninth Regiment of Cavalry."

Steward, T. G. *The Colored Regulars in the United States Army . . . Revolutionary War to 1899*. Philadelphia: 1904.

Unit Members. *Historical and Pictorial Review, 9th Cavalry Regiment, Second Cavalry Division of the United States Army*. Baton Rouge, Louisiana: 1941.

UNITED STATES ARMY IN WORLD WAR II

Lee, Ulysses G. *The Employment of Negro Troops*. 1966.

10th CAVALRY

Heraldic Items

BADGE

Description: On a heraldic wreath or and sable, a buffalo statant proper. On a scroll of the second fimbriated of the first the motto *Ready and Forward* of the like.

Symbolism: Black and gold have long been used as the regimental colors. The buffalo has likewise been the emblem of the regiment for many years, having its origin in the term *Buffalo Soldiers* applied by the Indians to Negro regiments.

The regimental badge, in lieu of a coat of arms, is used as the crest on the organizational color.

DISTINCTIVE INSIGNIA

The distinctive insignia is the badge of the regiment.

Lineage and Honors

LINEAGE

Constituted 28 July 1866 in the Regular Army as 10th Cavalry. Organized 21 September 1866 at Fort Leavenworth, Kansas. Assigned to 1st Cavalry Division 13 September 1921–18 December 1922. Assigned to 2d Cavalry Division 24 March 1923–15 August 1927. Assigned to 3d Cavalry Division 15 August 1927–10 October 1940. Assigned 10 October 1940 to 2d Cavalry Division. Inactivated 20 March 1944 in North Africa.

Redesignated 20 October 1950 as 510th Tank Battalion and relieved from assignment to 2d Cavalry Division. Activated 17 November 1950 at Camp Polk, Louisiana. Inactivated 1 May 1958 in Germany.

Reorganized and redesignated 25 June 1958 as 10th Cavalry, a parent regiment under the Combat Arms Regimental System (Headquarters and Headquarters Company, 510th Tank Battalion, redesignated as Headquarters and Headquarters Troop, 10th Cavalry).

201

314-902 O - 69 - 15

CAMPAIGN PARTICIPATION CREDIT

Indian Wars
Comanches
Apaches
New Mexico 1880
Texas 1880

War With Spain
Santiago

Philippine Insurrection
Without inscription

Mexican Expedition
Mexico 1916–1917

World War II
European-African-Middle Eastern
Theater without inscription

Vietnam
Counteroffensive, Phase II
Counteroffensive, Phase III
Tet Counteroffensive

DECORATIONS
None.

1st SQUADRON, 10th CAVALRY

RA

(4th Infantry Division)

LINEAGE

Constituted 28 July 1866 in the Regular Army as Company A, 10th Cavalry. Organized 18 February 1867 at Fort Leavenworth, Kansas. (Cavalry companies officially designated as troops in 1883.) (10th Cavalry assigned to 1st Cavalry Division 13 September 1921–18 December 1922; assigned to 2d Cavalry Division 24 March 1923–15 August 1927; assigned to 3d Cavalry Division 15 August 1927–10 October 1940; assigned to 2d Cavalry Division 10 October 1940.) Inactivated 20 March 1944 at Algiers, North Africa.

Redesignated 20 October 1950 as Company A, 510th Tank Battalion. (10th Cavalry concurrently relieved from assignment to 2d Cavalry Division.) Activated 17 November 1950 at Camp Polk, Louisiana. Inactivated 1 May 1958 in Germany. Redesignated 10 June 1958 as Troop A (Reconnaissance), 10th Cavalry. Activated 25 June 1958 at Fort Knox, Kentucky.

Reorganized and redesignated 1 September 1963 as Headquarters and Headquarters Troop, 1st Squadron, 10th Cavalry; concurrently, transferred (less personnel and equipment) from Fort Knox, Kentucky, to Fort Lewis, Washington, and assigned to 4th Infantry Division (organic elements concurrently constituted and activated).

CAMPAIGN PARTICIPATION CREDIT

Indian Wars
   *Comanches
   Apaches
   New Mexico 1880
   Texas 1880

War With Spain
   *Santiago

Philippine Insurrection
   Without inscription

Mexican Expedition
   *Mexico 1916–1917

World War II
   *European-African-Middle Eastern
      Theater without inscription

Vietnam
   *Counteroffensive, Phase II
   *Counteroffensive, Phase III
   *Tet Counteroffensive

DECORATIONS

None.

2d SQUADRON, 10th CAVALRY

RA

(7th Infantry Division)

LINEAGE

Constituted 28 July 1866 in the Regular Army as Company B, 10th Cavalry. Organized 1 April 1867 at Fort Leavenworth, Kansas. (Cavalry companies officially designated as troops in 1883.) (10th Cavalry assigned to 1st Cavalry Division 13 September 1921–18 December 1922; assigned to 2d Cavalry Division 24 March 1923–15 August 1927; assigned to 3d Cavalry Division 15 August 1927–10 October 1940; assigned to 2d Cavalry Division 10 October 1940.) Inactivated 20 March 1944 in North Africa.

Redesignated 20 October 1950 as Company B, 510th Tank Battalion (10th Cavalry concurrently relieved from assignment to 2d Cavalry Division.) Activated 17 November 1950 at Camp Polk, Louisiana.

Reorganized and redesignated 1 July 1957 as Headquarters and Headquarters Troop, 2d Reconnaissance Squadron, 10th Cavalry; concurrently, consolidated with 7th Reconnaissance Company (see ANNEX), transferred (less personnel and equipment) from Germany to Korea, and assigned to 7th Infantry Division (organic elements concurrently constituted and activated in Korea). Reorganized and redesignated 1 July 1963 as 2d Squadron, 10th Cavalry.

ANNEX

7th Cavalry Reconnaissance Troop constituted 1 January 1943 in the Regular Army and assigned to 7th Infantry Division. Activated 10 January 1943 at Camp San Luis Obispo, California. Reorganized and redesignated 7 November 1943 as 7th Cavalry Reconnaissance Troop, Mechanized. Redesignated 8 October 1945 as 7th Mechanized Cavalry Reconnaissance Troop. Redesignated 20 March 1949 as 7th Reconnaissance Company.

CAMPAIGN PARTICIPATION CREDIT

Indian Wars
  *Comanches
  Apaches
  New Mexico 1880
  *Texas 1880

War With Spain
  *Santiago

Philippine Insurrection
  Without inscription

Mexican Expedition
  *Mexico 1916–1917

World War II
  *European-African-Middle Eastern
    Theater without inscription

*Aleutian Islands (with arrowhead)
*Eastern Mandates
*Leyte
*Ryukyus (with arrowhead)

Korean War
  *UN defensive
  *UN offensive
  *CCF intervention
  *First UN counteroffensive
  *CCF spring offensive
  *UN summer-fall offensive
  *Second Korean winter
  *Korea, summer-fall 1952
  *Third Korean winter
  *Korea, summer 1953

DECORATIONS

*Presidential Unit Citation (Army), Streamer embroidered ATTU (7th Cavalry Reconnaissance Troop cited; WD GO 10, 1944)

*Presidential Unit Citation (Army), Streamer embroidered KWAJALEIN ATOLL (7th Cavalry Reconnaissance Troop cited; WD GO 88, 1944)

*Presidential Unit Citation (Navy), Streamer embroidered WONJU-HWACHON (7th Reconnaissance Company cited; DA GO 38, 1957)

*Navy Unit Commendation, Streamer embroidered PANMUNJOM (7th Reconnaissance Company cited; DA GO 38, 1951)

*Philippine Presidential Unit Citation, Streamer embroidered 17 OCTOBER 1944 TO 4 JULY 1945 (7th Cavalry Reconnaissance Troop cited; DA GO 47, 1950)

*Republic of Korea Presidential Unit Citation, Streamer embroidered IN-CHON (7th Reconnaissance Company cited; DA GO 35, 1951)

*Republic of Korea Presidential Unit Citation, Streamer embroidered KOREA (7th Reconnaissance Company cited; DA GO 22, 1956)

3d SQUADRON, 10th CAVALRY

AR

(inactive)

LINEAGE

Constituted 28 July 1866 in the Regular Army as Company C, 10th Cavalry. Organized 15 May 1867 at Fort Leavenworth, Kansas. (Cavalry companies officially designated as troops in 1883.) Troop C, 10th Cavalry, reorganized and redesignated 1 February 1928 as Machine Gun Troop, 10th Cavalry. (10th Cavalry assigned to 1st Cavalry Division 13 September 1921–18 December 1922; assigned to 2d Cavalry Division 24 March 1923–15 August 1927; assigned to 3d Cavalry Division 15 August 1927–10 October 1940; assigned to 2d Cavalry Division 10 October 1940.) Inactivated 20 March 1944 in North Africa. Disbanded 20 October 1950. (10th Cavalry concurrently relieved from assignment to 2d Cavalry Division.)

Reconstituted 25 June 1958 in the Regular Army. Redesignated 7 April 1959 as Headquarters and Headquarters Troop, 3d Reconnaissance Squadron, 10th Cavalry; concurrently, consolidated with Company C, 510th Tank Battalion (see ANNEX), withdrawn from the Regular Army, allotted to the Army Reserve, and assigned to 77th Infantry Division (organic elements concurrently constituted). Activated 1 May 1959 at Long Island City, New York. Reorganized and redesignated 26 March 1963 as 3d Squadron, 10th Cavalry.

ANNEX

Troop C, 10th Cavalry, constituted 1 February 1940 in the Regular Army. Activated 1 February 1941 at Fort Riley, Kansas, as an element of the 2d Cavalry Division. Inactivated 20 March 1944 in North Africa. Redesignated 20 October 1950 as Company C, 510th Tank Battalion, and relieved from assignment to 2d Cavalry Division. Activated 17 November 1950 at Camp Polk, Louisiana. Inactivated 1 May 1958 in Germany. Location changed 1 December 1964 to Fort Tilden, New York. Inactivated 30 December 1965 at Fort Tilden, New York, and relieved from assignment to 77th Infantry Division.

Home Area: First United States Army.

Campaign Participation Credit

Indian Wars
  *Comanches
   Apaches
  *New Mexico 1880
  *Texas 1880

War With Spain
  *Santiago

Philippine Insurrection
   Without inscription

Mexican Expedition
  *Mexico 1916–1917

World War II
  *European-African-Middle Eastern
   Theater without inscription

Decorations

None.

TROOP D, 10th CAVALRY

RA
(194th Armored Brigade)

LINEAGE

Constituted 28 July 1866 in the Regular Army as Company D, 10th Cavalry. Organized 1 June 1867 at Fort Leavenworth, Kansas. (Cavalry companies officially designated as troops in 1883.) Troop D, 10th Cavalry, demobilized 1 September 1921 at Fort Huachuca, Arizona.

Reconstituted 25 June 1958 in the Regular Army and redesignated as Headquarters and Headquarters Troop, 4th Reconnaissance Squadron, 10th Cavalry. Redesignated 1 September 1963 as Troop D, 10th Cavalry, and activated at Fort Knox, Kentucky. Assigned 15 April 1968 to 194th Armored Brigade.

CAMPAIGN PARTICIPATION CREDIT

Indian Wars
Comanches
New Mexico 1880

Mexican Expedition
Mexico 1916–1917

War With Spain
Santiago

DECORATIONS

None.

BIBLIOGRAPHY, 10TH CAVALRY

Bettis, Henry J., compiler. *A History of the 510th Tank Battalion (Hv) (Formerly the Tenth Cavalry Regiment)*. N.p.: 1953.

Cashin, Hershel V., *et al. Under Fire with the Tenth U.S. Cavalry . . . Review of the Negro's Participation in the Wars of the United States . . . Ninth and Tenth Cavalries . . . Indian Campaigns*. New York: 1899.

Downey, Fairfax. *Indian Fighting Army*. New York: 1941.

Glass, Edward L. N. *The History of the Tenth Cavalry, 1866–1921*. Tucson, Arizona: 1921.

Herr, John K., and Edward S. Wallace. *The Story of the U.S. Cavalry*. Boston: 1953.

Leckie, William H. *The Buffalo Soldiers. A Narrative of the Negro Cavalry in the West*. Norman, Oklahoma: 1967.

208

Rodenbough, Theo. F., and William L. Haskin, editors. *The Army of the United States*. New York: 1896. John Bigelow, Jr., "The Tenth Regiment of Cavalry."

Roster of non-commissioned officers of the Tenth U.S. Cavalry, with some regimental reminiscences, appendixes, etc., connected with the early history of the regiment. St. Paul: 1897.

Steward, T. C. *The Colored Regulars in the United States Army . . . Revolutionary War to 1899*. Philadelphia: 1904.

Thweatt, Hiram H., compiler. *What the Newspapers Say of the Negro Soldier in the Spanish-American War and the Return of the 10th Cavalry*. Thomasville, Georgia: circa 1908.

Unit Members. *Historical and Pictorial Review of the Tenth Cavalry Regiment*. Baton Rouge, Louisiana: 1941.

UNITED STATES ARMY IN WORLD WAR II

Lee, Ulysses G. *The Employment of Negro Troops*. 1966.

Wharfield, H. B., *10th Cavalry and Border Fights*. El Cajon, California: 1965.

Wharton, Harold. *With Scouts and Cavalry at Fort Apache*. Tucson: 1965.

11th ARMORED CAVALRY
(The Blackhorse Regiment)

HERALDIC ITEMS

COAT OF ARMS

Shield: Or, within an orle sable in chief two bolos saltirewise gules hilted azure and in base a cactus proper.

Crest: Upon a wreath of the color (or and sable) a horse's head erased sable.

Motto: Allons.

Symbolism: Organized in 1901, the regiment saw service in the Philippines, which is indicated by the crossed bolos with red blades and blue hilts. The regiment's excellent service on the Mexican border in 1916 is represented by the cactus. The regimental colors, black and yellow, are shown by the shield and the black border within the edge and by the color of the crest.

DISTINCTIVE INSIGNIA

The distinctive insignia is the shield, crest, and motto of the coat of arms.

LINEAGE AND HONORS

LINEAGE

Constituted 2 February 1901 in the Regular Army as 11th Cavalry. Organized 11 March 1901 at Fort Myer, Virginia. Assigned to 3d Cavalry Division August 1927–March 1933. Assigned to 2d Cavalry Division October 1933–October 1940. Inactivated 15 July 1942 at Fort Benning, Georgia; personnel and equipment transferred to 11th Armored Regiment (see ANNEX 1).

Headquarters and Headquarters Troop, 11th Cavalry, redesignated 19 April 1943 as Headquarters and Headquarters Troop, 11th Cavalry Group, Mechanized. Activated 5 May 1943 at Camp Anza, California. (Remainder of 11th Cavalry disbanded 26 October 1944.) Headquarters and Headquarters Troop, 11th Cavalry Group, Mechanized, converted and redesignated 1 May 1946 as Headquarters and Headquarters Troop, 11th Constabulary

Regiment. Reorganized and redesignated 2 February 1948 as Headquarters and Headquarters and Service Troop, 11th Constabulary Regiment. Converted and redesignated 30 November 1948 as Headquarters and Headquarters Company, 11th Armored Cavalry; concurrently, inactivated in Germany.

Organization of 11th Armored Cavalry (inactive) completed 30 November 1948 by reconstitution and/or redesignation of elements of the 11th Cavalry and Headquarters and Headquarters Troop, 1st Constabulary Regiment (see ANNEX 2). 11th Tank Battalion (see ANNEX 1) consolidated 8 January 1951 with 11th Armored Cavalry. 11th Armored Cavalry activated 1 August 1951 at Camp Carson, Colorado. 95th Tank Battalion (see ANNEX 1) consolidated 1 October 1958 with 3d Battalion, 11th Armored Cavalry. (Battalions and Companies redesignated 15 May 1960 as Squadrons and Troops.)

ANNEX 1

11th Armored Regiment constituted 11 July 1942 in the Army of the United States and assigned to 10th Armored Division. Activated 15 July 1942 at Fort Benning, Georgia, with personnel and equipment from 11th Cavalry.

Regiment broken up 20 September 1943 and its elements reorganized and redesignated as follows: 11th Armored Regiment (less 3d Battalion, Band, and Maintenance, Service, and Reconnaissance Companies) as 11th Tank Battalion; 3d Battalion as 712th Tank Battalion and relieved from assignment to 10th Armored Division; Reconnaissance Company as Troop E, 90th Cavalry Reconnaissance Squadron, Mechanized (separate lineage); Maintenance and Service Companies and Band disbanded.

11th Tank Battalion inactivated 13 October 1945 at Camp Patrick Henry, Virginia. Relieved from assignment to 10th Armored Division and consolidated 8 January 1951 with 11th Armored Cavalry.

712th Tank Battalion inactivated 27 October 1945 at Camp Kilmer, New Jersey. Reorganized and redesignated 1 September 1948 as 525th Medium Tank Battalion and allotted to the Regular Army. Activated 10 September 1948 at Fort Lewis, Washington. Inactivated 15 December 1948 at Fort Lewis, Washington. Redesignated 4 February 1950 as 95th Tank Battalion and assigned to 7th Armored Division. Activated 24 November 1950 at Camp Roberts, California. Inactivated 15 November 1953 at Camp Roberts, California. Consolidated 1 October 1958 with 3d Battalion, 11th Armored Cavalry.

ANNEX 2

Headquarters and Headquarters Detachment, 11th Tank Group, constituted 19 July 1943 in the Army of the United States. Activated 28 July 1943 at Camp Campbell, Kentucky. Reorganized and redesignated 5 December 1943 as Headquarters and Headquarters Company, 11th Armored Group. Converted and redesignated 1 May 1946 as Headquarters and Headquarters Troop, 1st Constabulary Regiment. Inactivated 20 September 1947 in Germany. Converted and redesignated 30 November 1948 as Headquarters and Headquarters Company, 3d Battalion, 11th Armored Cavalry.

CAMPAIGN PARTICIPATION CREDIT

Philippine Insurrection
    Samar 1902

Mexican Expedition
    Mexico 1916–1917

World War II
    Normandy
    Northern France

    Rhineland
    Ardennes-Alsace
    Central Europe

Vietnam
    Counteroffensive, Phase II
    Counteroffensive, Phase III
    Tet Counteroffensive

DECORATIONS

Troop K entitled to: Presidential Unit Citation (Army), Streamer embroidered FRANCE (Company B, 712th Tank Battalion, cited; DA GO 12, 1949)

Headquarters Troop, 3d Squadron, entitled to: Meritorious Unit Commendation, Streamer embroidered EUROPEAN THEATER (Headquarters Company, 712th Tank Battalion, cited; GO 643, 90th Infantry Division, 1945)

Headquarters Troop, 3d Squadron, and Troops I, K, and L each entitled to: French Croix de Guerre with Palm, Streamer embroidered MOSELLE-SAARE RIVERS (712th Tank Battalion cited; DA GO 43, 1950)

Headquarters Troop, 3d Squadron; Troops I, K, and L; Company M; and Howitzer Battery, 3d Squadron, entitled to: Meritorious Unit Commendation, Streamer embroidered VIETNAM 1966–1967 (3d Squadron, 11th Cavalry, cited; DA GO 32, 1968)

BIBLIOGRAPHY, 11TH ARMORED CAVALRY

Bonsteel, F. T. *The Eleventh Cavalry, 1901 to 1923.* Monterey, California: 1923.

Cobb, William W. "11th Cavalry Report," *Armor,* LXXXVI, No. 2 (March–April 1967).

Fifield, Robert W., *et al. 11th U.S. Cavalry, California-Mexican Border, 1941.* Los Angeles: 1941.

Haynes, George L., Jr., and James C. Williams. *The Eleventh Cavalry From the Roer to the Elbe, 1944–1945.* Nurnberg, Germany: 1945.

Herr, John K., and Edward S. Wallace. *The Story of the U.S. Cavalry.* Boston: 1953.

Tricoche, George Nestler. *La vie militaire a l'etranger. Notes d'un engage voluntaire au 11th United States Cavalry.* Paris: 1897.

Unit Members. *11th Armored Cavalry.* Fort Knox, Kentucky: 1956.

———. *11th Armored Cavalry, Germany, 1958.* Germany: 1958.

UNITED STATES ARMY IN WORLD WAR II

Blumenson, Martin. *Breakout and Pursuit.* 1961.

12th CAVALRY

HERALDIC ITEMS

COAT OF ARMS

Shield: Or, a cactus vert.

Crest: On a wreath or and vert, in front of a wreath of palm branches proper and superimposed upon a Melanesian war club and a kampilan in saltire gules, a sun in splendor of eight rays of the first, in chief issuant from a bar wavy azure a Japanese torii of the forth enclosing a horseshoe sable nailed of the first.

Motto: *Semper Paratus* (Always Ready).

Symbolism: The regiment was organized at Fort Sam Houston, Texas, in 1901, and spent its first two years at that post. The cactus shows the birthplace of the regiment as well as its service on the Mexican border.

The palm branches represent two Presidential Unit Citations awarded for action on Leyte. The sun, adapted from the arms of the Philippines, denotes an award of the Philippine Presidential Unit Citation. The kampilan, a weapon of the Moros, is for early tours of duty during the Philippine Insurrection. The war club represents service in New Guinea and the Bismarck Archipelago. The unit's claim that one of its enlisted men was among the first to enter Tokyo is noted by the horseshoe (suggesting cavalry) within the Japanese torii, or temple gateway.

DISTINCTIVE INSIGNIA

The distinctive insignia is the shield and motto of the coat of arms.

LINEAGE AND HONORS

LINEAGE

Constituted 2 February 1901 in the Regular Army as 12th Cavalry. Organized 8 February 1901 at Fort Sam Houston, Texas. Assigned to 2d Cavalry Division 24 March 1923–3 January 1933. Assigned 3 January 1933 to 1st Cavalry Division. Dismounted 28 February 1943 and reorganized 4 December 1943 partly under cavalry and partly under infantry tables of organization and

215

equipment. Reorganized wholly as infantry 20 July 1945 but retained cavalry designations. Inactivated 25 March 1949 at Otawa, Japan, and relieved from assignment to 1st Cavalry Division.

Reorganized 15 February 1957 as a parent regiment under the Combat Arms Regimental System.

CAMPAIGN PARTICIPATION CREDIT

World War II	*Vietnam*
New Guinea	Defense
Bismarck Archipelago	Counteroffensive
Leyte (with arrowhead)	Counteroffensive, Phase II
Luzon	Counteroffensive, Phase III
	Tet Counteroffensive

DECORATIONS

Presidential Unit Citation (Army), Streamer embroidered ORMOC VALLEY, LEYTE (Headquarters and Headquarters Troop, 12th Cavalry, cited; WD GO 108, 1946)

Presidential Unit Citation (Army), Streamer embroidered CENTRAL RANGE, LEYTE (1st Squadron, reinforced, cited; WD GO 110, 1946)

Presidential Unit Citation (Army), Streamer embroidered PLEIKU PROVINCE (1st and 2d Battalions cited; DA GO 40, 1967)

Philippine Presidential Unit Citation, Streamer embroidered 17 OCTOBER 1944 TO 4 JULY 1945 (12th Cavalry cited; DA GO 47, 1950)

1st BATTALION, 12th CAVALRY

RA

(1st Cavalry Division)

LINEAGE

Constituted 2 February 1901 in the Regular Army as Troop A, 12th Cavalry. Organized 25 March 1901 at Fort Sam Houston, Texas. (12th Cavalry assigned to 2d Cavalry Division 24 March 1923–3 January 1933; assigned 3 January 1933 to 1st Cavalry Division. Dismounted 28 February 1943 and reorganized 4 December 1943 partly under cavalry and partly under infantry tables of organization and equipment. Reorganized wholly as infantry 20 July 1945 but retained cavalry designations.) Inactivated 25 March 1949 in Japan (12th Cavalry concurrently relieved from assignment to 1st Cavalry Division).

Redesignated 15 February 1957 as Headquarters and Headquarters Troop, 1st Reconnaissance Squadron, 12th Cavalry, assigned to 1st Armored Division, and activated at Fort Polk, Louisiana; concurrently, consolidated with Headquarters and Headquarters and Service Company, 81st Reconnaissance Battalion (see ANNEX) (Companies A, B, C, and D, 81st Reconnaissance Battalion; concurrently, redesignated as Troops A, B, C, and D, 1st Reconnaissance Squadron, 12th Cavalry). Headquarters and Headquarters Troop, 1st Reconnaissance Squadron, 12th Cavalry, reorganized and redesignated 20 April 1959 as Troop A, 12th Cavalry (Troops A and B, 1st Reconnaissance Squadron, 12th Cavalry, concurrently inactivated; Troops C and D, 1st Reconnaissance Squadron, 12th Cavalry, inactivated 23 December 1957). Inactivated 3 February 1962 at Fort Hood, Texas, and relieved from assignment to 1st Armored Division.

Redesignated 15 July 1963 as Headquarters and Headquarters Company, 1st Battalion, 12th Cavalry, and assigned to 1st Cavalry Division (Troops A, B, and C, 1st Reconnaissance Squadron, 12th Cavalry, concurrently, redesignated as Companies A, B, and C, 1st Battalion, 12th Cavalry). Activated 1 September 1963 in Korea. Transferred (less personnel and equipment) 1 July 1965 from Korea to Fort Benning, Georgia, and reorganized.

ANNEX

7th Reconnaissance and Support Squadron (Mechanized) constituted 22 April 1940 in the Regular Army. Activated 1 June 1940 at Fort Knox,

314-902 O - 69 - 16

Kentucky. Reorganized and redesignated 15 July 1940 as 1st Reconnaissance Battalion (Armored) and assigned to 1st Armored Division. Redesignated 8 May 1941 as 81st Reconnaissance Battalion (Armored). Redesignated 1 January 1942 as 81st Armored Reconnaissance Battalion. Reorganized and redesignated 20 July 1944 as 81st Cavalry Reconnaissance Squadron, Mechanized.

Converted and redesignated 1 May 1946 as 81st Constabulary Squadron; concurrently, relieved from assignment to 1st Armored Division and assigned to 3d Constabulary Regiment. Inactivated 20 September 1947 in Germany and relieved from assignment to 3d Constabulary Regiment. Converted and redesignated 27 February 1951 as 81st Reconnaissance Battalion and assigned to 1st Armored Division. Activated 7 March 1951 at Fort Hood, Texas.

CAMPAIGN PARTICIPATION CREDIT

World War II
  *New Guinea
  *Bismarck Archipelago
    (with arrowhead)
  *Leyte (with arrowhead)
  *Luzon
  *Tunisia
  *Naples-Foggia
  *Anzio
  *Rome-Arno

  *North Apennines
  *Po Valley

Vietnam
  *Defense
  *Counteroffensive
  *Counteroffensive, Phase II
  *Counteroffensive, Phase III
  *Tet Counteroffensive

DECORATIONS

Presidential Unit Citation (Army), Streamer embroidered ORMOC VALLEY, LEYTE

*Presidential Unit Citation (Army), Streamer embroidered CENTRAL RANGE, LEYTE (1st Squadron, reinforced, cited; WD GO 110, 1946)

*Presidential Unit Citation (Army), Streamer embroidered PLEIKU PROVINCE (1st Battalion cited; DA GO 40, 1967)

*Philippine Presidential Unit Citation, Streamer embroidered 17 OCTOBER 1944 TO 4 JULY 1945 (12th Cavalry cited; DA GO 47, 1950)

*French Croix de Guerre with Palm, World War II, Streamer embroidered CENTRAL ITALY (81st Cavalry Reconnaissance Squadron cited; DA GO 43, 1950)

2d BATTALION, 12th CAVALRY

RA

(1st Cavalry Division)

LINEAGE

Constituted 2 February 1901 in the Regular Army as Troop B, 12th Cavalry. Organized 17 April 1901 at Fort Sam Houston, Texas. (12th Cavalry assigned to 2d Cavalry Division 24 March 1923–3 January 1933; assigned to 1st Cavalry Division 3 January 1933. Dismounted 28 February 1943 and reorganized 4 December 1943 partly under cavalry and partly under infantry tables of organization and equipment. Reorganized wholly as infantry 20 July 1945 but retained cavalry designations.) Inactivated 25 March 1949 in Japan (12th Cavalry concurrently relieved from assignment to 1st Cavalry Division).

Redesignated 15 February 1957 as Headquarters and Headquarters Company, 2d Battle Group, 12th Cavalry. Assigned 15 October 1957 to 1st Cavalry Division (organic elements concurrently constituted). Activated 15 November 1957 in Korea. Inactivated 1 September 1963 in Korea and relieved from assignment to 1st Cavalry Division. Redesignated 1 July 1965 as 2d Battalion, 12th Cavalry; concurrently, assigned to 1st Cavalry Division and activated at Fort Benning, Georgia.

CAMPAIGN PARTICIPATION CREDIT

World War II
*New Guinea
*Bismarck Archipelago
  (with arrowhead)
*Leyte (with arrowhead)
*Luzon

Vietnam
*Defense
*Counteroffensive
*Counteroffensive, Phase II
*Counteroffensive, Phase III
*Tet Counteroffensive

DECORATIONS

Presidential Unit Citation (Army), Streamer embroidered ORMOC VALLEY, LEYTE

*Presidential Unit Citation (Army), Streamer embroidered CENTRAL RANGE, LEYTE (1st Squadron, 12th Cavalry, reinforced, cited; WD GO 110, 1946)

*Presidential Unit Citation (Army), Streamer embroidered PLEIKU PROVINCE (2d Battalion cited; DA GO 40, 1967)

*Philippine Presidential Unit Citation, Streamer embroidered 17 OCTOBER 1944 TO 4 JULY 1945 (12th Cavalry cited; DA GO 47, 1950)

219

3d SQUADRON, 12th CAVALRY

RA

(3d Armored Division)

LINEAGE

Constituted 2 February 1901 in the Regular Army as Troop C, 12th Cavalry. Organized 22 April 1901 at Fort Sam Houston, Texas. (12th Cavalry assigned to 2d Cavalry Division 24 March 1923–3 January 1933.) Disbanded 1 February 1928 at Fort Brown, Texas.

Reconstituted 22 March 1940 and activated 1 August 1940 at Fort Brown, Texas, as an element of the 1st Cavalry Division. Dismounted 28 February 1943 and reorganized 4 December 1943 partly under cavalry and partly under infantry tables of organization and equipment. Reorganized wholly as infantry 20 July 1945 but retained cavalry designations. Inactivated 25 March 1949 in Japan (12th Cavalry concurrently relieved from assignment to 1st Cavalry Division).

Redesignated 15 February 1957 as Headquarters and Headquarters Troop, 3d Reconnaissance Squadron, 12th Cavalry. Activated 1 October 1957 in Germany and assigned to 3d Armored Division; concurrently, consolidated with Headquarters and Headquarters and Service Company, 83d Reconnaissance Battalion (see ANNEX). (Companies A, B, and C, 83d Reconnaissance Battalion, concurrently, redesignated as Troops A, B, and C, 3d Reconnaissance Squadron, 12th Cavalry; Troop D constituted and activated.) Reorganized and redesignated 1 September 1963 as 3d Squadron, 12th Cavalry.

ANNEX

3d Reconnaissance Battalion (Armored) constituted 16 January 1941 in the Regular Army and assigned to 3d Armored Division. Activated 15 April 1941 at Camp Polk, Louisiana. Redesignated 8 May 1941 as 83d Reconnaissance Battalion (Armored). Redesignated 1 January 1942 as 83d Armored Reconnaissance Battalion. Inactivated 10 November 1945 in Germany. Reorganized and redesignated 7 July 1947 as 83d Mechanized Cavalry Reconnaissance Squadron. Activated 15 July 1947 at Fort Knox, Kentucky. Reorganized and redesignated 30 July 1948 as 83d Reconnaissance Battalion.

220

CAMPAIGN PARTICIPATION CREDIT

World War II
  *New Guinea
  *Bismarck Archipelago
    (with arrowhead)
  *Leyte (with arrowhead)
  *Luzon

*Normandy
*Northern France
*Rhineland
*Ardennes-Alsace
*Central Europe

DECORATIONS

Presidential Unit Citation (Army), Streamer embroidered ORMOC VALLEY, LEYTE

*Presidential Unit Citation (Army), Streamer embroidered CENTRAL RANGE, LEYTE (1st Squadron, reinforced, cited; WD GO 110, 1946)

*Philippine Presidential Unit Citation, Streamer embroidered 17 OCTOBER 1944 TO 4 JULY 1945 (12th Cavalry cited; DA GO 47, 1950)

*French Croix de Guerre with Silver Star, World War II, Streamer embroidered ARDENNES (83d Armored Reconnaissance Battalion cited; DA GO 43, 1950)

*Belgian Fourragère 1940 (83d Armored Reconnaissance Battalion cited; DA GO 43, 1950)

*Cited in the Order of the Day of the Belgian Army for action in BELGIUM

*Cited in the Order of the Day of the Belgian Army for action in the ARDENNES

4th SQUADRON, 12th CAVALRY

LINEAGE

Constituted 2 February 1901 in the Regular Army as Troop D, 12th Cavalry. Organized 24 April 1901 at Fort Sam Houston, Texas. Redesignated 20 August 1921 as Headquarters Detachment, 6th Machine Gun Squadron. Demobilized 30 April 1924 at Fort Brown, Texas.

Reconstituted 16 November 1943 in the Regular Army and redesignated as Troop B, 12th Cavalry, an element of the 1st Cavalry Division. Activated 4 December 1943 at Brisbane, Australia. (12th Cavalry concurrently reorganized partly under cavalry and partly under infantry tables of organization and equipment. Reorganized wholly as infantry 20 July 1945 but retained cavalry designations.) Inactivated 25 March 1949 at Otawa, Japan. (12th Cavalry concurrently relieved from assignment to 1st Cavalry Division.)

Redesignated 15 February 1957 as Headquarters and Headquarters Troop, 4th Reconnaissance Squadron, 12th Cavalry. Redesignated 15 February 1962 as Headquarters and Headquarters Troop, 4th Squadron, 12th Cavalry; concurrently, assigned to 5th Infantry Division and activated at Fort Knox, Kentucky (organic elements concurrently constituted and activated).

CAMPAIGN PARTICIPATION CREDIT

World War II
  *New Guinea
  *Bismarck Archipelago
    (with arrowhead)

*Leyte (with arrowhead)
*Luzon

DECORATIONS

Presidential Unit Citation (Army), Streamer embroidered ORMOC VALLEY, LEYTE

*Presidential Unit Citation (Army), Streamer embroidered CENTRAL RANGE, LEYTE (1st Squadron, reinforced, cited; WD GO 110, 1946)

*Philippine Presidential Unit Citation, Streamer embroidered 17 OCTOBER 1944 to 4 July 1945 (12th Cavalry cited; DA GO 47, 1950)

5th SQUADRON, 12th CAVALRY

AR
(inactive)

LINEAGE

Constituted 2 February 1901 in the Regular Army as Troop E, 12th Cavalry. Organized 4 May 1901 at Fort Sam Houston, Texas. (12th Cavalry assigned to 2d Cavalry Division 24 March 1923–3 January 1933; assigned 3 January 1933 to 1st Cavalry Division. Dismounted 28 February 1943 and reorganized 4 December 1943 partly under cavalry and partly under infantry tables of organization and equipment. Reorganized wholly as infantry 20 July 1945 but retained cavalry designations.) Inactivated 25 March 1949 in Japan. (12th Cavalry concurrently relieved from assignment to 1st Cavalry Division.)

Redesignated 15 February 1957 as Headquarters and Headquarters Troop, 5th Reconnaissance Squadron, 12th Cavalry. Redesignated 15 March 1963 as Headquarters and Headquarters Troop, 5th Squadron, 12th Cavalry, and activated with Headquarters at San Antonio, Texas; concurrently, withdrawn from the Regular Army, allotted to the Army Reserve, and assigned to 90th Infantry Division (organic elements concurrently constituted and activated). Inactivated 31 December 1965 at San Antonio, Texas, and relieved from assignment to the 90th Infantry Division.

CAMPAIGN PARTICIPATION CREDIT

World War II
  *New Guinea
  *Bismarck Archipelago
    (with arrowhead)

*Leyte (with arrowhead)
*Luzon

DECORATIONS

Presidential Unit Citation (Army), Streamer embroidered ORMOC VALLEY, LEYTE

Presidential Unit Citation (Army), Streamer embroidered CENTRAL RANGE, LEYTE

*Philippine Presidential Unit Citation, Streamer embroidered 17 OCTOBER 1944 TO 4 JULY 1945 (12th Cavalry cited; DA GO 47, 1950)

Bibliography, 12th Cavalry

Cavalry School, U.S. Army. *Operations of the 81st Armored Reconnaissance Battalion in Tunisia*. Fort Riley, Kansas: 1944.

Department of the Army. AMERICAN FORCES IN ACTION series.

The Admiralties: Operations of the 1st Cavalry Division. Washington: 1945.

Herr, John K., and Edward S. Wallace. *The Story of the U.S. Cavalry*. Boston: 1953.

Schweitzer, C. L., editor. *12th U.S. Cavalry, Fort Bliss, Texas, 1941*. Los Angeles: 1941.

Unit Members. *Occupation Diary, First Cavalry Division 1945–1950*.

UNITED STATES ARMY IN WORLD WAR II

Cannon, M. Hamlin. *Leyte: The Return to the Philippines*. 1954.

Miller, John, jr. *CARTWHEEL: The Reduction of Rabaul*. 1959.

Smith, Robert R. *Triumph in the Philippines*. 1963.

Wright, B. C., comp. *The 1st Cavalry Division in World War II*. Japan: 1947.

13th ARMOR

(13th Horse)

HERALDIC ITEMS

BADGE

Description: Two cavalry sabres in saltire proper, overall a sun in splendor or charged with the numeral *13* sable. On a scroll or suspended from the hilts of the sabres the motto *It Shall Be Done* sable. All within a wreath of cactus on dexter side, palm on sinister side, proper.

Symbolism: The regiment was organized in 1901 at Fort Meade, South Dakota, and has served in the Philippines and along the Mexican border. The sun in splendor is taken from the flag of South Dakota; the wreath shows the Philippine and border service.

On the organizational flag the scroll of the regimental badge is omitted and the motto is placed on the scroll in the eagle's beak. This badge is in lieu of a coat of arms.

DISTINCTIVE INSIGNIA

The distinctive insignia is the regimental badge.

LINEAGE AND HONORS

LINEAGE

Constituted 2 February 1901 in the Regular Army as 13th Cavalry. Organized 1 May 1901 at Fort Meade, South Dakota. Assigned to 2d Cavalry Division 1 March 1933–18 August 1936. Reorganized and redesignated 16 September 1936 as 13th Cavalry, Mechanized. Reorganized and redesignated 15 July 1940 as 13th Armored Regiment and assigned to 1st Armored Division.

Regiment broken up 20 July 1944, and its elements reorganized and redesignated as elements of the 1st Armored Division as follows: Headquarters and Headquarters Company, Service Company, and Companies D, E, and F as 13th Tank Battalion; 3d Battalion and Maintenance Company as 4th Tank Battalion; Reconnaissance Company as Troop D, 81st Cavalry Reconnaissance

Squadron, Mechanized; Headquarters and Headquarters Companies, 1st and 2d Battalions, and Companies A, B, and C disbanded.

13th Tank Battalion converted and redesignated 1 May 1946 as 13th Constabulary Squadron; concurrently, relieved from assignment to 1st Armored Division and assigned to 10th Constabulary Regiment. Inactivated 20 September 1947 at Coburg, Germany, and relieved from assignment to 10th Constabulary Regiment. Converted and redesignated 27 February 1951 as 13th Medium Tank Battalion and assigned to 1st Armored Division. Activated 7 March 1951 at Fort Hood, Texas. Reorganized and redesignated 20 May 1953 as 13th Tank Battalion. Inactivated (less Company A) 15 February 1957 at Fort Polk, Louisiana (concurrently, Company A reorganized and redesignated as Headquarters and Headquarters Company, 1st Medium Tank Battalion, 13th Cavalry).

4th Tank Battalion converted and redesignated 1 May 1946 as 72d Constabulary Squadron; concurrently, relieved from assignment to 1st Armored Division and assigned to 10th Constabulary Regiment. Inactivated 20 September 1947 at Boblingen, Germany, and relieved from assignment to 10th Constabulary Regiment. Converted and redesignated 27 February 1951 as 4th Medium Tank Battalion and assigned to 1st Armored Division. Activated 7 March 1951 at Fort Hood, Texas. Reorganized and redesignated 20 May 1953 as 4th Tank Battalion. Inactivated 15 February 1957 at Fort Polk, Louisiana.

Troop D, 81st Cavalry Reconnaissance Squadron, Mechanized, reorganized and redesignated 1 May 1946 as Troop D, 81st Constabulary Squadron; concurrently, relieved from assignment to 1st Armored Division and assigned to 3d Constabulary Regiment. Inactivated 20 September 1947 in Germany, and relieved from assignment to 3d Constabulary Regiment. Redesignated 27 February 1951 as Company D, 81st Reconnaissance Battalion, and assigned to 1st Armored Division. Activated 7 March 1951 at Fort Hood, Texas. Inactivated 15 February 1957 at Fort Polk, Louisiana.

Headquarters and Headquarters Companies, 1st and 2d Battalions, and Companies A, B, and C, 13th Armored Regiment, reconstituted 15 February 1957 in the Regular Army.

13th and 4th Tank Battalions, Company D, 81st Reconnaissance Battalion, and reconstituted elements of the 13th Armored Regiment consolidated, reorganized, and redesignated 15 February 1957 as 13th Cavalry, a parent regiment under the Combat Arms Regimental System; 13th and 4th Tank Battalions and Company D, 81st Reconnaissance Battalion, concurrently relieved from assignment to 1st Armored Division (Headquarters, 13th Tank Battalion concurrently redesignated as Headquarters, 13th Cavalry). Reorganized and redesignated 3 February 1962 as 13th Armor.

CAMPAIGN PARTICIPATION CREDIT

Mexican Expedition
    Mexico 1916–1917

World War II
    Algeria-French Morocco
      (with arrowhead)

Tunisia
Naples-Foggia
Anzio
Rome-Arno
North Apennines
Po Valley

DECORATIONS

None.

1st BATTALION, 13th ARMOR

(13th Horse)

RA
(1st Armored Division)

LINEAGE

Constituted 2 February 1901 in the Regular Army as Troop K, 13th Cavalry. Organized 26 July 1901 at Fort Meade, South Dakota. Demobilized 3 September 1921 at Fort Clark, Texas. Reconstituted 15 July 1940 in the Regular Army and redesignated as Company D, 13th Armored Regiment, an element of the 1st Armored Division. Reorganized and redesignated 20 July 1944 as Company A, 13th Tank Battalion.

Converted and redesignated 1 May 1946 as Troop A, 13th Constabulary Squadron, an element of the 10th Constabulary Regiment. Inactivated 20 September 1947 in Germany (13th Constabulary Squadron concurrently relieved from assignment to 10th Constabulary Regiment). Converted and redesignated 27 February 1951 as Company A, 13th Medium Tank Battalion, an element of the 1st Armored Division. Activated 7 March 1951 at Fort Hood, Texas. Redesignated 20 May 1953 as Company A, 13th Tank Battalion.

Reorganized and redesignated 15 February 1957 as Headquarters and Headquarters Company, 1st Medium Tank Battalion (Patton), 13th Cavalry; remained assigned to 1st Armored Division (organic elements concurrently constituted and activated). Reorganized and redesignated 3 February 1962 as 1st Battalion, 13th Armor.

CAMPAIGN PARTICIPATION CREDIT

Mexican Expedition
  *Mexico 1916–1917

World War II
  *Algeria-French Morocco
    (with arrowhead)

*Tunisia
*Naples-Foggia
*Anzio
*Rome-Arno
*North Apennines
*Po Valley

DECORATIONS

None.

228

2d BATTALION, 13th ARMOR

(13th Horse)

RA

(1st Armored Division)

LINEAGE

Constituted 2 February 1901 in the Regular Army as Troop B, 13th Cavalry. Organized 14 May 1901 at Fort Meade, South Dakota. Redesignated 23 June 1901 as Troop E, 13th Cavalry. (13th Cavalry assigned to 2d Cavalry Division 1 March 1933–18 August 1936.) Reorganized and redesignated 16 September 1936 as Troop E, 13th Cavalry, Mechanized. Redesignated 15 July 1940 as Company E, 13th Armored Regiment, an element of the 1st Armored Division. Reorganized and redesignated 20 July 1944 as Company B, 13th Tank Battalion, an element of the 1st Armored Division.

Converted and redesignated 1 May 1946 as Troop B, 13th Constabulary Squadron, an element of the 10th Constabulary Regiment. Inactivated 20 September 1947 in Germany (13th Constabulary Squadron concurrently relieved from assignment to 10th Constabulary Regiment). Converted and redesignated 27 February 1951 as Company B, 13th Medium Tank Battalion, an element of the 1st Armored Division. Activated 7 March 1951 at Fort Hood, Texas. Redesignated 20 May 1953 as Company B, 13th Tank Battalion.

Inactivated 15 February 1957 at Fort Polk, Louisiana, and relieved from assignment to 1st Armored Division; concurrently, redesignated as Headquarters and Headquarters Company, 2d Medium Tank Battalion (Patton), 13th Cavalry.

Activated 1 October 1957 in Europe and assigned to 3d Armored Division (organic elements concurrently constituted and activated). Reorganized and redesignated 3 February 1962 as 2d Battalion, 13th Armor; concurrently, relieved from assignment to 3d Armored Division, transferred (less personnel and equipment) from United States Army, Europe, to Fort Hood, Texas, and assigned to 1st Armored Division.

229

Campaign Participation Credit

Mexican Expedition
   *Mexico 1916–1917

World War II
   *Algeria-French Morocco
      (with arrowhead)

*Tunisia
*Naples-Foggia
*Anzio
*Rome-Arno
*North Apennines
*Po Valley

Decorations

None.

BIBLIOGRAPHY, 13TH ARMOR

Abbott, H. P. *The Nazi "88" Made Believers.* Dayton, Ohio: 1946.

Department of the Army. AMERICAN FORCES IN ACTION series. *To Bizerte With the II Corps.* 1943.

Anzio Beachhead. 1947.

Embse, Charles B. V., with B. Smith. "Yank in a Tank," *American Magazine* (September, 1943).

Gardiner, Henry E. "We Fought at Kasserine," *Armored Cavalry Journal* (March–April, 1948).

Herr, John K., and Edward S. Wallace. *The Story of the U.S. Cavalry.* Boston: 1953.

History of the 13th Tank Battalion. Fort Hood, Texas: 1962.

Howe, George F. *The Battle History of the 1st Armored Division.* Washington: 1954.

19 Days From the Apennines to the Alps. Italy: 1945.

Painton, Frederick C. "Here Comes Gabriel; Fighting with a Yank Tank Crew," *Collier's* (17 July 1943).

"The Attack on our Cavalry at Parral," *Journal of the U.S. Cavalry Association* (November, 1916).

"The Cavalry Fight at Columbus," *Journal of the U.S. Cavalry Association* (November, 1916).

"The Columbus Raiders," *Journal of the U.S. Cavalry Association* (April, 1917).

Unit Members. *Historical and Pictorial Reviews, First Armored Division of the United States Army, Fort Knox, Kentucky.* Baton Rouge, Louisiana: 1941.

UNITED STATES ARMY IN WORLD WAR II

   Howe, George F. *Northwest Africa: Seizing the Initiative in the West.* 1957.

14th ARMORED CAVALRY

HERALDIC ITEMS

COAT OF ARMS

Shield: Or, a bend azure between a Moro kris paleways point up sable, and a rattlesnake coiled to strike proper.

Crest: On a wreath of the colors a dexter arm embowed habited azure, the hand gloved in a buckskin gauntlet proper, grasping a staff erect sable barbed or, therefrom a standard flotant of the last charged with a horseshoe heels upward encircling the Arabic numeral *14* in black.

Motto: *Suivez Moi* (Follow Me).

Symbolism: The shield is yellow for cavalry; the bend is in the color of the uniform worn at the time of the regiment's formation (1901). The kris is for Moro campaigns and the rattlesnake for service on the Mexican border.

DISTINCTIVE INSIGNIA

The distinctive insignia is the shield and motto of the coat of arms.

LINEAGE AND HONORS

LINEAGE

Constituted 2 February 1901 in the Regular Army as 14th Cavalry. Organized 19 February 1901 at Fort Leavenworth, Kansas. Inactivated 15 July 1942 at Fort Riley, Kansas; personnel and equipment transferred to 14th Armored Regiment (see ANNEX).

Headquarters, Headquarters Troop, and Service Troop, 14th Cavalry, reorganized and redesignated 12 July 1943 as Headquarters and Headquarters Troop, 14th Cavalry Group, and activated at Fort Lewis, Washington. Reorganized and redesignated 21 December 1943 as Headquarters and Headquarters Troop, 14th Cavalry Group, Mechanized. Remainder of 14th Cavalry disbanded 26 October 1944.

Headquarters and Headquarters Troop, 14th Cavalry Group, Mechanized, converted and redesignated 1 May 1946 as Headquarters and Headquarters

Troop, 14th Constabulary Regiment, and assigned to the United States Constabulary. Reorganized and redesignated 10 February 1948 as Headquarters and Headquarters and Service Troop, 14th Constabulary Regiment. Converted and redesignated 20 December 1948 as Headquarters and Headquarters Company, 14th Armored Cavalry; disbanded elements of 14th Cavalry concurrently reconstituted, redesignated as elements of 14th Armored Cavalry, and activated in Europe. 14th Armored Cavalry consolidated 8 January 1951 with 14th and 711th Tank Battalions (see ANNEX). (Battalions and companies redesignated 15 May 1960 as squadrons and troops.)

ANNEX

14th Armored Regiment constituted 11 July 1942 in the Regular Army and assigned to 9th Armored Division. Activated 15 July 1942 at Fort Riley, Kansas, with personnel and equipment from 14th Cavalry.

Regiment broken up 9 October 1943 and its elements reorganized and redesignated as follows: 14th Armored Regiment (less 3d Battalion, Band, and Maintenance, Service, and Reconnaissance Companies) as 14th Tank Battalion, and remained assigned to 9th Armored Division; 3d Battalion as 711th Tank Battalion, and relieved from assignment to 9th Armored Division; Reconnaissance Company as Troop E, 89th Cavalry Reconnaissance Squadron, Mechanized (separate lineage); Band and Maintenance and Service Companies disbanded.

14th Tank Battalion inactivated 13 October 1945 at Camp Patrick Henry, Virginia. Consolidated 8 January 1951 with 14th Armored Cavalry and relieved from assignment to 9th Armored Division.

711th Tank Battalion inactivated 21 January 1946 at Seattle Port of Embarkation, Washington. Consolidated 8 January 1951 with 3d Battalion, 14th Armored Cavalry.

CAMPAIGN PARTICIPATION CREDIT

Philippine Insurrection	*World War II*
Mindanao	Rhineland
Jolo	Ardennes-Alsace
	Central Europe
	Ryukyus
	Leyte

DECORATIONS

Presidential Unit Citation (Army), Streamer embroidered REMAGEN BRIDGE (14th Tank Battalion cited; WD GO 72, 1945)

Cited in the Order of the Day of the Belgian Army for action in the ARDENNES (14th Tank Battalion cited; DA GO 43, 1950)

Bibliography, 14th Armored Cavalry

Hechler, Kenneth Williams. *The Bridge at Remagen.* New York: 1957.

Unit Members. *14th Armored Cavalry 1901–1955.* Germany: 1956.

————. *14th Armored Cavalry Regiment 1901–1952.* Atlanta, Georgia: 1952.

————. *Historical and Pictorial Review 14th Cavalry . . . Camp Funston, Kansas, 1941.* Baton Rouge, Louisiana: 1941.

————. *Regimental Day, March 5, 1932 . . . Fourteenth Regiment of U.S. Cavalry.* Fort Des Moines, Iowa: 1932.

————. *The Bridge.* Bayreuth, Germany: 1945.

————. *The 14th Cavalry Group, Mechanized, in the European Theater of Operations.* N.p.: 1945.

UNITED STATES ARMY IN WORLD WAR II

Appleman, Roy E., *et al. Okinawa: The Last Battle.* 1948.

Cole, Hugh M. *The Ardennes: Battle of the Bulge.* 1965.

15th ARMOR

Heraldic Items

Coat of Arms

Shield: Per fess gules and argent in chief a lion passant or and in base a kris and kampilan saltirewise of the first hilted sable.

Crest: On a wreath of the colors a setting sun behind the Golden Gate all proper.

Motto: *Tous Pour Un, Un Pour Tous* (All for One, One for All).

Symbolism: The red and white divided shield represents the old cavalry guidon. Hard fighting in the Philippines is indicated by the crossed kris and kampilan of the Moro and Lake Lanao campaigns. In World War I the regiment was in France in the vicinity of Bordeaux, and the golden lion is taken from the arms of that city.

The birthplace of the regiment is indicated by the crest. The Golden Gate as used here portrays "through the portals of the past." It was one of the few structures left standing after the fire of 1906 and was removed and re-erected in Golden Gate Park, San Francisco. The translation of the motto *All for One, One for All* is indicative of the spirit of the regiment.

Distinctive Insignia

The distinctive insignia is the shield and motto of the coat of arms.

Lineage and Honors

Lineage

Constituted 2 February 1901 in the Regular Army as 15th Cavalry. Organized 12 February 1901 at Presidio of San Francisco, California. Assigned to 15th Cavalry Division December 1917–11 May 1918. Inactivated 18 October 1921 at Fort D. A. Russell, Wyoming. Activated 22 March 1942 at Fort Riley, Kansas, and redesignated as 15th Cavalry, Mechanized.

Regiment broken up 12 March 1944 and its elements reorganized and redesignated as Headquarters and Headquarters Troop, 15th Cavalry Group,

235

Mechanized, and 15th and 17th Cavalry Reconnaissance Squadrons, Mechanized.

Headquarters and Headquarters Troop, 15th Cavalry Group, Mechanized, converted and redesignated 1 May 1946 as Headquarters and Headquarters Troop, 15th Constabulary Regiment, and assigned to the United States Constabulary. Reorganized and redesignated 2 February 1948 as Headquarters and Headquarters and Service Troop, 15th Constabulary Regiment. Inactivated 20 December 1948 at Fussen, Germany, and relieved from assignment to the United States Constabulary. Redesignated 23 October 1950 as Headquarters and Headquarters Company, 15th Armored Cavalry Group. Activated 15 November 1950 at Camp Polk, Louisiana. Redesignated 25 September 1953 as Headquarters and Headquarters Company, 15th Armor Group. Inactivated 1 December 1955 at Fort Knox, Kentucky.

15th Cavalry Reconnaissance Squadron, Mechanized (less Troop E) converted and redesignated 1 May 1946 as 15th Constabulary Squadron and assigned to 15th Constabulary Regiment. Inactivated 20 December 1948 at Fussen, Germany, and relieved from assignment to 15th Constabulary Regiment. Activated 20 May 1949 at Weiden, Germany, and assigned to the United States Constabulary. Inactivated 15 December 1952 at Weiden, Germany, and relieved from assignment to the United States Constabulary. Redesignated 13 August 1954 as 15th Reconnaissance Battalion.

Troop E, 15th Cavalry Reconnaissance Squadron, Mechanized, converted and redesignated 1 May 1946 as Light Tank Troop, 15th Constabulary Regiment. Inactivated 28 February 1947 in Germany. Disbanded 25 February 1953. Reconstituted and redesignated 14 August 1954 as Troop L, 15th Cavalry.

17th Cavalry Reconnaissance Squadron, Mechanized, inactivated 20 January 1947 in Germany. Squadron (less Company F) redesignated 1 September 1948 as 501st Reconnaissance Battalion. Activated 25 September 1948 at Fort Sill, Oklahoma. Inactivated 25 January 1949 at Fort Sill, Oklahoma.

Company F, 17th Cavalry Reconnaissance Squadron, Mechanized, redesignated 1 September 1948 as 550th Light Tank Company. Redesignated 19 March 1951 as 550th Tank Company. Activated 6 April 1951 at Fort Benning, Georgia. Inactivated 25 June 1958 at Fort Campbell, Kentucky. Redesignated 1 October 1958 as Troop F, 15th Cavalry.

Headquarters and Headquarters Company, 15th Armor Group; 15th and 501st Reconnaissance Battalions; and Troops F and L, 15th Cavalry, consolidated and redesignated 1 April 1957–1 May 1959 as elements of the 15th Cavalry, a parent regiment under the Combat Arms Regimental System (Headquarters and Headquarters Company, 15th Armor Group, redesignated 1 May 1959 as Headquarters and Headquarters Troop, 15th Cavalry). Redesignated 1 July 1963 as 15th Armor.

Campaign Participation Credit

Philippine Insurrection
Mindanao
Luzon 1902

World War I
Without inscription

World War II
Normandy
Northern France
Rhineland
Central Europe

Decorations

None.

1st BATTALION, 15th ARMOR

LINEAGE

Constituted 2 February 1901 in the Regular Army as Troop A, 15th Cavalry. Organized 1 March 1901 at Presidio of San Francisco, California. Inactivated 18 October 1921 at Fort D. A. Russell, Wyoming. Activated 22 March 1942 at Fort Riley, Kansas, and redesignated as Troop A, 15th Cavalry, Mechanized.

Reorganized and redesignated 12 March 1944 as Troop A, 15th Cavalry Reconnaissance Squadron, Mechanized. Converted and redesignated 1 May 1946 as Troop A, 15th Constabulary Squadron. Inactivated 20 December 1948 at Fussen, Germany. Activated 20 May 1949 at Weiden, Germany. Inactivated 15 December 1952 at Weiden, Germany. Redesignated 13 August 1954 as Company A, 15th Reconnaissance Battalion.

Redesignated 1 July 1957 as Headquarters and Headquarters Troop, 1st Reconnaissance Squadron, 15th Cavalry; concurrently, consolidated with Headquarters and Headquarters and Service Troop, 82d Reconnaissance Battalion (see ANNEX), assigned to 2d Armored Division, and activated in Germany (concurrently, Companies A, B, and C, 82d Reconnaissance Battalion, redesignated as Troops A, B, and C, 1st Reconnaissance Squadron, 15th Cavalry. Troop D, 1st Reconnaissance Squadron, 15th Cavalry, concurrently constituted and activated). Redesignated 1 July 1963 as 1st Battalion, 15th Armor; concurrently, relieved from assignment to 2d Armored Division, transferred (less personnel and equipment) from Fort Hood, Texas, to Korea, assigned to 1st Cavalry Division and reorganized. Transferred (less personnel and equipment) 1 July 1965 from Korea to Fort Benning, Georgia; concurrently, inactivated at Fort Benning, Georgia, and relieved from assignment to 1st Cavalry Division.

ANNEX

2d Reconnaissance Battalion (Armored) constituted 15 July 1940 in the Regular Army, assigned to 2d Armored Division and activated at Fort Benning, Georgia. Redesignated 8 May 1941 as 82d Reconnaissance Battalion (Armored). Redesignated 1 January 1942 as 82d Armored Reconnaissance Battalion. Converted and redesignated 25 March 1946 as 82d Cavalry Reconnaissance Squadron, Mechanized. Redesignated 17 January 1949 as 82d Reconnaissance Battalion.

238

CAMPAIGN PARTICIPATION CREDIT

Philippine Insurrection
  *Mindanao
  *Luzon 1902

World War I
  *Without inscription

World War II
  *Algeria-French Morocco
    (with arrowhead)
  *Sicily (with arrowhead)
  *Normandy
  *Northern France
  *Rhineland
  *Ardennes-Alsace
  *Central Europe

DECORATIONS

*Presidential Unit Citation (Army), Streamer embroidered WESTPHALIAN PLAINS (82d Armored Reconnaissance Battalion cited; WD GO 84, 1945)

*Belgian Fourragère 1940 (82d Armored Reconnaissance Battalion cited; DA GO 43, 1950)

*Cited in the Order of the Day of the Belgian Army for action in BELGIUM

*Cited in the Order of the Day of the Belgian Army for action in the ARDENNES

2d BATTALION, 15th ARMOR

RA
(inactive)

LINEAGE

Constituted 2 February 1901 in the Regular Army as Troop B, 15th Cavalry. Organized 1 March 1901 at Presidio of San Francisco, California. Inactivated 18 October 1921 at Fort D. A. Russell, Wyoming. Activated 22 March 1942 at Fort Riley, Kansas, and redesignated as Troop B, 15th Cavalry, Mechanized.

Reorganized and redesignated 12 March 1944 as Troop B, 15th Cavalry Reconnaissance Squadron, Mechanized. Converted and redesignated 1 May 1946 as Troop B, 15th Constabulary Squadron. Inactivated 20 December 1948 at Fussen, Germany. Activated 20 May 1949 at Weiden, Germany. Inactivated 15 December 1952 at Weiden, Germany. Redesignated 13 August 1954 as Company B, 15th Reconnaissance Battalion.

Redesignated 1 April 1957 as Headquarters and Headquarters Troop, 2d Reconnaissance Squadron, 15th Cavalry; concurrently, consolidated with Headquarters and Headquarters and Service Company, 25th Reconnaissance Battalion (see ANNEX), assigned to 4th Armored Division, and activated at Fort Hood, Texas (concurrently, Companies A, B, and C, 25th Reconnaissance Battalion redesignated as Troops A, B, and C, 2d Reconnaissance Squadron, 15th Cavalry. Troop D, 2d Reconnaissance Squadron, 15th Cavalry, concurrently constituted and activated). Redesignated 1 August 1963 as 2d Battalion, 15th Armor; concurrently, relieved from assignment to 4th Armored Division, transferred (less personnel and equipment) from U.S. Army, Europe, to U.S. Army, Pacific, assigned to the 1st Cavalry Division and reorganized. Transferred (less personnel and equipment) 1 July 1965 from Korea to Fort Benning, Georgia; concurrently, inactivated at Fort Benning, Georgia, and relieved from assignment to 1st Cavalry Division.

ANNEX

4th Reconnaissance Battalion (Armored) constituted 13 January 1941 in the Regular Army and assigned to 4th Armored Division. Activated 15 April 1941 at Pine Camp, New York. Redesignated 8 May 1941 as 84th Reconnaissance Battalion (Armored). Redesignated 1 January 1942 as 84th Armored Reconnaissance Battalion. Converted and redesignated 10 September 1943 as 25th Cavalry Reconnaissance Squadron, Mechanized. Converted and redesignated 1 May 1946 as 25th Constabulary Squadron and relieved from assignment to 4th Armored Division. Inactivated 20 December 1948 at Straubing, Germany; concurrently, converted and redesignated as 25th Reconnaissance Battalion. Assigned 25 February 1953 to 4th Armored Division. Activated 15 June 1954 at Fort Hood, Texas.

CAMPAIGN PARTICIPATION CREDIT

Philippine Insurrection
  *Mindanao
  *Luzon 1902

World War I
  *Without inscription

World War II
  *Normandy
  *Northern France
  *Rhineland
  *Ardennes-Alsace
  *Central Europe

DECORATIONS

*Presidential Unit Citation (Army), Streamer embroidered ARDENNES (25th Cavalry Reconnaissance Squadron cited; WD GO 54, 1945)

*French Croix de Guerre with Palm, World War II, Streamer embroidered NORMANDY (25th Cavalry Reconnaissance Squadron cited; DA GO 43, 1950)

*French Croix de Guerre with Palm, World War II, Streamer embroidered MOSELLE RIVER (25th Cavalry Reconnaissance Squadron cited; DA GO 43, 1950)

*French Croix de Guerre, World War II, Fourragère (25th Cavalry Reconnaissance Squadron cited; DA GO 43, 1950)

3d BATTALION, 15th ARMOR

AR
(inactive)

LINEAGE

Constituted 2 February 1901 in the Regular Army as Troop C, 15th Cavalry. Organized 1 March 1901 at Presidio of San Francisco, California. Inactivated 18 October 1921 at Fort D. A. Russell, Wyoming. Activated 22 March 1942 at Fort Riley, Kansas, and redesignated as Troop C, 15th Cavalry, Mechanized.

Reorganized and redesignated 15 March 1944 as Troop C, 17th Cavalry Reconnaissance Squadron, Mechanized. Inactivated 20 January 1947 in Germany. Redesignated 1 September 1948 as Company C, 501st Reconnaissance Battalion. Activated 25 September 1948 at Fort Sill, Oklahoma. Inactivated 25 January 1949 at Fort Sill, Oklahoma.

Redesignated 10 April 1959 as Headquarters and Headquarters Troop, 3d Reconnaissance Squadron, 15th Cavalry; concurrently, withdrawn from the Regular Army, allotted to the Army Reserve, and assigned to 81st Infantry Division (organic elements concurrently constituted). Activated 1 May 1959 at Atlanta, Georgia.

Transferred (less personnel and equipment) 15 March 1963 from Third United States Army to Fourth United States Army; concurrently, redesignated as 3d Battalion, 15th Armor, relieved from assignment to 81st Infantry Division, assigned to 90th Infantry Division, and reorganized with Headquarters at Terminal, Texas. Inactivated 31 December 1965 at Terminal, Texas, and relieved from assignment to 90th Infantry Division.

CAMPAIGN PARTICIPATION CREDIT

Philippine Insurrection
  *Mindanao
  Luzon 1902

World War I
  *Without inscription

World War II
  *Normandy
  *Northern France
  *Rhineland
  *Central Europe

DECORATIONS

None.

242

4th BATTALION, 15th ARMOR

AR
(inactive)

LINEAGE

Constituted 2 February 1901 in the Regular Army as Troop D, 15th Cavalry. Organized 1 March 1901 at Presidio of San Francisco, California. Disbanded 16 September 1921 at Fort D. A. Russell, Wyoming. Reconstituted 22 March 1942 in the Regular Army and redesignated as Troop D, 15th Cavalry, Mechanized, and activated at Fort Riley, Kansas.

Reorganized and redesignated 15 March 1944 as Troop B, 17th Cavalry Reconnaissance Squadron, Mechanized. Inactivated 20 January 1947 in Germany. Redesignated 1 September 1948 as Company B, 501st Reconnaissance Battalion. Activated 25 September 1948 at Fort Sill, Oklahoma. Inactivated 25 January 1949 at Fort Sill, Oklahoma.

Redesignated 19 March 1959 as Headquarters and Headquarters Troop, 4th Reconnaissance Squadron, 15th Cavalry; concurrently, withdrawn from the Regular Army, allotted to the Army Reserve, and assigned to 90th Infantry Division (organic elements concurrently constituted). Activated 1 April 1959 at San Antonio, Texas. Reorganized and redesignated 15 March 1963 as 4th Battalion, 15th Armor. Inactivated 31 December 1965 at San Antonio, Texas, and relieved from assignment to 90th Infantry Division.

CAMPAIGN PARTICIPATION CREDIT

Philippine Insurrection
  *Mindanao
  Luzon 1902

World War I
  *Without inscription

World War II
  *Normandy
  *Northern France
  *Rhineland
  *Central Europe

DECORATIONS

None.

COMPANY E, 15th ARMOR

RA
(inactive)

LINEAGE

Constituted 2 February 1901 in the Regular Army as Troop E, 15th Cavalry. Organized 6 March 1901 at Presidio of San Francisco, California. Inactivated 18 October 1921 at Fort D. A. Russell, Wyoming. Activated 22 March 1942 at Fort Riley, Kansas, and redesignated as Troop E, 15th Cavalry, Mechanized.

Reorganized and redesignated 12 March 1944 as Company F, 15th Cavalry Reconnaissance Squadron, Mechanized. Converted and redesignated 1 May 1946 as Troop E, 15th Constabulary Squadron, an element of the 15th Constabulary Regiment. Inactivated 20 December 1948 at Fussen, Germany, and relieved from assignment to 15th Constabulary Regiment. Activated 20 May 1949 at Weiden, Germany, and assigned to the United States Constabulary. Inactivated 15 December 1952 and relieved from assignment to the United States Constabulary. Redesignated 13 August 1954 as Company D, 15th Reconnaissance Battalion.

Redesignated 1 May 1959 as Headquarters and Headquarters Troop, 5th Reconnaissance Squadron, 15th Cavalry. Redesignated 1 July 1963 as Headquarters and Headquarters Company, 5th Battalion, 15th Armor. Redesignated 4 January 1967 as Company E, 15th Armor. Activated 25 January 1967 at Fort Hood, Texas. Inactivated 1 July 1967 at Fort Hood, Texas.

CAMPAIGN PARTICIPATION CREDIT

Philippine Insurrection
Mindanao
Luzon 1902

World War II–EAME
Normandy
Northern France
Rhineland
Central Europe

DECORATIONS

None.

244

COMPANY F, 15th ARMOR

RA
(inactive)

LINEAGE

Constituted 2 February 1901 in the Regular Army as Troop F, 15th Cavalry. Organized 8 March 1901 at Presidio of San Francisco, California. Inactivated 18 October 1921 at Fort D. A. Russell, Wyoming. Activated 22 March 1942 at Fort Riley, Kansas, and redesignated as Troop F, 15th Cavalry, Mechanized.

Reorganized and redesignated 12 March 1944 as Troop F, 17th Cavalry Reconnaissance Squadron, Mechanized. Inactivated 20 January 1947 in Germany.

Redesignated 1 September 1948 as 550th Light Tank Company. Redesignated 19 March 1951 as 550th Tank Company. Activated 6 April 1951 at Fort Benning, Georgia. Inactivated 25 June 1958 at Fort Campbell, Kentucky.

Redesignated 1 October 1958 as Troop F, 15th Cavalry. Redesignated 1 May 1959 as Headquarters and Headquarters Troop, 6th Reconnaissance Squadron, 15th Cavalry. Redesignated 1 July 1963 as Headquarters and Headquarters Company, 6th Battalion, 15th Armor. Redesignated 4 January 1967 as Company F, 15th Armor. Activated 25 January 1967 at Fort Hood, Texas. Inactivated 1 July 1967 at Fort Hood, Texas.

CAMPAIGN PARTICIPATION CREDIT

Philippine Insurrection
Mindanao
Luzon 1902

World War II–EAME
Normandy
Northern France
Rhineland
Central Europe

DECORATIONS

None.

COMPANY G, 15th ARMOR

RA
(inactive)

LINEAGE

Constituted 2 February 1901 in the Regular Army as Troop G, 15th Cavalry. Organized 8 March 1901 at Presidio of San Francisco, California. Inactivated 18 October 1921 at Fort D. A. Russell, Wyoming.

Redesignated 1 May 1959 as Headquarters and Headquarters Troop, 7th Reconnaissance Squadron, 15th Cavalry. Redesignated 1 July 1963 as Headquarters and Headquarters Company, 7th Battalion, 15th Armor. Redesignated 4 January 1967 as Company G, 15th Armor. Activated 25 January 1967 at Fort Hood, Texas. Inactivated 10 June 1967 at Fort Hood, Texas.

CAMPAIGN PARTICIPATION CREDIT

Philippine Insurrection
Mindanao
Luzon 1902

DECORATIONS
None.

BIBLIOGRAPHY, 15TH ARMOR

Herr, John K., and Edward S. Wallace. *The Story of the U.S. Cavalry.* Boston: 1953.

Larson, Ross E. Fifteenth U.S. Cavalry History. Typescript. Fort D. A. Russell, Wyoming: 1923.

Unit Members. *Conquer, The Story of the Ninth Army, 1944–1945.* Washington: 1947.

————. *History of the XVI Corps From Its Activation to the End of the War in Europe.* Washington: 1947.

UNITED STATES ARMY IN WORLD WAR II
Blumenson, Martin. *Breakout and Pursuit.* 1961.

Wallace, William M. *History and Roster of the 15th Cavalry from Its Organization to 1904.* N.p.: circa 1904.

16th ARMOR

HERALDIC ITEMS

COAT OF ARMS

Shield: Or a bordure vert, on a chevron azure 16 mullets pierced of the field; on a canton embattled (for the 6th Cavalry) vert (for the 3d Cavalry) a staff erect attached thereto a standard flotant or charged with a horseshoe heels upward encircling the Arabic numeral *14* sable (for the 14th Cavalry).

Crest: On a wreath of the colors a rattlesnake coiled to strike proper.

Motto: Strike Hard.

Symbolism: The regiment was organized in 1916 with personnel from the 3d, 6th, and 14th Cavalry, which are represented by the canton. (The standard is from the crest of the coat of arms for the 14th Cavalry; green was the color of the facings of the Mounted Rifles, now the 3d Cavalry; the embattled partition line commemorates the first engagement of the 6th Cavalry when it assaulted artillery in earthworks at Williamsburg in 1862.)

            The shield is yellow (or), the cavalry color; the blue chevron is for the old blue uniform; the 16 mullets (spur rowels) indicate the numerical designation and mounted service. The green border and the rattlesnake crest symbolize the birth and subsequent service of the organization on the Mexican border. The motto has a direct reference to the crest.

DISTINCTIVE INSIGNIA

The distinctive insignia is the shield and motto of the coat of arms.

LINEAGE AND HONORS

LINEAGE

Constituted 1 July 1916 in the Regular Army as 16th Cavalry and organized at Fort Sam Houston, Texas. Inactivated 12 November 1921 at Forts Sam Houston and McIntosh, Texas. Activated 15 June 1942 at Camp Forrest, Tennessee, as 16th Cavalry, Mechanized.

Regiment broken up 22 December 1943 and its elements reorganized and redesignated as Headquarters and Headquarters Troop, 16th Cavalry Group, Mechanized, and 16th and 19th Cavalry Reconnaissance Squadrons, Mechanized.

Headquarters and Headquarters Troop, 16th Cavalry Group, Mechanized, converted and redesignated 1 May 1946 as Headquarters and Headquarters Troop, 16th Constabulary Squadron, and assigned to 4th Constabulary Regiment. (Troops of 16th Constabulary Squadron constituted and activated 1 May 1946.) Reorganized and redesignated 10 February 1948 as Headquarters and Headquarters and Service Troop, 16th Constabulary Squadron. Relieved 1 February 1949 from assignment to 4th Constabulary Regiment and assigned to the United States Constabulary. Inactivated 27 November 1950 at Grafenwohr, Germany. Converted and redesignated 9 March 1951 as Headquarters and Headquarters Company, 16th Armored Cavalry Group. (Troops of 16th Constabulary Squadron disbanded 9 March 1951.) Activated 1 April 1951 at Camp Cooke, California. Reorganized and redesignated 1 October 1953 as Headquarters and Headquarters Company, 16th Armor Group.

16th Cavalry Reconnaissance Squadron, Mechanized, inactivated 10 February 1946 at Camp Hood, Texas.

19th Cavalry Reconnaissance Squadron, Mechanized, inactivated 10 November 1945 at Camp Campbell, Kentucky. Reorganized 1 August 1946 at Fort Riley, Kansas, and redesignated as Headquarters and Headquarters Troop, 19th Cavalry Group, Mechanized. (Troops of 19th Cavalry Reconnaissance Squadron, Mechanized, absorbed in the reorganization on 1 August 1946.) Inactivated 6 November 1946 at Fort Riley, Kansas. Redesignated 2 January 1953 as Headquarters and Headquarters Company, 19th Armored Cavalry Group, and activated at Frankfurt, Germany. Redesignated 1 October 1953 as Headquarters and Headquarters Company, 19th Armor Group. Inactivated 1 July 1955 in Europe.

Headquarters and Headquarters Company, 16th Armor Group, 16th Cavalry Reconnaissance Squadron, Mechanized, and Headquarters and Headquarters Company, 19th Armor Group, consolidated 2 July 1955; consolidated unit designated as Headquarters and Headquarters Company, 16th Armor Group.

Former 16th Cavalry designated 1 March 1957 as a parent regiment under the Combat Arms Regimental System; concurrently, former troops withdrawn from 16th Armor Group and redesignated elements of the 16th Cavalry. 16th Cavalry redesignated 26 March 1963 as 16th Armor (Headquarters and Headquarters Company, 16th Armor Group, inactivated 15 April 1968; concurrently, redesignated as Headquarters and Headquarters Company, 16th Armor).

CAMPAIGN PARTICIPATION CREDIT

World War II
Rhineland
Central Europe

Vietnam
Defense
Counteroffensive
Counteroffensive, Phase II
Counteroffensive, Phase III
Tet Counteroffensive

DECORATIONS
None.

1st BATTALION, 16th ARMOR

RA
(inactive)

Constituted 1 July 1916 in the Regular Army as Troop A, 16th Cavalry. Organized 14 July 1916 at Fort Sam Houston, Texas. Inactivated 12 November 1921 at Fort Sam Houston, Texas. Activated 15 June 1942 at Camp Forrest, Tennessee, and redesignated as Troop A, 16th Cavalry, Mechanized.

Reorganized and redesignated 22 December 1943 as Troop A, 16th Cavalry Reconnaissance Squadron, Mechanized. Inactivated 10 February 1946 at Camp Hood, Texas. Consolidated 2 July 1955 with Headquarters Company, 16th Armor Group (then active) and retained latter designation.

Former Troop A (organized 14 July 1916), 16th Cavalry withdrawn 1 March 1957, and redesignated as Headquarters and Headquarters Troop, 1st Reconnaissance Squadron (Sky Cavalry), 16th Cavalry; assigned to 2d United States Army Missile Command, and activated at Fort Hood, Texas (organic elements concurrently constituted and activated). Inactivated 25 August 1961 at Fort Carson, Colorado. Redesignated 6 March 1964 as 1st Battalion, 16th Armor, and activated (less personnel) at Fort Bragg, North Carolina; concurrently, relieved from assignment to 2d United States Army Missile Command and assigned to 82d Airborne Division. Inactivated 15 August 1965 at Fort Bragg, North Carolina, and relieved from assignment to 82d Airborne Division.

CAMPAIGN PARTICIPATION CREDIT

World War II
  *Rhineland
  *Central Europe

DECORATIONS

None.

250

2d BATTALION, 16th ARMOR

RA
(inactive)

LINEAGE

Constituted 1 July 1916 in the Regular Army as Troop B, 16th Cavalry. Organized 14 July 1916 at Fort Sam Houston, Texas. Inactivated 12 November 1921 at Fort Sam Houston, Texas. Activated 15 June 1942 at Camp Forrest, Tennessee, and redesignated as Troop B, 16th Cavalry, Mechanized.

Reorganized and redesignated 22 December 1943 as Troop B, 16th Cavalry Reconnaissance Squadron, Mechanized. Inactivated 10 February 1946 at Camp Hood, Texas. Consolidated 2 July 1955 with Headquarters Company, 16th Armor Group (then active) and retained latter designation.

Former Troop B (organized 14 July 1916), 16th Cavalry withdrawn 24 June 1958 and redesignated as Headquarters and Headquarters Troop, 2d Reconnaissance Squadron (Sky Cavalry), 16th Cavalry, activated at Vicenza, Italy, and assigned to 1st United States Army Missile Command (organic elements concurrently constituted and activated). Inactivated 25 June 1959 in Italy and relieved from assignment to 1st United States Army Missile Command. Redesignated 21 January 1964 as 2d Battalion, 16th Armor, and assigned to 101st Airborne Division. Activated 3 February 1964 at Fort Campbell, Kentucky. Inactivated 21 May 1965 at Fort Campbell, Kentucky, and relieved from assignment to the 101st Airborne Division.

CAMPAIGN PARTICIPATION CREDIT

World War II
  *Rhineland
  *Central Europe

DECORATIONS

None.

COMPANY D, 16th ARMOR

RA

(173d Airborne Brigade)

LINEAGE

Constituted 1 July 1916 in the Regular Army as Troop D, 16th Cavalry. Organized 14 July 1916 at Fort Sam Houston, Texas. Inactivated 12 November 1921 at Fort Sam Houston, Texas. Activated 15 June 1942 at Camp Forrest, Tennessee, and redesignated as Troop D, 16th Cavalry, Mechanized.

Reorganized and redesignated 22 December 1943 as Troop B, 19th Cavalry Reconnaissance Squadron, Mechanized. Inactivated 10 November 1945 at Camp Campbell, Kentucky. Consolidated 2 July 1955 with Headquarters Company, 16th Armor Group (then active) and retained latter designation.

Former Troop D (organized 14 July 1916), 16th Cavalry, withdrawn 26 March 1963 and redesignated as Company D, 16th Armor, and assigned to 173d Airborne Brigade. Activated 25 June 1963 on Okinawa.

CAMPAIGN PARTICIPATION CREDIT

World War II-EAME
Rhineland
Central Europe

Vietnam
*Defense
*Counteroffensive
*Counteroffensive, Phase II
*Counteroffensive, Phase III
*Tet Counteroffensive

DECORATIONS

None.

BIBLIOGRAPHY, 16TH ARMOR

Allen, Robert S. *Lucky Forward, The History of Patton's Third U.S. Army.* New York: 1947.

Garbutt, Arthur I., editor. *19th Cavalry Reconnaissance Squadron, A Brief History.* Camp Campbell, Kentucky: 1945.

Herr, John K., and Edward S. Wallace. *The Story of the U.S. Cavalry.* Boston: 1953.

Unit Members. *After Action Report, Third U.S. Army, 1 August 1944– 9 May 1945.* 3 Volumes. Regensburg, Germany: 1945.

————. *A Souvenir Booklet for the Officers, Enlisted Men and Civilians Who Made History with the Third U.S. Army in the European Theater of Operations 1944–1945.* Bad Tolz, Germany: 1945.

Unit Members. *Fifteenth U.S. Army in Germany, 16 April–10 July 1945.* N.p.: 1945.

———. *History of the Fifteenth United States Army, 21 August 1944– 11 July 1945.* N.p.: 1946.

———. *Report of Operations, 12th Army Group.* 14 Volumes. Weisbaden, Germany: 1948.

———. *Third Army . . . A Brief Survey of Operations in Europe.* N.p.: 1945.

———. *16th Cavalry Group, Rhineland and Central Europe Campaigns.* Berlin: 1946.

Wallace, Brenton G. *Patton and his Third Army.* Harrisburg, Pennsylvania: 1946.

17th CAVALRY

Heraldic Items

Coat of Arms

Shield: Per bend tenné and vert, in sinister chief a demiunicorn and in dexter base a demihorse both rampant argent.

Crest: On a hurt wavy of six voided similarly or a winged spur argent.

Motto: Forward.

Symbolism: The regiment was organized in 1916 with personnel from the 1st, 3d, 6th, 8th, and 14th Cavalry. The shield is taken from the coats of arms of those regiments: the orange from the 1st, the green from the 3d, the unicorn from the 6th, the demihorse from the 8th, and the diagonal line from the 14th. The crest is the winged spur, emblematic of the motto of the flying cavalry; the background is the blue ribbon with the motto *Forward*.

Distinctive Insignia

The distinctive insignia is the crest of the coat of arms.

Lineage and Honors

Lineage

Constituted 1 July 1916 in the Regular Army as 17th Cavalry and organized at Fort Bliss, Texas. Inactivated 26 September 1921 at Presidio of Monterey, California. Redesignated 1 July 1940 as 17th Cavalry (Corps Reconnaissance).

Headquarters and Headquarters Troop, 17th Cavalry, consolidated 9 March 1951 with Headquarters and Headquarters Company, 17th Armored Group (see ANNEX), and redesignated as Headquarters and Headquarters Company, 17th Armored Cavalry Group (remaining troops of the 17th Cavalry concurrently disbanded). Activated 20 March 1951 at Camp Polk, Louisiana. Inactivated 4 May 1959 at Fort Stewart, Georgia.

Disbanded troops of the 17th Cavalry reconstituted in the Regular Army as follows: A, 1 September 1957; B, 25 April 1957; C, 1 March 1957; D through M, 4 May 1959. Reconstituted troops, 17th Cavalry, and Headquarters and Headquarters Company, 17th Armored Cavalry Group, redesignated by elements 4 May 1959 as 17th Cavalry, a parent regiment under the Combat

Arms Regimental System (Headquarters and Headquarters Company, 17th Armored Cavalry Group, concurrently redesignated as Headquarters and Headquarters Troop, 17th Cavalry).

ANNEX

Headquarters and Headquarters Company, 1st Armored Group, constituted 26 February 1943 in the Army of the United States. Activated 2 March 1943 at Fort Knox, Kentucky. Redesignated 20 November 1943 as Headquarters and Headquarters Company, 17th Armored Group. Inactivated 30 April 1946 in Europe.

CAMPAIGN PARTICIPATION CREDIT

World War II	Vietnam
Northern France	Defense
Rhineland	Counteroffensive
Ardennes-Alsace	Counteroffensive, Phase II
Central Europe	Counteroffensive, Phase III
	Tet Counteroffensive

DECORATIONS

Valorous Unit Award, Streamer embroidered BEN CAT (Troop E, 17th Cavalry, cited; GO 3525, U.S. Army, Vietnam, 13 July 1967)

1st SQUADRON, 17th CAVALRY

RA

(82d Airborne Division)

LINEAGE

Constituted 1 July 1916 in the Regular Army as Troop A, 17th Cavalry. Organized 9 July 1916 at Fort Bliss, Texas. Inactivated 26 September 1921 at Presidio of Monterey, California. Disbanded 9 March 1951.

Reconstituted 1 September 1957 in the Regular Army and consolidated with 82d Airborne Reconnaissance Company (see ANNEX); consolidated unit reorganized and designated as Troop A (Reconnaissance) (Aviation), 17th Cavalry; concurrently, assigned to 82d Airborne Division and activated at Fort Bragg, North Carolina.

Reorganized and redesignated 25 May 1964 as Headquarters and Headquarters Troop, 1st Squadron, 17th Cavalry (organic elements constituted 6 March 1964 in the Regular Army and activated 25 May 1964 at Fort Bragg, North Carolina).

ANNEX

Headquarters, 163d and 164th Infantry Brigades constituted 5 August 1917 in the National Army and assigned to 82d Division. Organized 6 September 1917 and 25 August 1917, respectively, at Camp Gordon, Georgia. Demobilized 26 May 1919 at Camp Mills, Long Island, New York. Reconstituted and redesignated 24 June 1921 as Headquarters and Headquarters Companies, 163d and 164th Infantry Brigades, respectively; allotted to the Organized Reserves and assigned to 82d Division. Organized in February 1922: 163d at Macon, Georgia, and 164th at Jacksonville, Florida.

Consolidated, converted, reorganized, and redesignated 30 January 1942 as 82d Reconnaissance Troop. Ordered into the active military service 25 March 1942 at Camp Claiborne, Louisiana. Redesignated 1 April 1942 as 82d Cavalry Reconnaissance Troop. Disbanded 15 August 1942 at Camp Claiborne, Louisiana.

Reconstituted 22 February 1945 in the Army of the United States and redesignated as Reconnaissance Platoon, 82d Airborne Division. Activated 1 March 1945 in France. Reorganized and redesignated 15 December 1947 as 82d Reconnaissance Company; concurrently, relieved from assignment to 82d Airborne Division. Allotted 3 March 1949 to Regular Army. Reorganized and redesignated 15 July 1950 as 82d Airborne Reconnaissance Company and assigned to 82d Airborne Division.

Campaign Participation Credit

World War I
  *St. Mihiel
  *Meuse-Argonne
  *Lorraine 1918

World War II
  Northern France
  *Rhineland

Ardennes-Alsace
  *Central Europe

Vietnam
  Troop B, 1st Squadron,
  is entitled to:
  Tet Counteroffensive

Decorations

None.

2d SQUADRON, 17th CAVALRY

RA

(101st Airborne Division)

LINEAGE

Constituted 1 July 1916 in the Regular Army as Troop B, 17th Cavalry. Organized 9 July 1916 at Fort Bliss, Texas. Inactivated 26 September 1921 at Presidio of Monterey, California. Disbanded 9 March 1951.

Reconstituted 25 April 1957 in the Regular Army and consolidated with 101st Airborne Reconnaissance Troop (see ANNEX); consolidated unit reorganized and designated as Troop B (Reconnaissance) (Aviation), 17th Cavalry, assigned to 101st Airborne Division and activated at Fort Campbell, Kentucky. Reorganized and redesignated 3 February 1964 as Headquarters and Headquarters Troop, 2d Squadron, 17th Cavalry (organic elements constituted 21 January 1964 in the Regular Army and activated 3 February 1964).

ANNEX

57th Cavalry Reconnaissance Troop, Mechanized, constituted 12 May 1944 in the Army of the United States. Activated 29 May 1944 at Fort McIntosh, Texas. Inactivated 29 November 1945 at Camp Bowie, Texas. Activated 31 December 1946 in the Philippine Islands. Inactivated 30 May 1947 in the Philippine Islands. Redesignated 19 March 1948 as 57th Reconnaissance Company. Activated 12 April 1948 at Fort Knox, Kentucky. Inactivated 2 June 1948 at Fort Knox, Kentucky.

Redesignated 10 August 1950 as 101st Airborne Reconnaissance Company and assigned to 101st Airborne Division. Activated 25 August 1950 at Camp Breckinridge, Kentucky. Inactivated 1 December 1953 at Camp Breckinridge, Kentucky. Activated 15 May 1954 at Fort Jackson, South Carolina. Redesignated 1 July 1956 as 101st Airborne Reconnaissance Troop.

CAMPAIGN PARTICIPATION CREDIT

World War II   Central Europe
   Northern France
   Rhineland   *Vietnam*
   Ardennes-Alsace   *Counteroffensive, Phase III
                                          *Tet Counteroffensive

DECORATIONS

Troop A, 2d Squadron, 17th Cavalry, is entitled to: Meritorius Unit Commendation, Streamer embroidered VIETNAM 1965–1966 (Troop A, 2d Squadron, 17th Cavalry, cited; GO 2337, U.S. Army, Vietnam, 24 May 1967 as amended by GO 6603, U.S. Army, Vietnam, 26 December 1967)

3d SQUADRON, 17th CAVALRY

RA

(nondivisional)

LINEAGE

Constituted 1 July 1916 in the Regular Army as Troop C, 17th Cavalry. Organized 9 July 1916 at Fort Bliss, Texas. Inactivated 26 September 1921 at Presidio of Monterey, California. Disbanded 9 March 1951.

Reconstituted 1 March 1957 in the Regular Army and consolidated with 11th Airborne Reconnaissance Company (see ANNEX); consolidated unit designated as Troop C (Reconnaissance) (Airborne), 17th Cavalry, assigned to 11th Airborne Division and activated in Europe. Relieved 1 July 1958 from assignment to 11th Airborne Division. Inactivated 15 November 1958 in Europe. Activated 15 March 1962 as Troop C (Air), 17th Cavalry, at Fort Knox, Kentucky. Inactivated 16 January 1963 at Fort Knox, Kentucky.

Redesignated 1 February 1963 as Headquarters and Headquarters Troop, 3d Squadron, 17th Cavalry, and assigned to 11th Air Assault Division (organic elements concurrently constituted in the Regular Army). (Troop B [Air], 3d Squadron, 17th Cavalry, activated 7 February 1963 at Fort Rucker, Alabama.) 3d Squadron (less Troop B), 17th Cavalry, activated 19 March 1964 at Fort Benning, Georgia. Relieved 30 June 1965 from assignment to 11th Air Assault Division. Inactivated 1 July 1965 at Fort Benning, Georgia. Activated 25 November 1966 at Fort Knox, Kentucky.

ANNEX

11th Tank Company constituted 16 November 1921 in the Regular Army. Activated 19 November 1921 at Camp George G. Meade, Maryland. Assigned 26 August 1941 to the Hawaiian Division. Relieved 1 October 1941 from assignment to the Hawaiian Division. Disbanded 23 April 1942 in Hawaii.

Reconstituted 10 September 1947 in the Regular Army. Activated 20 September 1947 in Europe. Inactivated 1 November 1948 in Germany. Redesignated 28 February 1949 as 11th Reconnaissance Company. Activated 30 April 1949 at Camp Campbell, Kentucky. Redesignated 15 July 1950 as 11th Airborne Reconnaissance Company and assigned to 11th Airborne Division.

Campaign Participation Credit

World War II
   *Central Pacific
   Northern France
   Rhineland
   Ardennes-Alsace
   Central Europe

Vietnam
   *Counteroffensive, Phase III
   *Tet Counteroffensive

Decorations

None.

TROOP D, 17th CAVALRY

RA
(199th Infantry Brigade)

LINEAGE

Constituted 1 July 1916 in the Regular Army as Troop D, 17th Cavalry. Organized 9 July 1916 at Fort Bliss, Texas. Demobilized 26 September 1921 at Presidio of Monterey, California. Disbanded 9 March 1951.

Reconstituted 4 May 1959 in the Regular Army as Troop D, 17th Cavalry. Activated 24 September 1962 at Fort Rucker, Alabama. Inactivated 24 February 1963 at Fort Rucker, Alabama. Activated 1 June 1966 at Fort Benning, Georgia, and assigned to 199th Infantry Brigade.

CAMPAIGN PARTICIPATION CREDIT

Vietnam
Counteroffensive
Counteroffensive, Phase II
Counteroffensive, Phase III
Tet Counteroffensive

DECORATIONS
None.

TROOP E, 17th CAVALRY

RA
(173d Airborne Brigade)

LINEAGE

Constituted 1 July 1916 in the Regular Army as Troop E, 17th Cavalry, and organized at Fort Bliss, Texas. Inactivated 26 September 1921 at Presidio of Monterey, California. Disbanded 9 March 1951.

Reconstituted 4 May 1959 in the Regular Army as Troop E, 17th Cavalry. Assigned 26 March 1963 to 173d Airborne Brigade. Activated 25 June 1963 on Okinawa.

CAMPAIGN PARTICIPATION CREDIT

Vietnam
  Defense
  Counteroffensive
  Counteroffensive, Phase II
  Counteroffensive, Phase III
  Tet Counteroffensive

DECORATIONS

Valorous Unit Award, Streamer embroidered BEN CAT (Troop E, 17th Cavalry, cited; GO 3525, U.S. Army, Vietnam, 13 July 1967)

264

TROOP F, 17th CAVALRY

RA
(196th Infantry Brigade)

LINEAGE

Constituted 1 July 1916 in the Regular Army as Troop F, 17th Cavalry, and organized at Fort Bliss, Texas. Inactivated 26 September 1921 at Presidio of Monterey, California. Disbanded 9 March 1951.

Reconstituted 4 May 1959 in the Regular Army as Troop F, 17th Cavalry. Assigned 10 September 1965 to 196th Infantry Brigade. Activated 15 September 1965 at Fort Devens, Massachusetts.

CAMPAIGN PARTICIPATION CREDIT

Vietnam
Counteroffensive, Phase II
Counteroffensive, Phase III
Tet Counteroffensive

DECORATIONS
None.

265

7th SQUADRON, 17th CAVALRY

RA

(nondivisional)

LINEAGE

Constituted 1 July 1916 in the Regular Army as Troop G, 17th Cavalry, and organized at Fort Bliss, Texas. Inactivated 26 September 1921 at Presidio of Monterey, California. Disbanded 9 March 1951.

Reconstituted 4 May 1959 in the Regular Army as Troop G, 17th Cavalry. Activated 6 December 1962 at Fort Ord, California. Inactivated 31 August 1965 at Fort Ord, California.

Redesignated 27 September 1966 as Headquarters and Headquarters Troop, 7th Squadron, 17th Cavalry (organic elements concurrently constituted). Activated 25 November 1966 at Fort Knox, Kentucky.

CAMPAIGN PARTICIPATION CREDIT

World War II
  Northern France
  Rhineland
  Ardennes-Alsace
  Central Europe

Vietnam
  *Counteroffensive, Phase III
  *Tet Counteroffensive

DECORATIONS

None.

266

TROOP H, 17th CAVALRY

RA
(198th Infantry Brigade)

LINEAGE

Constituted 1 July 1916 in the Regular Army as Troop H, 17th Cavalry, and organized at Fort Bliss, Texas. Demobilized 26 September 1921 at Presidio of Monterey, California.

Reconstituted 4 May 1959 in the Regular Army as Troop H, 17th Cavalry. Assigned 10 May 1967 to 198th Infantry Brigade and activated at Fort Hood, Texas.

CAMPAIGN PARTICIPATION CREDIT

Vietnam
  Counteroffensive, Phase III
  Tet Counteroffensive

DECORATIONS

None.

BIBLIOGRAPHY, 17TH CAVALRY

Dyer, George B. *XII Corps, Spearhead of Patton's Third Army*. Baton Rouge, Louisiana: 1947.

267

32d ARMOR

HERALDIC ITEMS

COAT OF ARMS

Shield: Or, a bend raguly gules.

Crest: On a wreath or and gules, five truncated pyramids fesswise conjoined in base argent supporting a lion rampant of the second langued azure and armed of the third, the dexter paw grasping a chain mace of the fourth and the sinister paw a pine tree eradicated proper.

Motto: Victory or Death.

Symbolism: The shield is yellow for cavalry. The bend raguly in red symbolizes the cutting firepower of the regiment.

The truncated pyramids simulate dragon's teeth (a type of tank obstacle) used to protect the Siegfried Line, the defenses of which were battered, pierced, and overrun by the unit, an action for which it was awarded the Presidential Unit Citation, alluded to by the chain mace (for armor) in the color (blue) of the citation award. The red lion and the uprooted pine tree refer to the Ardennes and Belgian campaigns for which the unit was cited in Orders of the Day of the Belgian Army and awarded the Belgian Fourragère, the predominating color of that award being red. The five truncated pyramids also refer to participation in five World War II campaigns.

DISTINCTIVE INSIGNIA

The distinctive insignia is the shield and motto of the coat of arms.

LINEAGE AND HONORS

LINEAGE

Constituted 13 January 1941 in the Regular Army as 2d Armored Regiment and assigned to 3d Armored Division. Activated 15 April 1941 at Camp Beauregard, Louisiana. Redesignated 8 May 1941 as 32d Armored Regiment. Inactivated 10 November 1945 in Germany.

Regiment broken up 7 July 1947 and reorganized and redesignated as follows: 32d Armored Regiment (less certain elements) as 32d Tank Battalion; Headquarters and Headquarters Company, 2d Battalion, and Companies B and G as Headquarters and Headquarters Company and Companies D and A, respectively, 7th Tank Battalion (concurrently, certain elements of the 33d Armored Regiment were redesignated elements of the 7th Tank Battalion); Reconnaissance Company as Troop D, 83d Mechanized Cavalry Reconnaissance Squadron, an element of the 3d Armored Division; Service Company as Service Company, 13th Armored Infantry Battalion, an element of the 3d Armored Division. Headquarters and Headquarters Company, 3d Battalion, and Companies C, H, and I and Maintenance Company disbanded.

32d Tank Battalion activated 15 July 1947 as an element of the 3d Armored Division at Fort Knox, Kentucky. Redesignated 30 July 1948 as 32d Medium Tank Battalion. Redesignated 15 March 1955 as 32d Tank Battalion. Relieved 1 October 1957 from assignment to 3d Armored Division; concurrently, Company D, 32d Tank Battalion, redesignated as Headquarters and Headquarters Company, 1st Medium Tank Battalion, 32d Armor, and assigned to 3d Armored Division; remainder of 32d Tank Battalion inactivated.

7th Tank Battalion activated 15 July 1947 as an element of the 3d Armored Division at Fort Knox, Kentucky. Redesignated 30 July 1948 as 7th Medium Tank Battalion. Redesignated 15 March 1955 as 7th Tank Battalion. Inactivated 1 October 1957 in Europe and relieved from assignment to 3d Armored Division.

Headquarters and Headquarters Company, 3d Battalion; Maintenance Company; and Companies C, H, and I, 32d Armored Regiment, reconstituted 28 May 1948 in the Regular Army and redesignated as 61st Heavy Tank Battalion. Activated 12 July 1948 as an element of the 9th Infantry Division at Fort Dix, New Jersey. Redesignated 25 May 1954 as 61st Tank Battalion. Inactivated 1 December 1957 at Fort Carson, Colorado, and relieved from assignment to 9th Infantry Division.

Troop D, 83d Mechanized Cavalry Reconnaissance Squadron, activated 15 July 1947 at Fort Knox, Kentucky. Redesignated 30 July 1948 as Company D, 83d Reconnaissance Battalion. Inactivated 1 October 1957 in Europe, and relieved from assignment to 3d Armored Division.

Service Company, 13th Armored Infantry Battalion, activated 15 July 1947 at Fort Knox, Kentucky. Redesignated 30 July 1948 as Company D, 13th Armored Infantry Battalion. Inactivated 1 October 1957 in Europe and relieved from assignment to the 3d Armored Division.

32d, 7th (less certain elements in 33d Armor), and 61st Tank Battalions; Company D, 83d Reconnaissance Battalion; and Company D, 13th Armored Infantry Battalion, consolidated and redesignated 1 December 1957 as 32d Armor, a parent regiment under the Combat Arms Regimental System (Headquarters and Headquarters and Service Company, 32d Tank Battalion, redesignated as Headquarters and Headquarters Company, 32d Armor).

CAMPAIGN PARTICIPATION CREDIT

World War II
    Normandy
    Northern France

Rhineland
Ardennes-Alsace
Central Europe

DECORATIONS

Presidential Unit Citation (Army), Streamer embroidered SIEGFRIED LINE (2d Battalion [with Companies B, E, and F assigned], 32d Armored Regiment, cited; WD GO 54, 1945)

Belgian Fourragère 1940 (32d Armored Regiment cited; DA GO 43, 1950)
    Cited in the Order of the Day of the Belgian Army for action in BELGIUM
    Cited in the Order of the Day of the Belgian Army for action in the ARDENNES

1st BATTALION, 32d ARMOR

RA
(3d Armored Division)

LINEAGE

Constituted 13 January 1941 in the Regular Army as Company A, 2d Armored Regiment, an element of the 3d Armored Division. Activated 15 April 1941 at Camp Beauregard, Louisiana. Redesignated 8 May 1941 as Company A, 32d Armored Regiment. Inactivated 10 November 1945 in Germany.

Redesignated 7 July 1947 as Company D, 32d Tank Battalion. Activated 15 July 1947 at Fort Knox, Kentucky, as an element of the 3d Armored Division. Redesignated 30 July 1948 as Company D, 32d Medium Tank Battalion. Redesignated 15 March 1955 as Company D, 32d Tank Battalion.

Reorganized and redesignated 1 October 1957 as Headquarters and Headquarters Company, 1st Medium Tank Battalion (Patton), 32d Armor, and remained assigned to 3d Armored Division (organic elements concurrently constituted and activated). Reorganized and redesignated 1 October 1963 as 1st Battalion, 32d Armor.

CAMPAIGN PARTICIPATION CREDIT

World War II
* *Normandy
* *Northern France
* *Rhineland
* *Ardennes-Alsace
* *Central Europe

DECORATIONS

Presidential Unit Citation (Army), Streamer embroidered SIEGFRIED LINE

*Belgian Fourragère 1940 (32d Armored Regiment cited; DA GO 43, 1950)

**Cited in the Order of the Day of the Belgian Army for action in BELGIUM

**Cited in the Order of the Day of the Belgian Army for action in the ARDENNES

2d BATTALION, 32d ARMOR

RA
(3d Armored Division)

LINEAGE

Constituted 13 January 1941 in the Regular Army as Company B, 2d Armored Regiment, an element of the 3d Armored Division. Activated 15 April 1941 at Camp Beauregard, Louisiana. Redesignated 8 May 1941 as Company B, 32d Armored Regiment. Transferred 26 June 1944 from 1st Battalion, 32d Armored Regiment, to 2d Battalion, 32d Armored Regiment. Inactivated 10 November 1945 in Germany.

Redesignated 7 July 1947 as Company D, 7th Tank Battalion. Activated 15 July 1947 at Fort Knox, Kentucky, as an element of the 3d Armored Division. Redesignated 30 July 1948 as Company D, 7th Medium Tank Battalion. Redesignated 15 March 1955 as Company D, 7th Tank Battalion.

Reorganized and redesignated 15 February 1957 as Headquarters and Headquarters Company, 2d Medium Tank Battalion, 32d Armor; concurrently, relieved from assignment to 3d Armored Division and assigned to 1st Armored Division (organic elements concurrently constituted and activated). Inactivated 23 December 1957 at Fort Polk, Louisiana. Relieved 12 March 1958 from assignment to 1st Armored Division. Activated 3 February 1962 in Germany and assigned to 3d Armored Division. Reorganized and redesignated 1 October 1963 as 2d Battalion, 32d Armor.

CAMPAIGN PARTICIPATION CREDIT

World War II
  *Normandy
  *Northern France
*Rhineland
*Ardennes-Alsace
*Central Europe

DECORATIONS

*Presidential Unit Citation (Army), Streamer embroidered SIEGFRIED LINE (2d Battalion [with Companies B, E, and F assigned], 32d Armored Regiment, cited; WD GO 54, 1945)

*Belgian Fourragère 1940 (32d Armored Regiment cited; DA GO 43, 1950)

*Cited in the Order of the Day of the Belgian Army for action in BELGIUM

*Cited in the Order of the Day of the Belgian Army for action in the ARDENNES

273

3d BATTALION, 32d ARMOR

RA
(3d Armored Division)

LINEAGE

Constituted 13 January 1941 in the Regular Army as Company C, 2d Armored Regiment, an element of the 3d Armored Division. Activated 15 April 1941 at Camp Beauregard, Louisiana. Redesignated 8 May 1941 as Company C, 32d Armored Regiment. Transferred 26 June 1944 from 1st Battalion, 32d Armored Regiment, to 3d Battalion, 32d Armored Regiment. Inactivated 10 November 1945 in Germany. Disbanded 7 July 1947.

Reconstituted 28 May 1948 in the Regular Army and redesignated as Company C, 61st Heavy Tank Battalion, an element of the 9th Infantry Division. Activated 12 July 1948 at Fort Dix, New Jersey. Redesignated 25 May 1954 as Company C, 61st Tank Battalion.

Inactivated 1 December 1957 at Fort Carson, Colorado; concurrently, redesignated as Headquarters and Headquarters Company, 3d Medium Tank Battalion (Patton), 32d Armor, and relieved from assignment to 9th Infantry Division. Activated 25 June 1958 at Fort Stewart, Georgia (organic elements constituted 10 June 1958 and activated 25 June 1958). Redesignated 1 September 1963 as 3d Battalion, 32d Armor; concurrently, transferred (less personnel and equipment) from Fort Stewart, Georgia, to Germany, assigned to 3d Armored Division, and reorganized.

CAMPAIGN PARTICIPATION CREDIT

World War II
*Normandy
*Northern France

*Rhineland
*Ardennes-Alsace
*Central Europe

DECORATIONS

Presidential Unit Citation (Army), Streamer embroidered SIEGFRIED LINE
*Belgian Fourragère 1940 (32d Armored Regiment cited; DA GO 43, 1950)

*Cited in the Order of the Day of the Belgian Army for action in BELGIUM

*Cited in the Order of the Day of the Belgian Army for action in ARDENNES

274

4th BATTALION, 32d ARMOR

AR
(nondivisional)

LINEAGE

Constituted 13 January 1941 in the Regular Army as Company D, 2d Armored Regiment, an element of the 3d Armored Division. Activated 15 April 1941 at Camp Beauregard, Louisiana. Redesignated 8 May 1941 as Company D, 32d Armored Regiment. Transferred 26 June 1944 from 2d Battalion, 32d Armored Regiment, to 1st Battalion, 32d Armored Regiment. Inactivated 10 November 1945 in Germany.

Redesignated 7 July 1947 as Company A, 32d Tank Battalion. Activated 15 July 1947 at Fort Knox, Kentucky, as an element of the 3d Armored Division. Redesignated 30 July 1948 as Company A, 32d Medium Tank Battalion. Redesignated 15 March 1955 as Company A, 32d Tank Battalion. Inactivated 1 October 1957 in Germany (32d Tank Battalion concurrently relieved from assignment to 3d Armored Division).

Redesignated 1 December 1957 as Headquarters and Headquarters Company, 4th Medium Tank Battalion, 32d Armor. Withdrawn from Regular Army 24 April 1959, concurrently allotted to the Army Reserve and assigned to Fifth United States Army (organic elements concurrently constituted). Activated 1 May 1959 with Headquarters at Jeffersonville, Indiana. Reorganized and redesignated 13 March 1964 as 4th Battalion, 32d Armor.

Home Area: Fifth United States Army.

CAMPAIGN PARTICIPATION CREDIT

World War II
  *Normandy
  *Northern France
*Rhineland
*Ardennes-Alsace
*Central Europe

DECORATIONS

Presidential Unit Citation (Army), Streamer embroidered SIEGFRIED LINE
  *Belgian Fourragère 1940 (32d Armored Regiment cited; DA GO 43, 1950)
    *Cited in the Order of the Day of the Belgian Army for action in BELGIUM
    *Cited in the Order of the Day of the Belgian Army for action in ARDENNES

275

5th BATTALION, 32d ARMOR

RA
(24th Infantry Division)

LINEAGE

Constituted 13 January 1941 in the Regular Army as Company E, 2d Armored Regiment, an element of the 3d Armored Division. Activated 15 April 1941 at Camp Beauregard, Louisiana. Redesignated 8 May 1941 as Company E, 32d Armored Regiment. Inactivated 10 November 1945 in Germany.

Redesignated 7 July 1947 as Company B, 32d Tank Battalion. Activated 15 July 1947 at Fort Knox, Kentucky, as an element of the 3d Armored Division. Redesignated 30 July 1948 as Company B, 32d Medium Tank Battalion. Redesignated 15 March 1955 as Company B, 32d Tank Battalion. Inactivated 1 October 1957 in Germany (32d Tank Battalion concurrently relieved from assignment to the 3d Armored Division).

Redesignated 1 December 1957 as Headquarters and Headquarters Company, 5th Medium Tank Battalion, 32d Armor (organic elements constituted 21 June 1963 in the Regular Army). Activated 1 September 1963 in Germany. Reorganized and redesignated 5 May 1964 as 5th Battalion, 32d Armor. Assigned 1 May 1966 to the 24th Infantry Division.

CAMPAIGN PARTICIPATION CREDIT

World War II
  *Normandy
  *Northern France

*Rhineland
*Ardennes-Alsace
*Central Europe

DECORATIONS

*Presidential Unit Citation (Army), Streamer embroidered SIEGFRIED LINE (2d Battalion [with Companies B, E, and F assigned], 32d Armored Regiment, cited; WD GO 54, 1945)

*Belgian Fourragère 1940 (32d Armored Regiment cited; DA GO 43, 1950)

*Cited in the Order of the Day of the Belgian Army for action in BELGIUM

*Cited in the Order of the Day of the Belgian Army for action in ARDENNES

276

6th BATTALION, 32d ARMOR

RA
(nondivisional)

Constituted 13 January 1941 in the Regular Army as Company F, 2d Armored Regiment, an element of the 3d Armored Division. Activated 15 April 1941 at Camp Beauregard, Louisiana. Redesignated 8 May 1941 as Company F, 32d Armored Regiment. Inactivated 10 November 1945 in Germany.

Redesignated 7 July 1947 as Company C, 32d Tank Battalion. Activated 15 July 1947 at Fort Knox, Kentucky, as an element of the 3d Armored Division. Redesignated 30 July 1948 as Company C, 32d Medium Tank Battalion. Redesignated 15 March 1955 as Company C, 32d Tank Battalion. Inactivated 1 October 1957 in Germany (32d Tank Battalion concurrently relieved from assignment to 3d Armored Division).

Redesignated 1 December 1957 as Headquarters and Headquarters Company, 6th Medium Tank Battalion, 32d Armor. Redesignated 10 June 1966 as Headquarters and Headquarters Company, 6th Battalion, 32d Armor (organic elements concurrently constituted). Activated 22 June 1966 at Fort Knox, Kentucky.

CAMPAIGN PARTICIPATION CREDIT

World War II
    *Normandy
    *Northern France

*Rhineland
*Ardennes-Alsace
*Central Europe

DECORATIONS

*Presidential Unit Citation (Army), Streamer embroidered SIEGFRIED LINE (2d Battalion [with Companies B, E, and F assigned], 32d Armored Regiment, cited; WD GO 54, 1945)

*Belgian Fourragère 1940

    *Cited in the Order of the Day of the Belgian Army for action in BELGIUM

    *Cited in the Order of the Day of the Belgian Army for action in the ARDENNES

277

Bibliography, 32d Armor

Department of the Army. AMERICAN FORCES IN ACTION series. *St-Lo*. 1946.

Rock, William R. *3d Armored Division (Spearhead)*, *A History of the 3d Armored Division*. Germany: 1958.

Unit Members. *A History of the Third Armored Division, April 1941–July 1958*. Germany: 1958.

———. *Call Me Spearhead, Saga of the Third Armored "Spearhead" Division*. Paris: 1944.

———. *Conquer, The Story of the Ninth Army*. Washington: 1947.

———. *Historical and Pictorial Review, Third Armored Division of the United States Army*. Baton Rouge, Louisiana: 1942.

———. *Spearhead in the West, 1941–45, The Third Armored Division*. Europe: 1945.

———. *Spearheading with the Third Armored Division in the Bulge, Duren-Cologne . . . East to the Elbe*. Europe: 1945. Sequel to *Call Me Spearhead*.

UNITED STATES ARMY IN WORLD WAR II

Blumenson, Martin. *Breakout and Pursuit*. 1961.

Cole, Hugh M. *The Lorraine Campaign*. 1950.

———. *The Ardennes: Battle of the Bulge*. 1965.

Harrison, Gordon A. *Cross-Channel Attack*. 1951.

MacDonald, Charles B. *The Siegfried Line Campaign*. 1963.

33d ARMOR

HERALDIC ITEMS

COAT OF ARMS

Shield: Vert, in orle thirty-three plates.

Crest: On a wreath argent and vert, a mound of the last charged in base with a broken meat hook of the first and supporting a castle of two towers of the like, the castle wall embattled of five and charged with a lion rampant sable, armed and langued gules, beneath an escutcheon tierced per pale of the second, the fourth, and the second, charged with a mullet or.

Motto: Men of War.

Symbolism: The shield is the green and white of the Armored Force. The thirty-three plates designate the number of the regiment. The white (silver) castle on a green mound is taken from the coat of arms of Mons, Belgium. Only two of the castle towers are shown, representing the two attacks on Mons in 1944 spearheaded by the unit. The capture of Mons from the German Seventh Army is alluded to by the meat hook (a charge found in German heraldry), the broken pieces of which simulate the numeral 7. The liberation of Mons is symbolized by the black lion taken from the coat of arms of Hainaut Province. The award of the French Croix de Guerre with Silver Gilt Star is symbolized by the green, red, and green shield with gold star. The five embattlements of the castle wall represent participation in five World War II campaigns.

DISTINCTIVE INSIGNIA

The distinctive insignia is the shield and motto of the coat of arms.

LINEAGE AND HONORS

LINEAGE

Constituted 13 January 1941 in the Regular Army as 3d Armored Regiment and assigned to 3d Armored Division. Activated 15 April 1941 at Camp

Beauregard, Louisiana. Redesignated 8 May 1941 as 33d Armored Regiment. Inactivated 10 November 1945 in Europe.

Regiment broken up 7 July 1947, and reorganized and redesignated as follows: 33d Armored Regiment (less certain elements) as 33d Tank Battalion; Headquarters and Headquarters Company, 3d Battalion, and Companies G and H as Service Company and Companies B and C, respectively, 7th Tank Battalion (remainder of 7th Tank Battalion from elements of the 32d Armored Regiment); Reconnaissance Company as Troop E, 83d Mechanized Cavalry Reconnaissance Squadron (hereafter separate lineage). Headquarters and Headquarters Company, 2d Battalion, Companies B, C, and I, and Service and Maintenance Companies disbanded.

7th and 33d Tank Battalions activated 15 July 1947 at Fort Knox, Kentucky, and assigned to 3d Armored Division. Reorganized and redesignated 30 July 1948 as 7th and 33d Medium Tank Battalions. Reorganized and re-designated 15 March 1955 as 7th and 33d Tank Battalions. Inactivated 1 October 1957 in Europe; concurrently, relieved (less Company D, 7th Tank Battalion) from assignment to 3d Armored Division.

Headquarters and Headquarters Company, 2d Battalion; Service Company; and Companies B, C, and I, 33d Armored Regiment, reconstituted 28 May 1948 in the Regular Army and redesignated as Headquarters, Headquarters and Service Company, and Companies B, C, and A, respectively, 62d Heavy Tank Battalion. Assigned 18 June 1948 to 10th Infantry Division. Activated 1 July 1948 at Fort Riley, Kansas. Reorganized and redesignated 15 June 1954 as 62d Tank Battalion. Inactivated 7 July 1957 in Germany. Relieved 1 October 1957 from assignment to 10th Infantry Division.

33d and 62d Tank Battalions and elements of the 7th Tank Battalion con-solidated and redesignated 1 October 1957 as 33d Armor, a parent regiment under the Combat Arms Regimental System (Headquarters, Headquarters and Service Company, 33d Tank Battalion, concurrently redesignated as Head-quarters and Headquarters Company, 33d Armor).

CAMPAIGN PARTICIPATION CREDIT

World War II
Normandy
Northern France

Rhineland
Ardennes-Alsace
Central Europe

DECORATIONS

Presidential Unit Citation (Army), Streamer embroidered HASTENRATH-SCHERPENSEL (Headquarters and Headquarters Company, 1st Battalion, 33d Armored Regiment, and Companies A, F, and I cited; WD GO 66, 1945)

French Croix de Guerre with Silver-Gilt Star, World War II, Streamer embroidered MONS (33d Armored Regiment cited; DA GO 43, 1950)

Belgian Fourragère 1940 (33d Armored Regiment cited; DA GO 43, 1950)

Cited in the Order of the Day of the Belgian Army for action 3–13 September 1944 in BELGIUM

Cited in the Order of the Day of the Belgian Army for action 20–25 December 1944 in the ARDENNES

1st BATTALION, 33d ARMOR

RA

(3d Armored Division)

Constituted 13 January 1941 in the Regular Army as Company A, 3d Armored Regiment, an element of the 3d Armored Division. Activated 15 April 1941 at Camp Beauregard, Louisiana. Redesignated 8 May 1941 as Company A, 33d Armored Regiment. Inactivated 10 November 1945 in Germany.

Redesignated 7 July 1947 as Company D, 33d Tank Battalion. Activated 15 July 1947 at Fort Knox, Kentucky, as an element of the 3d Armored Division. Redesignated 30 July 1948 as Company D, 33d Medium Tank Battalion. Redesignated 15 March 1955 as Company D, 33d Tank Battalion.

Reorganized and redesignated 1 October 1957 as Headquarters and Headquarters Company, 1st Medium Tank Battalion (Patton), 33d Armor, and remained assigned to 3d Armored Division (organic elements concurrently constituted and activated). Reorganized and redesignated 1 October 1963 as 1st Battalion, 33d Armor.

CAMPAIGN PARTICIPATION CREDIT

World War II
  *Normandy
  *Northern France

*Rhineland
*Ardennes-Alsace
*Central Europe

DECORATIONS

*Presidential Unit Citation (Army), Streamer embroidered HASTENRATH-SCHERPENSEL (Headquarters and Headquarters Company, 1st Battalion, 33d Armored Regiment, and Companies A, F, and I cited; WD GO 66, 1945)

*French Croix de Guerre with Silver-Gilt Star, World War II, Streamer embroidered MONS (33d Armored Regiment cited; DA GO 43, 1950)

*Belgian Fourragère 1940 (33d Armored Regiment cited; DA GO 43, 1950)

*Cited in the Order of the Day of the Belgian Army for action 3–13 September 1944 in BELGIUM

*Cited in the Order of the Day of the Belgian Army for action 20–25 December 1944 in the ARDENNES

*Cited in the Order of the Day of the Belgian Army for action 17–25 January 1945 in BELGIUM (1st and 2d Battalions [with Companies A, B, C, D, E, F, and I] and 1st Platoon, Reconnaissance Company, 33d Armored Regiment, cited; DA GO 43, 1950)

*Cited in the Order of the Day of the Belgian Army for action 3–13 September 1944 along the MEUSE RIVER (1st Battalion [with Companies A, F, and I] and 3d Platoon, Reconnaissance Company, 33d Armored Regiment, cited; DA GO 43, 1950)

2d BATTALION, 33d ARMOR

RA
(3d Armored Division)

LINEAGE

Constituted 13 January 1941 in the Regular Army as Company B, 3d Armored Regiment, an element of the 3d Armored Division. Activated 15 April 1941 at Camp Beauregard, Louisiana. Redesignated 8 May 1941 as Company B, 33d Armored Regiment. Transferred 26 June 1944 from 1st Battalion, 33d Armored Regiment, to 2d Battalion, 33d Armored Regiment. Inactivated 10 November 1945 in Germany. Disbanded 7 July 1947.

Reconstituted 28 May 1948 in the Regular Army and redesignated as Company B, 62d Heavy Tank Battalion. (62d Heavy Tank Battalion assigned 18 June 1948 to 10th Infantry Division.) Activated 1 July 1948 at Fort Riley, Kansas. Redesignated 15 June 1954 as Company B, 62d Tank Battalion.

Reorganized and redesignated 15 February 1957 as Headquarters and Headquarters Company, 2d Medium Tank Battalion (Patton), 33d Armor; concurrently, relieved from assignment to 10th Infantry Division, transferred (less personnel and equipment) from Germany to Fort Polk, Louisiana, and assigned to 1st Armored Division (organic elements constituted 11 February 1957 and activated 15 February 1957). Inactivated 23 December 1957 at Fort Polk, Louisiana. Redesignated 12 March 1958 as 2d Heavy Tank Battalion, 33d Armor, and relieved from assignment to 1st Armored Division. Activated 1 May 1958 in Germany. Reorganized and redesignated 10 December 1962 as 2d Medium Tank Battalion, 33d Armor. Reorganized and redesignated 1 October 1963 as 2d Battalion, 33d Armor, and assigned to 3d Armored Division.

CAMPAIGN PARTICIPATION CREDIT

World War II
*Normandy
*Northern France

*Rhineland
*Ardennes-Alsace
*Central Europe

DECORATIONS

Presidential Unit Citation (Army), Streamer embroidered HASTENRATH-SCHERPENSEL

*French Croix de Guerre with Silver-Gilt Star, World War II, Streamer embroidered MONS (33d Armored Regiment cited; DA GO 43, 1950)

284

*Belgian Fourragère 1940 (33d Armored Regiment cited; DA GO 43, 1950)

*Cited in the Order of the Day of the Belgian Army for action 3–13 September 1944 in BELGIUM

*Cited in the Order of the Day of the Belgian Army for action 20–25 December 1944 in the ARDENNES

*Cited in the Order of the Day of the Belgian Army for action 17–25 January 1945 in BELGIUM (1st and 2d Battalions [with Companies A, B, D, E, and I] and 1st Platoon, Reconnaissance Company, 33d Armored Regiment, cited; DA GO 43, 1950)

*Cited in the Order of the Day of the Belgian Army for action 3–13 September 1944 along the MEUSE RIVER (1st Battalion [with Companies A, F, and I] and 3d Platoon, Reconnaissance Company, 33d Armored Regiment, cited; DA GO 43, 1950)

3d BATTALION, 33d ARMOR

RA

(3d Armored Division)

Constituted 13 January 1941 in the Regular Army as Company C, 3d Armored Regiment, an element of the 3d Armored Division. Activated 15 April 1941 at Camp Beauregard, Louisiana. Redesignated 8 May 1941 as Company C, 33d Armored Regiment. Transferred 26 June 1944 from 1st Battalion, 33d Armored Regiment, to 3d Battalion, 33d Armored Regiment. Inactivated 10 November 1945 in Germany. Disbanded 7 July 1947.

Reconstituted 28 May 1948 in the Regular Army and redesignated as Company C, 62d Heavy Tank Battalion. (62d Heavy Tank Battalion assigned 18 June 1948 to 10th Infantry Division.) Activated 1 July 1948 at Fort Riley, Kansas. Redesignated 15 June 1954 as Company C, 62d Tank Battalion.

Inactivated 1 October 1957 in Germany; concurrently, redesignated as Headquarters and Headquarters Company, 3d Medium Tank Battalion (Patton), 33d Armor, and relieved from assignment to 10th Infantry Division. Activated 25 June 1958 at Fort Knox, Kentucky (organic elements constituted 10 June 1958 and activated 25 June 1958). Reorganized and redesignated 1 July 1963 as 3d Battalion, 33d Armor; concurrently, transferred (less personnel and equipment) from Fort Knox, Kentucky, to United States Army, Europe, and assigned to 3d Armored Division.

CAMPAIGN PARTICIPATION CREDIT

World War II
*Normandy
*Northern France
*Rhineland
*Ardennes-Alsace
*Central Europe

DECORATIONS

Presidential Unit Citation (Army), Streamer embroidered HASTENRATH-SCHERPENSEL

*French Croix de Guerre with Silver-Gilt Star, World War II, Streamer embroidered MONS (33d Armored Regiment cited; DA GO 43, 1950)

*Belgian Fourragère 1940 (33d Armored Regiment cited; DA GO 43, 1950)

*Cited in the Order of the Day of the Belgian Army for action 3–13 September 1944 in BELGIUM

*Cited in the Order of the Day of the Belgian Army for action 20–25 December 1944 in the ARDENNES

4th BATTALION, 33d ARMOR

(205th Infantry Brigade)
RA

Constituted 13 January 1941 in the Regular Army as Company D, 3d Armored Regiment, an element of the 3d Armored Division. Activated 15 April 1941 at Camp Beauregard, Louisiana. Redesignated 8 May 1941 as Company D, 33d Armored Regiment. Inactivated 10 November 1945 in Germany.

Reorganized and redesignated 7 July 1947 as Company A, 33d Tank Battalion. Activated 15 July 1947 at Fort Knox, Kentucky, as an element of the 3d Armored Division. Redesignated 30 July 1948 as Company A, 33d Medium Tank Battalion. Redesignated 15 March 1955 as Company A, 33d Tank Battalion.

Inactivated 1 October 1957 in Europe; concurrently, redesignated as Headquarters and Headquarters Company, 4th Medium Tank Battalion, 33d Armor, and relieved from assignment to 3d Armored Division. Withdrawn from the Regular Army 20 April 1959, allotted to the Army Reserve, and assigned to 103d Infantry Division (organic elements concurrently constituted). Activated 18 May 1959 with Headquarters at Fort Snelling, Minnesota. Reorganized and redesignated 15 February 1963 as 4th Battalion, 33d Armor; concurrently, relieved from assignment to 103d Infantry Division and assigned to 205th Infantry Brigade.

Home Area: Fifth United States Army.

CAMPAIGN PARTICIPATION CREDIT

World War II
  *Normandy
  *Northern France
*Rhineland
*Ardennes-Alsace
*Central Europe

DECORATIONS

Presidential Unit Citation (Army), Streamer embroidered HASTENRATH-SCHERPENSEL

*French Croix de Guerre with Silver-Gilt Star, World War II, Streamer embroidered MONS (33d Armored Regiment cited; DA GO 43, 1950)

*Belgian Fourragère 1940 (33d Armored Regiment cited; DA GO 43, 1950)

*Cited in the Order of the Day of the Belgian Army for action in BELGIUM

*Cited in the Order of the Day of the Belgian Army for action in the ARDENNES

5th BATTALION, 33d ARMOR

RA

(194th Armored Brigade)

LINEAGE

Constituted 13 January 1941 in the Regular Army as Company E, 3d Armored Regiment, an element of the 3d Armored Division. Activated 15 April 1941 at Camp Beauregard, Louisiana. Redesignated 8 May 1941 as Company E, 33d Armored Regiment. Inactivated 10 November 1945 in Germany.

Redesignated 7 July 1947 as Company B, 33d Tank Battalion. Activated 15 July 1947 at Fort Knox, Kentucky, as an element of the 3d Armored Division. Reorganized and redesignated 30 July 1948 as Company B, 33d Medium Tank Battalion. Reorganized and redesignated 15 March 1955 as Company B, 33d Tank Battalion.

Inactivated 1 October 1957 in Germany; concurrently, redesignated as Headquarters and Headquarters Company, 5th Medium Tank Battalion, 33d Armor, and relieved from assignment to 3d Armored Division (organic elements constituted 10 May 1963). Activated 1 July 1963 at Fort Knox, Kentucky. Redesignated 24 September 1963 as 5th Battalion, 33d Armor. Assigned 15 April 1968 to 194th Armored Brigade.

CAMPAIGN PARTICIPATION CREDIT

World War II
*Normandy
*Northern France

*Rhineland
*Ardennes-Alsace
*Central Europe

DECORATIONS

Presidential Unit Citation (Army), Streamer embroidered HASTENRATH-SCHERPENSEL

*French Croix de Guerre with Silver-Gilt Star, World War II, Streamer embroidered MONS (33d Armored Regiment cited; DA GO 43, 1950)

*Belgian Fourragère 1940 (33d Armored Regiment cited; DA GO 43, 1950)

*Cited in the Order of the Day of the Belgian Army for action 3–13 September 1944 in BELGIUM

*Cited in the Order of the Day of the Belgian Army for action 20–25 December 1944 in the ARDENNES

BIBLIOGRAPHY, 33D ARMOR

Department of the Army. AMERICAN FORCES IN ACTION series. *St-Lo*. 1946.

Roberts, A. Eaton. *Five Stars to Victory. The Exploits of Task Force Lovelady . . . 33d Armored Regiment . . . Against Germany, 1944–1945.* Birmingham, Alabama: 1949.

Rock, William R. *3d Armored Division (Spearhead), A History of the 3d Armored Division.* Germany: 1958.

Unit Members. *A History of the Third Armored Division, April 1941– July 1958.* Germany: 1958.

————. *Call Me Spearhead, Saga of the Third Armored "Spearhead" Division.* Paris: 1944.

————. *Conquer, The Story of the Ninth Army.* Washington: 1947.

————. *Historical and Pictorial Review, Third Armored Division of the United States Army.* Baton Rouge, Louisiana: 1942.

————. *Spearhead in the West, 1941–45, The Third Armored Division.* Europe: 1945.

————. *Spearheading with the Third Armored Division in the Bulge, Duren-Cologne . . . East to the Elbe.* Europe: 1945. Sequel to *Call Me Spearhead.*

UNITED STATES ARMY IN WORLD WAR II
Blumenson, Martin. *Breakout and Pursuit.* 1961.
Cole, Hugh M. *The Ardennes: Battle of the Bulge.* 1965.
————. *The Lorraine Campaign.* 1950.
Harrison, Gordon A. *Cross-Channel Attack.* 1951.
MacDonald, Charles B. *The Siegfried Line Campaign.* 1963.

34th ARMOR

Heraldic Items

Coat of Arms

Shield: Azure, an arm embowed proper and couped at the shoulder raised and armed with a buckler or having seven rivets of the field three and four.

Crest: On a wreath or and azure, in front of a tower gules masoned of the first and emitting from each side a stream of water of the second, three spears one in pale and two in saltire with shafts of the first and points of the second those points in saltire each charged with a fleur-de-lis of the first, over all in pale an escutcheon barry of ten argent and of the second.

Motto: The Strong Arm for Victory.

Symbolism: The buckler represents the armored protective device. The arm embowed is raised in the attitude of striking.

The red tower gushing water to each side alludes to the bitter fighting at the Roer River dams, for which a Presidential Unit Citation was awarded. The spears symbolize the advance through Normandy, northern France, and Germany. The shield, bearing a part of the arms of Luxembourg, represents the award of the Luxembourg Croix de Guerre for participation in the liberation of that country.

Distinctive Insignia

The distinctive insignia is the shield of the coat of arms.

Lineage and Honors

Lineage

Constituted 28 August 1941 in the Regular Army as 34th Armored Regiment and assigned to 5th Armored Division. Activated 1 October 1941 at Fort Knox, Kentucky. Regiment broken up 20 September 1943 and its elements reorganized and redesignated as follows: Regimental Headquarters and Headquarters Company and 2d Battalion as 34th Tank Battalion, an element of the

5th Armored Division; 1st Battalion as 772d Tank Battalion and relieved from assignment to 5th Armored Division; 3d Battalion as 10th Tank Battalion, an element of the 5th Armored Division; Reconnaissance Company as Troop D, 85th Cavalry Reconnaissance Squadron, Mechanized, an element of the 5th Armored Division; Maintenance Company and Service Company disbanded.

34th Tank Battalion inactivated 8 October 1945 at Camp Myles Standish, Massachusetts. Redesignated 18 June 1948 as 34th Medium Tank Battalion. Activated 6 July 1948 at Camp Chaffee, Arkansas. Inactivated 1 February 1950 at Camp Chaffee, Arkansas. Activated 1 September 1950 at Camp Chaffee, Arkansas. Inactivated 16 March 1956 at Camp Chaffee, Arkansas. Relieved 27 March 1957 from assignment to 5th Armored Division.

772d Tank Battalion inactivated 14 November 1945 at Camp Shelby, Mississippi. Redesignated 16 January 1947 as 306th Tank Battalion; concurrently, withdrawn from the Regular Army and allotted to the Organized Reserves. Headquarters and Headquarters Company activated 5 February 1947 at Seattle, Washington (organic companies activated 25 June 1947 at Seattle, Washington). Reorganized and redesignated 2 May 1949 as 306th Heavy Tank Battalion. Inactivated 15 September 1950 at Seattle, Washington. Disbanded 20 February 1952. Reconstituted 27 March 1957; concurrently, withdrawn from the Army Reserve (formerly Organized Reserves) and allotted to the Regular Army.

10th Tank Battalion inactivated 9 October 1945 at Camp Myles Standish, Massachusetts. Redesignated 18 June 1948 as 10th Medium Tank Battalion. Activated 6 July 1948 at Camp Chaffee, Arkansas. Inactivated 1 February 1950 at Camp Chaffee, Arkansas. Activated 1 September 1950 at Camp Chaffee, Arkansas. Inactivated 16 March 1956 at Camp Chaffee, Arkansas. Relieved 27 March 1957 from assignment to 5th Armored Division.

Troop D, 85th Cavalry Reconnaissance Squadron, Mechanized, redesignated 25 August 1945 as Troop D, 85th Mechanized Cavalry Reconnaissance Squadron. Inactivated 11 October 1945 at Camp Kilmer, New Jersey. Redesignated 18 June 1948 as Company D, 85th Reconnaissance Battalion. Activated 6 July 1948 at Camp Chaffee, Arkansas. Inactivated 1 February 1950 at Camp Chaffee, Arkansas. Activated 1 September 1950 at Camp Chaffee, Arkansas. Inactivated 16 March 1956 at Camp Chaffee, Arkansas.

Maintenance Company, 34th Armored Regiment, and Service Company, 34th Armored Regiment, reconstituted 27 March 1957.

34th and 10th Medium Tank Battalions and 306th Heavy Tank Battalion; Company D, 85th Reconnaissance Battalion; and reconstituted companies of 34th Armored Regiment consolidated and redesignated 27 March 1957 as 34th Armor, a parent regiment under the Combat Arms Regimental System (Headquarters and Headquarters and Service Company, 34th Medium Tank Battalion, redesignated as Headquarters and Headquarters Company, 34th Armor).

CAMPAIGN PARTICIPATION CREDIT

World War II
    Normandy
    Northern France
    Rhineland
    Ardennes-Alsace
    Central Europe

Vietnam
    Counteroffensive, Phase II
    Counteroffensive, Phase III
    Tet Counteroffensive

DECORATIONS

Presidential Unit Citation (Army), Streamer embroidered ROER RIVER DAMS (10th Tank Battalion cited; WD GO 31, 1947)

Luxembourg Croix de Guerre, Streamer embroidered LUXEMBOURG (10th and 34th Tank Battalions and 85th Cavalry Reconnaissance Squadron cited; DA GO 43, 1950 and DA GO 44, 1951)

1st BATTALION, 34th ARMOR

LINEAGE

Constituted 28 August 1941 in the Regular Army as Company A, 34th Armored Regiment, an element of the 5th Armored Division. Activated 1 October 1941 at Fort Knox, Kentucky. Redesignated 20 September 1943 as Company A, 772d Tank Battalion and relieved from assignment to 5th Armored Division. Inactivated 14 November 1945 at Camp Shelby, Mississippi.

Redesignated 16 January 1947 as Company A, 306th Tank Battalion; concurrently, withdrawn from the Regular Army, allotted to the Organized Reserves, and assigned to Sixth Army. Activated 25 June 1947 at Seattle, Washington. (Organized Reserves redesignated in 1948 as the Organized Reserve Corps; in 1952, as the Army Reserve.) Reorganized and redesignated 2 May 1949 as Company A, 306th Heavy Tank Battalion. Inactivated 15 September 1950 at Seattle, Washington. Disbanded 20 February 1952.

Reconstituted and redesignated 27 March 1957 as Company A, 34th Armor; concurrently, withdrawn from the Army Reserve and allotted to the Regular Army. Redesignated 1 April 1957 as Headquarters and Headquarters Company, 1st Medium Tank Battalion (Patton), 34th Armor; concurrently, assigned to 4th Infantry Division and activated at Fort Lewis, Washington (organic elements concurrently constituted and activated). Reorganized and redesignated 1 October 1963 as 1st Battalion, 34th Armor. Inactivated 14 October 1965 at Fort Lewis, Washington.

CAMPAIGN PARTICIPATION CREDIT

World War II
  Normandy
  Northern France
  *Rhineland
  Ardennes-Alsace
  *Central Europe

DECORATIONS

Presidential Unit Citation (Army), Streamer embroidered ROER RIVER DAMS

2d BATTALION, 34th ARMOR

RA

(25th Infantry Division)

Constituted 28 August 1941 in the Regular Army as Company B, 34th Armored Regiment, an element of the 5th Armored Division. Activated 1 October 1941 at Fort Knox, Kentucky. Redesignated 20 September 1943 as Company B, 772d Tank Battalion and relieved from assignment to 5th Armored Division. Inactivated 14 November 1945 at Camp Shelby, Mississippi.

Redesignated 16 January 1947 as Company B, 306th Tank Battalion; concurrently, withdrawn from the Regular Army, allotted to the Organized Reserves, and assigned to Sixth Army. Activated 25 June 1947 at Seattle, Washington. (Organized Reserves redesignated in 1948 as the Organized Reserve Corps; in 1952, as the Army Reserve.) Reorganized and redesignated 2 May 1949 as Company B, 306th Heavy Tank Battalion. Inactivated 15 September 1950 at Seattle, Washington. Disbanded 20 February 1952.

Reconstituted and redesignated 27 March 1957 as Company B, 34th Armor; concurrently, withdrawn from the Army Reserve and allotted to the Regular Army. Activated 1 June 1957 at Fort Ord, California. Inactivated 25 April 1961 at Fort Ord, California. Redesignated 21 August 1963 as Headquarters and Headquarters Company, 2d Battalion, 34th Armor, and assigned to 4th Infantry Division (organic elements concurrently constituted). Activated 1 October 1963 at Fort Irwin, California. Relieved 1 August 1967 from assignment to 4th Infantry Division and assigned to 25th Infantry Division.

CAMPAIGN PARTICIPATION CREDIT

World War II
Normandy
Northern France
*Rhineland
Ardennes-Alsace
*Central Europe

Vietnam
*Counteroffensive, Phase II
*Counteroffensive, Phase III
*Tet Counteroffensive

DECORATIONS

Presidential Unit Citation (Army), Streamer embroidered ROER RIVER DAMS

3d MEDIUM TANK BATTALION, 34th ARMOR

RA
(inactive)

LINEAGE

Constituted 28 August 1941 in the Regular Army as Company C, 34th Armored Regiment, an element of the 5th Armored Division. Activated 1 October 1941 at Fort Knox, Kentucky. Redesignated 20 September 1943 as Company C, 772d Tank Battalion and relieved from assignment to 5th Armored Division. Inactivated 14 November 1945 at Camp Shelby, Mississippi.

Redesignated 16 January 1947 as Company C, 306th Tank Battalion; concurrently, withdrawn from the Regular Army, allotted to the Organized Reserves, and assigned to Sixth Army. Activated 25 June 1947 at Seattle, Washington. (Organized Reserves redesignated in 1948 as the Organized Reserve Corps; in 1952, as the Army Reserve.) Reorganized and redesignated 2 May 1949 as Company C, 306th Heavy Tank Battalion. Inactivated 15 September 1950 at Seattle, Washington. Disbanded 20 February 1952.

Reconstituted 27 March 1957 and redesignated as Headquarters and Headquarters Company, 3d Medium Tank Battalion (Patton), 34th Armor; concurrently, withdrawn from Army Reserve and allotted to the Regular Army. Activated 1 July 1958 in Germany and assigned to 24th Infantry Division (organic elements constituted 5 June 1958 and activated 1 July 1958). Inactivated 1 February 1963 in Germany and relieved from assignment to 24th Infantry Division.

CAMPAIGN PARTICIPATION CREDIT

World War II
Normandy
Northern France

*Rhineland
Ardennes-Alsace
*Central Europe

DECORATIONS

Presidential Unit Citation (Army), Streamer embroidered ROER RIVER DAMS

296

COMPANY D, 34th ARMOR

RA
(inactive)

LINEAGE

Constituted 28 August 1941 in the Regular Army as Company D, 34th Armored Regiment, an element of the 5th Armored Division. Activated 1 October 1941 at Fort Knox, Kentucky. Redesignated 20 September 1943 as Company A, 34th Tank Battalion, an element of the 5th Armored Division. Inactivated 8 October 1945 at Camp Myles Standish, Massachusetts. Redesignated 18 June 1948 as Company A, 34th Medium Tank Battalion. Activated 6 July 1948 at Camp Chaffee, Arkansas. Inactivated 1 February 1950 at Camp Chaffee, Arkansas. Activated 1 September 1950 at Camp Chaffee, Arkansas. Inactivated 16 March 1956 at Camp Chaffee, Arkansas.

Redesignated 27 March 1957 as Headquarters and Headquarters Company, 4th Medium Tank Battalion, 34th Armor, and relieved from assignment to 5th Armored Division. Redesignated 8 November 1957 as Company D (Walker), 34th Armor. Activated 15 November 1957 at Fort Kobbe, Canal Zone. Inactivated 8 August 1962 at Fort Kobbe, Canal Zone.

CAMPAIGN PARTICIPATION CREDIT

World War II-EAME
   Normandy
   Northern France

Rhineland
Ardennes-Alsace
Central Europe

DECORATIONS

Luxembourg Croix de Guerre, Streamer embroidered LUXEMBOURG (34th Tank Battalion cited; DA GO 43, 1950 and DA GO 44, 1951)

297

COMPANY E, 34th ARMOR

RA
(inactive)

Constituted 28 August 1941 in the Regular Army as Company E, 34th Armored Regiment, an element of the 5th Armored Division. Activated 1 October 1941 at Fort Knox, Kentucky. Redesignated 20 September 1943 as Company B, 34th Tank Battalion, an element of the 5th Armored Division. Inactivated 8 October 1945 at Camp Myles Standish, Massachusetts.

Redesignated 18 June 1948 as Company B, 34th Medium Tank Battalion. Activated 6 July 1948 at Camp Chaffee, Arkansas. Inactivated 1 February 1950 at Camp Chaffee, Arkansas. Activated 1 September 1950 at Camp Chaffee, Arkansas. Inactivated 16 March 1956 at Camp Chaffee, Arkansas.

Redesignated 27 March 1957 as Headquarters and Headquarters Company, 5th Medium Tank Battalion, 34th Armor, and relieved from assignment to 5th Armored Division. Redesignated 3 January 1958 as Company E, 34th Armor. Activated 22 January 1958 at Fort Sill, Oklahoma. Inactivated 25 March 1961 at Fort Sill, Oklahoma.

CAMPAIGN PARTICIPATION CREDIT

World War II–EAME
Normandy
Northern France

Rhineland
Ardennes-Alsace
Central Europe

DECORATIONS

Luxembourg Croix de Guerre, Streamer embroidered LUXEMBOURG (34th Tank Battalion cited; DA GO 43, 1950 and DA GO 44, 1951)

298

COMPANY F, 34th ARMOR

RA
(inactive)

Constituted 28 August 1941 in the Regular Army as Company F, 34th Armored Regiment, an element of the 5th Armored Division. Activated 1 October 1941 at Fort Knox, Kentucky. Redesignated 20 September 1943 as Company C, 34th Tank Battalion, an element of the 5th Armored Division. Inactivated 8 October 1945 at Camp Myles Standish, Massachusetts.

Redesignated 18 June 1948 as Company C, 34th Medium Tank Battalion. Activated 6 July 1948 at Camp Chaffee, Arkansas. Inactivated 1 February 1950 at Camp Chaffee, Arkansas. Activated 1 September 1950 at Camp Chaffee, Arkansas. Inactivated 16th March 1956 at Camp Chaffee, Arkansas.

Redesignated 27 March 1957 as Headquarters and Headquarters Company, 6th Medium Tank Battalion, 34th Armor, and relieved from assignment to 5th Armored Division. Redesignated 12 February 1958 as Company F, 34th Armor, and assigned to 2d Infantry Brigade. Activated 15 February 1958 at Fort Devens, Massachusetts. Inactivated 19 February 1962 at Fort Devens, Massachusetts. Relieved 20 April 1962 from assignment to 2d Infantry Brigade.

CAMPAIGN PARTICIPATION CREDIT

World War II–EAME
Normandy
Northern France

Rhineland
Ardennes-Alsace
Central Europe

DECORATIONS

Luxembourg Croix de Guerre, Streamer embroidered LUXEMBOURG (34th Tank Battalion cited; DA GO 43, 1950 and DA GO 44, 1951)

299

COMPANY G, 34th ARMOR

RA
(inactive)

LINEAGE

Constituted 28 August 1941 in the Regular Army as Company G, 34th Armored Regiment, an element of the 5th Armored Division. Activated 1 October 1941 at Fort Knox, Kentucky. Redesignated 20 September 1943 as Company A, 10th Tank Battalion, an element of the 5th Armored Division. Inactivated 9 October 1945 at Camp Myles Standish, Massachusetts.

Redesignated 18 June 1948 as Company A, 10th Medium Tank Battalion. Activated 6 July 1948 at Camp Chaffee, Arkansas. Inactivated 1 February 1950 at Camp Chaffee, Arkansas. Activated 1 September 1950 at Camp Chaffee, Arkansas. Inactivated 16 March 1956 at Camp Chaffee, Arkansas.

Redesignated 27 March 1957 as Headquarters and Headquarters Company, 7th Medium Tank Battalion, 34th Armor, and relieved from assignment to 5th Armored Division. Redesignated 12 February 1958 as Company G, 34th Armor, and assigned to 2d Infantry Brigade. Activated 15 February 1958 at Fort Devens, Massachusetts. Inactivated 20 April 1962 at Fort Devens, Massachusetts, and relieved from assignment to 2d Infantry Brigade.

CAMPAIGN PARTICIPATION CREDIT

World War II–EAME
   Normandy
   Northern France

Rhineland
Ardennes-Alsace
Central Europe

DECORATIONS

Presidential Unit Citation (Army), Streamer embroidered ROER RIVER DAMS (10th Tank Battalion cited; WD GO 31, 1947)

Luxembourg Croix de Guerre, Streamer embroidered LUXEMBOURG (10th Tank Battalion cited; DA GO 43, 1950 and DA GO 44, 1951)

French Croix de Guerre with Silver-Gilt Star, World War II, Streamer embroidered WALLENDORF (10th Tank Battalion cited; DA GO 43, 1950)

8th MEDIUM TANK BATTALION, 34th ARMOR

RA
(inactive)

LINEAGE

Constituted 28 August 1941 in the Regular Army as Company H, 34th Armored Regiment, an element of the 5th Armored Division. Activated 1 October 1941 at Fort Knox, Kentucky. Redesignated 20 September 1943 as Company B, 10th Tank Battalion, an element of the 5th Armored Division. Inactivated 9 October 1945 at Camp Myles Standish, Massachusetts.

Redesignated 18 June 1948 as Company B, 10th Medium Tank Battalion. Activated 6 July 1948 at Camp Chaffee, Arkansas. Inactivated 1 February 1950 at Camp Chaffee, Arkansas. Activated 1 September 1950 at Camp Chaffee, Arkansas. Inactivated 16 March 1956 at Camp Chaffee, Arkansas.

Redesignated 27 March 1957 as Headquarters and Headquarters Company, 8th Medium Tank Battalion, 34th Armor, and relieved from assignment to 5th Armored Division. Redesignated 10 June 1958 as Company H (Walker), 34th Armor. Activated 25 June 1958 at Fort Knox, Kentucky.

Reorganized and redesignated 12 December 1958 as Headquarters and Headquarters Company, 8th Medium Tank Battalion (Patton), 34th Armor (organic elements concurrently constituted and activated). Inactivated 24 September 1963 at Fort Knox, Kentucky.

CAMPAIGN PARTICIPATION CREDIT

World War II
  *Normandy
  *Northern France

*Rhineland
*Ardennes-Alsace
*Central Europe

DECORATIONS

*Presidential Unit Citation (Army), Streamer embroidered ROER RIVER DAMS (10th Tank Battalion cited; WD GO 31, 1947)

*Luxembourg Croix de Guerre, Streamer embroidered LUXEMBOURG (10th Tank Battalion cited; DA GO 43, 1950 and DA GO 44, 1951)

*French Croix de Guerre with Silver-Gilt Star, World War II, Streamer embroidered WALLENDORF (10th Tank Battalion cited; DA GO 43, 1950)

9th BATTALION, 34th ARMOR

AR
(187th Infantry Brigade)

Constituted 28 August 1941 in the Regular Army as Company I, 34th Armored Regiment, an element of the 5th Armored Division. Activated 1 October 1941 at Fort Knox, Kentucky. Reorganized and redesignated 20 September 1943 as Company C, 10th Tank Battalion, an element of the 5th Armored Division. Inactivated 9 October 1945 at Camp Myles Standish, Massachusetts.

Redesignated 18 June 1948 as Company C, 10th Medium Tank Battalion. Activated 6 July 1948 at Camp Chaffee, Arkansas. Inactivated 1 February 1950 at Camp Chaffee, Arkansas. Activated 1 September 1950 at Camp Chaffee, Arkansas. Inactivated 16 March 1956 at Camp Chaffee, Arkansas.

Redesignated 27 March 1957 as Headquarters and Headquarters Company, 9th Medium Tank Battalion, 34th Armor, and relieved from assignment to 5th Armored Division. Withdrawn from the Regular Army 6 April 1959, allotted to the Army Reserve, and assigned to 94th Infantry Division (organic elements concurrently constituted). Activated 1 May 1959 with Headquarters at Boston, Massachusetts.

Reorganized and redesignated 7 January 1963 as 9th Battalion, 34th Armor, relieved from assignment to 94th Infantry Division, and assigned to 187th Infantry Brigade.

Home Area: First United States Army.

CAMPAIGN PARTICIPATION CREDIT

World War II
    *Normandy
    *Northern France

*Rhineland
*Ardennes-Alsace
*Central Europe

DECORATIONS

*Presidential Unit Citation (Army), Streamer embroidered ROER RIVER DAMS (10th Tank Battalion cited; WD GO 31, 1947)

*Luxembourg Croix de Guerre, Streamer embroidered LUXEMBOURG (10th Tank Battalion cited; DA GO 43, 1950 and DA GO 44, 1951)

*French Croix de Guerre with Silver-Gilt Star, World War II, Streamer embroidered WALLENDORF

Bibliography, 34th Armor

Unit Members. *Paths of Armor, Normandy, Northern France, Ardennes, Alsace, Rhineland, Central Europe. A History of 5th Armored Division.* Atlanta, Georgia: 1950.

————. *The Road to Germany, the Story of the 5th Armored Division.* Paris: 1944.

————. *The Victory Division in Europe, Story of the Fifth Armored Division.* Europe: 1945.

UNITED STATES ARMY IN WORLD WAR II

Blumenson, Martin. *Breakout and Pursuit.* 1961.

Cole, Hugh M. *The Lorraine Campaign.* 1950.

MacDonald, Charles B. *The Siegfried Line Campaign.* 1963.

MacDonald, Charles B., and Sidney T. Mathews. *Three Battles: Arnaville, Altuzzo, and Schmidt.* 1952.

35th ARMOR

Heraldic Items

Coat of Arms

Shield: Vert, an armadillo passant argent, langued gules.

Crest: On a wreath of the colors, argent and vert, a fleur-de-lis gules in front of a palm branch of the first.

Motto: *Vincere Vel Mori* (To Conquer or Die).

Symbolism: The shield is green, the color of the Armored Force. The armadillo, being characterized by the qualities of invulnerability, protection, and cunning endurance, alludes to the elements that are vital if the organization is to pursue successfully its duties. The palm is for military victory. The fleur-de-lis commemorates World War II service in France. The color red symbolizes courage.

Distinctive Insignia

The distinctive insignia is the shield, crest, and motto of the coat of arms.

Lineage and Honors

Lineage

Constituted 13 January 1941 in the Regular Army as 5th Armored Regiment and assigned to 4th Armored Division. Activated 15 April 1941 at Pine Camp, New York. Redesignated 8 May 1941 as 35th Armored Regiment.

Regiment broken up 10 September 1943 and its elements reorganized and redesignated as follows: Regimental Headquarters and Headquarters Company and 2d Battalion as 35th Tank Battalion, an element of the 4th Armored Division; 1st Battalion as 771st Tank Battalion and relieved from assignment to 4th Armored Division; 3d Battalion as 8th Tank Battalion, an element of the 4th Armored Division; Reconnaissance Company as Troop D, 25th Cavalry Reconnaissance Squadron, Mechanized, an element of the 4th Armored Division; Maintenance and Service Companies disbanded.

35th Tank Battalion relieved 1 May 1946 from assignment to 4th Armored Division; concurrently, converted and redesignated as 35th Constabulary Squad-

305

ron and assigned to 5th Constabulary Regiment. Inactivated 20 September 1947 at Augsburg, Germany. Converted and redesignated 11 December 1951 as 35th Tank Battalion and relieved from assignment to 5th Constabulary Regiment. Assigned 25 February 1953 to 4th Armored Division. Activated 15 June 1954 at Fort Hood, Texas. Inactivated 1 April 1957 at Fort Hood, Texas, and relieved from assignment to 4th Armored Division.

771st Tank Battalion (less Company D and Service Company) converted and redesignated 1 May 1946 as 71st Constabulary Squadron and assigned to 10th Constabulary Regiment. Inactivated 20 September 1947 at Hessenthal, Germany. Converted and redesignated 11 December 1951 as 771st Tank Battalion and relieved from assignment to 10th Constabulary Regiment. (Company D, 771st Tank Battalion, redesignated 1 May 1946 as Light Tank Troop, 10th Constabulary Regiment. Inactivated 28 February 1947. Disbanded 25 February 1953. Reconstituted 1 April 1957 in the Regular Army.) (Service Company, 771st Tank Battalion, redesignated 1 May 1946 as Service Troop, 10th Constabulary Regiment. Inactivated 20 September 1947. Disbanded 25 February 1953. Reconstituted 1 April 1957 in the Regular Army.)

8th Tank Battalion relieved 1 May 1946 from assignment to 4th Armored Division; concurrently, converted and redesignated as 8th Constabulary Squadron and assigned to 5th Constabulary Regiment. Inactivated 20 September 1947 at Landshut, Germany. Converted and redesignated 11 December 1951 as 8th Tank Battalion and relieved from assignment to 5th Constabulary Regiment. Redesignated 25 February 1953 as 508th Tank Battalion and assigned to 4th Armored Division. Activated 15 June 1954 at Fort Hood, Texas. Inactivated 1 April 1957 at Fort Hood, Texas, and relieved from assignment to 4th Armored Division.

Troop D, 25th Cavalry Reconnaissance Squadron, Mechanized, redesignated 15 September 1945 as Troop D, 25th Mechanized Cavalry Reconnaissance Squadron. Relieved 1 May 1946 from assignment to 4th Armored Division; concurrently, converted and redesignated as Troop D, 25th Constabulary Squadron, an element of the 11th Constabulary Regiment. Inactivated 20 December 1948 in Germany; concurrently, converted and redesignated as Company D, 25th Reconnaissance Battalion, and relieved from assignment to 11th Constabulary Regiment. Assigned 25 February 1953 to 4th Armored Division. Activated 15 June 1954 at Fort Hood, Texas. Inactivated 1 April 1957 at Fort Hood, Texas, and relieved from assignment to 4th Armored Division.

35th, 771st, and 508th Tank Battalions; Company D, 25th Reconnaissance Battalion; Light Tank Troop, 10th Constabulary Regiment; and Service Troop, 10th Constabulary Regiment, consolidated and redesignated 1 April 1957 as 35th Armor, a parent regiment under the Combat Arms Regimental System

(Headquarters and Headquarters and Service Company, 35th Tank Battalion, redesignated as Headquarters and Headquarters Company, 35th Armor).

CAMPAIGN PARTICIPATION CREDIT

World War II
Normandy
Northern France

Rhineland
Ardennes-Alsace
Central Europe

DECORATIONS

Presidential Unit Citation (Army), Streamer embroidered ARDENNES (35th and 8th Tank Battalions and 25th Cavalry Reconnaissance Squadron cited; WD GO 54, 1945)

French Croix de Guerre with Palm, World War II, Streamer embroidered NORMANDY (35th and 8th Tank Battalions and 25th Cavalry Reconnaissance Squadron cited; DA GO 43, 1950)

French Croix de Guerre with Palm, World War II, Streamer embroidered MOSELLE RIVER (35th and 8th Tank Battalions and 25th Cavalry Reconnaissance Squadron cited; DA GO 43, 1950)

French Croix de Guerre, World War II, Fourragère (35th and 8th Tank Battalions and 25th Cavalry Reconnaissance Squadron cited; DA GO 43, 1950)

1st BATTALION, 35th ARMOR

RA
(4th Armored Division)

LINEAGE

Constituted 13 January 1941 in the Regular Army as Company A, 5th Armored Regiment, an element of the 4th Armored Division. Activated 15 April 1941 at Pine Camp, New York. Redesignated 8 May 1941 as Company A, 35th Armored Regiment.

Redesignated 10 September 1943 as Company A, 771st Tank Battalion and relieved from assignment to 4th Armored Division. Converted and redesignated 1 May 1946 as Troop A, 71st Constabulary Squadron, an element of the 10th Constabulary Regiment. Inactivated 20 September 1947 in Germany. Converted and redesignated 11 December 1951 as Company A, 771st Tank Battalion, and relieved from assignment to 10th Constabulary Regiment.

Redesignated 1 April 1957 as Headquarters and Headquarters Company, 1st Medium Tank Battalion (Patton), 35th Armor; concurrently, assigned to 4th Armored Division and activated at Fort Hood, Texas (organic elements concurrently constituted and activated). Reorganized and redesignated 20 August 1963 as 1st Battalion, 35th Armor.

CAMPAIGN PARTICIPATION CREDIT

World War II
  Normandy
  Northern France

*Rhineland
*Ardennes-Alsace
*Central Europe

DECORATIONS

Presidential Unit Citation (Army), Streamer embroidered ARDENNES

2d MEDIUM TANK BATTALION, 35th ARMOR

RA
(inactive)

LINEAGE

Constituted 13 January 1941 in the Regular Army as Company B, 5th Armored Regiment, an element of the 4th Armored Division. Activated 15 April 1941 at Pine Camp, New York. Redesignated 8 May 1941 as Company B, 35th Armored Regiment.

Redesignated 10 September 1943 as Company B, 771st Tank Battalion, and relieved from assignment to 4th Armored Division. Converted and redesignated 1 May 1946 as Troop B, 71st Constabulary Squadron, an element of the 10th Constabulary Regiment. Inactivated 20 September 1947 in Germany. Converted and redesignated 11 December 1951 as Company B, 771st Tank Battalion, and relieved from assignment to 10th Constabulary Regiment. Redesignated 1 April 1957 as Company B, 35th Armored Regiment.

Redesignated 1 July 1957 as Headquarters and Headquarters Company, 2d Medium Tank Battalion (Patton), 35th Armor; concurrently, assigned to 2d Armored Division and activated in Germany (organic elements concurrently constituted and activated). Inactivated 1 July 1963 at Fort Hood, Texas, and relieved from assignment to 2d Armored Division.

CAMPAIGN PARTICIPATION CREDIT

World War II
Normandy
Northern France

*Rhineland
*Ardennes-Alsace
*Central Europe

DECORATIONS

Presidential Unit Citation (Army), Streamer embroidered ARDENNES

3d BATTALION, 35th ARMOR

RA
(4th Armored Division)

LINEAGE

Constituted 13 January 1941 in the Regular Army as Company C, 5th Armored Regiment, an element of the 4th Armored Division. Activated 15 April 1941 at Pine Camp, New York. Redesignated 8 May 1941 as Company C, 35th Armored Regiment.

Redesignated 10 September 1943 as Company C, 771st Tank Battalion, and relieved from assignment to 4th Armored Division. Converted and redesignated 1 May 1946 as Troop C, 71st Constabulary Squadron, an element of the 10th Constabulary Regiment. Inactivated 20 September 1947 in Germany. Converted and redesignated 11 December 1951 as Company C, 771st Tank Battalion, and relieved from assignment to 10th Constabulary Regiment.

Redesignated 1 April 1957 as Headquarters and Headquarters Company, 3d Medium Tank Battalion, 35th Armor. Activated 1 May 1958 in Germany (organic elements constituted 12 March 1958 and activated 1 May 1958). Assigned 5 June 1963 to 4th Armored Division. Reorganized and redesignated 1 August 1963 as 3d Battalion, 35th Armor.

CAMPAIGN PARTICIPATION CREDIT

World War II
Normandy
Northern France

*Rhineland
*Ardennes-Alsace
*Central Europe

DECORATIONS

Presidential Unit Citation (Army), Streamer embroidered ARDENNES

4th BATTALION, 35th ARMOR

RA

(4th Armored Division)

LINEAGE

Constituted 13 January 1941 in the Regular Army as Company D, 5th Armored Regiment, an element of the 4th Armored Division. Activated 15 April 1941 at Pine Camp, New York. Redesignated 8 May 1941 as Company D, 35th Armored Regiment.

Redesignated 10 September 1943 as Company A, 35th Tank Battalion, an element of the 4th Armored Division. Converted and redesignated 1 May 1946 as Troop A, 35th Constabulary Squadron, an element of the 5th Constabulary Regiment. Inactivated 20 September 1947 at Augsburg, Germany, and relieved from assignment to 5th Constabulary Regiment. Converted and redesignated 11 December 1951 as Company A, 35th Tank Battalion. (35th Tank Battalion assigned 25 February 1953 to 4th Armored Division.) Activated 15 June 1945 at Fort Hood, Texas.

Inactivated 1 April 1957 at Fort Hood, Texas; concurrently, relieved from assignment to 4th Armored Division and redesignated as Headquarters and Headquarters Company, 4th Medium Tank Battalion, 35th Armor. Withdrawn from the Regular Army 11 May 1959, allotted to the Army Reserve, and assigned to 102d Infantry Division (organic elements concurrently constituted). Activated 1 June 1959 at St. Louis, Missouri. Inactivated 1 April 1963 at St. Louis, Missouri, and relieved from assignment to 102d Infantry Division. Redesignated 1 July 1963 as 4th Battalion, 35th Armor; concurrently, withdrawn from the Army Reserve, allotted to the Regular Army, assigned to the 4th Armored Division, and activated in Germany.

CAMPAIGN PARTICIPATION CREDIT

World War II
*Normandy
*Northern France
*Rhineland
*Ardennes-Alsace
*Central Europe

311

Decorations

*Presidential Unit Citation (Army), Streamer embroidered ARDENNES (35th Tank Battalion cited; WD GO 54, 1945)

*French Croix de Guerre with Palm, World War II, Streamer embroidered NORMANDY (35th Tank Battalion cited; DA GO 43, 1950)

*French Croix de Guerre with Palm, World War II, Streamer embroidered MOSELLE RIVER (35th Tank Battalion cited; DA GO 43, 1950)

*French Croix de Guerre, World War II, Fourragère (35th Tank Battalion cited; DA GO 43, 1950)

5th BATTALION, 35th ARMOR

AR
(nondivisional)

LINEAGE

Constituted 13 January 1941 in the Regular Army as Company E, 5th Armored Regiment, an element of the 4th Armored Division. Activated 15 April 1941 at Pine Camp, New York. Redesignated 8 May 1941 as Company E, 35th Armored Regiment.

Redesignated 10 September 1943 as Company B, 35th Tank Battalion, an element of the 4th Armored Division. Converted and redesignated 1 May 1946 as Troop B, 35th Constabulary Squadron, an element of the 5th Constabulary Regiment. Inactivated 20 September 1947 at Augsburg, Germany, and relieved from assignment to 5th Constabulary Regiment. Converted and redesignated 11 December 1951 as Company B, 35th Tank Battalion. (35th Tank Battalion assigned 25 February 1953 to 4th Armored Division.) Activated 15 June 1954 at Fort Hood, Texas.

Inactivated 1 April 1957 at Fort Hood, Texas; concurrently, relieved from assignment to 4th Armored Division and redesignated as Headquarters and Headquarters Company, 5th Medium Tank Battalion, 35th Armor. Withdrawn from the Regular Army 24 March 1959, allotted to the Army Reserve, and assigned to Fourth United States Army (organic elements concurrently constituted). Activated 1 April 1959 with Headquarters, at Albuquerque, New Mexico. Reorganized and redesignated 29 April 1964 as 5th Battalion, 35th Armor. (Location changed 1 January 1966 to Laredo, Texas.)

Home Area: Fourth United States Army.

CAMPAIGN PARTICIPATION CREDIT

World War II
  *Normandy
  *Northern France

*Rhineland
*Ardennes-Alsace
*Central Europe

DECORATIONS

*Presidential Unit Citation (Army), Streamer embroidered ARDENNES (35th Tank Battalion cited; WD GO 54, 1945)

*French Croix de Guerre with Palm, World War II, Streamer embroidered NORMANDY (35th Tank Battalion cited; DA GO 43, 1950)

*French Croix de Guerre with Palm, World War II, Streamer embroidered MOSELLE RIVER (35th Tank Battalion cited; DA GO 43, 1950)

*French Croix de Guerre, World War II, Fourragère (35th Tank Battalion cited; DA GO 43, 1950)

6th BATTALION, 35th ARMOR

AR
(inactive)

LINEAGE

Constituted 13 January 1941 in the Regular Army as Company F, 5th Armored Regiment, an element of the 4th Armored Division. Activated 15 April 1941 at Pine Camp, New York. Redesignated 8 May 1941 as Company F, 35th Armored Regiment.

Redesignated 10 September 1943 as Company C, 35th Tank Battalion. Converted and redesignated 1 May 1946 as Troop C, 35th Constabulary Squadron, an element of the 5th Constabulary Regiment. Inactivated 20 September 1947 at Augsburg, Germany, and relieved from assignment to 5th Constabulary Regiment. Converted and redesignated 11 December 1951 as Company C, 35th Tank Battalion. (35th Tank Battalion assigned 25 February 1953 to 4th Armored Division.) Activated 15 June 1954 at Fort Hood, Texas.

Inactivated 1 April 1957 at Fort Hood, Texas; concurrently, relieved from assignment to 4th Armored Division and redesignated as Headquarters and Headquarters Company, 6th Medium Tank Battalion, 35th Armor. Redesignated 26 March 1963 as Headquarters and Headquarters Company, 6th Battalion, 35th Armor; concurrently, withdrawn from the Regular Army, allotted to the Army Reserve, and assigned to 102d Infantry Division (organic elements concurrently constituted). Activated 1 April 1963 with Headquarters at St. Louis, Missouri. Inactivated 31 December 1965 at St. Louis, Missouri, and relieved from assignment to 102d Infantry Division.

CAMPAIGN PARTICIPATION CREDIT

World War II
  *Normandy
  *Northern France

*Rhineland
*Ardennes-Alsace
*Central Europe

DECORATIONS

*Presidential Unit Citation (Army), Streamer embroidered ARDENNES (35th Tank Battalion cited; WD GO 54, 1945)

*French Croix de Guerre with Palm, World War II, Streamer embroidered NORMANDY (35th Tank Battalion cited; DA GO 43, 1950)

*French Croix de Guerre with Palm, World War II, Streamer embroidered MOSELLE RIVER (35th Tank Battalion cited; DA GO 43, 1950)

*French Croix de Guerre, World War II, Fourragère (35th Tank Battalion cited; DA GO 43, 1950)

7th BATTALION, 35th ARMOR

AR

(inactive)

Constituted 13 January 1941 in the Regular Army as Company G, 5th Armored Regiment, an element of the 4th Armored Division. Activated 15 April 1941 at Pine Camp, New York. Redesignated 8 May 1941 as Company G, 35th Armored Regiment.

Redesignated 10 September 1943 as Company A, 8th Tank Battalion, and relieved from assignment to 4th Armored Division. Converted and redesignated 1 May 1946 as Troop A, 8th Constabulary Squadron, an element of the 5th Constabulary Regiment. Inactivated 20 September 1947 in Germany and relieved from assignment to 5th Constabulary Regiment. Converted and redesignated 11 December 1951 as Company A, 8th Tank Battalion. Redesignated 25 February 1953 as Company A, 508th Tank Battalion, an element of the 4th Armored Division. Activated 15 June 1954 at Fort Hood, Texas.

Inactivated 1 April 1957 at Fort Hood, Texas; concurrently, relieved from assignment to 4th Armored Division and redesignated as Headquarters and Headquarters Company, 7th Medium Tank Battalion, 35th Armor. Redesignated 26 March 1963 as Headquarters and Headquarters Company, 7th Battalion, 35th Armor; concurrently, withdrawn from the Regular Army, allotted to the Army Reserve, and assigned to 102d Infantry Division (organic elements concurrently constituted). Activated 1 April 1963 with Headquarters at St. Louis, Missouri. Inactivated 31 December 1965 at St. Louis, Missouri, and relieved from assignment to 102d Infantry Division.

CAMPAIGN PARTICIPATION CREDIT

World War II
  *Normandy
  *Northern France
  *Rhineland

*Ardennes-Alsace
*Central Europe

315

DECORATIONS

*Presidential Unit Citation (Army), Streamer embroidered ARDENNES (8th Tank Battalion cited; WD GO 54, 1945)

*French Croix de Guerre with Palm, World War II, Streamer embroidered NORMANDY (8th Tank Battalion cited; DA GO 43, 1950)

*French Croix de Guerre with Palm, World War II, Streamer embroidered MOSELLE RIVER (8th Tank Battalion cited; DA GO 43, 1950)

*French Croix de Guerre, World War II, Fourragère (8th Tank Battalion cited; DA GO 43, 1950)

BIBLIOGRAPHY, 35TH ARMOR

Castagna, Edwin. *The History of the 771st Tank Battalion*. Berkeley, California: 1946.

Department of the Army. AMERICAN FORCES IN ACTION series.

   Small Unit Actions. 1946.

Draper, Theodore. *The 84th Infantry Division in the Battle of Ardennes*. Europe: 1945. 771st Tank Battalion supported 84th Infantry Division, December 1944–May 1945.

————. *The 84th Infantry Division in the Battle of Germany, November 1944–May 1945*. New York: 1946.

Harrison, Gordon A. *Attack on Singling by Elements of 4th Armored Division*. History Section, European Theater of Operations: 1945.

Koyen, Kenneth A. *The Fourth Armored Division From the Beach to Bavaria, the Story of the Fourth Armored Division in Combat*. Munich, Germany: 1945.

Mick, Allan H., editor. *With the 102d Infantry Division Through Germany*. Washington: 1947. 771st Tank Battalion supported 102d Infantry Division, November–December 1944.

The Armor School. *Armor in the Exploitation (the Fourth Armored Division Across France to the Moselle River)*. Fort Knox, Kentucky: 1949.

Unit Members. *The Nancy Bridgehead*. Fort Knox, Kentucky: 1946.

————. *What They Said About the 4th Armored Division*. Germany: 1945.

UNITED STATES ARMY IN WORLD WAR II

   Blumenson, Martin. *Breakout and Pursuit*. 1961.

   Cole, Hugh M. *The Ardennes: Battle of the Bulge*. 1965.

   ————. *The Lorraine Campaign*. 1950.

37th ARMOR

HERALDIC ITEMS

COAT OF ARMS

Shield: Argent, a wyvern glissant, sans legs, tail nowed vert, langued, eyed and barbed gules.

Crest: On a wreath argent and vert, between two triton shells gules and surmounting an annulet sable fimbriated of the first flamant of the third, three spearheads of the first each bearing in base an ermine spot of the fourth.

Motto: Courage Conquers.

Symbolism: The shield is green and white, the colors of the Armored Force. The wyvern represents the deadliness of the tank. The three spearheads stand for three World War II decoration streamers, NORMANDY, MOSELLE RIVER, and ARDENNES, and for the regiment's claim to the title, "Point of the Spearhead." The ermine spots are from the arms of Nantes, Brittany. The annulet ringed with flames represents Bastogne surrounded by enemy fire. The triton shells, used as war trumpets by the early inhabitants of Pacific islands, are scarlet, the color of the Meritorious Unit Commendation streamer awarded for service in the Pacific theater.

DISTINCTIVE INSIGNIA

The distinctive insignia is the shield and motto of the coat of arms.

LINEAGE AND HONORS

LINEAGE

Constituted 13 January 1941 in the Regular Army as 7th Armored Regiment and assigned to 4th Armored Division. Activated 15 April 1941 at Pine Camp, New York. Redesignated 8 May 1941 as 37th Armored Regiment.

Regiment broken up 10 September 1943 and its elements reorganized and redesignated as follows: Regimental Headquarters and Headquarters Company, 1st Battalion, and Company D as 37th Tank Battalion, an element of the 4th Armored Division; 3d Battalion as 706th Tank Battalion and relieved from assignment to 4th Armored Division; Reconnaissance Company as Troop E, 25th Cavalry Reconnaissance Squadron, Mechanized, an element of the 4th Armored Division (hereafter separate lineage); 2d Battalion (less Company D), absorbed in 37th Tank Battalion; Maintenance and Service Companies disbanded.

37th Tank Battalion relieved 1 May 1946 from assignment to 4th Armored Division; concurrently, converted and redesignated as 37th Constabulary Squadron and assigned to 3d Constabulary Regiment. Inactivated 20 September 1947 at Weilburg, Germany. Converted and redesignated 11 December 1951 as 37th Tank Battalion and relieved from assignment to 3d Constabulary Regiment. Assigned 25 February 1953 to 4th Armored Division. Activated 15 June 1954 at Fort Hood, Texas. Relieved 1 April 1957 from assignment to 4th Armored Division; concurrently, battalion (less Company A) inactivated at Fort Hood, Texas (Company A reorganized and redesignated as Headquarters and Headquarters Company, 1st Medium Tank Battalion, 37th Armor).

706th Tank Battalion inactivated 20 September 1946 on Luzon, Philippine Islands. Redesignated 25 March 1949 as 71st Heavy Tank Battalion; concurrently, assigned to 1st Cavalry Division and activated at Chigasaki, Honshu, Japan (Company A, only, filled). Reorganized and redesignated 5 August 1950 as 71st Tank Battalion. Inactivated 16 October 1950 in Korea and relieved from assignment to 1st Cavalry Division. Redesignated 14 August 1951 as 706th Tank Battalion. Assigned 25 February 1953 to 12th Armored Division. Relieved 1 April 1957 from assignment to 12th Armored Division.

Headquarters and Headquarters Company, and Companies E and F, 2d Battalion, 37th Armored Regiment; and Service Company, 37th Armored Regiment, reconstituted 1 April 1957 in the Regular Army.

37th and 706th Tank Battalions and reconstituted elements of the 37th Armored Regiment consolidated and redesignated 1 April 1957 as 37th Armor, a parent regiment under the Combat Arms Regimental System (Headquarters and Headquarters and Service Company, 37th Tank Battalion, redesignated as Headquarters and Headquarters Company, 37th Armor).

CAMPAIGN PARTICIPATION CREDIT

World War II
  Normandy
  Northern France
  Rhineland
  Ardennes-Alsace
  Central Europe
  Western Pacific

Leyte
Ryukyus

Korean War
  UN defensive
  UN offensive

DECORATIONS

Presidential Unit Citation (Army), Streamer embroidered ARDENNES (37th Tank Battalion cited; WD GO 54, 1945)

Meritorious Unit Commendation, Streamer embroidered PACIFIC THEATER (706th Tank Battalion cited; WD GO 14, 77th Inf Div, 1946)

French Croix de Guerre with Palm, World War II, Streamer embroidered NORMANDY (37th Tank Battalion cited; DA GO 43, 1950)

French Croix de Guerre with Palm, World War II, Streamer embroidered MOSELLE RIVER (37th Tank Battalion cited; DA GO 43, 1950)

French Croix de Guerre, World War II, Fourragère (37th Tank Battalion cited; DA GO 43, 1950)

1st BATTALION, 37th ARMOR

RA

(4th Armored Division)

LINEAGE

Constituted 13 January 1941 in the Regular Army as Company A, 7th Armored Regiment, an element of the 4th Armored Division. Activated 15 April 1941 at Pine Camp, New York. Redesignated 8 May 1941 as Company A, 37th Armored Regiment.

Reorganized and redesignated 10 September 1943 as Company A, 37th Tank Battalion. Converted and redesignated 1 May 1946 as Troop A, 37th Constabulary Squadron (37th Tank Battalion concurrently relieved from assignment to 4th Armored Division). Inactivated 20 September 1947 at Weilburg, Germany. Converted and redesignated 11 December 1951 as Company A, 37th Tank Battalion. (37th Tank Battalion assigned 25 February 1953 to 4th Armored Division.) Activated 15 June 1954 at Fort Hood, Texas.

Reorganized and redesignated 1 April 1957 as Headquarters and Headquarters Company, 1st Medium Tank Battalion (Patton), 37th Armor, and remained assigned to 4th Armored Division (organic elements concurrently constituted and activated). Reorganized and redesignated 12 August 1963 as 1st Battalion, 37th Armor.

CAMPAIGN PARTICIPATION CREDIT

World War II
  *Normandy
  *Northern France
  *Rhineland
  *Ardennes-Alsace
  *Central Europe

Western Pacific
  Leyte
  Ryukyus

Korean War
  UN defensive
  UN offensive

DECORATIONS

*Presidential Unit Citation (Army), Streamer embroidered ARDENNES (37th Tank Battalion cited; WD GO 54, 1945)

Meritorious Unit Commendation, Streamer embroidered PACIFIC THEATER

*French Croix de Guerre with Palm, World War II, Streamer embroidered NORMANDY (37th Tank Battalion cited; DA GO 43, 1950)

*French Croix de Guerre with Palm, World War II, Streamer embroidered MOSELLE RIVER (37th Tank Battalion cited; DA GO 43, 1950)

*French Croix de Guerre, World War II, Fourragère (37th Tank Battalion cited; DA GO 43, 1950)

320

2d BATTALION, 37th ARMOR

RA

(4th Armored Division)

Constituted 13 January 1941 in the Regular Army as Company B, 7th Armored Regiment, an element of the 4th Armored Division. Activated 15 April 1941 at Pine Camp, New York. Redesignated 8 May 1941 as Company B, 37th Armored Regiment.

Reorganized and redesignated 10 September 1943 as Company B, 37th Tank Battalion. Converted and redesignated 1 May 1946 as Troop B, 37th Constabulary Squadron (37th Tank Battalion concurrently relieved from assignment to 4th Armored Division). Inactivated 20 September 1947 at Weilburg, Germany. Converted and redesignated 11 December 1951 as Company B, 37th Tank Battalion. (37th Tank Battalion assigned 25 February 1953 to 4th Armored Division.) Activated 15 June 1954 at Fort Hood, Texas.

Inactivated 1 April 1957 at Fort Hood, Texas; concurrently, redesignated as Headquarters and Headquarters Company, 2d Medium Tank Battalion (Patton), 37th Armor, and relieved from assignment to 4th Armored Division. Activated 1 July 1957 in Germany and assigned to 2d Armored Division (organic elements concurrently constituted and activated). Relieved 1 July 1963 from assignment to 2d Armored Division; concurrently, transferred (less personnel and equipment) from Fort Hood, Texas, to United States Army, Europe, assigned to 4th Armored Division, and reorganized. Reorganized and redesignated 26 August 1963 as 2d Battalion, 37th Armor.

CAMPAIGN PARTICIPATION CREDIT

World War II
 *Normandy
 *Northern France
 *Rhineland
 *Ardennes-Alsace
 *Central Europe
 Western Pacific

Leyte
Ryukyus

Korean War
 UN defensive
 UN offensive

DECORATIONS

*Presidential Unit Citation (Army), Streamer embroidered ARDENNES (37th Tank Battalion cited; WD GO 54, 1945)

Meritorious Unit Commendation, Streamer embroidered PACIFIC THEATER

*French Croix de Guerre with Palm, World War II, Streamer embroidered NORMANDY (37th Tank Battalion cited; DA GO 43, 1950)

*French Croix de Guerre with Palm, World War II, Streamer embroidered MOSELLE RIVER (37th Tank Battalion cited; DA GO 43, 1950)

*French Croix de Guerre, World War II, Fourragère (37th Tank Battalion cited; DA GO 43, 1950)

3d BATTALION, 37th ARMOR

RA
(4th Armored Division)

Constituted 13 January 1941 in the Regular Army as Company C, 7th Armored Regiment, an element of the 4th Armored Division. Activated 15 April 1941 at Pine Camp, New York. Redesignated 8 May 1941 as Company C, 37th Armored Regiment.

Reorganized and redesignated 10 September 1943 as Company C, 37th Tank Battalion. Converted and redesignated 1 May 1946 as Troop C, 37th Constabulary Squadron (37th Tank Battalion concurrently relieved from assignment to 4th Armored Division). Inactivated 20 September 1947 at Weilburg, Germany. Converted and redesignated 11 December 1951 as Company C, 37th Tank Battalion. (37th Tank Battalion assigned 25 February 1953 to 4th Armored Division.) Activated 15 June 1954 at Fort Hood, Texas.

Inactivated 1 April 1957 at Fort Hood, Texas; concurrently, redesignated as Headquarters and Headquarters Company, 3d Medium Tank Battalion (Patton), 37th Armor, and relieved from assignment to 4th Armored Division. Activated 1 May 1958 in Germany (organic elements constituted 12 March 1958 and activated 1 May 1958 in Germany). Assigned 17 June 1963 to 4th Armored Division. Reorganized and redesignated 1 August 1963 as 3d Battalion, 37th Armor.

CAMPAIGN PARTICIPATION CREDIT

World War II
  *Normandy
  *Northern France
  *Rhineland
  *Ardennes-Alsace
  *Central Europe
  Western Pacific

Leyte
Ryukyus

Korean War
  UN defensive
  UN offensive

323

DECORATIONS

*Presidential Unit Citation (Army), Streamer embroidered ARDENNES
(37th Tank Battalion cited; WD GO 54, 1945)

Meritorious Unit Commendation, Streamer embroidered PACIFIC THEATER

*French Croix de Guerre with Palm, World War II, Streamer embroidered
NORMANDY (37th Tank Battalion cited; DA GO 43, 1950)

*French Croix de Guerre with Palm, World War II, Streamer embroidered
MOSELLE RIVER (37th Tank Battalion cited; DA GO 43, 1950)

*French Croix de Guerre, World War II, Fourragère (37th Tank Battalion
cited; DA GO 43, 1950)

4th BATTALION, 37th ARMOR

RA

(194th Armored Brigade)

LINEAGE

Constituted 13 January 1941 in the Regular Army as Company D, 7th Armored Regiment, an element of the 4th Armored Division. Activated 15 April 1941 at Pine Camp, New York. Redesignated 8 May 1941 as Company D, 37th Armored Regiment.

Reorganized and redesignated 10 September 1943 as Company D, 37th Tank Battalion. Converted and redesignated 1 May 1946 as Troop D, 37th Constabulary Squadron (37th Tank Battalion concurrently relieved from assignment to 4th Armored Division). Inactivated 20 September 1947 in Germany. Disbanded 11 December 1951.

Reconstituted 25 February 1953 in the Regular Army, converted, and redesignated as Company D, 37th Tank Battalion, an element of the 4th Armored Division. Activated 15 June 1954 at Fort Hood, Texas.

Inactivated 1 April 1957 at Fort Hood, Texas; concurrently, redesignated as Headquarters and Headquarters Company, 4th Medium Tank Battalion, 37th Armor, and relieved from assignment to 4th Armored Division. Redesignated 10 June 1958 as Company D (Patton), 37th Armor. Activated 25 June 1958 at Fort Knox, Kentucky. Reorganized and redesignated 12 December 1958 as Headquarters and Headquarters Company, 4th Tank Battalion (Composite), 37th Armor (organic elements constituted 6 November 1958 and activated 12 December 1958). Reorganized and redesignated 25 June 1960 as 4th Medium Tank Battalion, 37th Armor. Reorganized and redesignated 24 September 1963 as 4th Battalion, 37th Armor. Assigned 15 April 1968 to 194th Armored Brigade.

CAMPAIGN PARTICIPATION CREDIT

World War II
*Normandy
*Northern France
*Rhineland
*Ardennes-Alsace
*Central Europe
  Western Pacific

Leyte
Ryukyus

Korean War
  UN defensive
  UN offensive

325

DECORATIONS

*Presidential Unit Citation (Army), Streamer embroidered ARDENNES (37th Tank Battalion cited; WD GO 54, 1945)

Meritorious Unit Commendation, Streamer embroidered PACIFIC THEATER

*French Croix de Guerre with Palm, World War II, Streamer embroidered NORMANDY (37th Tank Battalion cited; DA GO 43, 1950)

*French Croix de Guerre with Palm, World War II, Streamer embroidered MOSELLE RIVER (37th Tank Battalion cited; DA GO 43, 1950)

*French Croix de Guerre, World War II, Fourragère (37th Tank Battalion cited; DA GO 43, 1950)

5th MEDIUM TANK BATTALION, 37th ARMOR

AR

(inactive)

LINEAGE

Constituted 13 January 1941 in the Regular Army as Company G, 7th Armored Regiment, an element of the 4th Armored Division. Activated 15 April 1941 at Pine Camp, New York. Redesignated 8 May 1941 as Company G, 37th Armored Regiment.

Reorganized and redesignated 10 September 1943 as Company A, 706th Tank Battalion, and relieved from assignment to 4th Armored Division. Inactivated 30 September 1946 in Luzon, Philippine Islands.

Redesignated 25 March 1949 as Company A, 71st Heavy Tank Battalion; concurrently, activated at Chigasaki, Honshu, Japan, and assigned to 1st Cavalry Division. Reorganized and redesignated 5 August 1950 as Company A, 71st Tank Battalion. Inactivated 16 October 1950 in Korea (71st Tank Battalion concurrently relieved from assignment to 1st Cavalry Division). Redesignated 14 August 1951 as Company A, 706th Tank Battalion. (706th Tank Battalion assigned 25 February 1953 to the 12th Armored Division.)

Redesignated 1 April 1957 as Headquarters and Headquarters Company, 5th Medium Tank Battalion, 37th Armor, and relieved from assignment to 12th Armored Division. Withdrawn from the Regular Army 19 March 1959, allotted to the Army Reserve, and assigned to 90th Infantry Division (organic elements concurrently constituted). Activated 1 April 1959 with Headquarters at Laredo, Texas. Inactivated 27 March 1963 at Laredo, Texas, and relieved from assignment to 90th Infantry Division.

CAMPAIGN PARTICIPATION CREDIT

World War II
  *Western Pacific
  *Leyte
  *Ryukyus
  Normandy
  Northern France
  Rhineland

Ardennes-Alsace
Central Europe

Korean War
  *UN defensive
  *UN offensive

DECORATIONS

Presidential Unit Citation (Army), Streamer embroidered ARDENNES

*Presidential Unit Citation (Army), Streamer embroidered DEFENSE OF KOREA (Company A, 71st Heavy Tank Battalion, cited; DA GO 45, 1950, as amended by DA GO 77, 1951)

*Meritorious Unit Commendation, Streamer embroidered PACIFIC THEATER (706th Tank Battalion cited; WD GO 14, 77th Inf Div, 1946)

*Philippine Presidential Unit Citation, Streamer embroidered 17 OCTOBER 1944 TO 4 JULY 1945 (706th Tank Battalion cited; DA GO 47, 1950)

*Republic of Korea Presidential Unit Citation, Streamer embroidered WAEGWAN-TAEGU (71st Heavy Tank Battalion cited; DA GO 35, 1951)

BIBLIOGRAPHY, 37TH ARMOR

Department of the Army. AMERICAN FORCES IN ACTION series.
   Guam. 1946. 706th Tank Battalion mentioned.
   Small Unit Actions. 1946.
Harrison, Gordon A. *Attack on Singling by Elements of 4th Armored Division.* History Section, European Theater of Operations: 1945.
Koyen, Kenneth A. *The Fourth Armored Division From the Beach to Bavaria, the Story of the Fourth Armored Division in Combat.* Munich, Germany: 1945.
The Armor School. *Armor in the Exploitation (the Fourth Armored Division Across France to the Moselle River).* Fort Knox, Kentucky: 1949.
Unit Members. *Historical and Pictorial Review, 37th Armored Regiment, . . . Pine Camp, New York.* Baton Rouge, Louisiana: 1942.
———. *The Nancy Bridgehead.* Fort Knox, Kentucky: 1946.
———. *What They Said About the 4th Armored Division.* Germany: 1945.
UNITED STATES ARMY IN WORLD WAR II
   Blumenson, Martin. *Breakout and Pursuit.* 1961.
   Cannon, M. Hamlin. *Leyte: The Return to the Philippines.* 1954.
   Cole, Hugh M. *The Ardennes: Battle of the Bulge.* 1965.
   ———. *The Lorraine Campaign.* 1950.

40th ARMOR

HERALDIC ITEMS

COAT OF ARMS

Shield: Vert, a demidinosaur (Tyrannosaurus) rampant couped argent, eyed gules, langued azure holding in its sinister claw a sword erect of the second, inflamed proper.

Crest: On a wreath argent and vert, behind a lion rampant gules, armed and langued azure, grasping a fir tree sinister bendwise eradicated of the first a portcullis sable cloué argent.

Motto: By Force and Valor.

Symbolism: The dinosaur, with its scaly armored hide and dangerous tail capable of destroying everything in its path, is symbolic of the destroying functions of the regiment, and the flaming sword represents the zeal of the men in the performance of their duties.

The uprooted tree stands for the regiment's action in the Hurtgen Forest in World War II, for which the unit was awarded the Presidential Unit Citation. The lion, from the arms of Belgium, is symbolic of action in the Ardennes, for which the unit was awarded the Belgian Fourragère. The portcullis with five spikes symbolizes the fortifications of Europe and the regiment's five campaign credits. The portcullis and fir tree also stand for postwar service of battalions of the regiment in Germany and Alaska, the portcullis alluding to the Iron Curtain in Germany and the white fir to the snow-covered forests of Alaska.

DISTINCTIVE INSIGNIA

The distinctive insignia is the shield and motto of the coat of arms.

LINEAGE AND HONORS

LINEAGE

Constituted 13 January 1941 in the Regular Army as 4th Armored Regiment and assigned to 3d Armored Division. Activated 15 April 1941 at Camp Beauregard, Louisiana. Redesignated 8 May 1941 as 40th Armored

314-902 O - 69 - 23

Regiment. Inactivated 1 January 1942 at Camp Beauregard, Louisiana, and relieved from assignment to 3d Armored Division. Activated 2 March 1942 at Camp Polk, Louisiana, and assigned to 7th Armored Division.

Regiment broken up 20 September 1943 and its elements reorganized and redesignated as follows: Regimental Headquarters and Headquarters Company, 1st Battalion, and Company D as 40th Tank Battalion, an element of the 7th Armored Division; 3d Battalion as 709th Tank Battalion and relieved from assignment to 7th Armored Division; Reconnaissance Company as Troop E, 87th Cavalry Reconnaissance Squadron, an element of the 7th Armored Division; 2d Battalion (less Company D) absorbed in 40th Tank Battalion; Maintenance and Service Companies disbanded.

40th Tank Battalion reorganized and redesignated 25 July 1945 as 40th Amphibian Tractor Battalion and relieved from assignment to 7th Armored Division. Inactivated 22 February 1946 at Camp Kilmer, New Jersey. Redesignated 25 June 1948 as 40th Heavy Tank Battalion and assigned to 4th Infantry Division. Activated 6 July 1948 at Ford Ord, California. Redesignated 18 November 1950 as 40th Tank Battalion; concurrently, transferred (less personnel and equipment) from Fort Ord, California, to Fort Benning, Georgia, and reorganized. Inactivated 1 April 1957 at Fort Lewis, Washington, and relieved from assignment to 4th Infantry Division.

709th Tank Battalion inactivated 10 April 1946 at Camp Kilmer, New Jersey. Redesignated 30 July 1948 as 86th Heavy Tank Battalion, assigned to 3d Armored Division, and activated at Fort Knox, Kentucky. Redesignated 15 April 1953 as 709th Tank Battalion. Inactivated 1 October 1957 in Germany and relieved from assignment to 3d Armored Division.

Troop E, 87th Cavalry Reconnaissance Squadron, Mechanized, inactivated 9 October 1945 at Camp Shank, New York. Disbanded 4 November 1950. Reconstituted 15 October 1957 in the Regular Army.

Headquarters and Headquarters Company, 2d Battalion, 40th Armored Regiment; Companies E and F, 40th Armored Regiment; and Service Company, 40th Armored Regiment, reconstituted 15 October 1957 in the Regular Army.

40th and 709th Tank Battalions; Troop E, 87th Cavalry Reconnaissance Squadron, Mechanized; and the reconstituted elements of the 40th Armored Regiment consolidated, reorganized, and redesignated 15 October 1957 as 40th Armor, a parent regiment under the Combat Arms Regimental System (Headquarters and Headquarters and Service Company, 40th Tank Battalion, redesignated as Headquarters and Headquarters Company, 40th Armor).

CAMPAIGN PARTICIPATION CREDIT

World War II
  Normandy
  Northern France

Rhineland
Ardennes-Alsace
Central Europe

DECORATIONS

Presidential Unit Citation (Army), Streamer embroidered HURTGEN FOR-EST (709th Tank Battalion [less Company C] cited; WD GO 21, 1947)

Belgian Fourragère 1940 (40th Tank Battalion and 87th Cavalry Reconnaissance Squadron cited; DA GO 43, 1950)

Cited in the Order of the Day of the Belgian Army for action in the ARDENNES

Cited in the Order of the Day of the Belgian Army for action in BELGIUM

COMPANY A, 40th ARMOR

RA

(171st Infantry Brigade)

Constituted 13 January 1941 in the Regular Army as Company A, 4th Armored Regiment, an element of the 3d Armored Division. Activated 15 April 1941 at Camp Beauregard, Louisiana. Redesignated 8 May 1941 as Company A, 40th Armored Regiment. Inactivated 1 January 1942 at Camp Beauregard, Louisiana (40th Armored Regiment concurrently relieved from assignment to 3d Armored Division). Activated 2 March 1942 at Camp Polk, Louisiana (40th Armored Regiment concurrently assigned to 7th Armored Division).

Redesignated 20 September 1943 as Company A, 40th Tank Battalion, and remained assigned to 7th Armored Division. Reorganized and redesignated 25 July 1945 as Company A, 40th Amphibian Tractor Battalion (40th Amphibian Tractor Battalion concurrently relieved from assignment to 7th Armored Division). Inactivated 22 February 1946 at Camp Kilmer, New Jersey. Redesignated 25 June 1948 as Company A, 40th Heavy Tank Battalion, an element of the 4th Infantry Division. Activated 6 July 1948 at Fort Ord, California. Redesignated 18 November 1950 as Company A, 40th Tank Battalion; concurrently, transferred (less personnel and equipment) from Fort Ord, California, to Fort Benning, Georgia, and reorganized. Inactivated 1 April 1957 at Fort Lewis, Washington (40th Tank Battalion concurrently relieved from assignment to 4th Infantry Division).

Redesignated 15 October 1957 as Headquarters and Headquarters Company, 1st Medium Tank Battalion, 40th Armor. Redesignated 16 December 1957 as Company A (Walker), 40th Armor, and activated at Ladd Air Force Base, Alaska. Assigned 20 May 1963 to 171st Infantry Brigade.

CAMPAIGN PARTICIPATION CREDIT

World War II–EAME
Northern France
Rhineland

Ardennes-Alsace
Central Europe

DECORATIONS

Belgian Fourragère 1940 (40th Tank Battalion cited; DA GO 43, 1950)

Cited in the Order of the Day of the Belgian Army for action December 1944 in the ARDENNES

Cited in the Order of the Day of the Belgian Army for action January 1945 in BELGIUM

COMPANY B, 40th ARMOR

RA
(nondivisional)

LINEAGE

Constituted 13 January 1941 in the Regular Army as Company B, 4th Armored Regiment, an element of the 3d Armored Division. Activated 15 April 1941 at Camp Beauregard, Louisiana. Redesignated 8 May 1941 as Company B, 40th Armored Regiment. Inactivated 1 January 1942 at Camp Beauregard, Louisiana (40th Armored Regiment concurrently relieved from assignment to 3d Armored Division). Activated 2 March 1942 at Camp Polk, Louisiana (40th Armored Regiment concurrently assigned to 7th Armored Division).

Redesignated 20 September 1943 as Company B, 40th Tank Battalion, and remained assigned to 7th Armored Division. Reorganized and redesignated 25 July 1945 as Company B, 40th Amphibian Tractor Battalion (40th Amphibian Tractor concurrently relieved from assignment to 7th Armored Division). Inactivated 22 February 1946 at Camp Kilmer, New Jersey, Redesignated 25 June 1948 as Company B, 40th Heavy Tank Battalion, an element of the 4th Infantry Division. Activated 6 July 1948 at Fort Ord, California. Redesignated 18 November 1950 as Company B, 40th Tank Battalion; concurrently, transferred (less personnel and equipment) from Fort Ord, California, to Fort Benning, Georgia, and reorganized. Inactivated 1 April 1957 at Fort Lewis, Washington (40th Tank Battalion concurrently relieved from assignment to 4th Infantry Division).

Redesignated 1 July 1957 as Headquarters and Headquarters Company, 2d Medium Tank Battalion (Patton), 40th Armor; concurrently, assigned to 7th Infantry Division and activated in Korea (organic elements concurrently constituted and activated). Inactivated 1 July 1963 in Korea, and relieved from assignment to 7th Infantry Division. Headquarters and Headquarters Company, 2d Medium Tank Battalion, 40th Armor, redesignated 9 October 1963 as Company B, 40th Armor. Activated 24 October 1963 at Fort Sill, Oklahoma.

CAMPAIGN PARTICIPATION CREDIT

World War II-EAME
Northern France
Rhineland

Ardennes-Alsace
Central Europe

DECORATIONS

Belgian Fourragère 1940 (40th Tank Battalion cited; DA GO 43, 1950)

Cited in the Order of the Day of the Belgian Army for action December 1944 in the ARDENNES

Cited in the Order of the Day of the Belgian Army for action January 1945 in BELGIUM

3d MEDIUM TANK BATTALION, 40th ARMOR

RA
(inactive)

LINEAGE

Constituted 13 January 1941 in the Regular Army as Company C, 4th Armored Regiment, an element of the 3d Armored Division. Activated 15 April 1941 at Camp Beauregard, Louisiana. Redesignated 8 May 1941 as Company C, 40th Armored Regiment. Inactivated 1 January 1942 at Camp Beauregard, Louisiana (40th Armored Regiment concurrently relieved from assignment to 3d Armored Division). Activated 2 March 1942 at Camp Polk, Louisiana (40th Armored Regiment concurrently assigned to 7th Armored Division).

Redesignated 20 September 1943 as Company C, 40th Tank Battalion, and remained assigned to 7th Armored Division. Disbanded 25 July 1945 in Germany.

Reconstituted 25 June 1948 in the Regular Army and redesignated as Company C, 40th Heavy Tank Battalion, an element of the 4th Infantry Division. Activated 6 July 1948 at Fort Ord, California. Redesignated 18 November 1950 as Company C, 40th Tank Battalion. Inactivated 1 April 1957 at Fort Lewis, Washington (40th Tank Battalion concurrently relieved from assignment to the 4th Infantry Division).

Redesignated 15 October 1957 as Headquarters and Headquarters Company, 3d Medium Tank Battalion (Patton), 40th Armor, and assigned to 1st Cavalry Division (organic elements concurrently constituted). Activated 1 December 1957 in Korea. Relieved 15 July 1963 from assignment to 1st Cavalry Division. Inactivated 1 September 1963 in Korea.

CAMPAIGN PARTICIPATION CREDIT

World War II	
Normandy	*Rhineland
*Northern France	*Ardennes-Alsace
	*Central Europe

DECORATIONS

Presidential Unit Citation (Army), Streamer embroidered HURTGEN FOREST
*Belgian Fourragère 1940 (40th Tank Battalion cited; DA GO 43, 1950)
    *Cited in the Order of the Day of the Belgian Army for action December 1944 in the ARDENNES
    *Cited in the Order of the Day of the Belgian Army for action January 1945 in BELGUIM

COMPANY D, 40th ARMOR

RA

(172d Infantry Brigade)

LINEAGE

Constituted 13 January 1941 in the Regular Army as Company D, 4th Armored Regiment, an element of the 3d Armored Division. Activated 15 April 1941 at Camp Beauregard, Louisiana. Redesignated 8 May 1941 as Company D, 40th Armored Regiment. Inactivated 1 January 1942 at Camp Beauregard, Louisiana (40th Armored Regiment concurrently relieved from assignment to 3d Armored Division). Activated 2 March 1942 at Camp Polk, Louisiana (40th Armored Regiment concurrently assigned to 7th Armored Division).

Redesignated 20 September 1943 as Company D, 40th Tank Battalion, and remained assigned to 7th Armored Division. Disbanded 25 July 1945 in Germany.

Reconstituted 10 February 1955 in the Regular Army and activated in Germany as an element of the 4th Infantry Division. Transferred (less personnel and equipment) 30 June 1956 from Germany to Fort Lewis, Washington, and reorganized. Inactivated 1 April 1957 at Fort Lewis, Washington (40th Tank Battalion concurrently relieved from assignment to 4th Infantry Division).

Redesignated 15 October 1957 as Headquarters and Headquarters Company, 4th Medium Tank Battalion, 40th Armor. Redesignated 16 December 1957 as Company D, 40th Armor, and activated in Alaska. Assigned 1 July 1963 to 172d Infantry Brigade.

CAMPAIGN PARTICIPATION CREDIT

World War II-EAME
    Northern France
    Rhineland

    Ardennes-Alsace
    Central Europe

DECORATIONS

French Croix de Guerre with Silver Star, World War II, Streamer embroidered BELGIUM (Company D, 40th Tank Battalion, cited; DA GO 43, 1950)

Belgian Fourragère 1940 (40th Tank Battalion cited; DA GO 43, 1950)

Cited in the Order of the Day of the Belgian Army in action December 1944 in the ARDENNES

Cited in the Order of the Day of the Belgian Army for action January 1945 in BELGIUM

336

5th BATTALION, 40th ARMOR

AR
(inactive)

LINEAGE

Constituted 13 January 1941 in the Regular Army as Company E, 4th Armored Regiment, an element of the 3d Armored Division. Activated 15 April 1941 at Camp Beauregard, Louisiana. Redesignated 8 May 1941 as Company E, 40th Armored Regiment. Inactivated 1 January 1942 at Camp Beauregard, Louisiana (40th Armored Regiment concurrently relieved from assignment to 3d Armored Division). Activated 2 March 1942 at Camp Polk, Louisiana (40th Armored Regiment concurrently assigned to 7th Armored Division).

Absorbed in 40th Tank Battalion 20 September 1943 at Fort Benning, Georgia, in reorganization and redesignation of elements of the 40th Armored Regiment as 40th Tank Battalion, an element of the 7th Armored Division (40th Tank Battalion [less Companies C and D] reorganized and redesignated 25 July 1945 as 40th Amphibian Tractor Battalion; Companies C and D concurrently disbanded. 40th Amphibian Tractor Battalion inactivated 22 February 1946 at Camp Kilmer, New Jersey; redesignated 25 June 1948 as 40th Heavy Tank Battalion and assigned to 4th Infantry Division; activated 6 July 1948 at Fort Ord, California; redesignated 18 November 1950 as 40th Tank Battalion, transferred [less personnel and equipment] from Fort Ord, California, to Fort Benning, Georgia, and reorganized; inactivated 1 April 1957 at Fort Lewis, Washington, and relieved from assignment to 4th Infantry Division).

Former Company E, 40th Armored Regiment, reconstituted 15 October 1957 in the Regular Army and redesignated as Headquarters and Headquarters Company, 5th Medium Tank Battalion (Patton), 40th Armor. Activated 25 June 1958 at Camp Irwin, California (organic elements constituted 10 June 1958 and activated 25 June 1958). Inactivated 19 February 1962 at Fort Irwin, California.

Redesignated 27 March 1963 as 5th Battalion, 40th Armor; concurrently, withdrawn from the Regular Army, allotted to the Army Reserve, and assigned to 63d Infantry Division. Activated 1 April 1963 with Headquarters at San Bernardino, California. Inactivated 31 December 1965 at San Bernardino, California, and relieved from assignment to 63d Infantry Division.

337

CAMPAIGN PARTICIPATION CREDIT

World War II
   Normandy
    *Northern France

                               *Rhineland
                               *Ardennes-Alsace
                               *Central Europe

DECORATIONS

Presidential Unit Citation (Army), Streamer embroidered HURTGEN FOREST

*Belgian Fourragère 1940 (40th Tank Battalion cited; DA GO 43, 1950)

   *Cited in the Order of the Day of the Belgian Army for action December 1944 in the ARDENNES

   *Cited in the Order of the Day of the Belgian Army for action January 1945 in BELGIUM

COMPANY F, 40th ARMOR

RA

(Berlin Brigade)

LINEAGE

Constituted 13 January 1941 in the Regular Army as Company F, 4th Armored Regiment, an element of the 3d Armored Division. Activated 15 April 1941 at Camp Beauregard, Louisiana. Redesignated 8 May 1941 as Company F, 40th Armored Regiment. Inactivated 1 January 1942 at Camp Beauregard, Louisiana (40th Armored Regiment concurrently relieved from assignment to 3d Armored Division). Activated 2 March 1942 at Camp Polk, Louisiana (40th Armored Regiment concurrently assigned to 7th Armored Division).

Absorbed in 40th Tank Battalion 20 September 1943 at Fort Benning, Georgia, in reorganization and redesignation of elements of the 40th Armored Regiment as 40th Tank Battalion, an element of the 7th Armored Division (40th Tank Battalion [less Companies C and D] reorganized and redesignated 25 July 1945 as 40th Amphibian Tractor Battalion; Companies C and D concurrently disbanded. 40th Amphibian Tractor Battalion inactivated 22 February 1946 at Camp Kilmer, New Jersey; redesignated 25 June 1948 as 40th Heavy Tank Battalion and assigned to 4th Infantry Division; activated 6 July 1948 at Fort Ord, California; redesignated 18 November 1950 as 40th Tank Battalion, transferred [less personnel and equipment] from Fort Ord, California, to Fort Benning, Georgia, and reorganized; inactivated 1 April 1957 at Fort Lewis, Washington, and relieved from assignment to 4th Infantry Division).

Former Company F, 40th Armored Regiment, reconstituted 15 October 1957 in the Regular Army and redesignated as Headquarters and Headquarters Company, 6th Medium Tank Battalion, 40th Armor. Redesignated 2 May 1958 as Company F (Patton), 40th Armor. Activated 1 June 1958 in Germany. Assigned 1 September 1963 to Berlin Brigade.

CAMPAIGN PARTICIPATION CREDIT

World War II-EAME
Northern France
Rhineland

Ardennes-Alsace
Central Europe

DECORATIONS

Belgian Fourragère 1940 (40th Tank Battalion cited; DA GO 43, 1950)
Cited in the Order of the Day of the Belgian Army for action December 1944 in the ARDENNES
Cited in the Order of the Day of the Belgian Army for action January 1945 in BELGIUM

7th BATTALION, 40th ARMOR

LINEAGE

Constituted 27 February 1942 in the Regular Army as Company G, 40th Armored Regiment. Activated 2 March 1942 at Camp Polk, Louisiana (40th Armored concurrently assigned to 7th Armored Division).

Reorganized and redesignated 20 September 1943 as Company A, 709th Tank Battalion, and relieved from assignment to 7th Armored Division. Inactivated 10 April 1946 at Camp Kilmer, New Jersey.

Redesignated 30 July 1948 as Company A, 86th Heavy Tank Battalion, an element of the 3d Armored Division and activated at Fort Knox, Kentucky. Redesignated 15 April 1953 as Company A, 709th Tank Battalion. Inactivated 1 October 1957 in Germany (709th Tank Battalion concurrently relieved from assignment to 3d Armored Division).

Redesignated 15 October 1957 as Headquarters and Headquarters Company, 7th Medium Tank Battalion, 40th Armor. Withdrawn from the Regular Army 31 March 1959, allotted to the Army Reserve, and assigned to 63d Infantry Division (organic elements concurrently constituted). Activated 1 May 1959 at El Monte, California. Redesignated 1 April 1963 as 7th Battalion, 40th Armor. Inactivated 31 December 1965 at El Monte, California, and relieved from assignment to 63d Infantry Division.

CAMPAIGN PARTICIPATION CREDIT

World War II
  *Normandy
  *Northern France

  *Rhineland
  *Ardennes-Alsace
  *Central Europe

DECORATIONS

*Presidential Unit Citation (Army), Streamer embroidered HURTGEN FOREST (709th Tank Battalion [less Company C] cited; WD GO 21, 1947)

341

8th BATTALION, 40th ARMOR

AR
(191st Infantry Brigade)

Constituted 27 February 1942 in the Regular Army as Company H, 40th Armored Regiment. Activated 2 March 1942 at Camp Polk Louisiana (40th Armored concurrently assigned to 7th Armored Division).

Reorganized and redesignated 20 September 1943 as Company B, 709th Tank Battalion, and relieved from assignment to 7th Armored Division. Inactivated 10 April 1946 at Camp Kilmer, New Jersey.

Redesignated 30 July 1948 as Company B, 86th Heavy Tank Battalion, an element of 3d Armored Division and activated at Fort Knox, Kentucky. Redesignated 15 April 1953 as Company B, 709th Tank Battalion. Inactivated 1 October 1957 in Germany (709th Tank Battalion concurrently relieved from assignment to 3d Armored Division).

Redesignated 15 October 1957 as Headquarters and Headquarters Company, 8th Medium Tank Battalion, 40th Armor. Withdrawn from the Regular Army 29 April 1959, allotted to the Army Reserve, and assigned to 96th Infantry Division (organic elements concurrently constituted). Activated 20 May 1959 with Headquarters at Tucson, Arizona. Redesignated 15 February 1963 as 8th Tank Battalion, 40th Armor; concurrently, relieved from assignment to 96th Infantry Division and assigned to 191st Infantry Brigade. Redesignated 12 September 1963 as 8th Battalion, 40th Armor.

Home Area: Sixth United States Army.

Campaign Participation Credit

World War II
  *Normandy
  *Northern France

*Rhineland
*Ardennes-Alsace
*Central Europe

Decorations

*Presidential Unit Citation (Army), Streamer embroidered HURTGEN FOREST (709th Tank Battalion [less Company C] cited; WD GO 21, 1947)

Bibliography, 40th Armor

Griesbach, Marc F. *Combat History of the Eighth Infantry Division in World War II*. Baton Rouge, Louisiana: 1946. 709th Tank Battalion included.

The Armored School. *The Defense of St. Vith, Belgium, 17–23 December 1944*. Fort Knox, Kentucky: 1949.

Unit Members. *From the Beaches to the Baltic, the Story of the 7th Armored Division*. Germany: 1945.

————. *History of the 5th Medium Tank Battalion (Patton), 40th Armor*. Camp Irwin, California: 1958.

————. *Roll Out the Barrel. A History of 7th Armored Division*. Paris: circa 1945.

————. *The Lucky Seventh*. Camp Roberts, California: 1953.

————. *The Seventh Armored Division in the Battle of St. Vith*. Baltimore: 1948.

UNITED STATES ARMY IN WORLD WAR II

Blumenson, Martin. *Breakout and Pursuit*. 1961.

Cole, Hugh M. *The Ardennes: Battle of the Bulge*. 1965.

————. *The Lorraine Campaign*. 1950.

MacDonald, Charles B., and Sidney T. Mathews. *Three Battles: Arnaville, Altuzzo, and Schmidt*. 1952.

MacDonald, Charles B. *The Siegfried Line Campaign*. 1963.

63d ARMOR

HERALDIC ITEMS

COAT OF ARMS

Shield: Vert, a bend wavy or between a fleur-de-lis and a lion rampant argent, on a canton of the last a mullet of the first within a square one point to chief of the third superimposed on a septfoil of the first.

Crest: On a wreath or and vert a dragon sejant gules gorged with a collar sable rimmed of the first and grasping in his dexter claw a morning star of the fourth.

Motto: Seek, Strike, Destroy.

Symbolism: Green is used for armor. The wavy band is from the arms of the Rheinprovinz and indicates service in that area and in Central Europe, while the fleur-de-lis is for service in France and the French citation for Colleville. The rampant lion from the arms of Belgium represents the Belgian citations for Mons and Eupen-Malmedy. The canton represents descent from the 745th Tank Battalion, from which these honors were inherited, seven being represented by the septfoil, four by the square, and five by the star. The Siegfried Line is symbolized by a dragon, the collar about his throat signifying the capture of the line after it was breached by armor units. The morning star, a type of medieval club, alludes to the reduction of the city of Aachen.

DISTINCTIVE INSIGNIA

The distinctive insignia is the shield of the coat of arms.

LINEAGE AND HONORS

LINEAGE

Constituted 3 May 1942 in the Army of the United States as the 745th Tank Battalion. Activated 15 August 1942 at Camp Bowie, Texas. Inactivated 27 October 1945 at Camp Kilmer, New Jersey.

Redesignated 14 September 1948 as 63d Heavy Tank Battalion, allotted to the Regular Army, and assigned to 1st Infantry Division. Activated

345

10 October 1948 in Germany. Reorganized and redesignated 10 October 1950 as 63d Tank Battalion. Inactivated 15 February 1957 at Fort Riley, Kansas, and relieved from assignment to 1st Infantry Division.

Reorganized and redesignated 25 January 1963 as 63d Armor, a parent regiment under the Combat Arms Regimental System.

CAMPAIGN PARTICIPATION CREDIT

World War II
  Normandy (with arrowhead)
  Northern France

Rhineland
Ardennes-Alsace
Central Europe

DECORATIONS

French Croix de Guerre with Palm, World War II, Streamer embroidered NORMANDY (745th Tank Battalion cited; DA GO 43, 1950)

Belgian Fourragère 1940 (745th Tank Battalion cited; DA GO 43, 1950)

Cited in the Order of the Day of the Belgian Army for action near MONS

Cited in the Order of the Day of the Belgian Army for action near EUPEN-MALMEDY

1st BATTALION, 63d ARMOR

RA
(1st Infantry Division)

LINEAGE

Constituted 3 May 1942 in the Army of the United States as Company A, 745th Tank Battalion. Activated 15 August 1942 at Camp Bowie, Texas. Inactivated 27 October 1945 at Camp Kilmer, New Jersey.

Redesignated 14 September 1948 as Company A, 63d Heavy Tank Battalion, an element of the 1st Infantry Division and allotted to the Regular Army. Activated 10 October 1948 in Germany. Reorganized and redesignated 10 October 1950 as Company A, 63d Tank Battalion. Inactivated 15 February 1957 at Fort Riley, Kansas (63d Tank Battalion concurrently relieved from assignment to 1st Infantry Division).

Redesignated 25 January 1963 as Headquarters and Headquarters Company, 1st Medium Tank Battalion, 63d Armor, and assigned to 1st Infantry Division (organic elements concurrently constituted). Activated 1 July 1963 at Fort Riley, Kansas. Reorganized and redesignated 2 January 1964 as 1st Battalion, 63d Armor.

CAMPAIGN PARTICIPATION CREDIT

World War II
*Normandy (with arrowhead)
*Northern France
*Rhineland
*Ardennes-Alsace
*Central Europe

DECORATIONS

*French Croix de Guerre with Palm, World War II, Streamer embroidered NORMANDY (745th Tank Battalion cited; DA GO 43, 1950)

*Belgian Fourragère 1940 (745th Tank Battalion cited; DA GO 43, 1950)

*Cited in the Order of the Day of the Belgian Army for action near MONS

*Cited in the Order of the Day of the Belgian Army for action near EUPEN-MALMEDY

2d BATTALION, 63d ARMOR

RA
(1st Infantry Division)
(inactive)

LINEAGE

Constituted 3 May 1942 in the Army of the United States as Company B, 745th Tank Battalion. Activated 15 August 1942 at Camp Bowie, Texas. Inactivated 27 October 1945 at Camp Kilmer, New Jersey.

Redesignated 14 September 1948 as Company B, 63d Heavy Tank Battalion, an element of the 1st Infantry Division and allotted to the Regular Army. Activated 10 October 1948 in Germany. Reorganized and redesignated 10 October 1950 as Company A, 63d Tank Battalion. Inactivated 15 February 1957 at Fort Riley, Kansas (63d Tank Battalion concurrently relieved from assignment to 1st Infantry Division).

Redesignated 25 January 1963 as Headquarters and Headquarters Company, 2d Battalion, 63d Armor, and assigned to 1st Infantry Division (organic elements concurrently constituted). Activated 2 January 1964 at Fort Riley, Kansas. Inactivated 15 September 1965 at Fort Riley, Kansas.

CAMPAIGN PARTICIPATION CREDIT

World War II
   *Normandy (with arrowhead)
   *Northern France

*Rhineland
*Ardennes-Alsace
*Central Europe

DECORATIONS

*French Croix de Guerre with Palm, World War II, Streamer embroidered NORMANDY (745th Tank Battalion cited; DA GO 43, 1950)

*Belgian Fourragère 1940 (745th Tank Battalion cited; DA GO 43, 1950)

   *Cited in the Order of the Day of the Belgian Army for action near MONS

   *Cited in the Order of the Day of the Belgian Army for action near EUPEN-MALMEDY

BIBLIOGRAPHY, 63D ARMOR

Department of the Army. AMERICAN FORCES IN ACTION series.
   Omaha Beachhead. 1945.
   Small Unit Actions. 1946.

Howenstine, Harold D., and George E. Troll, editors. *History of the 745th Tank Battalion, August 1942 to June 1945*. Nurnberg, Germany: 1945.

Hurkala, John. *The Fighting First Division: A True History of World War II*. New York: 1958.

Knickerbocker, H. R., *et al*. *Danger Forward, the Story of the First Division in World War II* . . . . Washington: 1948.

UNITED STATES ARMY IN WORLD WAR II

Blumenson, Martin. *Breakout and Pursuit*. 1961.

Cole, Hugh M. *The Ardennes: Battle of the Bulge*. 1965.

Harrison, Gordon A. *Cross-Channel Attack*. 1951.

MacDonald, Charles B. *The Siegfried Line Campaign*. 1963.

64th ARMOR

HERALDIC ITEMS

COAT OF ARMS

Shield: Argent, the head of a fighting African elephant sable, tusks proper.

Crest: On a wreath of the colors argent and sable mounted on a trophy base or charged with a Korean taeguk two elephant tusks proper supporting a Catherine wheel gules charged on the hub with a bezant, all in front of a mount of three peaks vert.

Motto: We Pierce.

Symbolism: The elephant symbolizes the heavy assault of a tank battalion. Elephants were used in ancient times to lead the attack in a manner comparable to the present-day use of armored organizations.

The Catherine wheel with its hooked spikes symbolizes the armored tracked vehicle and its function, the spikes further representing eight battle honors for the Korean War and the gold disc in the center referring to the award of the Bravery Gold Medal of Greece. The elephant tusks in a trophy base decorated with a Korean taeguk are symbolic of two awards of the Korean Presidential Unit Citation. The three peaks allude to service in the North Apennines in World War II, and the valley between the tusks to the Po Valley Campaign.

DISTINCTIVE INSIGNIA

The distinctive insignia is the shield and motto of the coat of arms.

LINEAGE AND HONORS

LINEAGE

Constituted 13 January 1941 in the Regular Army as 78th Tank Battalion. Redesignated 8 May 1941 as 758th Tank Battalion (Light). Activated 1 June 1941 at Fort Knox, Kentucky. Reorganized and redesignated 3 May 1945 at 758th Light Tank Battalion. Inactivated 22 September 1945 at Viareggio, Italy.

351

Redesignated 23 May 1946 as 758th Tank Battalion. Activated 14 June 1946 at Fort Knox, Kentucky. Reorganized and redesignated 15 January 1948 as 758th Heavy Tank Battalion.

Redesignated 3 November 1949 as 64th Heavy Tank Battalion and assigned to 2d Armored Division. Relieved 13 August 1950 from assignment to 2d Armored Division and assigned to 3d Infantry Division. Reorganized and redesignated 6 March 1951 as 64th Tank Battalion. Inactivated 1 July 1957 at Fort Benning, Georgia, and relieved from assignment to 3d Infantry Division.

Redesignated 25 January 1963 as 64th Armor, a parent regiment under the Combat Arms Regimental System.

CAMPAIGN PARTICIPATION CREDIT

World War II
  North Apennines
  Po Valley

Korean War
  CCF intervention
  First UN counteroffensive

CCF spring offensive
UN summer-fall offensive
Second Korean winter
Korea, summer-fall 1952
Third Korean winter
Korea, summer 1953

DECORATIONS

Republic of Korea Presidential Unit Citation, Streamer embroidered UIJONGBU CORRIDOR TO SEOUL (64th Tank Battalion cited; DA GO 20, 1953)

Republic of Korea Presidential Unit Citation, Streamer embroidered IRON TRIANGLE (64th Tank Battalion cited; DA GO 29, 1954)

Chryssoun Aristion Andrias (Bravery Gold Medal of Greece), Streamer embroidered KOREA (64th Tank Battalion cited; DA GO 2, 1956).

1st BATTALION, 64th ARMOR

RA

(3d Infantry Division)

LINEAGE

Constituted 13 January 1941 in the Regular Army as Company A, 78th Tank Battalion. Redesignated 8 May 1941 as Company A, 758th Tank Battalion (Light). Activated 1 June 1941 at Fort Knox, Kentucky. Reorganized and redesignated 3 May 1945 as Company A, 758th Light Tank Battalion. Inactivated 22 September 1945 at Viareggio, Italy.

Redesignated 23 May 1946 as Company A, 758th Tank Battalion. Activated 14 June 1946 at Fort Knox, Kentucky. Reorganized and redesignated 15 January 1948 as Company A, 758th Heavy Tank Battalion.

Redesignated 3 November 1949 as Company A, 64th Heavy Tank Battalion, an element of the 2d Armored Division. (64th Heavy Tank Battalion relieved 13 August 1950 from assignment to 2d Armored Division and assigned to 3d Infantry Division.) Reorganized and redesignated 6 March 1951 as Company A, 64th Tank Battalion. Inactivated 1 July 1957 at Fort Benning, Georgia (64th Tank Battalion concurrently relieved from assignment to 3d Infantry Division).

Redesignated 1 April 1963 as Headquarters and Headquarters Company, 1st Battalion, 64th Armor, assigned to 3d Infantry Division and activated in Germany (organic elements concurrently constituted and activated).

CAMPAIGN PARTICIPATION CREDIT

World War II
  *North Apennines
  *Po Valley

Korean War
  *CCF intervention
  *First UN counteroffensive

*CCF spring offensive
*UN summer-fall offensive
*Second Korean winter
*Korea, summer-fall 1952
*Third Korean winter
*Korea, summer 1953

DECORATIONS

*Presidential Unit Citation (Army), Streamer embroidered KUMSONG, KOREA (Company A, 64th Tank Battalion, cited; DA GO 11, 1954)

*Republic of Korea Presidential Unit Citation, Streamer embroidered UIJONGBU CORRIDOR TO SEOUL (64th Tank Battalion cited; DA GO 20, 1953)

*Republic of Korea Presidential Unit Citation, Streamer embroidered IRON TRIANGLE (64th Tank Battalion cited; DA GO 29, 1954)

*Chryssoun Aristion Andrias (Bravery Gold Medal of Greece), Streamer embroidered KOREA (64th Tank Battalion cited; DA GO 2, 1956)

2d BATTALION, 64th ARMOR

RA
(3d Infantry Division)

Lineage

Constituted 13 January 1941 in the Regular Army as Company B, 78th Tank Battalion. Redesignated 8 May 1941 as Company B, 758th Tank Battalion (Light). Activated 1 June 1941 at Fort Knox, Kentucky. Reorganized and redesignated 3 May 1945 as Company B, 758th Light Tank Battalion. Inactivated 22 September 1945 at Viareggio, Italy.

Redesignated 23 May 1946 as Company B, 758th Tank Battalion. Activated 14 June 1946 at Fort Knox, Kentucky. Reorganized and redesignated 15 January 1948 as Company B, 758th Heavy Tank Battalion.

Redesignated 3 November 1949 as Company B, 64th Heavy Tank Battalion, an element of the 2d Armored Division. (64th Heavy Tank Battalion relieved 13 August 1950 from assignment to 2d Armored Division and assigned to 3d Infantry Division.) Reorganized and redesignated 6 March 1951 as Company B, 64th Tank Battalion. Inactivated 1 July 1957 at Fort Benning, Georgia (64th Tank Battalion concurrently relieved from assignment to 3d Infantry Division).

Redesignated 25 January 1963 as Headquarters and Headquarters Company, 2d Battalion, 64th Armor. Assigned 18 April 1963 to 3d Infantry Division (organic elements concurrently constituted). Activated 17 June 1963 in Germany.

Campaign Participation Credit

World War II
*North Apennines
*Po Valley

Korean War
*CCF intervention
*First UN counteroffensive

*CCF spring offensive
*UN summer-fall offensive
*Second Korean winter
*Korea, summer-fall 1952
*Third Korean winter
*Korea, summer 1953

Decorations

*Republic of Korea Presidential Unit Citation, Streamer embroidered UIJONGBU CORRIDOR TO SEOUL (64th Tank Battalion cited; DA GO 20, 1953)

*Republic of Korea Presidential Unit Citation, Streamer embroidered IRON TRIANGLE (64th Tank Battalion cited; DA GO 29, 1954)

*Chryssoun Aristion Andrias (Bravery Gold Medal of Greece), Streamer embroidered KOREA (64th Tank Battalion cited; DA GO 2, 1956)

3d BATTALION, 64th ARMOR

RA

(3d Infantry Division)

LINEAGE

Constituted 13 January 1941 in the Regular Army as Company C, 78th Tank Battalion. Redesignated 8 May 1941 as Company C, 758th Tank Battalion (Light). Activated 1 June 1941 at Fort Knox, Kentucky. Reorganized and redesignated 3 May 1945 as Company C, 758th Light Tank Battalion. Inactivated 22 September 1945 at Viareggio, Italy.

Redesignated 23 May 1946 as Company C, 758th Tank Battalion. Activated 14 June 1946 at Fort Knox, Kentucky. Reorganized and redesignated 15 January 1948 as Company C, 758th Heavy Tank Battalion.

Redesignated 3 November 1949 as Company C, 64th Heavy Tank Battalion, an element of the 2d Armored Division (64th Heavy Tank Battalion relieved 13 August 1950 from assignment to 2d Armored Division and assigned to 3d Infantry Division). Reorganized and redesignated 6 March 1951 as Company C, 64th Tank Battalion. Inactivated 1 July 1957 at Fort Benning, Georgia (64th Tank Battalion concurrently relieved from assignment to 3d Infantry Division).

Redesignated 25 January 1963 as Headquarters and Headquarters Company, 3d Battalion, 64th Armor. Assigned 18 April 1963 to 3d Infantry Division (organic elements concurrently constituted). Activated 17 June 1963 in Germany.

CAMPAIGN PARTICIPATION CREDIT

World War II
  *North Apennines
  *Po Valley

Korean War
  *CCF intervention
  *First UN counteroffensive

*CCF spring offensive
*UN summer-fall offensive
*Second Korean winter
*Korea, summer-fall 1952
*Third Korean winter
*Korea, summer 1953

DECORATIONS

*Republic of Korea Presidential Unit Citation, Streamer embroidered KOREA 1950–1952 (Company C, 64th Tank Battalion, cited; DA GO 41, 1955)

*Republic of Korea Presidential Unit Citation, Streamer embroidered UIJONGBU CORRIDOR TO SEOUL (64th Tank Battalion cited; DA GO 20, 1953)

*Republic of Korea Presidential Unit Citation, Streamer embroidered IRON TRIANGLE (64th Tank Battalion cited; DA GO 29, 1954)

*Chryssoun Aristion Andrias (Bravery Gold Medal of Greece), Streamer embroidered KOREA (64th Tank Battalion cited; DA GO 2, 1956)

4th BATTALION, 64th ARMOR

RA
(3d Infantry Division)

LINEAGE

Constituted 23 May 1946 in the Regular Army as Company D, 758th Tank Battalion. Activated 14 June 1946 at Fort Knox, Kentucky. Inactivated 15 January 1948 at Fort Knox, Kentucky. Disbanded 1 December 1950.

Reconstituted 27 October 1954, redesignated as Company D, 64th Tank Battalion, an element of the 3d Infantry Division. Activated 2 December 1954 at Fort Benning, Georgia. Inactivated 1 July 1957 at Fort Benning, Georgia (64th Tank Battalion concurrently relieved from assignment to 3d Infantry Division).

Redesignated 1 May 1966 as Headquarters and Headquarters Company, 4th Battalion, 64th Armor; concurrently, assigned to 3d Infantry Division and activated in Germany (organic elements concurrently constituted and activated).

CAMPAIGN PARTICIPATION CREDIT

World War II
North Apennines
Po Valley

Korean War
CCF intervention
First UN counteroffensive

CCF spring offensive
UN summer-fall offensive
Second Korean winter
Korea, summer-fall 1952
Third Korean winter
Korea, summer 1953

DECORATIONS

None.

BIBLIOGRAPHY, 64TH ARMOR

Department of the Army
Korea, 1950. Washington: 1952.
Dolcater, Max W., *et al. 3d Infantry Division in Korea.* Tokyo, Japan: 1953.
Gugeler, Russell A. *Combat Actions in Korea.* Washington: 1954.
Miller, John, jr., O. J. Carroll, and M. E. Tackley. *Korea 1951–1953.* Washington: 1956.
Westover, John G. *Combat Support in Korea.* Washington: 1955.
UNITED STATES ARMY IN THE KOREAN WAR
Appleman, Roy E. *South to the Naktong, North to the Yalu.* 1961.
Hermes, Walter G. *Truce Tent and Fighting Front.* 1966.

357

66th ARMOR
(Iron Knights)

Heraldic Items

Coat of Arms

Shield: Tierced in pairle reversed gules, azure and or; in chief a label of three points argent. On dexter side an inescutcheon of the second fimbriated, semé-de-lis, overall a saltire all of the last.

Crest: On a wreath of the three colors a wyvern without wings sinister couchant reguardant argent, grasping in its dexter claw a pine tree inverted and eradicated proper. On its neck a label of three points azure.

Motto: Semper in Hostes.

Symbolism: The coat of arms was originally approved for the 15th Tank Battalion, part of which was in the old 304th Tank Brigade. Therefore the shield and crest of the 304th Tank Brigade are used with the label added for difference. The shield is of the colors of the Tank Corps shoulder sleeve insignia. The brigade was organized at Langres, France, in 1918, and the arms of Langres are shown on an inescutcheon differenced by a silver border and changing the cross from red to silver. The wyvern is from the original insignia of the French Tank Corps. The uprooted pine tree commemorates the activities of the brigade in the Argonne forest during the Meuse-Argonne operations.

Distinctive Insignia

The distinctive insignia is the shield of the coat of arms.

Lineage and Honors

Lineage

Organized in August 1918 as Headquarters and Headquarters Companies, 1st and 2d Provisional Brigades, Tank Corps, in the American Expeditionary Forces in France. Redesignated 6 November 1918 as Headquarters and Headquarters Companies, 304th and 305th Brigades, Tank Corps, respectively. Consolidated and redesignated 22 June 1921 as Headquarters and Headquarters Company, 1st Tank Group.

Reorganized and redesiganted 1 September 1929 as Headquarters and Headquarters Company, 1st Tank Regiment; concurrently, remainder of 1st Tank Regiment organized by redesignation of existing units as follows: 16th Tank Battalion as 1st Battalion (16th Tank Battalion organized in 1918 as Headquarters and Headquarters Company, 327th Battalion, Tank Corps, and Company C, 1st Separate Battalion, Heavy Tank Service, 65th Engineers); 15th Tank Battalion as 2d Battalion (15th Tank Battalion organized in 1918 as elements of the 1st Battalion, Tank Center and Company A, 1st Separate Battalion, Heavy Tank Service, 65th Engineers); 18th Tank Battalion as 3d Battalion (18th Tank Battalion organized in 1918 as 329th Battalion, Tank Corps, and Headquarters and Headquarters Company, 328th Battalion, Tank Corps); 21st Tank Maintenance Company as Service Company (21st Tank Maintenance Company organized in 1918 as 316th Repair and Salvage Company, Tank Corps).

1st Tank Regiment converted, reorganized, and redesignated 25 October 1932 as 66th Infantry (Light Tanks). Converted, reorganized, and redesignated 15 July 1940 as 66th Armored Regiment and assigned to 2d Armored Division.

Regiment broken up 25 March 1946 and its elements reorganized and redesignated as follows: Regimental Headquarters and Headquarters Company; 1st Battalion Headquarters and Headquarters Company; Service Company; Medical Detachment; and Companies A, B, C, and D as 66th Tank Battalion, an element of the 2d Armored Division. 2d and 3d Battalion Headquarters and Headquarters Companies and Companies E and F as 6th Tank Battalion, an element of the 2d Armored Division (concurrently, certain elements of the 67th Armored Regiment were redesignated as elements of the 6th Tank Battalion). Reconnaissance Company as Troop D, 82d Mechanized Cavalry Reconnaissance Squadron, an element of the 2d Armored Division. Service Company as Service Company, 12th Armored Infantry Battalion, an element of the 2d Armored Division. Band as Band, 2d Armored Division (separate lineage). Maintenance Company and Companies G, H, and I disbanded.

66th Tank Battalion redesignated 5 January 1949 as 66th Medium Tank Battalion. Redesignated 1 April 1953 as 66th Tank Battalion. Inactivated (less Companies A and B), 1 July 1957 in Germany and relieved from assignment to 2d Armored Division. Company A, 66th Tank Battalion, concurrently, redesignated as Headquarters and Headquarters Company, 1st Medium Tank Battalion, 66th Armor, and remained assigned to 2d Armored Division. Company B, 66th Tank Battalion, concurrently, redesignated as Headquarters and Headquarters Company, 2d Medium Tank Battalion, 66th Armor, transferred (less personnel and equipment) from Germany to Fort Hood, Texas, relieved from assignment to 2d Armored Division, assigned to 4th Armored Division, and reorganized.

6th Tank Battalion redesignated 31 January 1949 as 6th Medium Tank Battalion. Relieved 14 July 1950 from assignment to 2d Armored Division and assigned 6 October 1950 to 24th Infantry Division. Redesignated 10 November 1951 as 6th Tank Battalion. Inactivated 5 June 1958 in Korea and relieved from assignment to 24th Infantry Division.

Troop D, 82d Mechanized Cavalry Reconnaissance Squadron, redesignated 17 January 1948 as Company D, 82d Reconnaissance Battalion. Inactivated 1 July 1957 in Germany and relieved from assignment to 2d Armored Division.

Service Company, 12th Armored Infantry Battalion, redesignated 11 October 1948 as Company D, 12th Armored Infantry Battalion. Inactivated 1 July 1957 in Germany and relieved from assignment to 2d Armored Division.

Maintenance Company and Companies G, H, and I, 66th Armored Regiment, reconstituted 1 July 1957 in the Regular Army.

6th (less Companies C and D) and 66th Tank Battalions; Company D, 82d Reconnaissance Battalion; Company D, 12th Armored Infantry Battalion; and reconstituted elements of the 66th Armored Regiment consolidated and redesignated 12 October 1959 as 66th Armor, a parent regiment under the Combat Arms Regimental System (Headquarters, 66th Tank Battalion, redesignated as Headquarters, 66th Armor) (Companies C and D, 6th Tank Battalion, redesignated as elements of the 67th Armor—separate lineages).

CAMPAIGN PARTICIPATION CREDIT

World War I
Somme Offensive
St. Mihiel
Meuse-Argonne

World War II
Algeria-French Morocco
(with arrowhead)
Sicily
Normandy
Northern France
Rhineland

Ardennes-Alsace
Central Europe

Korean War
UN defensive
UN offensive
CCF intervention
First UN counteroffensive
CCF spring offensive
UN summer-fall offensive
Second Korean winter
Korea, summer 1953

DECORATIONS

Presidential Unit Citation (Army), Streamer embroidered NORMANDY (2d Battalion, 66th Armored Regiment, cited; WD GO 82, 1945)

Presidential Unit Citation (Army), Streamer embroidered VIRE RIVER (3d Battalion, 66th Armored Regiment, cited; WD GO 82, 1945)

Presidential Unit Citation (Army), Streamer embroidered ROER RIVER (1st Battalion, 66th Armored Regiment, cited; WD GO 2, 1946)

Belgian Fourragère 1940 (66th Armored Regiment cited; DA GO 43, 1950)

Cited in the Order of the Day of the Belgian Army for action in BELGIUM

Cited in the Order of the Day of the Belgian Army for action in the ARDENNES

1st BATTALION, 66th ARMOR

(Iron Knights)

RA

(2d Armored Division)

LINEAGE

Constituted in February 1918 as Company C, 1st Separate Battalion, Heavy Tank Service, 65th Engineers, and organized at Camp Upton, New York. Redesignated 16 March 1918 as Company C, 1st Heavy Battalion, Tank Service. Redesignated 16 April 1918 as Company C, 41st Heavy Battalion, Tank Corps. Redesignated 25 April 1918 as Company C, 301st Battalion, Tank Corps, American Expeditionary Forces. Reorganized and redesignated 22 June 1921 as Companies A, B, and C, 16th Tank Battalion (hereafter separate lineages; see 2d and 3d Battalions, 66th Armor).

Company A, 16th Tank Battalion, redesignated 1 September 1929 as Company A, 1st Tank Regiment. Converted, reorganized and redesignated 25 October 1932 as Company A, 66th Infantry (Light Tanks). Converted, reorganized and redesignated 15 July 1940 as Company A, 66th Armored Regiment, and element of the 2d Armored Division. Transferred in June 1944 from 1st Battalion to 2d Battalion, 66th Armored Regiment.

Redesignated 25 March 1946 as Company A, 66th Tank Battalion, and remained assigned to 2d Armored Division. Redesignated 5 January 1949 as Company A, 66th Medium Tank Battalion. Redesignated 1 April 1953 as Company A, 66th Tank Battalion.

Reorganized and redesignated 1 July 1957 as Headquarters and Headquarters Company, 1st Medium Tank Battalion (Patton), 66th Armor, and assigned to 2d Armored Division (organic elements concurrently constituted and activated). Reorganized and redesignated 1 July 1963 as 1st Battalion, 66th Armor.

CAMPAIGN PARTICIPATION CREDIT

World War I
  *Somme Offensive
  St. Mihiel
  Meuse-Argonne

World War II
  *Algeria-French Morocco
    (with arrowhead)
  *Sicily
  *Normandy
  *Northern France
  *Rhineland

  *Ardennes-Alsace
  *Central Europe

Korean War
  UN defensive
  UN offensive
  CCF intervention
  First UN counteroffensive
  CCF spring offensive
  UN summer-fall offensive
  Second Korean winter
  Korea, summer 1953

DECORATIONS

*Presidential Unit Citation (Army), Streamer embroidered PIVITSHEIDE (Company A, 66th Armored Regiment, cited; DA GO 21, 1947)

*Presidential Unit Citation (Army), Streamer embroidered NORMANDY (2d Battalion, 66th Armored Regiment, cited; WD GO 82, 1945)

Presidential Unit Citation (Army), Streamer embroidered VIRE RIVER

Presidential Unit Citation (Army), Streamer embroidered ROER RIVER

*Belgian Fourragère 1940 (66th Armored Regiment cited; DA GO 43, 1950)

*Cited in the Order of the Day of the Belgian Army for action in September 1944 in BELGIUM

*Cited in the Order of the Day of the Belgian Army for action in December 1944 in the ARDENNES

2d BATTALION, 66th ARMOR

(Iron Knights)

RA
(2d Armored Division)

Constituted in February 1918 as Company C, 1st Separate Battalion, Heavy Tank Service, 65th Engineers, and organized at Camp Upton, New York. Redesignated 16 March 1918 as Company C, 1st Heavy Battalion, Tank Service. Redesignated 16 April 1918 as Company C, 41st Heavy Battalion, Tank Corps. Redesignated 25 April 1918 as Company C, 301st Battalion, Tank Corps, American Expeditionary Forces. Reorganized and redesignated 22 June 1921 as Companies A, B, and C, 16th Tank Battalion (hereafter separate lineages; see 1st and 3d Battalions, 66th Armor).

Company B, 16th Tank Battalion, redesignated 1 September 1929 as Company B, 1st Tank Regiment. Converted, reorganized, and redesignated 25 October 1932 as Company B, 66th Infantry (Light Tanks). Converted, reorganized and redesignated 15 July 1940 as Company B, 66th Armored Regiment, an element of the 2d Armored Division. Transferred in June 1944 from 1st Battalion to 3d Battalion, 66th Armored Regiment.

Redesignated 25 March 1946 as Company B, 66th Tank Battalion, and remained assigned to 2d Armored Division. Redesignated 5 January 1949 as Company B, 66th Medium Tank Battalion. Redesignated 1 April 1953 as Company B, 66th Tank Battalion.

Redesignated 1 April 1957 as Headquarters and Headquarters Company, 2d Medium Tank Battalion (Patton), 66th Armor; transferred (less personnel and equipment) from Germany to Fort Hood, Texas, and reorganized; relieved from assignment to 2d Armored Division and assigned to 4th Armored Division (organic elements concurrently constituted and activated). (A new Company B, 66th Tank Battalion, constituted and activated 1 April 1957. Disbanded 1 July 1957.) Redesignated 1 July 1963 as 2d Battalion, 66th Armor; concurrently, relieved from assignment to 4th Armored Division, transferred (less personnel and equipment) from United States Army, Europe, to Fort Hood, Texas, assigned to 2d Armored Division, and reorganized.

CAMPAIGN PARTICIPATION CREDIT

World War I
  *Somme Offensive
  St. Mihiel
  Meuse-Argonne

World War II
  *Algeria-French Morocco
    (with arrowhead)
  *Sicily
  *Normandy
  *Northern France
  *Rhineland

  *Ardennes-Alsace
  *Central Europe

Korean War
  UN defensive
  UN offensive
  CCF intervention
  First UN counteroffensive
  CCF spring offensive
  UN summer-fall offensive
  Second Korean winter
  Korea, summer 1953

DECORATIONS

Presidential Unit Citation (Army), Streamer embroidered NORMANDY

*Presidential Unit Citation (Army), Streamer embroidered VIRE RIVER (3d Battalion, 66th Armored Regiment, cited; WD GO 82, 1945)

Presidential Unit Citation (Army), Streamer embroidered ROER RIVER

*Belgian Fourragère 1940 (66th Armored Regiment cited; DA GO 43, 1950)

  *Cited in the Order of the Day of the Belgian Army for action in September 1944 in BELGIUM

  *Cited in the Order of the Day of the Belgian Army for action in December 1944 in the ARDENNES

3d BATTALION, 66th ARMOR
(Iron Knights)

RA
(2d Armored Division)
(inactive)

LINEAGE

Constituted in February 1918 as Company C, 1st Separate Battalion, Heavy Tank Service, 65th Engineers, and organized at Camp Upton, New York. Redesignated 16 March 1918 as Company C, 1st Heavy Battalion, Tank Service. Redesignated 16 April 1918 as Company C, 41st Heavy Battalion, Tank Corps. Redesignated 25 April 1918 as Company C, 301st Battalion, Tank Corps, American Expeditionary Forces. Reorganized and redesignated 22 June 1921 as Companies A, B, and C, 16th Tank Battalion (hereafter separate lineages; see 1st and 2d Battalions, 66th Armor).

Company C, 16th Tank Battalion, redesignated 1 September 1929 as Company C, 1st Tank Regiment. Converted, reorganized, and redesignated 25 October 1932 as Company C, 66th Infantry (Light Tanks). Converted, reorganized, and redesignated 15 July 1940 as Company C, 66th Armored Regiment, an element of the 2d Armored Division.

Redesignated 25 March 1946 as Company C, 66th Tank Battalion, and remained assigned to 2d Armored Division. Redesignated 5 January 1949 as Company C, 66th Medium Tank Battalion. Redesignated 1 April 1953 as Company C, 66th Tank Battalion. Inactivated 1 July 1957 in Germany and relieved from assignment to 2d Armored Division.

Redesignated 10 June 1958 as Headquarters and Headquarters Company, 3d Medium Tank Battalion (Patton), 66th Armor (organic elements concurrently constituted). Activated 25 June 1958 at Fort Benning, Georgia. Inactivated 25 June 1959 at Fort Benning, Georgia.

Headquarters and Headquarters Company reorganized and redesignated 9 September 1959 as Company C, 66th Armor, and assigned to 1st Infantry Brigade (remainder of 3d Medium Tank Battalion, 66th Armor, concurrently disbanded). Activated 24 September 1959 at Fort Benning, Georgia. Relieved 20 September 1962 from assignment to 1st Infantry Brigade. Inactivated 24 September 1962 at Fort Benning, Georgia.

Redesignated 8 August 1963 as Headquarters and Headquarters Company, 3d Battalion, 66th Armor, and assigned to 2d Armored Division (organic elements concurrently constituted). Activated 12 August 1963 at Fort Hood, Texas. Inactivated 15 October 1965 at Fort Hood, Texas.

CAMPAIGN PARTICIPATION CREDIT

World War I
  *Somme Offensive
  St. Mihiel
  Meuse-Argonne

World War II
  *Algeria-French Morocco
    (with arrowhead)
  *Sicily
  *Normandy
  *Northern France
  *Rhineland

  *Ardennes-Alsace
  *Central Europe

Korean War
  UN defensive
  UN offensive
  CCF intervention
  First UN counteroffensive
  CCF spring offensive
  UN summer-fall offensive
  Second Korean winter
  Korea, summer 1953

DECORATIONS

Presidential Unit Citation (Army), Streamer embroidered NORMANDY

Presidential Unit Citation (Army), Streamer embroidered VIRE RIVER

*Presidential Unit Citation (Army), Streamer embroidered ROER RIVER (1st Battalion, 66th Armored Regiment, cited; WD GO 2, 1946)

*Belgian Fourragère 1940 (66th Armored Regiment cited; DA GO 43, 1950)

*Cited in the Order of the Day of the Belgian Army for action in September 1944 in BELGIUM

*Cited in the Order of the Day of the Belgian Army for action in December 1944 in the ARDENNES

COMPANY D, 66th ARMOR

(Iron Knights)

RA
(inactive)

LINEAGE

Constituted 25 April 1918 as Company A, Tank Service Detachment, American Expeditionary Forces, and organized in France. Redesignated 6 June 1918 as Company A, 326th Battalion, Tank Corps. Redesignated 12 September 1918 as Company A, 344th Battalion, Tank Corps.

Reorganized and redesignated 22 June 1921 as Company A, 15th Tank Battalion. Redesignated 1 September 1929 as Company D, 1st Tank Regiment. Converted, reorganized, and redesignated 25 October 1932 as Company D, 66th Infantry (Light Tanks). Converted, reorganized, and redesignated 15 July 1940 as Company D, 66th Armored Regiment, an element of the 2d Armored Division.

Redesignated 25 March 1946 as Company D, 66th Tank Battalion, and remained assigned to 2d Armored Division. Redesignated 15 January 1949 as Company D, 66th Medium Tank Battalion. Redesignated 1 April 1953 as Company D, 66th Tank Battalion. Inactivated 1 July 1957 in Germany and relieved from assignment to 2d Armored Division.

Redesignated 10 June 1958 as Company D, 66th Armor. Activated 25 June 1958 at Fort Campbell, Kentucky. Inactivated 24 July 1965 at Fort Campbell, Kentucky.

CAMPAIGN PARTICIPATION CREDIT

World War I
St. Mihiel
Meuse-Argonne

World War II–EAME
Algeria-French Morocco
(with arrowhead)

Sicily
Normandy
Northern France
Rhineland
Ardennes-Alsace
Central Europe

DECORATIONS

Presidential Unit Citation (Army), Streamer embroidered NORMANDY (2d Battalion, 66th Armored Regiment, cited; WD GO 82, 1945)

French Croix de Guerre with Palm, World War II, Streamer embroidered ST LO (2d Battalion, 66th Armored Regiment, cited; DA GO 43, 1950)

Belgian Fourragère 1940 (66th Armored Regiment cited; DA GO 43, 1950)

Cited in the Order of the Day of the Belgian Army for action in September 1944 in BELGIUM

Cited in the Order of the Day of the Belgian Army for action in December 1944 in the ARDENNES

5th BATTALION, 66th ARMOR

(Iron Knights)

AR
(nondivisional)
(inactive)

LINEAGE

Constituted 17 February 1918 as Company A, 1st Separate Battalion, Heavy Tank Service, 65th Engineers, and organized at Camp Upton, New York. Redesignated 16 March 1918 as Company A, 1st Heavy Battalion, Tank Service. Redesignated 16 April 1918 as Company A, 41st Heavy Battalion, Tank Corps. Redesignated 25 April 1918 as Company A, 301st Battalion, Tank Corps, in the American Expeditionary Forces.

Reorganized and redesignated 22 June 1921 as Company B, 15th Tank Battalion. Redesignated 1 September 1929 as Company E, 1st Tank Regiment. Converted, reorganized, and redesignated 25 October 1932 as Company E, 66th Infantry (Light Tanks). Converted, reorganized, and redesignated 15 July 1940 as Company E, 66th Armored Regiment, an element of the 2d Armored Division.

Reorganized and redesignated 25 March 1946 as Company A, 6th Tank Battalion. Redesignated 31 January 1949 as Company A, 6th Medium Tank Battalion. (6th Medium Tank Battalion relieved 14 July 1950 from assignment to 2d Armored Division; assigned 6 October 1950 to 24th Infantry Division.) Redesignated 10 November 1951 as Company A, 6th Tank Battalion. Inactivated 5 June 1958 in Korea and relieved from assignment to 24th Infantry Division.

Redesignated 2 April 1959 as Headquarters and Headquarters Company, 5th Medium Tank Battalion, 66th Armor; concurrently, withdrawn from the Regular Army, allotted to the Army Reserve, and assigned to Second United States Army (organic elements concurrently constituted). Activated 15 May 1959 at Rockville, Maryland. Redesignated 22 April 1964 as the 5th Battalion, 66th Armor. Relieved 1 January 1966 from assignment to Second United States Army and assigned to First United States Army; concurrently location of Headquarters changed to Baltimore, Maryland. Inactivated 31 January 1968 at Baltimore, Maryland.

Home Area: First United States Army.

CAMPAIGN PARTICIPATION CREDIT

World War I
*Somme Offensive
St. Mihiel
Meuse-Argonne

World War II
*Algeria-French Morocco
  (with arrowhead)
*Sicily
*Normandy
*Northern France
*Rhineland

*Ardennes-Alsace
*Central Europe

Korean War
*UN defensive
*UN offensive
*CCF intervention
*First UN counteroffensive
*CCF spring offensive
*UN summer-fall offensive
*Second Korean winter
*Korea, summer 1953

DECORATIONS

*Presidential Unit Citation (Army), Streamer embroidered NORMANDY (2d Battalion, 66th Armored Regiment, cited; WD GO 82, 1945)

Presidential Unit Citation (Army), Streamer embroidered VIRE RIVER

Presidential Unit Citation (Army), Streamer embroidered ROER RIVER

*French Croix de Guerre with Palm, World War II, Streamer embroidered ST LO (2d Battalion, 66th Armored Regiment, cited; DA GO 43, 1950)

*Belgian Fourragère 1940 (66th Armored Regiment cited; DA GO 43, 1950)

*Cited in the Order of the Day of the Belgian Army for action in BELGIUM

*Cited in the Order of the Day of the Belgian Army for action in the ARDENNES

*Republic of Korea Presidential Unit Citation, Streamer embroidered KOREA (6th Tank Battalion cited, DA GO 50, 1954)

6th BATTALION, 66th ARMOR

(Iron Knights)

AR
(inactive)

LINEAGE

Constituted 25 April 1918 as Company C, 1st Battalion, Tank Center, and organized in England. Redesignated 6 June 1918 as Company C, 326th Tank Battalion. Redesignated 12 September 1918 as Company C, 344th Tank Battalion.

Redesignated 28 February 1921 as Company C, 15th Tank Battalion. Reorganized and redesignated 1 September 1929 as Company F, 1st Tank Regiment. Converted, reorganized, and redesignated 25 October 1932 as Company F, 66th Infantry (Light Tanks). Converted, reorganized, and redesignated 15 July 1940 as Company F, 66th Armored Regiment, an element of the 2d Armored Division.

Reorganized and redesignated 25 March 1946 as Company B, 6th Tank Battalion, and remained assigned to 2d Armored Division. Reorganized and redesignated 31 January 1949 as Company B, 6th Medium Tank Battalion. (6th Medium Tank Battalion relieved 14 July 1950 from assignment to 2d Armored Division; assigned 6 October 1950 to 24th Infantry Division.) Reorganized and redesignated 10 November 1951 as Company B, 6th Tank Battalion. Inactivated 5 June 1958 in Korea and relieved from assignment to 24th Infantry Division.

Redesignated 6 June 1958 as Headquarters and Headquarters Company, 6th Tank Battalion, 66th Armor. Redesignated 25 March 1963 as Headquarters and Headquarters Company, 6th Battalion, 66th Armor; concurrently, withdrawn from the Regular Army, allotted to the Army Reserve, and assigned to 77th Infantry Division (organic elements concurrently constituted). Activated 26 March 1963 at Bronx, New York. Inactivated 30 December 1965 at Fort Tilden, New York, and relieved from assignment to the 77th Infantry Division.

373

CAMPAIGN PARTICIPATION CREDIT

World War I
  *Somme Offensive
  *St. Mihiel
  *Meuse-Argonne

World War II
  Algeria-French Morocco
    (with arrowhead)
  *Sicily
  *Normandy
  *Northern France
  *Rhineland

  *Ardennes-Alsace
  *Central Europe

Korean War
  *UN defensive
  *UN offensive
  *CCF intervention
  *First UN counteroffensive
  *CCF spring offensive
  *UN summer-fall offensive
  *Second Korean winter
  *Korea, summer 1953

DECORATIONS

*Presidential Unit Citation (Army), Streamer embroidered NORMANDY (2d Battalion, 66th Armored Regiment, cited; WD GO 82, 1945)

Presidential Unit Citation (Army), Streamer embroidered VIRE RIVER

Presidential Unit Citation (Army), Streamer embroidered ROER RIVER

*French Croix de Guerre with Palm, World War II, Streamer embroidered ST LO (2d Battalion, 66th Armored Regiment, cited; DA GO 43, 1950)

*Belgian Fourragère 1940 (66th Armored Regiment cited; DA GO 43, 1950)

*Cited in the Order of the Day of the Belgian Army for action in BELGIUM

*Cited in the Order of the Day of the Belgian Army for action in the ARDENNES

*Republic of Korea Presidential Unit Citation, Streamer embroidered KOREA (6th Tank Battalion cited; DA GO 50, 1954)

7th BATTALION, 66th ARMOR

(Iron Knights)

AR
(inactive)

LINEAGE

Constituted in May 1918 as Company A, 329th Battalion, Tank Corps, and organized at Camp Colt, Pennsylvania. Redesignated 1 July 1921 as Company A, 18th Tank Battalion. Inactivated 29 July 1922 at Camp Meade, Maryland.

Redesignated 1 September 1929 as Company G, 1st Tank Regiment. Activated 16 September 1931 at Fort Devens, Massachusetts. Converted, reorganized, and redesignated 25 October 1932 as Company G, 66th Infantry (Light Tanks).

Converted, reorganized, and redesignated 15 July 1940 as Company G, 66th Armored Regiment, an element of the 2d Armored Division. Disbanded 25 March 1946 at Camp Hood, Texas, and relieved from assignment to 2d Armored Division.

Reconstituted 1 July 1957 in the Regular Army. Redesignated 6 June 1958 as Headquarters and Headquarters Company, 7th Tank Battalion, 66th Armor. Redesignated 25 March 1963 as Headquarters and Headquarters Company, 7th Battalion, 66th Armor; concurrently, withdrawn from the Regular Army, allotted to the Army Reserve, and assigned to 77th Infantry Division (organic elements concurrently constituted). Activated 26 March 1963 with Headquarters at Fort Tilden, New York. Inactivated 30 December 1965 at Staten Island, New York, and relieved from assignment to 77th Infantry Division.

CAMPAIGN PARTICIPATION CREDIT

World War I
  Somme Offensive
  St. Mihiel
  Meuse-Argonne

World War II
  Algeria-French Morocco
    (with arrowhead)
  *Sicily
  *Normandy
  *Northern France
  *Rhineland

*Ardennes-Alsace
*Central Europe

Korean War
  UN defensive
  UN offensive
  CCF intervention
  First UN counteroffensive
  CCF spring offensive
  UN summer-fall offensive
  Second Korean winter
  Korea, summer 1953

375

DECORATIONS

*Presidential Unit Citation (Army), Streamer embroidered NORMANDY (2d Battalion, 66th Armored Regiment, cited; WD GO 82, 1945)

Presidential Unit Citation (Army), Streamer embroidered VIRE RIVER

Presidential Unit Citation (Army), Streamer embroidered ROER RIVER

*French Croix de Guerre with Palm, World War II, Streamer embroidered ST LO (2d Battalion, 66th Armored Regiment, cited; DA GO 43, 1950)

*Belgian Fourragère 1940 (66th Armored Regiment cited; DA GO 43, 1950)

*Cited in the Order of the Day of the Belgian Army for action in BELGIUM

*Cited in the Order of the Day of the Belgian Army for action in the ARDENNES

BIBLIOGRAPHY, 66TH ARMOR

Barth, George B. *Tropic Lightning and Taro Leaf in Korea.* N.p.: 1953.

Department of the Army. AMERICAN FORCES IN ACTION series.

Omaha Beachhead. 1945.

Utah Beach to Cherbourg. 1947.

St-Lo. 1946.

Department of the Army

Korea, 1950. Washington: 1952.

Miller, John, jr., O. J. Carroll, and M. E. Tackley. *Korea 1951–1953.* Washington: 1956.

Stadtmauer, Saul A., editor. *A Pictorial History of the Victory Division in Korea.* Tokyo, Japan: 1953.

Unit Members. *A History of the Second Armored Division, 1940–1946.* Atlanta, Georgia: 1946.

————. *Brief History of the 6th Tank Battalion (Medium), 1918–1953, Organization Day March 25.* Japan: 1952.

————. *Hell on Wheels, War Against the Axis, 1942–1945.* N.p.: 1945.

————. *24th Infantry Division, A Brief History. The Story of the 24th Division's Actions in the Korean Conflict.* Tokyo, Japan: 1954.

UNITED STATES ARMY IN THE KOREAN WAR

Appleman, Roy E. *South to the Naktong, North to the Yalu.* 1961.

UNITED STATES ARMY IN WORLD WAR II

Blumenson, Martin. *Breakout and Pursuit.* 1961.

Cole, Hugh M. *The Ardennes: Battle of the Bulge.* 1965.

Harrison, Gordon A. *Cross-Channel Attack.* 1951.

Garland, Albert N., and Howard McGaw Smith. *Sicily and the Surrender of Italy.* 1965.

Howe, George F. *Northwest Africa: Seizing the Initiative in the West.* 1957.

MacDonald, Charles B. *The Siegfried Line Campaign.* 1963.

67th ARMOR

HERALDIC ITEMS

COAT OF ARMS

Shield: Per fess gules and or, a mount azure erupting and smoking proper.

Crest: On a wreath of the colors a lion rampant sable.

Motto: None.

Symbolism: The personnel of the 17th Tank Battalion, from which this regiment descends, were in the old 305th Tank Brigade and therefore adopted the undifferenced arms and crest of that brigade. The erupting mount symbolizes the antitank mines that caused heavy losses within the 17th Tank Battalion. The crest is taken from the ancient arms of Picardy, where the brigade saw all of its action. The colors of the shield commemorate the insignia worn by the brigade.

DISTINCTIVE INSIGNIA

The distinctive insignia is the shield of the coat of arms.

LINEAGE AND HONORS

LINEAGE

Constituted 1 September 1929 in the Regular Army as 2d Tank Regiment; concurrently, organized (with only one active battalion) as follows: Headquarters and Headquarters Company, newly constituted (inactive). 1st Battalion by redesignation of 19th Tank Battalion (inactive) (19th Tank Battalion constituted 24 March 1923 in the Regular Army). 2d Battalion by redesignation of 17th Tank Battalion (active) (17th Tank Battalion organized in 1918 as 303d Battalion, Tank Corps, and elements of the 1st Separate Battalion, Heavy Tank Service, 65th Engineers). 3d Battalion, newly constituted (inactive).

(2d Battalion [less Company F] inactivated 15 September 1931 at Fort George G. Meade, Maryland.)

2d Tank Regiment redesignated 31 October 1932 as 67th Infantry (Medium Tanks). (Headquarters and Headquarters Company, 2d Battalion, and Company D activated 1 October 1939 at Fort Benning, Georgia.) Regiment activated 5 June 1940 at Fort Benning, Georgia. Reorganized and redesignated 15 July 1940 as 67th Armored Regiment and assigned to 2d Armored Division.

Regiment broken up 25 March 1946 and its elements reorganized and redesignated as follows: Regimental Headquarters and Headquarters Company; 3d Battalion Headquarters and Headquarters Company; and Companies D, G, H, and I as 67th Tank Battalion, an element of the 2d Armored Division. Companies A and C as Companies D and C, respectively, of 6th Tank Battalion, an element of the 2d Armored Division (concurrently, certain elements of the 66th Armored Regiment were redesignated elements of the 6th Tank Battalion). Reconnaissance Company as Troop E, 82d Mechanized Cavalry Reconnaissance Squadron (separate lineage). Remaining elements of the 67th Armored Regiment disbanded.

67th Tank Battalion redesignated 11 October 1948 as 67th Medium Tank Battalion. Redesignated 1 April 1953 as 67th Tank Battalion. Inactivated 1 July 1957 in Germany and relieved from assignment to 2d Armored Division.

6th Tank Battalion redesignated 31 January 1949 as 6th Medium Tank Battalion. Relieved 14 July 1950 from assignment to 2d Armored Division. Assigned 6 October 1950 to 24th Infantry Division. Redesignated 10 November 1951 as 6th Tank Battalion. Company D, 6th Tank Battalion, redesignated 1 July 1957 as Headquarters and Headquarters Company, 1st Medium Tank Battalion, 67th Armor, relieved from assignment to 24th Infantry Division, assigned to 2d Armored Division, transferred (less personnel and equipment) from Korea to Germany, and reorganized. 6th Tank Battalion inactivated 5 June 1958 in Korea and relieved from assignment to 24th Infantry Division (a new Company D, 6th Tank Battalion, constituted 1 July 1957, was disbanded 5 June 1958).

Headquarters and Headquarters Companies, 1st and 2d Battalions, 67th Armored Regiment; Companies B, E, and F, 67th Armored Regiment; and Maintenance and Service Companies, 67th Armored Regiment, reconstituted 6 February 1947; concurrently, consolidated and redesignated as 321st Mechanized Cavalry Reconnaissance Squadron, allotted to the Organized Reserves and assigned to First Army. Activated 21 February 1947 at Boston, Massachusetts. Redesignated 21 October 1948 as 1st Battalion, 304th Armored Cavalry. (Organized Reserves redesignated in 1948 as the Organized Reserve Corps.) Inactivated 31 July 1950 at Boston, Massachusetts. Redesignated 17 October 1950 as 57th Medium Tank Battalion; concurrently, withdrawn from the Organized Reserve Corps and allotted to the Regular Army. Assigned 20 October 1950 to 2d Armored Division. Activated 10 November 1950 at Fort Hood, Texas. Redesignated 1 April 1953 as 57th Tank Battalion. Inactivated 1 July 1957 in Germany and relieved from assignment to 2d Armored Division.

67th and 57th Tank Battalions and Company D, 6th Tank Battalion, consolidated, reorganized, and redesignated 1 July 1957 as 67th Armor, a parent regiment under the Combat Arms Regimental System (Headquarters, 67th Tank Battalion, redesignated as Headquarters, 67th Armor). (Company C, 6th Tank Battalion, redesignated 6 June 1958 as Headquarters and Headquarters Company, 3d Medium Tank Battalion, 67th Armor.)

CAMPAIGN PARTICIPATION CREDIT

World War I
  Somme Offensive

World War II
  Algeria-French Morocco
    (with arrowhead)
  Sicily (with arrowhead)

Normandy
Northern France
Rhineland
Ardennes-Alsace
Central Europe

DECORATIONS

Presidential Unit Citation (Army), Streamer embroidered NORMANDY (67th Armored Regiment [less 3d Battalion] cited; DA GO 28, 1948)

Presidential Unit Citation (Army), Streamer embroidered SIEGFRIED LINE (3d Battalion, 67th Armored Regiment, cited; WD GO 108, 1945)

Belgian Fourragère 1940 (67th Armored Regiment cited; DA GO 43, 1950)

Cited in the Order of the Day of the Belgian Army for action in BELGIUM

Cited in the Order of the Day of the Belgian Army for action in the ARDENNES

1st BATTALION, 67th ARMOR

LINEAGE

Constituted 24 March 1923 in the Regular Army as Company A, 19th Tank Battalion, Heavy. Redesignated 1 September 1929 as Company A, 2d Tank Regiment. Redesignated 31 October 1932 as Company A, 67th Infantry (Medium Tanks).

Activated 5 June 1940 at Fort Benning, Georgia. Redesignated 15 July 1940 as Company A, 67th Armored Regiment, an element of the 2d Armored Division. Redesignated 25 March 1946 as Company D, 6th Tank Battalion, an element of the 2d Armored Division. Redesignated 31 January 1949 as Company D, 6th Medium Tank Battalion. (6th Medium Tank Battalion relieved 14 July 1950 from assignment to 2d Armored Division and assigned 6 October 1950 to 24th Infantry Division.) Redesignated 10 November 1951 as Company D, 6th Tank Battalion.

Redesignated 1 July 1957 as Headquarters and Headquarters Company, 1st Medium Tank Battalion, 67th Armor, relieved from assignment to 24th Infantry Division, assigned to 2d Armored Division, transferred (less personnel and equipment) from Korea to Germany, and reorganized (organic elements concurrently constituted and activated). Reorganized and redesignated 1 July 1963 as 1st Battalion, 67th Armor.

CAMPAIGN PARTICIPATION CREDIT

World War I
  Somme Offensive

World War II
  *Algeria-French Morocco (with arrowhead)
  *Tunisia
  *Sicily (with arrowhead)
  *Normandy
  *Northern France
  *Rhineland
  *Ardennes-Alsace

*Central Europe

Korean War
  *UN defensive
  *UN offensive
  *CCF intervention
  *First UN counteroffensive
  *CCF spring offensive
  *UN summer-fall offensive
  *Second Korean winter
  *Korea, summer 1953

382

Decorations

*Presidential Unit Citation (Army), Streamer embroidered NORMANDY (67th Armored Regiment [less 3d Battalion] cited; DA GO 28, 1948)

*Presidential Unit Citation (Army), Streamer embroidered SIEGFRIED LINE

*Presidential Unit Citation (Army), Streamer embroidered KOKSU-RI (Company D, 6th Medium Tank Battalion, cited; DA GO 36, 1951)

*Belgian Fourragère 1940 (67th Armored Regiment cited; DA GO 43, 1950)

*Cited in the Order of the Day of the Belgian Army for action September 1944 in BELGIUM

*Cited in the Order of the Day of the Belgian Army for action December 1944 in the ARDENNES

*Republic of Korea Presidential Unit Citation, Streamer embroidered KOREA (6th Tank Battalion cited; DA GO 50, 1954)

2d BATTALION, 67th ARMOR

RA
(2d Armored Division)

LINEAGE

Constituted 24 March 1923 in the Regular Army as Company B, 19th Tank Battalion, Heavy. Redesignated 1 September 1929 as Company B, 2d Tank Regiment. Redesignated 31 October 1932 as Company B, 67th Infantry (Medium Tanks).

Activated 5 June 1940 at Fort Benning, Georgia, as an element of the 2d Armored Division. Redesignated 15 July 1940 as Company B, 67th Armored Regiment. Transferred in June 1944 from 1st Battalion, 67th Armored Regiment, to 2d Battalion, 67th Armored Regiment. Disbanded 25 March 1946 at Camp Hood, Texas.

Reconstituted 6 February 1947 in the Organized Reserves and redesignated as Troop B, 321st Mechanized Cavalry Reconnaissance Squadron. Activated 21 February 1947 at Boston, Massachusetts. (Organized Reserves redesignated in 1948 as the Organized Reserve Corps.) Redesignated 21 October 1948 as Company B, 304th Armored Cavalry Regiment. Inactivated 31 July 1950 at Boston, Massachusetts.

Redesignated 17 August 1950 as Company B, 57th Medium Tank Battalion; concurrently, withdrawn from the Organized Reserve Corps and allotted to the Regular Army. Activated 10 November 1950 at Fort Hood, Texas. Redesignated 1 April 1953 as Company B, 57th Tank Battalion.

Redesignated 1 April 1957 as Headquarters and Headquarters Company, 2d Medium Tank Battalion (Patton), 67th Armor, and assigned to 4th Armored Division; transferred (less personnel and equipment) from Germany to Fort Hood, Texas, and reorganized (organic elements concurrently constituted and activated). Redesignated 1 July 1963 as 2d Battalion, 67th Armor; concurrently relieved from assignment to 4th Armored Division, assigned to 2d Armored Division; transferred (less personnel and equipment) from Germany to Fort Hood, Texas, and reorganized.

384

CAMPAIGN PARTICIPATION CREDIT

World War I
   Somme Offensive

World War II
   *Algeria-French Morocco (with
     arrowhead)
   *Sicily (with arrowhead)

*Normandy
*Northern France
*Rhineland
*Ardennes-Alsace
*Central Europe

DECORATIONS

*Presidential Unit Citation (Army), Streamer embroidered NORMANDY (67th Armored Regiment [less 3d Battalion] cited; DA GO 28, 1948)

Presidential Unit Citation (Army), Streamer embroidered SIEGFRIED LINE

*Belgian Fourragère 1940 (67th Armored Regiment cited; DA GO 43, 1950)

*Cited in the Order of the Day of the Belgian Army for action during September 1944 in BELGUIM

*Cited in the Order of the Day of the Belgian Army for action during December 1944 in the ARDENNES

3d MEDIUM TANK BATTALION, 67th ARMOR

AR
(inactive)

Constituted 24 March 1923 in the Regular Army as Company C, 19th Tank Battalion, Heavy. Redesignated 1 September 1929 as Company C, 2d Tank Regiment. Redesignated 31 October 1932 as Company C, 67th Infantry (Medium Tanks).

Activated 5 June 1940 at Fort Benning, Georgia. Redesignated 15 July 1940 as Company C, 67th Armored Regiment, an element of the 2d Armored Division. Transferred 30 June 1944 from 1st Battalion, 67th Armored Regiment, to 3d Battalion, 67th Armored Regiment.

Redesignated 25 March 1946 as Company C, 6th Tank Battalion, an element of the 2d Armored Division. Redesignated 31 January 1949 as Company C, 6th Medium Tank Battalion. (6th Medium Tank Battalion relieved 14 July 1950 from assignment to 2d Armored Division and assigned 6 October 1950 to 24th Infantry Division.) Redesignated 10 November 1951 as Company C, 6th Tank Battalion. Inactivated 5 June 1958 in Korea and relieved from assignment to 24th Infantry Division.

Redesignated 6 June 1958 as Headquarters and Headquarters Company, 3d Medium Tank Battalion, 67th Armor. Withdrawn from the Regular Army 17 April 1959, allotted to the Army Reserve, and assigned to Third United States Army (organic elements concurrently constituted). Activated 1 June 1959 with Headquarters at Tallahassee, Florida. Inactivated 1 May 1964 at Tallahassee, Florida.

CAMPAIGN PARTICIPATION CREDIT

World War I
Somme Offensive

World War II
*Algeria-French Morocco
  (with arrowhead)
*Sicily (with arrowhead)
*Normandy
*Northern France
*Rhineland
*Ardennes-Alsace

*Central Europe

Korean War
*UN defensive
*UN offensive
*CCF intervention
*First UN counteroffensive
*CCF spring offensive
*UN summer-fall offensive
*Second Korean winter
*Korea, summer 1953

DECORATIONS

Presidential Unit Citation (Army), Streamer embroidered NORMANDY

*Presidential Unit Citation (Army), Streamer embroidered SIEGFRIED LINE (3d Battalion, 67th Armored Regiment, cited; WD GO 28, 1948)

*Republic of Korea Presidential Unit Citation, Streamer embroidered KOREA 1952–1953 (Company C, 6th Tank Battalion, cited; DA GO 24, 1954)

*Republic of Korea Presidential Unit Citation, Streamer embroidered 1952 (6th Tank Battalion cited; DA GO 50, 1954)

*Belgian Fourragère 1940 (67th Armored Regiment cited; DA GO 54, 1950)

*Cited in the Order of the Day of the Belgian Army for action in BELGIUM

*Cited in the Order of the Day of the Belgian Army for action in the ARDENNES

4th BATTALION, 67th ARMOR

AR

(nondivisional)

Organized in May 1918 as Companies B and C, 303d Battalion, Tank Corps, at Camp Colt, Pennsylvania. Consolidated and redesignated 22 June 1921 as Company C, 17th Tank Battalion. Redesignated 1 September 1929 as Company D, 2d Tank Regiment. Inactivated 15 September 1931 at Fort George G. Meade, Maryland.

Redesignated 31 October 1932 as Company D, 67th Infantry (Medium Tanks). Activated 1 October 1939 at Fort Benning, Georgia.

Reorganized and redesignated 15 July 1940 as Company D, 67th Armored Regiment, an element of the 2d Armored Division. Transferred 30 June 1944 from 2d Battalion, 67th Armored Regiment, to 1st Battalion, 67th Armored Regiment. Reorganized and redesignated 25 March 1946 as Company D, 67th Tank Battalion, an element of the 2d Armored Division. Redesignated 11 October 1948 as Company D, 67th Medium Tank Battalion. Redesignated 1 April 1953 as Company D, 67th Tank Battalion. Inactivated 1 July 1957 in Germany and relieved from assignment to 2d Armored Division.

Redesignated 20 March 1959 as Headquarters and Headquarters Company, 4th Medium Tank Battalion, 67th Armor; concurrently, withdrawn from the Regular Army, allotted to the Army Reserve, and assigned to Second United States Army. Activated 17 April 1959 with Headquarters at Wheeling, West Virginia (organic elements constituted 30 March 1959 and activated 17 April 1959). Reorganized and redesignated 24 April 1964 as 4th Battalion, 67th Armor. Relieved 1 January 1966 from assignment to Second United States Army and assigned to First United States Army.

Home Area: First United States Army.

CAMPAIGN PARTICIPATION CREDIT

World War I
Somme Offensive

World War II
*Algeria-French Morocco
(with arrowhead)
*Sicily (with arrowhead)

*Normandy
*Northern France
*Rhineland
*Ardennes-Alsace
*Central Europe

DECORATIONS

*Presidential Unit Citation (Army), Streamer embroidered NORMANDY (67th Armored Regiment [less 3d Battalion] cited; DA GO 28, 1948)

Presidential Unit Citation (Army), Streamer embroidered SIEGFRIED LINE

*Belgian Fourragère 1940 (67th Armored Regiment cited; DA GO 43, 1950)

*Cited in the Order of the Day of the Belgian Army for action in BELGIUM

*Cited in the Order of the Day of the Belgian Army for action in the ARDENNES

5th BATTALION, 67th ARMOR

AR
(nondivisional)

LINEAGE

Organized in May 1918 as Company A, 303d Battalion, Tank Corps, at Camp Colt, Pennsylvania. Redesignated 22 June 1921 as Company A, 17th Tank Battalion. Redesignated 1 September 1929 as Company E, 2d Tank Regiment. Inactivated 15 September 1931 at Fort George G. Meade, Maryland.

Redesignated 31 October 1932 as Company E, 67th Infantry (Medium Tanks). Activated 1 October 1939 at Fort Benning, Georgia.

Reorganized and redesignated 15 July 1940 as Company E, 67th Armored Regiment, an element of the 2d Armored Division. Disbanded 25 March 1946 at Camp Hood, Texas.

Reconstituted 6 February 1947 in the Organized Reserves and redesignated as Troop E, 321st Mechanized Cavalry Reconnaissance Squadron; concurrently, assigned to First United States Army. Activated 21 February 1947 at Boston, Massachusetts. (Organized Reserves redesignated in 1948 as the Organized Reserve Corps; in 1952 as the Army Reserve.) Reorganized and redesignated 9 December 1949 as Assault Gun Company, 1st Battalion, 304th Armored Cavalry. Inactivated 31 July 1950 at Boston, Massachusetts. Disbanded 17 August 1950.

Reconstituted 1 July 1957, withdrawn from the Army Reserve, allotted to the Regular Army, and redesignated as Headquarters and Headquarters Company, 5th Tank Battalion, 67th Armor. Redesignated 13 March 1964 as Headquarters and Headquarters Company, 5th Battalion, 67th Armor, withdrawn from the Regular Army, allotted to the Army Reserve, and assigned to Third United States Army (organic elements concurrently constituted). Activated 1 May 1964 with Headquarters at Tallahassee, Florida.

Home Area: Third United States Army.

CAMPAIGN PARTICIPATION CREDIT

World War I
  Somme Offensive

World War II
  *Algeria-French Morocco
    (with arrowhead)
  *Sicily (with arrowhead)

*Normandy
*Northern France
*Rhineland
*Ardennes-Alsace
*Central Europe

390

DECORATIONS

*Presidential Unit Citation (Army), Streamer embroidered NORMANDY (67th Armored Regiment [less 3d Battalion] cited; DA GO 28, 1948)

Presidential Unit Citation (Army), Streamer embroidered SIEGFRIED LINE (3d Battalion, 67th Armored Regiment, cited; WD GO 108, 1945)

*French Croix de Guerre with Palm, World War II, Streamer embroidered GRIMESNIL (Company E, 67th Armored Regiment, cited; DA GO 43, 1950)

*Belgian Fourragère 1940 (67th Armored Regiment cited; DA GO 43, 1950)

*Cited in the Order of the Day of the Belgian Army for action in BELGIUM

*Cited in the Order of the Day of the Belgian Army for action in the ARDENNES

BIBLIOGRAPHY, 67TH ARMOR

Department of the Army. AMERICAN FORCES IN ACTION series.
Omaha Beachhead. 1945.
Utah Beach to Cherbourg. 1947.
St-Lo. 1946.
Unit Members. A History of the Second Armored Division, 1940–1946. Atlanta, Georgia: 1946.
———. Brief History of the 6th Tank Battalion (Medium), 1918–1953, Organization Day March 25. Japan: 1952.
———. Hell on Wheels, War Against the Axis, 1942–1945. N.p.: 1945.
———. History, 67th Armored Regiment. Germany: 1945.
UNITED STATES ARMY IN THE KOREAN WAR
Appleman, Roy E. South to the Naktong, North to the Yalu. 1961.
UNITED STATES ARMY IN WORLD WAR II
Blumenson, Martin. Breakout and Pursuit. 1961.
Cole, Hugh M. The Ardennes: Battle of the Bulge. 1965.
Garland, Albert N., and Howard McGaw Smyth. Sicily and the Surrender of Italy. 1965.
Harrison, Gordon A. Cross-Channel Attack. 1951.
Howe, George F. Northwest Africa: Seizing the Initiative in the West. 1957.
MacDonald, Charles B. The Siegfried Line Campaign. 1963.

68th ARMOR

HERALDIC ITEMS

COAT OF ARMS

Shield: Azure, a lion passant argent.

Crest: On a wreath argent and vert, a sector of a disc azure bordered of the first surmounted by an anchor sable the stock banded of six, three and three, silver, vert and silver, the flukes gules and issuing from the stock thereof a demi-fleur-de-lis of the first the center petal of the third, on the shank of the anchor a taeguk gules and azure, overall palewise a lightning flash gold.

Motto: *Ventre à Terre.*

Symbolism: The colors, blue and white, associate the regiment with the infantry. The lion symbolizes the power of a tank regiment.

     The anchor, a symbol of support, stands for service during World War II with the 4th Marine Division at Saipan and Tinian for which the Presidential Unit Citation streamer (Navy) was awarded. The flukes of the anchor, simulating arrowheads for assault landings, are red in reference to the heavy casualties sustained in those actions. The lightning flash alludes to the speed and firepower of armor organizations. The fleur-de-lis is for service in France and the taeguk for service in Korea. The blue and white base represents the shores of Europe, the Pacific islands, and Korea.

DISTINCTIVE INSIGNIA

The distinctive insignia is the shield and motto of the coat of arms.

LINEAGE AND HONORS

LINEAGE

Constituted 1 October 1933 in the Regular Army as 68th Infantry (Light Tanks). (1st and 2d Battalions activated 1 January 1940 at Fort Benning, Georgia, by redesignation of the 1st through 7th Tank Companies [organized in 1918] as companies of 68th Infantry. 1st Battalion inactivated 5 June 1940 at Fort Benning, Georgia.)

393

68th Infantry (Light Tanks) redesignated 15 July 1940 as 68th Armored Regiment and assigned to 2d Armored Division. Activated (less 2d Battalion— already active) 1 August 1940 at Fort Benning, Georgia. Inactivated 8 January 1942 at Fort Benning, Georgia, and relieved from assignment to 2d Armored Division. Activated 15 February 1942 at Fort Knox, Kentucky, and assigned to 6th Armored Division.

Regiment broken up 20 September 1943 and its elements reorganized and redesignated as follows: Regimental Headquarters and Headquarters Company and 2d Battalion as 68th Tank Battalion, an element of the 6th Armored Division; 1st Battalion as 773d Tank Battalion and relieved from assignment to 6th Armored Division; 3d Battalion as 15th Tank Battalion, an element of the 6th Armored Division; Reconnaissance Company as Troop D, 86th Cavalry Reconnaissance Squadron, Mechanized, an element of the 6th Armored Division; Band, Maintenance and Service Companies disbanded.

68th Tank Battalion relieved 19 July 1945 from assignment to 6th Armored Division. Inactivated 29 December 1945 at Camp Patrick Henry, Virginia. Redesignated 21 August 1950 as 68th Medium Tank Battalion and assigned to 6th Armored Division. Activated 5 September 1950 at Fort Leonard Wood, Missouri. Inactivated 16 March 1956 at Fort Leonard Wood, Missouri. Relieved 1 July 1957 from assignment to 6th Armored Division.

773d Tank Battalion reorganized and redesignated 27 October 1943 as 773d Amphibian Tank Battalion. Reorganized and redesignated 10 January 1944 as 773d Amphibian Tractor Battalion. Inactivated 15 April 1946 at Yokohama, Japan. Redesignated 24 December 1946 as 56th Amphibian Tractor Battalion. Redesignated 18 April 1949 as 56th Amphibious Tank and Tractor Battalion. Activated 10 May 1949 at Fort Worden, Washington. Inactivated 15 December 1954 in Japan.

15th Tank Battalion relieved 19 July 1945 from assignment to 6th Armored Division. Inactivated by elements 22–25 February 1946 at New York Port of Embarkation, New York. Headquarters and Headquarters Company, 15th Tank Battalion, redesignated 1 August 1946 as 15th Tank Company and activated at Fort Riley, Kansas. Inactivated 6 November 1946 at Fort Riley, Kansas. Activated 1 May 1947 at Duino, Italy. Inactivated 1 December 1949 in Europe. Redesignated 21 August 1950 as Headquarters and Headquarters Company, 15th Medium Tank Battalion. Battalion activated 5 September 1950 as an element of the 6th Armored Division at Fort Leonard Wood, Missouri. Inactivated 16 March 1956 at Fort Leonard Wood, Missouri. Relieved 1 July 1957 from assignment to 6th Armored Division.

Troop D, 86th Cavalry Reconnaissance Squadron, Mechanized, inactivated 19 September 1945 at Camp Myles Standish, Massachusetts. Redesignated 21 August 1950 as Company D, 86th Reconnaissance Battalion. Activated 5

September 1950 at Fort Leonard Wood, Missouri. Inactivated 16 March 1956 at Fort Leonard Wood, Missouri.

Maintenance Company and Service Company, 68th Armored Regiment, reconstituted 1 July 1957 in the Regular Army.

68th and 15th Tank Battalions; 56th Amphibious Tank and Tractor Battalion; Company D, 86th Reconnaissance Battalion; and Maintenance and Service Companies, 68th Armored Regiment, consolidated, reorganized and redesignated 1 July 1957 as 68th Armor, a parent regiment under the Combat Arms Regimental System (Headquarters and Headquarters and Service Company, 68th Tank Battalion, redesignated as Headquarters and Headquarters Company, 68th Armor).

CAMPAIGN PARTICIPATION CREDIT

World War I
 St. Mihiel
 Meuse-Argonne

World War II
 Normandy
 Northern France
 Rhineland

Ardennes-Alsace
Central Europe
Western Pacific
 (with arrowhead)
Ryukyus (with arrowhead)

Korean War
 Korea, summer 1953

DECORATIONS

Presidential Unit Citation (Navy), Streamer embroidered SAIPAN and TINIAN (773d Amphibian Tractor Battalion cited; DA GO 73, 1948)

1st BATTALION, 68th ARMOR

RA
(8th Infantry Division)

LINEAGE

Organized 7 June 1918 as Company A, 327th Battalion, Tank Corps, American Expeditionary Forces, in France. Redesignated 12 September 1918 as Company A, 345th Battalion, Tank Corps. Redesignated 8 January 1921 as 1st Tank Company and allotted to the Regular Army.

Redesignated 1 January 1940 as Company A, 68th Infantry (Light Tanks). Inactivated 5 June 1940 at Fort Benning, Georgia. Redesignated 15 July 1940 as Company A, 68th Armored Regiment, an element of the 2d Armored Division. Activated 1 August 1940 at Fort Benning, Georgia. Inactivated 8 January 1942 at Fort Benning, Georgia (68th Armored Regiment concurrently relieved from assignment to 2d Armored Division). Activated 15 February 1942 at Fort Knox, Kentucky, as an element of the 6th Armored Division.

Reorganized and redesignated 20 September 1943 as Company A, 773d Tank Battalion, and relieved from assignment to 6th Armored Division. Reorganized and redesignated 27 October 1943 as Company A, 773d Amphibian Tank Battalion. Redesignated 10 January 1944 as Company A, 773d Amphibian Tractor Battalion. Inactivated 15 April 1946 at Yokohama, Japan.

Redesignated 24 December 1946 as Company A, 56th Amphibian Tractor Battalion. Redesignated 18 April 1949 as Company A, 56th Amphibious Tank and Tractor Battalion. Activated 10 May 1949 at Fort Worden, Washington. Inactivated 15 December 1954 in Japan.

Redesignated 1 July 1957 as Headquarters and Headquarters Company, 1st Medium Tank Battalion (Patton), 68th Armor; concurrently, assigned to 3d Infantry Division and activated at Fort Benning, Georgia (organic companies concurrently constituted and activated). Reorganized and redesignated 1 April 1963 as 1st Battalion, 68th Armor; concurrently, relieved from assignment to 3d Infantry Division and assigned to 8th Infantry Division.

396

CAMPAIGN PARTICIPATION CREDIT

World War I
  *St. Mihiel
  *Meuse-Argonne

World War II
  Normandy
  Northern France
  Rhineland
  Ardennes-Alsace

Central Europe
  *Western Pacific (with arrowhead)
  *Ryukyus (with arrowhead)

Korean War
  *UN defensive (with arrowhead)
  *UN offensive
  *CCF intervention
  *Korea, summer 1953

DECORATIONS

*Presidential Unit Citation (Navy), Streamer embroidered SAIPAN and TINIAN (773d Amphibian Tractor Battalion cited; DA GO 73, 1948)

*Presidential Unit Citation (Navy), Streamer embroidered INCHON (Company A, 56th Amphibious Tank and Tractor Battalion, cited; DA GO 63, 1952)

*Republic of Korea Presidential Unit Citation, Streamer embroidered INCHON TO HUNGNAM (Company Λ, 56th Amphibious Tank and Tractor Battalion, cited; DA GO 8, 1952)

*Republic of Korea Presidential Unit Citation, Streamer embroidered KOREA (56th Amphibious Tank and Tractor Battalion cited; DA GO 23, 1954)

2d BATTALION, 68th ARMOR

RA

(8th Infantry Division)

LINEAGE

Organized in April 1918 as Company C, 328th Battalion, Tank Corps, at Camp Colt, Pennsylvania. Redesignated 8 January 1921 as 4th Tank Company, and assigned to 4th Division, and allotted to the Regular Army. Inactivated 27 September 1921 at Fort Lewis, Washington. Activated 15 September 1931 at Fort McClellan, Alabama.

Redesignated 1 January 1940 as Company B, 68th Infantry (Light Tanks), and relieved from assignment to 4th Division. Inactivated 5 June 1940 at Fort Benning, Georgia. Redesignated 15 July 1940 as Company B, 68th Armored Regiment, an element of the 2d Armored Division. Activated 1 August 1940 at Fort Benning, Georgia. Inactivated 8 January 1942 at Fort Benning, Georgia (68th Armored Regiment concurrently relieved from assignment to 2d Armored Division). Activated 15 February 1942 at Fort Knox, Kentucky, as an element of the 6th Armored Division.

Reorganized and redesignated 20 September 1943 as Company B, 773d Tank Battalion, and relieved from assignment to 6th Armored Division. Reorganized and redesignated 27 October 1943 as Company B, 773d Amphibian Tank Battalion. Redesignated 10 January 1944 as Company B, 773d Amphibian Tractor Battalion. Inactivated 15 April 1946 in Japan.

Redesignated 24 December 1946 as Company B, 56th Amphibian Tractor Battalion. Redesignated 18 April 1949 as Company B, 56th Amphibious Tank and Tractor Battalion. Activated 10 May 1949 at Fort Worden, Washington. Inactivated 15 December 1954 in Japan.

Redesignated 1 July 1957 as Headquarters and Headquarters Company, 2d Medium Tank Battalion (Patton), 68th Armor. Assigned 1 August 1957 to 8th Infantry Division and activated in Germany (organic companies concurrently constituted and activated). Reorganized and redesignated 1 April 1963 as 2d Battalion, 68th Armor.

CAMPAIGN PARTICIPATION CREDIT

World War I
St. Mihiel
Meuse-Argonne

World War II
Normandy
Northern France
Rhineland

Ardennes-Alsace
Central Europe
*Western Pacific (with arrowhead)
*Ryukyus (with arrowhead)

Korean War
*Korea, summer 1953

DECORATIONS

*Presidential Unit Citation (Navy), Streamer embroidered SAIPAN and TINIAN (773d Amphibian Tractor Battalion cited; DA GO 73, 1948)

*Republic of Korea Presidential Unit Citation, Streamer embroidered KOREA (56th Amphibious Tank and Tractor Battalion cited; DA GO 23, 1954)

3d BATTALION, 68th ARMOR

RA
(8th Infantry Division)

LINEAGE

Organized 16 April 1918 as Company B, 1st Tank Center, American Expeditionary Forces, in France from Provisional Company B, Tank Service (organized 17 February 1918). Redesignated 6 June 1918 as Company B, 326th Battalion, Tank Corps. Redesignated 1 September 1918 as Company B, 344th Battalion, Tank Corps. Redesignated 8 January 1921 as 5th Tank Company and allotted to the Regular Army.

Consolidated 1 January 1940 with 6th Tank Company (see ANNEX), reorganized and redesignated as Company C, 68th Infantry (Light Tanks). Inactivated 5 June 1940 at Fort Benning, Georgia. Redesignated 15 July 1940 as Company C, 68th Armored Regiment, an element of the 2d Armored Division. Activated 1 August 1940 at Fort Benning, Georgia. Inactivated 8 January 1942 at Fort Benning, Georgia (68th Armored Regiment concurrently relieved from assignment to 2d Armored Division). Activated 15 February 1942 at Fort Knox, Kentucky, as an element of the 6th Armored Division.

Reorganized and redesignated 20 September 1943 as Company C, 773d Tank Battalion, and relieved from assignment to 6th Armored Division. Redesignated 27 October 1943 as Company C, 773d Amphibian Tank Battalion. Redesignated 10 January 1944 as Company C, 773d Amphibian Tractor Battalion. Inactivated 15 April 1946 in Japan.

Redesignated 24 December 1946 as Company C, 56th Amphibian Tractor Battalion. Redesignated 18 April 1949 as Company C, 56th Amphibious Tank and Tractor Battalion. Activated 10 May 1949 at Fort Worden, Washington. Inactivated 15 December 1954 in Japan.

Redesignated 1 July 1957 as Headquarters and Headquarters Company, 3d Medium Tank Battalion (Patton), 68th Armor. Assigned 1 December 1957 to 9th Infantry Division and activated at Fort Carson, Colorado (organic companies concurrently constituted and activated). Inactivated 31 January 1962 at Fort Carson, Colorado. Redesignated 27 March 1963 as 3d Battalion, 68th Armor; concurrently, relieved from assignment to 9th Infantry Division and assigned to 8th Infantry Division. Activated 1 April 1963 in Germany.

400

ANNEX

Company B, 328th Battalion, Tank Corps, organized in April 1918 at Camp Colt, Pennsylvania. Redesignated 8 January 1921 as 6th Tank Company and allotted to the Regular Army.

CAMPAIGN PARTICIPATION CREDIT

World War I
  *St. Mihiel
  *Meuse-Argonne

World War II
  Normandy
  Northern France
  Rhineland

Ardennes-Alsace
Central Europe
*Western Pacific (with arrowhead)
*Ryukyus (with arrowhead)

Korean War
  *Korea, summer 1953

DECORATIONS

*Presidential Unit Citation (Navy), Streamer embroidered SAIPAN and TINIAN (773d Amphibian Tractor Battalion cited; DA GO 73, 1948)

*Republic of Korea Presidential Unit Citation, Streamer embroidered KOREA (56th Amphibious Tank and Tractor Battalion cited; DA GO 23, 1954)

4th BATTALION, 68th ARMOR

RA

(nondivisional)

LINEAGE

Organized 7 June 1918 as Company C, 327th Battalion, Tank Corps, American Expeditionary Forces in France. Redesignated 12 September 1918 as Company C, 345th Battalion, Tank Corps. Redesignated 8 January 1921 as 2d Tank Company and allotted to the Regular Army.

Redesignated 1 January 1940 as Company D, 68th Infantry (Light Tanks). Redesignated 15 July 1940 as Company D, 68th Armored Regiment, an element of 2d Armored Division. Inactivated 8 January 1942 at Fort Benning, Georgia (68th Armored Regiment concurrently relieved from assignment to 2d Armored Division). Activated 15 February 1942 at Fort Knox, Kentucky, as an element of the 6th Armored Division.

Reorganized and redesignated 20 September 1943 as Company A, 68th Tank Battalion, an element of the 6th Armored Division. (68th Tank Battalion relieved 19 July 1945 from assignment to 6th Armored Division.) Inactivated 29 December 1945 at Camp Patrick Henry, Virginia. Redesignated 21 August 1950 as Company A, 68th Medium Tank Battalion, an element of the 6th Armored Division. Activated 5 September 1950 at Fort Leonard Wood, Missouri. Inactivated 16 March 1956 at Fort Leonard Wood, Missouri.

Redesignated 1 July 1957 as Headquarters and Headquarters Company, 4th Medium Tank Battalion, 68th Armor, and relieved from assignment to 6th Armored Division. Redesignated 20 May 1958 as Headquarters, Headquarters and Service Company, 4th Medium Tank Battalion (Patton), 68th Armor. Activated 13 June 1958 at Fort Bragg, North Carolina (organic elements constituted 24 July 1957; activated 13 June 1958). Reorganized and redesignated 5 May 1964 as 4th Battalion, 68th Armor. Transferred (less personnel and equipment) 1 July 1965 from Fort Bragg, North Carolina, to Fort Stewart, Georgia, and reorganized.

402

CAMPAIGN PARTICIPATION CREDIT

World War I
  *St. Mihiel
  *Meuse-Argonne

World War II
  *Normandy
  *Northern France
  *Rhineland

*Ardennes-Alsace
*Central Europe
  Western Pacific (with arrowhead)
  Ryukyus (with arrowhead)

Korean War
  Korea, summer 1953

DECORATIONS

*Presidential Unit Citation (Army), Streamer embroidered LANDROFF, FRANCE (Company A, 68th Tank Battalion, cited; WD GO 81, 1946)

Presidential Unit Citation (Navy), Streamer embroidered SAIPAN and TINIAN

5th BATTALION, 68th ARMOR

RA

(8th Infantry Division)

Organized in April 1918 as Company A, 328th Battalion, Tank Corps, at Camp Colt, Pennsylvania. Redesignated 8 January 1921 as 3d Tank Company and allotted to the Regular Army.

Redesignated 1 January 1940 as Company E, 68th Infantry (Light Tanks). Redesignated 15 July 1940 as Company E, 68th Armored Regiment, an element of the 2d Armored Division. Inactivated 8 January 1942 at Fort Benning, Georgia (68th Armored Regiment concurrently relieved from assignment to 2d Armored Division). Activated 15 February 1942 at Fort Knox, Kentucky, as an element of the 6th Armored Division.

Reorganized and redesignated 20 September 1943 as Company B, 68th Tank Battalion, an element of the 6th Armored Division. (68th Tank Battalion relieved 19 July 1945 from assignment to 6th Armored Division.) Inactivated 29 December 1945 at Camp Patrick Henry, Virginia. Redesignated 21 August 1950 as Company B, 68th Medium Tank Battalion, an element of the 6th Armored Division. Activated 5 September 1950 at Fort Leonard Wood, Missouri. Inactivated 16 March 1956 at Fort Leonard Wood, Missouri.

Redesignated 1 July 1957 as Headquarters and Headquarters Company, 5th Medium Tank Battalion, 68th Armor, and relieved from assignment to 6th Armored Division. Withdrawn from the Regular Army 7 April 1959, allotted to the Army Reserve, and assigned to 77th Infantry Division (organic elements concurrently constituted). Activated 1 May 1959 at Bronx, New York. Inactivated 26 March 1963 at Bronx, New York, and relieved from assignment to 77th Infantry Division.

Redesignated 1 April 1966 as 5th Battalion, 68th Armor; concurrently, withdrawn from the Army Reserve, allotted to the Regular Army, assigned to 8th Infantry Division, and activated in Germany.

404

Campaign Participation Credit

World War I
St. Mihiel

World War II
  *Normandy
  *Northern France
  *Rhineland

*Ardennes-Alsace
*Central Europe
  Western Pacific (with arrowhead)
  Ryukyus (with arrowhead)

Korean War
  Korea, summer 1953

Decorations

*Presidential Unit Citation (Army), Streamer embroidered HAN-SUR-NIED, FRANCE (Company B, 68th Tank Battalion, cited; WD GO 55, 1945)

Presidential Unit Citation (Navy), Streamer embroidered SAIPAN and TINIAN

6th BATTALION, 68th ARMOR

AR

(nondivisional)

LINEAGE

Organized 7 June 1918 as Company B, 327th Battalion, Tank Corps, American Expeditionary Forces, in France. Redesignated 12 September 1918 as Company B, 345th Battalion, Tank Corps. Redesignated 8 January 1921 as 7th Tank Company and allotted to the Regular Army. Inactivated 6 September 1921 at Camp Meade, Maryland.

Redesignated 1 January 1940 as Company F, 68th Infantry (Light Tanks), and activated at Fort Benning, Georgia. Redesignated 15 July 1940 as Company F, 68th Armored Regiment, an element of the 2d Armored Division. Inactivated 8 January 1942 at Fort Benning, Georgia (68th Armored Regiment concurrently relieved from assignment to 2d Armored Division). Activated 15 February 1942 at Fort Knox, Kentucky, as an element of the 6th Armored Division.

Reorganized and redesignated 20 September 1943 as Company C, 68th Tank Battalion, an element of the 6th Armored Division (68th Tank Battalion relieved 19 July 1945 from assignment to 6th Armored Division). Inactivated 29 December 1945 at Camp Patrick Henry, Virginia. Redesignated 21 August 1950 as Company C, 68th Medium Tank Battalion, an element of the 6th Armored Division. Activated 5 September 1950 at Fort Leonard Wood, Missouri. Inactivated 16 March 1956 at Fort Leonard Wood, Missouri.

Redesignated 1 July 1957 as Headquarters and Headquarters Company, 6th Medium Tank Battalion, 68th Armor, and relieved from assignment to 6th Armored Division. Withdrawn from the Regular Army 17 March 1959, allotted to the Army Reserve, and assigned to 79th Infantry Division (organic elements concurrently constituted). Activated 20 April 1959 with Headquarters at Allentown, Pennsylvania. Reorganized and redesignated 7 January 1963 as 6th Battalion, 68th Armor; concurrently, relieved from assignment to 79th Infantry Division, assigned to Second United States Army, and location of Headquarters changed to Bethlehem, Pennsylvania. Relieved 1 January 1966 from assignment to Second United States Army and assigned to First United States Army.

Home Area: First United States Army.

CAMPAIGN PARTICIPATION CREDIT

World War I
*St. Mihiel
*Meuse-Argonne

World War II
*Normandy
*Northern France
*Rhineland

*Ardennes-Alsace
*Central Europe
Western Pacific (with arrowhead)
Ryukyus (with arrowhead)

Korean War
Korea, summer 1953

DECORATIONS

Presidential Unit Citation (Navy), Streamer embroidered SAIPAN and TINIAN

7th BATTALION, 68th ARMOR

LINEAGE

Constituted 1 October 1933 in the Regular Army as Company G, 68th Infantry (Light Tanks). Redesignated 15 July 1940 as Company G, 68th Armored Regiment, an element of 2d Armored Division. Activated 13 August 1940 at Fort Benning, Georgia. Inactivated 8 January 1942 at Fort Benning, Georgia (68th Armored Regiment concurrently relieved from assignment to 2d Armored Division). Activated 15 February 1942 at Fort Knox, Kentucky, as an element of the 6th Armored Division.

Reorganized and redesignated 20 September 1943 as Company A, 15th Tank Battalion, an element of the 6th Armored Division. (68th Tank Battalion relieved 19 July 1945 from assignment to 6th Armored Division.) Inactivated 25 February 1946 at Camp Kilmer, New Jersey. Redesignated 5 September 1950 as Company A, 15th Medium Tank Battalion, and activated at Fort Leonard Wood, Missouri, as an element of the 6th Armored Division. Inactivated 16 March 1956 at Fort Leonard Wood, Missouri.

Redesignated 1 July 1957 as Headquarters and Headquarters Company, 7th Medium Tank Battalion, 68th Armor, and relieved from assignment to 6th Armored Division. Withdrawn from the Regular Army 19 March 1959, allotted to the Army Reserve, and assigned to 83d Infantry Division (organic elements concurrently constituted). Activated 20 March 1959 with Headquarters at Salem, Ohio. Reorganized and redesignated 15 April 1963 as 7th Battalion, 68th Armor. Inactivated 31 December 1965 and relieved from assignment to 83d Infantry Division.

CAMPAIGN PARTICIPATION CREDIT

World War I
St. Mihiel
Meuse-Argonne

World War II
*Normandy
*Northern France
*Rhineland

*Ardennes-Alsace
*Central Europe
Western Pacific (with arrowhead)
Ryukyus (with arrowhead)

Korean War
Korea, summer 1953

DECORATIONS

Presidential Unit Citation (Navy), Streamer embroidered SAIPAN and TINIAN

408

8th BATTALION, 68th ARMOR

AR
(inactive)

LINEAGE

Constituted 1 October 1933 in the Regular Army as Company H, 68th Infantry (Light Tanks). Redesignated 15 July 1940 as Company H, 68th Armored Regiment, an element of the 2d Armored Division. Activated 13 August 1940 at Fort Benning, Georgia. Inactivated 8 January 1942 at Fort Benning, Georgia (68th Armored Regiment concurrently relieved from assignment to 2d Armored Division). Activated 15 February 1942 at Fort Knox, Kentucky, as an element of the 6th Armored Division.

Reorganized and redesignated 20 September 1943 as Company B, 15th Tank Battalion, an element of the 6th Armored Division. (68th Tank Battalion relieved 19 July 1945 from assignment to 6th Armored Division.) Inactivated 22 February 1946 at Camp Kilmer, New Jersey. Redesignated 5 September 1950 as Company B, 15th Medium Tank Battalion, and activated at Fort Leonard Wood, Missouri, as an element of the 6th Armored Division. Inactivated 16 March 1956 at Fort Leonard Wood, Missouri.

Redesignated 1 July 1957 as Headquarters and Headquarters Company, 8th Medium Tank Battalion, 68th Armor, and relieved from assignment to 6th Armored Division. Redesignated 15 April 1963 as Headquarters and Headquarters Company, 8th Battalion, 68th Armor; concurrently, withdrawn from the Regular Army, allotted to the Army Reserve, assigned to 83d Infantry Division, and activated with Headquarters at Columbus, Ohio (organic elements constituted 27 March 1963 in the Army Reserve and activated 15 April 1963). Inactivated 31 December 1965 at Columbus, Ohio, and relieved from assignment to the 83d Infantry Division.

CAMPAIGN PARTICIPATION CREDIT

World War I
St. Mihiel
Meuse-Argonne

World War II
*Normandy
*Northern France
*Rhineland

*Ardennes-Alsace
*Central Europe
Western Pacific (with arrowhead)
Ryukyus (with arrowhead)

Korean War
Korea, summer 1953

409

Decorations

Presidential Unit Citation (Navy), Streamer embroidered saipan and tinian

Bibliography, 68th Armor

Byrd, Charles D. *The 15th Tank Battalion, A Record of Action*. Germany: 1945.

Miller, John, jr., O. J. Carroll, and M. E. Tackley. *Korea 1951–1953*. Washington: 1956.

Unit Members. *A Pictorial History of the Super 6th, 6th Armored Division, February 15, 1942–February 15, 1944*. Los Angeles: 1944.

————. *Combat History of the 6th Armored Division in the European Theater of Operations, 18 July 1944–8 May 1945*. Yadkinville, North Carolina: 1945.

————. *"Super Sixth" Meets Russians*. N.p.: 1945.

————. *The 68th Tank Battalion in Combat*. Minden, Nebraska: 1945.

UNITED STATES ARMY IN WORLD WAR II

Blumenson, Martin. *Breakout and Pursuit*. 1961.

Cole, Hugh M. *The Ardennes: Battle of the Bulge*. 1965.

————. *The Lorraine Campaign*. 1950.

69th ARMOR

HERALDIC ITEMS

COAT OF ARMS

Shield: Per bend argent and vert on the first a panther passant on division line, head to chief sable.

Crest: On a wreath of the colors argent and vert between two ruined towers sable, the dexter charged with a fleur-de-lis or and the sinister with an anchor of the like, a cubit arm in armor, the hand in a gauntlet proper grasping two lightning flashes fesswise gules.

Motto: *Vitesse et Puissance* (Speed and Power).

Symbolism: The shield is in the green and white of the Armored Force. The panther is symbolic of the tremendous power and striking ability of the regiment. Being always alert, the black variety of panther is considered the most dangerous of all the feline family.

The two ruined towers, bearing a fleur-de-lis and an anchor, allude to two areas, Europe and the Pacific; for the latter area, part of the organization was awarded three Presidential Unit Citations (Navy) and the Navy Unit Commendation. The gauntlet and lightning flashes symbolize armor and striking power.

DISTINCTIVE INSIGNIA

The distinctive insignia is the shield and motto of the coat of arms.

LINEAGE AND HONORS

LINEAGE

Constituted 15 July 1940 in the Regular Army as 69th Armored Regiment and assigned to 1st Armored Division. Activated 31 July 1940 at Fort Knox, Kentucky. Inactivated 10 January 1942 at Fort Knox, Kentucky. Relieved 15 February 1942 from assignment to 1st Armored Division, assigned to 6th Armored Division, and activated at Fort Knox, Kentucky.

411

Regiment broken up 20 September 1943 and its elements reorganized and redesignated as follows: Regimental Headquarters and Headquarters Company, Regimental Medical Detachment, 1st Battalion Headquarters and Headquarters Company, and Companies A, B, C, and D as 69th Tank Battalion, an element of the 6th Armored Division; 3d Battalion as 708th Tank Battalion and relieved from assignment to 6th Armored Division; Reconnaissance Company as Troop E, 86th Cavalry Reconnaissance Squadron, Mechanized; 2d Battalion (less Company D), absorbed in 69th Tank Battalion. Maintenance and Service Companies disbanded.

69th Tank Battalion reorganized and redesignated 10 July 1945 as 69th Amphibian Tractor Battalion and relieved from assignment to 6th Armored Division. Inactivated 8 March 1946 at Camp Kilmer, New Jersey. Redesignated 21 August 1950 as 69th Medium Tank Battalion and assigned to 6th Armored Division. Activated 5 September 1950 at Fort Leonard Wood, Missouri. Inactivated 16 March 1956 at Fort Leonard Wood, Missouri. Relieved 1 February 1957 from assignment to 6th Armored Division.

708th Tank Battalion reorganized and redesignated 27 October 1943 as 708th Amphibian Tank Battalion. (Reorganized 1 January 1944 as a provisional tractor battalion.) Inactivated 25 January 1946 in the Philippine Islands. Reorganized and redesignated 28 July 1950 as 89th Medium Tank Battalion. Activated 7 August 1950 in Korea. Redesignated 14 November 1951 as 89th Tank Battalion and assigned to 25th Infantry Division. Inactivated 1 February 1957 in Hawaii and relieved from assignment to 25th Infantry Division.

Troop E, 86th Cavalry Reconnaissance Squadron, Mechanized, inactivated 19 September 1945 at Camp Myles Standish, Massachusetts. Disbanded 21 August 1950. Reconstituted 1 February 1957 in the Regular Army.

Headquarters and Headquarters Company, 2d Battalion, 69th Armored Regiment; Companies E and F, and Maintenance and Service Companies, 69th Armored Regiment, reconstituted 1 February 1957 in the Regular Army.

69th and 89th Tank Battalions; Troop E, 86th Cavalry Reconnaissance Squadron, Mechanized; and the reconstituted elements of the 69th Armored Regiment consolidated, reorganized and redesignated 1 February 1957 as 69th Armor, a parent regiment under the Combat Arms Regimental System (Headquarters, 69th Medium Tank Battalion, redesignated as Headquarters, 69th Armor).

CAMPAIGN PARTICIPATION CREDIT

World War II
  Normandy
  Northern France
  Rhineland
  Ardennes-Alsace
  Central Europe
  Eastern Mandates
  Western Pacific
    (with arrowhead)
  Ryukyus (with arrowhead)

Korean War
  UN defensive
  UN offensive

  CCF intervention
  First UN counteroffensive
  CCF spring offensive
  UN summer-fall offensive
  Second Korean winter
  Korea, summer-fall 1952
  Third Korean winter
  Korea, summer 1953

Vietnam
  Counteroffensive
  Counteroffensive, Phase II
  Counteroffensive, Phase III
  Tet Counteroffensive

DECORATIONS

Presidential Unit Citation (Navy), Streamer embroidered SAIPAN and TINIAN (708th Amphibious Tank Battalion cited; DA GO 73, 1948)

Presidential Unit Citation (Navy), Streamer embroidered OKINAWA (708th Amphibian Tank Battalion cited; DA GO 73, 1948)

Presidential Unit Citation (Navy), Streamer embroidered WONJU-HWACHON (89th Medium Tank Battalion cited; DA GO 38, 1957)

Navy Unit Commendation, Streamer embroidered PANMUNJOM (89th Tank Battalion cited; DA GO 38, 1957)

1st BATTALION, 69th ARMOR

RA

(25th Infantry Division)

LINEAGE

Constituted 15 July 1940 in the Regular Army as Company A, 69th Armored Regiment, an element of the 1st Armored Division. Activated 31 July 1940 at Fort Knox, Kentucky. Inactivated 10 January 1942 at Fort Knox, Kentucky. Activated 15 February 1942 at Fort Knox, Kentucky (69th Armored Regiment concurrently relieved from assignment to 1st Armored Division and assigned to 6th Armored Division).

Reorganized and redesignated 20 September 1943 as Company A, 69th Tank Battalion. Reorganized and redesignated 10 July 1945 as Company A, 69th Amphibian Tractor Battalion and relieved from assignment to 6th Armored Division. Inactivated 8 March 1946 at Camp Kilmer, New Jersey. Redesignated 21 August 1950 as Company A, 69th Medium Tank Battalion, an element of the 6th Armored Division. Activated 5 September 1950 at Fort Leonard Wood, Missouri. Inactivated 16 March 1956 at Fort Leonard Wood, Missouri. (69th Tank Battalion relieved 1 February 1957 from assignment to 6th Armored Division.)

Redesignated 15 February 1957 as Headquarters and Headquarters Company, 1st Medium Tank Battalion (Patton), 69th Armor; concurrently, assigned to 1st Infantry Division and activated at Fort Riley, Kansas (organic elements concurrently constituted and activated). Relieved 1 July 1963 from assignment to 1st Infantry Division, transferred (less personnel and equipment) from Fort Riley, Kansas, to United States Army, Pacific, assigned to 25th Infantry Division, and reorganized in Hawaii. Reorganized and redesignated 5 August 1963 as 1st Battalion, 69th Armor.

414

CAMPAIGN PARTICIPATION CREDIT

World War II
  *Normandy
  *Northern France
  *Rhineland
  *Ardennes-Alsace
  *Central Europe
   Eastern Mandates
   Western Pacific
     (with arrowhead)
   Ryukyus (with arrowhead)

Korean War
   UN defensive
   UN offensive

CCF intervention
First UN counteroffensive
CCF spring offensive
UN summer-fall offensive
Second Korean winter
Korea, summer-fall 1952
Third Korean winter
Korea, summer 1953

Vietnam
  *Counteroffensive
  *Counteroffensive, Phase II
  *Counteroffensive, Phase III
  *Tet Counteroffensive

DECORATIONS

Presidential Unit Citation (Navy), Streamer embroidered SAIPAN and TINIAN

Presidential Unit Citation (Navy), Streamer embroidered OKINAWA

Presidential Unit Citation (Navy), Streamer embroidered WONJU-HWACHON

Navy Unit Commendation, Streamer embroidered PANMUNJOM

2d MEDIUM TANK BATTALION, 69th ARMOR

RA

(inactive)

LINEAGE

Constituted 15 July 1940 in the Regular Army as Company B, 69th Armored Regiment, an element of the 1st Armored Division. Activated 31 July 1940 at Fort Knox, Kentucky. Inactivated 10 January 1942 at Fort Knox, Kentucky. Activated 15 February 1942 at Fort Knox, Kentucky (69th Armored Regiment concurrently relieved from assignment to 1st Armored Division and assigned to 6th Armored Division).

Reorganized and redesignated 20 September 1943 as Company B, 69th Tank Battalion. Reorganized and redesignated 10 July 1945 as Company B, 69th Amphibian Tractor Battalion, and relieved from assignment to 6th Armored Division. Inactivated 8 March 1946 at Camp Kilmer, New Jersey. Redesignated 21 August 1950 as Company B, 69th Medium Tank Battalion, and assigned to 6th Armored Division. Activated 5 September 1950 at Fort Leonard Wood, Missouri. Inactivated 16 March 1956 at Fort Leonard Wood, Missouri. Relieved 1 February 1957 from assignment to 6th Armored Division.

Redesignated 1 July 1957 as Headquarters and Headquarters Company, 2d Medium Tank Battalion (Patton), 69th Armor (organic elements concurrently constituted). Assigned 8 July 1957 to 10th Infantry Division and activated in Germany. Relieved 14 June 1958 from assignment to 10th Infantry Division, assigned to 2d Infantry Division, and reorganized at Fort Benning, Georgia. Inactivated 1 March 1963 at Fort Benning, Georgia, and relieved from assignment to 2d Infantry Division.

CAMPAIGN PARTICIPATION CREDIT

World War II
- *Normandy
- *Northern France
- *Rhineland
- *Ardennes-Alsace
- *Central Europe
- Eastern Mandates
- Western Pacific
  (with arrowhead)
- Ryukyus (with arrowhead)

Korean War
- UN defensive
- UN offensive
- CCF intervention
- First UN counteroffensive
- CCF spring offensive
- UN summer-fall offensive
- Second Korean winter
- Korea, summer-fall 1952
- Third Korean winter
- Korea, summer 1953

416

DECORATIONS

Presidential Unit Citation (Navy), Streamer embroidered SAIPAN and TINIAN

Presidential Unit Citation (Navy), Streamer embroidered OKINAWA

Presidential Unit Citation. (Navy), Streamer embroidered WONJU-HWACHON

Navy Unit Commendation, Streamer embroidered PANMUNJOM

3d MEDIUM TANK BATTALION, 69th ARMOR

RA

(inactive)

LINEAGE

Constituted 15 July 1940 in the Regular Army as Company H, 69th Armored Regiment, an element of the 1st Armored Division. Activated 31 July 1940 at Fort Knox, Kentucky. Inactivated 10 January 1942 at Fort Knox, Kentucky. Activated 15 February 1942 at Fort Knox, Kentucky (69th Armored Regiment concurrently relieved from assignment to 1st Armored Division and assigned to 6th Armored Division).

Reorganized and redesignated 20 September 1943 as Company C, 69th Tank Battalion. Absorbed 10 July 1945 into 69th Amphibian Tractor Battalion and relieved from assignment to 6th Armored Division. Inactivated 8 March 1946 at Camp Kilmer, New Jersey. Redesignated 21 August 1950 as Company C, 69th Medium Tank Battalion, an element of the 6th Armored Division. Activated 5 September 1950 at Fort Leonard Wood, Missouri. Inactivated 16 March 1956 at Fort Leonard Wood, Missouri. Redesignated 14 January 1957 as Company C, 69th Tank Battalion (69th Tank Battalion relieved 1 February 1957 from assignment to 6th Armored Division).

Reorganized and redesignated 15 February 1957 as Headquarters and Headquarters Company, 3d Medium Tank Battalion (Patton), 69th Armor; concurrently, assigned to 25th Infantry Division and activated in Hawaii (organic elements concurrently constituted and activated). Inactivated 1 July 1963 in Hawaii and relieved from assignment to 25th Infantry Division.

CAMPAIGN PARTICIPATION CREDIT

World War II
*Normandy
*Northern France
*Rhineland
*Ardennes-Alsace
*Central Europe
Eastern Mandates
Western Pacific (with arrowhead)
Ryukyus (with arrowhead)

Korean War
UN defensive
UN offensive
CCF intervention
First UN counteroffensive
CCF spring offensive
UN summer-fall offensive
Second Korean winter
Korea, summer-fall 1952
Third Korean winter
Korea, summer 1953

418

DECORATIONS

*Presidential Unit Citation (Army), Streamer embroidered BASTOGNE (Company C, 69th Tank Battalion, cited; WD GO 80, 1945)

Presidential Unit Citation (Navy), Streamer embroidered SAIPAN and TINIAN

Presidential Unit Citation (Navy), Streamer embroidered OKINAWA

Presidential Unit Citation (Navy), Streamer embroidered WONJU-HWACHON

Navy Unit Commendation, Streamer embroidered PANMUNJOM

4th BATTALION, 69th ARMOR

RA

(197th Infantry Brigade)

LINEAGE

Constituted 15 July 1940 in the Regular Army as Company D, 69th Armored Regiment, an element of the 1st Armored Division. Activated 31 July 1940 at Fort Knox, Kentucky. Inactivated 10 January 1942 at Fort Knox, Kentucky. Activated 15 February 1942 at Fort Knox, Kentucky (69th Armored Regiment concurrently relieved from assignment to 1st Armored Division and assigned to 6th Armored Division).

Reorganized and redesignated 20 September 1943 as Company D, 69th Tank Battalion. Absorbed 10 July 1945 into 69th Amphibian Tractor Battalion and relieved from assignment to 6th Armored Division. Inactivated 8 March 1946 at Camp Kilmer, New Jersey. Redesignated 21 August 1950 as Company D, 69th Medium Tank Battalion, and assigned to 6th Armored Division. Activated 5 September 1950 at Fort Leonard Wood, Missouri. Inactivated 16 March 1956 at Fort Leonard Wood, Missouri.

Redesignated 1 February 1957 as Headquarters and Headquarters Company, 4th Medium Tank Battalion, 69th Armor, and relieved from assignment to 6th Armored Division. Redesignated 10 June 1958 as Company D (Patton), 69th Armor. Activated 25 July 1958 at Fort Benning, Georgia, as an element of the 1st Infantry Brigade. Relieved 20 September 1962 from assignment to 1st Infantry Brigade and assigned to 197th Infantry Brigade.

Reorganized and redesignated 24 September 1962 as Headquarters and Headquarters Company, 4th Battalion, 69th Armor (organic elements constituted 20 September 1962 and activated 24 September 1962).

CAMPAIGN PARTICIPATION CREDIT

World War II
- *Normandy
- *Northern France
- *Rhineland
- *Ardennes-Alsace
- *Central Europe
- Eastern Mandates
- Western Pacific (with arrowhead)
- Ryukyus (with arrowhead)

Korean War
- UN defensive
- UN offensive
- CCF intervention
- First UN counteroffensive
- CCF spring offensive
- UN summer-fall offensive
- Second Korean winter
- Korea, summer-fall 1952
- Third Korean winter
- Korea, summer 1953

DECORATIONS

Presidential Unit Citation (Navy), Streamer embroidered SAIPAN and TINIAN

Presidential Unit Citation (Navy), Streamer embroidered OKINAWA

Presidential Unit Citation (Navy), Streamer embroidered WONJU-HWACHON

Navy Unit Commendation, Streamer embroidered PANMUNJOM

5th BATTALION, 69th ARMOR

AR
(inactive)

LINEAGE

Constituted 15 July 1940 in the Regular Army as Company G, 69th Armored Regiment, an element of the 1st Armored Division. Activated 31 July 1940 at Fort Knox, Kentucky. Inactivated 10 January 1942 at Fort Knox, Kentucky. (69th Armored Regiment relieved 15 February 1942 from assignment to 1st Armored Division and assigned to 6th Armored Division.) Activated 1 March 1942 at Fort Knox, Kentucky.

Reorganized and redesignated 20 September 1943 as Company A, 708th Tank Battalion, and relieved from assignment to 6th Armored Division. Reorganized and redesignated 27 October 1943 as Company A, 708th Amphibian Tank Battalion. Inactivated 25 January 1946 in the Philippine Islands.

Redesignated 28 July 1950 as Company A, 89th Medium Tank Battalion. Activated 7 August 1950 in Korea. Redesignated 14 November 1951 as Company A, 89th Tank Battalion (89th Tank Battalion concurrently assigned to 25th Infantry Division).

Inactivated 1 February 1957 in Hawaii; concurrently, relieved from assignment to 25th Infantry Division and redesignated as Headquarters and Headquarters Company, 5th Medium Tank Battalion, 69th Armor. Withdrawn 10 April 1959 from the Regular Army, allotted to the Army Reserve, and assigned to 81st Infantry Division (organic elements concurrently constituted). Activated 1 May 1959 with Headquarters at Athens, Georgia. Reorganized and redesignated 1 April 1963 as 5th Battalion, 69th Armor. Inactivated 31 December 1965 at Athens, Georgia, and relieved from assignment to 81st Infantry Division.

CAMPAIGN PARTICIPATION CREDIT

World War II
  *Eastern Mandates
  *Western Pacific (with arrowhead)
  *Ryukyus (with arrowhead)
  Normandy
  Northern France
  Rhineland
  Ardennes-Alsace
  Central Europe

Korean War
  *UN defensive

*UN offensive
*CCF intervention
*First UN counteroffensive
*CCF spring offensive
*UN summer-fall offensive
*Second Korean winter
*Korea, summer-fall 1952
*Third Korean winter
*Korea, summer 1953

422

DECORATIONS

*Presidential Unit Citation (Army), Streamer embroidered NAM RIVER (Company A, 89th Medium Tank Battalion, cited; DA GO 49, 1951)

*Presidential Unit Citation (Navy), Streamer embroidered SAIPAN and TINIAN (708th Amphibian Tank Battalion cited; DA GO 73, 1948)

*Presidential Unit Citation (Navy), Streamer embroidered OKINAWA (708th Amphibian Tank Battalion cited; DA GO 73, 1948)

*Presidential Unit Citation (Navy), Streamer embroidered WONJU-HWACHON (89th Medium Tank Battalion cited; DA GO 38, 1957)

*Navy Unit Commendation, Streamer embroidered PANMUNJOM (89th Tank Battalion cited; DA GO 38, 1957)

*Republic of Korea Presidential Unit Citation, Streamer embroidered MUNSAN-NI (89th Tank Battalion cited; DA GO 19, 1955)

6th BATTALION, 69th ARMOR

AR
(inactive)

LINEAGE

Constituted 15 July 1940 in the Regular Army as Company H, 69th Armored Regiment, an element of the 1st Armored Division. Activated 31 July 1940 at Fort Knox, Kentucky. Inactivated 10 January 1942 at Fort Knox, Kentucky. (69th Armored Regiment relieved 15 February 1942 from assignment to 1st Armored Division and assigned to 6th Armored Division.) Activated 1 March 1942 at Fort Knox, Kentucky.

Reorganized and redesignated 20 September 1943 as Company B, 708th Tank Battalion; concurrently, relieved from assignment to 6th Armored Division. Reorganized and redesignated 27 October 1943 as Company B, 708th Amphibian Tank Battalion. Inactivated 25 January 1946 in the Philippine Islands.

Redesignated 28 July 1950 as Company B, 89th Medium Tank Battalion. Activated 7 August 1950 in Korea. Redesignated 14 November 1951 as Company B, 89th Tank Battalion (89th Tank Battalion concurrently assigned to 25th Infantry Division).

Inactivated 1 February 1957 in Hawaii; concurrently, relieved from assignment to 25th Infantry Division and redesignated as Headquarters and Headquarters Company, 6th Medium Tank Battalion, 69th Armor. Redesignated 26 March 1963 as Headquarters and Headquarters Company, 6th Battalion, 69th Armor; concurrently, withdrawn from the Regular Army, allotted to the Army Reserve, and assigned to 81st Infantry Division (organic elements concurrently constituted). Activated 1 April 1963 with Headquarters at Waycross, Georgia. Inactivated 31 December 1965 at Waycross, Georgia, and relieved from assignment to 81st Infantry Division.

CAMPAIGN PARTICIPATION CREDIT

World War II
  *Eastern Mandates
  *Western Pacific (with arrowhead)
  *Ryukyus (with arrowhead)
  Normandy
  Northern France
  Rhineland
  Ardennes-Alsace
  Central Europe

Korean War
  *UN defensive
  *UN offensive
  *CCF intervention
  *First UN counteroffensive
  *CCF spring offensive
  *UN summer-fall offensive
  *Second Korean winter
  *Korea, summer-fall 1952
  *Third Korean winter
  *Korea, summer 1953

DECORATIONS

*Presidential Unit Citation (Navy), Streamer embroidered SAIPAN and TINIAN (708th Amphibian Tank Battalion cited; DA GO 73, 1948)

*Presidential Unit Citation (Navy), Streamer embroidered OKINAWA (708th Amphibious Tank Battalion cited; DA GO 73, 1948)

*Presidential Unit Citation (Navy), Streamer embroidered WONJU-HWACHON (89th Medium Tank Battalion cited; DA GO 38, 1957)

*Navy Unit Commendation, Streamer embroidered PANMUNJOM (89th Tank Battalion cited; DA GO 38, 1957)

*Republic of Korea Presidential Unit Citation, Streamer embroidered MUNSAN-NI (89th Tank Battalion cited; DA GO 19, 1955)

BIBLIOGRAPHY, 69TH ARMOR

Barth, George B. *Tropic Lightning and Taro Leaf in Korea.* N.p. 1953.

David, Allan A., ed. *Battleground Korea, The Story of the 25th Infantry Division.* Tokyo, Japan: 1952.

Department of the Army
Korea, 1950. Washington: 1952.

Miller, John, jr., O. J. Carroll, and M. E. Tackley. *Korea 1951–1953.* Washington: 1956.

Pullen, Richard T., *et al.,* eds. *25th Infantry Division. Tropic Lightning in Korea.* Atlanta, Georgia: 1954.

Unit Members. *A Pictorial History of the Super 6th, 6th Armored Division February 15, 1942– February 15, 1944.* Los Angeles: 1944.

———. *Brest to Bastogne.* Paris: 1945.

———. *Combat History of the 6th Armored Division in the European Theater of Operations, 18 July 1944–8 May 1945.* Yadkinville, North Carolina: 1945.

———. *"Super Sixth" Meets Russians.* N.p.: 1945.

———. *Thrust! The Story of the 89th Tank Battalion.* N.p.: 1953.

Westover, John G. *Combat Support in Korea.* Washington: 1955.

UNITED STATES ARMY IN THE KOREAN WAR
Appleman, Roy E. *South to the Naktong, North to the Yalu.* 1961.

UNITED STATES ARMY IN WORLD WAR II
Blumenson, Martin. *Breakout and Pursuit.* 1961.

Cole, Hugh M. *The Ardennes: Battle of the Bulge.* 1965.

———. *The Lorraine Campaign.* 1950.

70th ARMOR

HERALDIC ITEMS

COAT OF ARMS

Shield: Vert, five spearheads paleways in chevron or.

Crest: On a wreath or and vert, supported by two lions rampant sable langued gules a Korean gateway of the last with doors closed of the third secured by a bar with two holders of the first.

Motto: Strike Swiftly.

Symbolism: The shield is green with five gold spearheads representing a platoon of five tanks entering combat in a flying wedge formation.

The two lions refer to the arms of Normandy and of Belgium, where the unit served with distinction in World War II. The closed and bolted Korean gateway commemorates action in repulsing the enemy's attempt to pierce the Pusan Perimeter at Taegu in the Korean War.

DISTINCTIVE INSIGNIA

The distinctive insignia is the shield and motto of the coat of arms.

LINEAGE AND HONORS

LINEAGE

Constituted 15 July 1940 in the Regular Army as 70th Tank Battalion and activated at Fort George G. Meade, Maryland. Inactivated 1 June 1946 in Germany. Activated 1 August 1946 at Fort Knox, Kentucky. Reorganized and redesignated 14 June 1948 as 70th Medium Tank Battalion. Reorganized and redesignated 31 December 1948 as 70th Heavy Tank Battalion.

Reorganized and redesignated 2 May 1950 as 70th Tank Battalion. Assigned 10 November 1951 to 1st Cavalry Division. Inactivated 15 October 1957 in Korea and relieved from assignment to 1st Cavalry Division.

Redesignated 25 January 1963 as 70th Armor, a parent regiment under the Combat Arms Regimental System.

427

CAMPAIGN PARTICIPATION CREDIT

World War II
　　Algeria-French Morocco
　　Sicily (with arrowhead)
　　Normandy (with arrowhead)
　　Northern France
　　Rhineland
　　Ardennes-Alsace
　　Central Europe

Korean War
　　UN defensive
　　UN offensive
　　CCF intervention
　　First UN counteroffensive
　　CCF spring offensive
　　UN summer-fall offensive
　　Second Korean winter

DECORATIONS

Presidential Unit Citation (Army), Streamer embroidered COTENTIN PENINSULA (70th Tank Battalion cited; WD GO 85, 1944)

Presidential Unit Citation (Army), Streamer embroidered HURTGEN FOREST (Companies C and D, 70th Tank Battalion, cited; WD GO 36, 1946)

Belgian Fourragère 1940 (70th Tank Battalion cited; DA GO 43, 1950)

Cited in the Order of the Day of the Belgian Army for action at ST VITH

Cited in the Order of the Day of the Belgian Army for action in the ARDENNES

Chryssoun Aristion Andrias (Bravery Gold Medal of Greece), Streamer embroidered KOREA (70th Tank Battalion cited; DA GO 2, 1956)

Republic of Korea Presidential Unit Citation, Streamer embroidered TAEGU (70th Tank Battalion cited; DA GO 55, 1954)

1st BATTALION, 70th ARMOR

RA

(24th Infantry Division)

LINEAGE

Constituted 15 July 1940 in the Regular Army as Company A, 70th Tank Battalion, and activated at Fort George G. Meade, Maryland. Inactivated 1 June 1946 in Germany. Activated 1 August 1946 at Fort Knox, Kentucky. Reorganized and redesignated 14 June 1948 as Company A, 70th Medium Tank Battalion. Reorganized and redesignated 31 December 1948 as Company A, 70th Heavy Tank Battalion.

Reorganized and redesignated 2 May 1950 as Company A, 70th Tank Battalion. (70th Tank Battalion assigned 10 November 1951 to 1st Cavalry Division.) Inactivated 15 October 1957 in Korea and relieved from assignment to 1st Cavalry Division.

Redesignated 21 January 1963 as Headquarters and Headquarters Company, 1st Battalion, 70th Armor, and assigned to 24th Infantry Division (organic elements concurrently constituted). Activated 1 February 1963 in Germany.

CAMPAIGN PARTICIPATION CREDIT

World War II
  *Algeria-French Morocco
  *Tunisia
  *Sicily (with arrowhead)
  *Normandy (with arrowhead)
  *Northern France
  *Rhineland
  *Ardennes-Alsace
  *Central Europe

Korean War
  *UN defensive
  *UN offensive
  *CCF intervention
  *First UN counteroffensive
  *CCF spring offensive
  *UN summer-fall offensive
  *Second Korean winter

DECORATIONS

*Presidential Unit Citation (Army), Streamer embroidered COTENTIN PENINSULA (70th Tank Battalion cited; WD GO 85, 1944)

Presidential Unit Citation (Army), Streamer embroidered HURTGEN FOREST

*Presidential Unit Citation (Army), Streamer embroidered KOKSU-RI (Company A, 70th Tank Battalion, cited; DA GO 36, 1951)

*Belgian Fourragère 1940 (70th Tank Battalion cited; DA GO 43, 1950)

429

*Cited in the Order of the Day of the Belgian Army for action at ST VITH

*Cited in the Order of the Day of the Belgian Army for action in the ARDENNES

*Chryssoun Aristion Andrias (Bravery Gold Medal of Greece), Streamer embroidered KOREA (70th Tank Battalion cited; DA GO 2, 1956)

*Republic of Korea Presidenital Unit Citation, Streamer embroidered TAEGU (70th Tank Battalion cited; DA GO 55, 1954)

2d BATTALION, 70th ARMOR

RA

(24th Infantry Division)

LINEAGE

Constituted 15 July 1940 in the Regular Army as Company B, 70th Tank Battalion, and activated at Fort George G. Meade, Maryland. Inactivated 1 June 1946 in Germany. Activated 1 August 1946 at Fort Knox, Kentucky. Reorganized and redesignated 14 June 1948 as Company B, 70th Medium Tank Battalion. Reorganized and redesignated 31 December 1948 as Company B, 70th Heavy Tank Battalion.

Reorganized and redesignated 2 May 1950 as Company B, 70th Tank Battalion. (70th Tank Battalion assigned 10 November 1951 to 1st Cavalry Division.) Inactivated 15 October 1957 in Korea and relieved from assignment to 1st Cavalry Division.

Redesignated 21 January 1963 as Headquarters and Headquarters Company, 2d Battalion, 70th Armor, and assigned to 24th Infantry Division (organic elements concurrently constituted). Activated 1 February 1963 in Germany.

CAMPAIGN PARTICIPATION CREDIT

World War II
* *Algeria-French Morocco
* *Sicily (with arrowhead)
* *Normandy (with arrowhead)
* *Northern France
* *Rhineland
* *Ardennes-Alsace
* *Central Europe

Korean War
* *UN defensive
* *UN offensive
* *CCF intervention
* *First UN counteroffensive
* *CCF spring offensive
* *UN summer-fall offensive
* *Second Korean winter

DECORATIONS

*Presidential Unit Citation (Army), Streamer embroidered COTENTIN PENINSULA (70th Tank Battalion cited; WD GO 84, 1944)

Presidential Unit Citation (Army), Streamer embroidered HURTGEN FOREST

*Belgian Fourragère
*Cited in the Order of the Day of the Belgian Army for action at ST VITH
*Cited in the Order of the Day of the Belgian Army for action in the ARDENNES

*Chryssoun Aristion Andrias (Bravery Gold Medal of Greece), Streamer embroidered KOREA (70th Tank Battalion cited; DA GO 2, 1956)

*Republic of Korea Presidential Unit Citation, Streamer embroidered TAEGU (70th Tank Battalion cited; DA GO 55, 1954)

431

3d BATTALION, 70th ARMOR

RA

(24th Infantry Division)

LINEAGE

Constituted 15 July 1940 in the Regular Army as Company C, 70th Tank Battalion, and activated at Fort George G. Meade, Maryland. Inactivated 1 June 1946 in Germany. Activated 1 August 1946 at Fort Knox, Kentucky. Reorganized and redesignated 14 June 1948 as Company C, 70th Medium Tank Battalion. Reorganized and redesignated 31 December 1948 as Company C, 70th Heavy Tank Battalion.

Reorganized and redesignated 2 May 1950 as Company C, 70th Tank Battalion. (70th Tank Battalion assigned 10 November 1951 to 1st Cavalry Division.) Inactivated 15 October 1957 in Korea and relieved from assignment to 1st Cavalry Division.

Redesignated 21 January 1963 as Headquarters and Headquarters Company, 3d Battalion, 70th Armor, and assigned to 24th Infantry Division (organic elements concurrently constituted). Activated 1 February 1963 in Germany.

CAMPAIGN PARTICIPATION CREDIT

World War II
  *Algeria-French Morocco
  *Sicily (with arrowhead)
  *Normandy (with arrowhead)
  *Northern France
  *Rhineland
  *Ardennes-Alsace
  *Central Europe

Korean War
  *UN defensive
  *UN offensive
  *CCF intervention
  *First UN counteroffensive
  *CCF spring offensive
  *UN summer-fall offensive
  *Second Korean winter

DECORATIONS

*Presidential Unit Citation (Army), Streamer embroidered COTENTIN PENINSULA (70th Tank Battalion cited; WD GO 85, 1944)

*Presidential Unit Citation (Army), Streamer embroidered HURTGEN FOREST (Company C, 70th Tank Battalion, cited; WD GO 36, 1946)

*Presidential Unit Citation (Army), Streamer embroidered YONGCHON (Company C, 70th Tank Battalion, cited; DA GO 74, 1952)

*Belgian Fourragère 1940 (70th Tank Battalion cited; DA GO 43, 1950)

  *Cited in the Order of the Day of the Belgian Army for action at ST VITH

  *Cited in the Order of the Day of the Belgian Army for action in the ARDENNES

432

*Chryssoun Aristion Andrias (Bravery Gold Medal of Greece), Streamer embroidered KOREA (70th Tank Battalion cited; DA GO 2, 1956)

*Republic of Korea Presidential Unit Citation, Streamer embroidered TAEGU (70th Tank Battalion cited; DA GO 55, 1954)

BIBLIOGRAPHY, 70TH ARMOR

Department of the Army
  Korea, 1950. Washington: 1952.
Department of the Army. AMERICAN FORCES IN ACTION series.
  Utah Beach to Cherbourg. 1947.
Gugeler, Russell A. *Combat Actions in Korea.* Washington: 1954.
Mahr, Warren C., compiler. *1st Cavalry Division 1952–1954.* Atlanta, Georgia: 1954.
Miller, John, jr., O. J. Carroll, and M. E. Tackley. *Korea 1951–1953.* Washington: 1956.
Unit Members. *History of the 70th Tank Battalion, 5 June 1940–22 May 1946.* Louisville, Kentucky: 1950.
———. *1st Cavalry Division "The First Team."* Japan: 1959.
———. *The First Team: The First Cavalry Division 18 July 1950–18 January 1952.* Atlanta, Georgia: circa 1952.
UNITED STATES ARMY IN THE KOREAN WAR
  Appleman, Roy E. *South to the Naktong, North to the Yalu.* 1961.
UNITED STATES ARMY IN WORLD WAR II
  Blumenson, Martin. *Breakout and Pursuit.* 1961.
  Cole, Hugh M. *The Ardennes: Battle of the Bulge.* 1965.
  Garland, Albert N., and Howard McGaw Smyth. *Sicily and the Surrender of Italy.* 1965.
  Harrison, Gordon A. *Cross-Channel Attack.* 1951.
  Howe, George F. *Northwest Africa: Seizing the Initiative in the West.* 1957.
  MacDonald, Charles B. *The Siegfried Line Campaign.* 1963.
Westover, John G. *Combat Support in Korea.* Washington: 1955.

72d ARMOR

HERALDIC ITEMS

COAT OF ARMS

Shield: Or, a dragon passant with wings elevated and addorsed, vert, armed and langued gules, charged on the wing with a fleur-de-lis of the first and in chief three hurts (light blue).

Crest: On a wreath or and vert, issuing from a wavy bar azure bearing a wavy barrulet argent, tongues of flame proper supporting at top the Yin Yang symbol gules and of the third, overall a spiked mace (Morning Star) of the fourth.

Motto: Crusaders.

Symbolism: The principal colors of the shield are those of armor. The dragon is represented as a strong and fierce creature covered with invulnerable plates of mail and in heraldry is properly applied to the overthrow of an enemy. The fleur-de-lis charged on the wing symbolizes the campaigns in Europe and the three blue roundels represent the Korean operations.

The crest commemorates participation in the Korean War with special emphasis on the action on the Naktong River Line. The Yin Yang symbol in red and blue alludes to Korea. The Naktong River Line is represented by the wavy blue, white, blue bar, for water. The spiked mace is used as a symbol for armor and is placed over the Naktong River Line and the Yin Yang symbols to represent the holding, counterattacking, and hurling back of the enemy from the Naktong line. The savage nature of this action is alluded to by the flames rising from the Naktong River Line and engulfing the mace. The type of mace used—morning star—is an allusion to the time of the enemy's crossing of the line, his repulse, and his final withdrawal. The Presidential Unit Citation awarded for the action is symbolized to by the wavy blue stripe, which simulates a streamer and, in conjunction with the white stripe, refers to Korean service.

435

The distinctive insignia is the shield and motto of the coat of arms.

LINEAGE AND HONORS

LINEAGE

Constituted 14 January 1943 in the Army of the United States as 5th Armored Regiment. Activated 15 July 1943 at Camp Chaffee, Arkansas, and assigned to 16th Armored Division.

Regiment broken up 3 September 1943 and reorganized and redesignated as follows: 5th Armored Regiment (less 1st and 3d Battalions, Maintenance, Service and Reconnaissance Companies, and Band) as 5th Tank Battalion and remained assigned to 16th Armored Division; 1st Battalion as 717th Tank Battalion and relieved from assignment to 16th Armored Division; 3d Battalion as 26th Tank Battalion and remained assigned to 16th Armored Division; Reconnaissance Company as Troop D, 23d Cavalry Reconnaissance Squadron, Mechanized, an element of the 16th Armored Division; Maintenance and Service Companies and Band disbanded.

5th Tank Battalion inactivated 16 October 1945 at Camp Shanks, New York. Relieved 8 February 1951 from assignment to 16th Armored Division and allotted to the Regular Army. Activated 2 March 1951 at Fort Leonard Wood, Missouri. Inactivated 16 March 1956 at Fort Leonard Wood, Missouri.

717th Tank Battalion reorganized and redesignated 6 April 1948 as 717th Heavy Tank Battalion. Reorganized and redesignated (less Company D) 15 October 1948 as 72d Heavy Tank Battalion, allotted to the Regular Army, and assigned to 2d Infantry Division (Company D concurrently redesignated as Company D, 2d Engineer Combat Battalion—separate lineage). Reorganized and redesignated 6 June 1950 as 72d Tank Battalion. (New Company D, 72d Tank Battalion, constituted 27 September 1954 and activated 10 October 1954 at Fort Lewis, Washington.) Relieved 8 November 1957 from assignment to 2d Infantry Division. Inactivated 25 June 1958 at Camp Irwin, California.

26th Tank Battalion inactivated 16 October 1945 at Camp Myles Standish, Massachusetts. Disbanded 23 March 1953. Reconstituted 25 January 1963 in the Regular Army.

Troop D, 23d Cavalry Reconnaissance Squadron, Mechanized, inactivated 15 October 1945 at Camp Shanks, New York. Redesignated 13 August 1954 as Company D, 23d Reconnaissance Battalion, and allotted to the Regular Army.

5th, 72d, and 26th Tank Battalions and Company D, 23d Reconnaissance Battalion, consolidated, reorganized, and redesignated 25 January 1963 as 72d Armor, a parent regiment under the Combat Arms Regimental System.

CAMPAIGN PARTICIPATION CREDIT

World War II
Rhineland
Central Europe

Korean War
UN defensive
UN offensive
CCF intervention

First UN counteroffensive
CCF spring offensive
UN summer-fall offensive
Second Korean winter
Korea, summer-fall 1952
Third Korean winter
Korea, summer 1953

DECORATIONS

Presidential Unit Citation (Army), Streamer embroidered HONGCHON (72d Tank Battalion cited; DA GO 72, 1951)

Presidential Unit Citation (Army), Streamer embroidered YONGSAN (72d Tank Battalion cited; DA GO 81, 1951)

Republic of Korea Presidential Unit Citation, Streamer embroidered NAKTONG RIVER LINE (72d Tank Battalion cited; DA GO 35, 1951)

Republic of Korea Presidential Unit Citation, Streamer embroidered KOREA (72d Tank Battalion cited; DA GO 10, 1954)

1st BATTALION, 72d ARMOR

RA

(2d Infantry Division)

LINEAGE

Constituted 14 January 1943 in the Army of the United States as Company A, 5th Armored Regiment. Activated 15 July 1943 at Camp Chaffee, Arkansas, as an element of the 16th Armored Division.

Reorganized and redesignated 3 September 1943 as Company A, 717th Tank Battalion, and relieved from assignment to 16th Armored Division. Reorganized and redesignated 6 April 1948 as Company A, 717th Heavy Tank Battalion.

Reorganized and redesignated 15 October 1948 as Company A, 72d Heavy Tank Battalion, and allotted to the Regular Army (72d Heavy Tank Battalion concurrently assigned to 2d Infantry Division). Reorganized and redesignated 6 June 1950 as Company A, 72d Tank Battalion. (72d Tank Battalion relieved 8 November 1957 from assignment to 2d Infantry Division.) Inactivated 25 June 1958 at Camp Irwin, California.

Redesignated 25 January 1963 as Headquarters and Headquarters Company, 1st Battalion, 72d Armor, and assigned to 2d Infantry Division (organic elements concurrently constituted). Activated 1 March 1963 at Fort Benning, Georgia. Transferred (less personnel and equipment) 1 July 1965 from Fort Benning, Georgia, to Korea and reorganized.

CAMPAIGN PARTICIPATION CREDIT

World War II
  *Rhineland
  *Central Europe

Korean War
  *UN defensive
  *UN offensive
  *CCF intervention

*First UN counteroffensive
*CCF spring offensive
*UN summer-fall offensive
*Second Korean winter
*Korea, summer-fall 1952
*Third Korean winter
*Korea, summer 1953

438

DECORATIONS

*Presidential Unit Citation (Army), Streamer embroidered HONGCHON (72d Tank Battalion cited; DA GO 72, 1951)

*Presidential Unit Citation (Army), Streamer embroidered YONGSAN (72d Tank Battalion cited; DA GO 81, 1951)

*Presidential Unit Citation . (Army), Streamer embroidered KAPYONG (Company A, 72d Tank Battalion, cited; DA GO 47, 1952)

*Republic of Korea Presidential Unit Citation, Streamer embroidered NAKTONG RIVER LINE (72d Tank Battalion cited; DA GO 35, 1951)

*Republic of Korea Presidential Unit Citation, Streamer embroidered KOREA (72d Tank Battalion cited; DA GO 10, 1954)

2d BATTALION, 72d ARMOR

RA

(2d Infantry Division)

LINEAGE

Constituted 14 January 1943 in the Army of the United States as Company B, 5th Armored Regiment. Activated 15 July 1943 at Camp Chaffee, Arkansas, as an element of the 16th Armored Division.

Reorganized and redesignated 3 September 1943 as Company B, 717th Tank Battalion, and relieved from assignment to 16th Armored Division. Reorganized and redesignated 6 April 1948 as Company B, 717th Heavy Tank Battalion.

Reorganized and redesignated 15 October 1948 as Company B, 72d Heavy Tank Battalion, and allotted to the Regular Army (72d Heavy Tank concurrently assigned to 2d Infantry Division). Reorganized and redesignated 6 June 1950 as Company B, 72d Tank Battalion. (72d Tank Battalion relieved 8 November 1957 from assignment to 2d Infantry Division.) Inactivated 25 June 1958 at Camp Irwin, California.

Redesignated 25 January 1963 as Headquarters and Headquarters Company, 2d Battalion, 72d Armor, and assigned to 2d Infantry Division (organic elements concurrently constituted). Activated 25 March 1963 at Fort Stewart, Georgia. Transferred (less personnel and equipment) 1 July 1965 from Fort Stewart, Georgia, to Korea and reorganized.

CAMPAIGN PARTICIPATION CREDIT

World War II
*Rhineland
*Central Europe

Korean War
*UN defensive
*UN offensive
*CCF intervention

*First UN counteroffensive
*CCF spring offensive
*UN summer-fall offensive
*Second Korean winter
*Korea, summer-fall 1952
*Third Korean winter
*Korea, summer 1953

DECORATIONS

*Presidential Unit Citation (Army), Streamer embroidered HONGCHON (72d Tank Battalion cited; DA GO 72, 1951)

*Presidential Unit Citation (Army), Streamer embroidered YONGSAN (72d Tank Battalion cited; DA GO 81, 1951)

440

*Republic of Korea Presidential Unit Citation, Streamer embroidered
NAKTONG RIVER LINE (72d Tank Battalion cited; DA GO 35, 1951)

*Republic of Korea Presidential Unit Citation, Streamer embroidered
KOREA (72d Tank Battalion cited; DA GO 10, 1954)

BIBLIOGRAPHY, 72D ARMOR

Department of the Army
  Korea, 1950. 1952.

Gugeler, Russell A. *Combat Actions in Korea.* Washington: 1954.

Miller, John, jr., O. J. Carroll, and M. E. Tackley. *Korea 1951–1953.*
Washington: 1956.

Munroe, Clark C., *et al. The Second United States Infantry Division in
Korea, 1950 1951.* Tokyo, Japan: 1952.

Unit Members. *16th Armored Division.* Atlanta, Georgia: 1944.

———. *717th Tank Battalion Record.* San Angelo, Texas: 1946.

———. *The Second United States Infantry Division in Korea, 1951–1952.*
Tokyo, Japan: 1953.

———. *The Second United States Infantry Division in Korea, 1 Jan 53–
31 Dec 53.* Tokyo, Japan: 1954.

UNITED STATES ARMY IN THE KOREAN WAR
  Appleman, Roy E. *South to the Naktong, North to the Yalu.* 1961.

  Hermes, Walter G. *Truce Tent and Fighting Front.* 1966.

Webb, Raymond E. *72d Tank Battalion in Korea, 1950–1952.* Tokyo,
Japan: 1952.

Westover, John G. *Combat Support in Korea.* Washington: 1955.

73d ARMOR

HERALDIC ITEMS

COAT OF ARMS

Shield: Per fess azure and gules, on a fess or a hand in armor grasping a bolt of lightning, both vert.

Crest: On a wreath of the colors or and azure, issuing from a flame of six tongues, three to dexter and three to sinister, charged with an arrowhead argent within a crescent vert, the head of a mace formed by a Korean taeguk.

Motto: Honor, Fidelity, Courage.

Symbolism: The shield is divided red and blue per fess, with a fess of gold thereon, the three colors of the shoulder sleeve insignia of the armored tank forces. The lightning bolt is symbolic of the striking power of the regiment.

The six tongues of the flame represent the unit's six decorations. For action during World War II, the crescent and arrowhead symbolize the Algeria-French Morocco and Southern France assaults; the colors red and green are used to represent the French Croix de Guerre awarded for the Italian campaigns; and the mace in the arms of Colmar suggested the mace head to refer to that campaign. The taeguk represents the Korean War and the three Republic of Korea Presidential Unit Citations. The mace also alludes to the striking power of armor.

DISTINCTIVE INSIGNIA

The distinctive insignia consists of the shield and motto of the coat of arms.

LINEAGE AND HONORS

LINEAGE

Constituted 13 January 1941 in the Regular Army as 76th Tank Battalion. Redesignated 8 May 1941 as 756th Tank Battalion. Activated 1 June 1941 at Fort Lewis, Washington. Inactivated 8 February 1946 at Camp Kilmer,

New Jersey. Activated 1 August 1946 at Fort Benning, Georgia. Reorganized and redesignated 15 January 1948 as 756th Heavy Tank Battalion.

Redesignated 10 January 1949 as 73d Heavy Tank Battalion and assigned to 3d Infantry Division. Redesignated 14 July 1950 as 73d Tank Battalion and relieved from assignment to 3d Infantry Division. Assigned 10 November 1951 to 7th Infantry Division. Inactivated 1 July 1957 in Korea and relieved from assignment to 7th Infantry Division.

Redesignated 2 October 1962 as 73d Armor, a parent regiment under the Combat Arms Regimental System.

CAMPAIGN PARTICIPATION CREDIT

World War II
Algeria-French Morocco (with arrowhead)
Naples-Foggia
Rome-Arno
Southern France (with arrowhead)
Rhineland
Ardennes-Alsace
Central Europe

Korean War
UN defensive
UN offensive
CCF intervention
First UN counteroffensive
CCF spring offensive
UN summer-fall offensive
Second Korean winter
Korea, summer-fall 1952
Third Korean winter
Korea, summer 1953

DECORATIONS

Presidential Unit Citation (Army), Streamer embroidered COLMAR (756th Tank Battalion cited; WD GO 44, 1945)

French Croix de Guerre with Palm, World War II, Streamer embroidered CENTRAL ITALY (756th Tank Battalion cited; DA GO 43, 1950)

French Croix de Guerre with Silver-Gilt Star, World War II, Streamer embroidered ITALY (756th Tank Battalion cited; DA GO 43, 1950)

Republic of Korea Presidential Unit Citation, Streamer embroidered IN-CHON TO SEOUL (73d Tank Battalion cited; DA GO 75, 1954)

Republic of Korea Presidential Unit Citation, Streamer embroidered KOREA 1950–1952 (73d Tank Battalion cited; DA GO 41, 1955)

Republic of Korea Presidential Unit Citation, Streamer embroidered KOREA 1951–1953 (73d Tank Battalion cited; DA GO 22, 1956)

1st BATTALION, 73d ARMOR

RA
(7th Infantry Division)

LINEAGE

Constituted 13 January 1941 in the Regular Army as Company A, 76th Tank Battalion. Redesignated 8 May 1941 as Company A, 756th Tank Battalion. Activated 1 June 1941 at Fort Lewis, Washington. Inactivated 8 February 1946 at Camp Kilmer, New Jersey. Activated 1 August 1946 at Fort Benning, Georgia. Reorganized and redesignated 15 January 1948 as Company A, 756th Heavy Tank Battalion.

Reorganized and redesignated 10 January 1949 as Company A, 73d Heavy Tank Battalion (73d Heavy Tank Battalion concurrently assigned to 3d Infantry Division). (73d Tank Battalion assigned 10 November 1951 to 7th Infantry Division.) Inactivated 1 July 1957 in Korea (73d Tank Battalion concurrently relieved from assignment to 7th Infantry Division).

Redesignated 7 June 1963 as Headquarters and Headquarters Company, 1st Battalion, 73d Armor (organic elements concurrently constituted). Activated 1 July 1963 in Korea and assigned to 7th Infantry Division.

CAMPAIGN PARTICIPATION CREDIT

World War II
- *Algeria-French Morocco (with arrowhead)
- *Naples-Foggia
- *Rome-Arno
- *Southern France (with arrowhead)
- *Rhineland
- *Ardennes-Alsace
- *Central Europe

Korean War
- *UN defensive
- *UN offensive
- *CCF intervention
- *First UN counteroffensive
- *CCF spring offensive
- *UN summer-fall offensive
- *Second Korean winter
- *Korea, summer-fall 1952
- *Third Korean winter
- *Korea, summer 1953

445

DECORATIONS

*Presidential Unit Citation (Army), Streamer embroidered COLMAR (756th Tank Battalion cited; WD GO 44, 1945)

*French Croix de Guerre with Palm, World War II, Streamer embroidered CENTRAL ITALY (756th Tank Battalion cited; DA GO 43, 1950)

*French Croix de Guerre with Silver-Gilt Star, World War II, Streamer embroidered ITALY (756th Tank Battalion cited; DA GO 43, 1950)

*Republic of Korea Presidential Unit Citation, Streamer embroidered INCHON TO SEOUL (73d Tank Battalion cited; DA GO 75, 1954)

*Republic of Korea Presidential Unit Citation, Streamer embroidered KOREA 1950–1952 (73d Tank Battalion cited; DA GO 41, 1955)

*Republic of Korea Presidential Unit Citation, Streamer embroidered KOREA 1951–1953 (73d Tank Battalion cited; DA GO 22, 1956)

COMPANY D, 73d ARMOR

RA
(nondivisional)

LINEAGE

Constituted 13 January 1941 in the Regular Army as Company D, 76th Tank Battalion. Redesignated 8 May 1941 as Company D, 756th Tank Battalion. Organized 15 December 1943 at Naples, Italy. Inactivated 8 February 1946 at Camp Kilmer, New Jersey. Activated 1 August 1946 at Fort Benning, Georgia. Disbanded 1 December 1950 at Fort Benning, Georgia.

Reconstituted 3 December 1954 in the Regular Army and redesignated as Company D, 73d Tank Battalion, an element of the 7th Infantry Division. Activated 27 December 1954 in Korea. Inactivated 1 July 1957 in Korea (73d Tank Battalion concurrently relieved from assignment to 7th Infantry Division).

Redesignated 2 October 1962 as Headquarters and Headquarters Company, 4th Battalion, 73d Armor, and assigned to 194th Armored Brigade (organic companies concurrently constituted). Activated 21 December 1962 at Fort Ord, California.

Inactivated 4 January 1968 at Fort Ord, California, and relieved from assignment to 194th Armored Brigade; concurrently, Headquarters and Headquarters Company, 4th Battalion, 73d Armor, redesignated as Company D, 73d Armor, and activated at Fort Ord, California.

CAMPAIGN PARTICIPATION CREDIT

World War II
Naples-Foggia
Rome-Arno
Southern France (with arrowhead)

Rhineland
Ardennes-Alsace
Central Europe

DECORATIONS

Presidential Unit Citation (Army), Streamer embroidered COLMAR (756th Tank Battalion cited; WD GO 44, 1945)

French Croix de Guerre with Palm, World War II, Streamer embroidered CENTRAL ITALY (756th Tank Battalion cited; DA GO 43, 1950)

French Croix de Guerre with Silver-Gilt Star, World War II, Streamer embroidered ITALY (756th Tank Battalion cited; DA GO 43, 1950)

447

BIBLIOGRAPHY, 73D ARMOR

Department of the Army
  Korea, 1950. 1952.
Gugeler, Russell A. *Combat Actions in Korea*. Washington: 1954.
Miller, John, jr., O. J. Carroll, and M. E. Tackley. *Korea 1951–1953*. Washington: 1956.
Unit Members. *Bayonet, a History of the 7th Infantry Division*. Tokyo, Japan: 1951.
————. *The Seventh Infantry Division in Korea*. Atlanta, Georgia: 1954.

UNITED STATES ARMY IN THE KOREAN WAR
  Appleman, Roy E. *South to the Naktong, North to the Yalu*. 1961.

UNITED STATES ARMY IN WORLD WAR II
  Howe, George F. *Northwest Africa: Seizing the Initiative in the West*. 1957.
Westover, John G. *Combat Support in Korea*. Washington: 1955.

77th ARMOR

HERALDIC ITEMS

COAT OF ARMS

Shield: Azure, on a mount a tiger sejant argent, armed and langued gules, supporting a battle-axe in pale of the second, embrued of the third.

Crest: On a wreath argent and azure in front of a wreath of laurel proper and below two lances in saltire of the first a volcano sable enflamed overall proper and charged in base with an hourglass divided per fess gules and of the second and fimbriated of the first, above the flames a fleur-de-lis of the second charged with a mullet or.

Motto: *Insiste Firmiter.*

Symbolism: The carnivorous tiger is symbolic of the enemy-devouring qualities of the regiment. The battle-axe symbolizes the offensive mission of a tank battalion.

The volcano is an allusion to Mt. Etna the most distinctive feature of Sicily where the unit first saw action. The eruption of flames refers to subsequent participation in thirteen campaigns in Italy, France, Germany, and Korea. Two awards of the French Croix de Guerre with Palm are identified by the surrounding branches of laurel, while a third award with Silver Gilt Star is marked by the star on the fleur-de-lis which refers to the assault landing in Southern France. Crossed lances denote the courage and aggressive spirit displayed throughout many campaigns. The red and blue hourglass shape is an adaptation of the shoulder sleeve insignia of the 7th Division with which the unit served in Korea through six campaigns, twice receiving the Korean Presidential Unit Citation.

DISTINCTIVE INSIGNIA

The distinctive insignia consists of the shield and motto of the coat of arms.

449

Lineage and Honors

Lineage

Constituted 13 January 1941 in the Regular Army as 73d Tank Battalion (Medium). Redesignated 8 May 1941 as 753d Tank Battalion (Medium). Activated 1 June 1941 at Fort Benning, Georgia. Reorganized and redesignated 29 March 1944 as 753d Tank Battalion. Inactivated 9–15 January 1946 at Camp Patrick Henry, Virginia.

Activated 1 August 1946 at Fort Knox, Kentucky. Inactivated 15 October 1946 at Fort Knox, Kentucky.

Redesignated 20 March 1949 as 77th Heavy Tank Battalion, assigned to 7th Infantry Division and activated in Japan. Reorganized and redesignated 5 August 1950 as 77th Tank Battalion. Inactivated 10 November 1951 in Korea and relieved from assignment to 7th Infantry Division.

Redesignated 24 January 1962 as 77th Armor, a parent regiment under the Combat Arms Regimental System.

Campaign Participation Credit

World War II	*Korean War*
Sicily (with arrowhead)	UN defensive
Naples-Foggia	UN offensive
Rome-Arno	CCF intervention
Southern France (with arrowhead)	First UN counteroffensive
Rhineland	CCF spring offensive
Ardennes-Alsace	UN summer-fall offensive
Central Europe	

Decorations

French Croix de Guerre with Palm, World War II, Streamer embroidered CENTRAL ITALY (753d Tank Battalion cited; DA GO 43, 1950)

French Croix de Guerre with Palm, World War II, Streamer embroidered VOSGES (753d Tank Battalion cited; DA GO 43, 1950)

French Croix de Guerre with Silver-Gilt Star, World War II, Streamer embroidered MOUNT MAJO (753d Tank Battalion cited; DA GO 43, 1950)

French Croix de Guerre, World War II, Fourragère (753d Tank Battalion cited; DA GO 43, 1950)

Republic of Korea Presidential Unit Citation, Streamer embroidered SEOUL (77th Tank Battalion cited; DA GO 35, 1951)

Republic of Korea Presidential Unit Citation, Streamer embroidered KOREA (77th Tank Battalion cited; DA GO 22, 1956)

1st BATTALION, 77th ARMOR

RA

(5th Infantry Division)

LINEAGE

Constituted 13 January 1941 in the Regular Army as Company A, 73d Tank Battalion (Medium). Redesignated 8 May 1941 as Company A, 753d Tank Battalion (Medium). Activated 1 June 1941 at Fort Benning, Georgia. Reorganized and redesignated 29 March 1944 as Company A, 753d Tank Battalion. Inactivated 9 January 1946 at Camp Patrick Henry, Virginia.

Activated 1 August 1946 at Fort Knox, Kentucky. Inactivated 15 October 1946 at Fort Knox, Kentucky.

Redesignated 20 March 1949 as Company A, 77th Heavy Tank Battalion, an element of the 7th Infantry Division, and activated in Japan. Redesignated 5 August 1950 as Company A, 77th Tank Battalion. Inactivated 10 November 1951 in Korea and relieved from assignment to 7th Infantry Division.

Redesignated 19 February 1962 as Headquarters and Headquarters Company, 1st Battalion, 77th Armor; concurrently, assigned to 5th Infantry Division and activated at Fort Carson, Colorado (organic elements concurrently constituted and activated).

CAMPAIGN PARTICIPATION CREDIT

World War II
  *Sicily (with arrowhead)
  *Naples-Foggia
  *Rome-Arno
  *Southern France (with arrowhead)
  *Rhineland
  *Ardennes-Alsace
  *Central Europe

Korean War
  *UN defensive
  *UN offensive
  *CCF intervention
  *First UN counteroffensive
  *CCF spring offensive
  *UN summer-fall offensive

DECORATIONS

*French Croix de Guerre with Palm, World War II, Streamer embroidered CENTRAL ITALY (753d Tank Battalion cited; DA GO 43, 1950)

*French Croix de Guerre with Palm, World War II, Streamer embroidered VOSGES (753d Tank Battalion cited; DA GO 43, 1950)

*French Croix de Guerre with Silver-Gilt Star, World War II, Streamer embroidered MOUNT MAJO (753d Tank Battalion cited; DA GO 43, 1950)

451

*French Croix de Guerre, World War II, Fourragère (753d Tank Battalion cited; DA GO 43, 1950)

*Republic of Korea Presidental Unit Citation, Streamer embroidered SEOUL (77th Tank Battalion cited; DA GO 35, 1951)

*Republic of Korea Presidential Unit Citation, Streamer embroidered KOREA (77th Tank Battalion cited; DA GO 22, 1956)

2d BATTALION, 77th ARMOR

RA
(inactive)

Constituted 13 January 1941 in the Regular Army as Company B, 73d Tank Battalion (Medium). Redesignated 8 May 1941 as Company B, 753d Tank Battalion (Medium). Activated 1 June 1941 at Fort Benning, Georgia. Reorganized and redesignated 29 March 1944 as Company B, 753d Tank Battalion. Inactivated 9 January 1946 at Camp Patrick Henry, Virginia.

Activated 1 August 1946 at Fort Knox, Kentucky. Inactivated 15 October 1946 at Fort Knox, Kentucky.

Redesignated 20 March 1949 as Company B, 77th Heavy Tank Battalion, an element of the 7th Infantry Division, and activated in Japan. Redesignated 5 August 1950 as Company B, 77th Tank Battalion. Inactivated 10 November 1951 in Korea and relieved from assignment to 7th Infantry Division.

Redesignated 19 February 1962 as Headquarters and Headquarters Company, 2d Battalion, 77th Armor; concurrently, assigned to 5th Infantry Division and activated at Fort Irwin, California (organic elements concurrently constituted and activated). Inactivated 1 October 1963 at Fort Irwin, California, and relieved from assignment to 5th Infantry Division.

CAMPAIGN PARTICIPATION CREDIT

World War II
  *Sicily (with arrowhead)
  *Naples-Foggia
  *Rome-Arno
  *Southern France (with arrowhead)
  *Rhineland
  *Ardennes-Alsace
  *Central Europe

Korean War
  *UN defensive
  *UN offensive
  *CCF intervention
  *First UN counteroffensive
  *CCF spring offensive
  *UN summer-fall offensive

DECORATIONS

*French Croix de Guerre with Palm, World War II, Streamer embroidered CENTRAL ITALY (753d Tank Battalion cited; DA GO 43, 1950)

*French Croix de Guerre with Palm, World War II, Streamer embroidered VOSGES (753d Tank Battalion cited; DA GO 43, 1950)

*French Croix de Guerre with Silver-Gilt Star, World War II, Streamer embroidered MOUNT MAJO (753d Tank Battalion cited; DA GO 43, 1950)

*French Croix de Guerre, World War II, Fourragère (753d Tank Battalion cited; DA GO 43, 1950)

*Republic of Korea Presidential Unit Citation, Streamer embroidered SEOUL (77th Tank Battalion cited; DA GO 35, 1951)

*Republic of Korea Presidential Unit Citation, Streamer embroidered KOREA (77th Tank Battalion cited; DA GO 22, 1956)

3d BATTALION, 77th ARMOR

RA

(5th Infantry Division)

LINEAGE

Constituted 13 January 1941 in the Regular Army as Company C, 73d Tank Battalion (Medium). Redesignated 8 May 1941 as Company C, 753d Tank Battalion (Medium). Activated 1 June 1941 at Fort Benning, Georgia. Reorganized and redesignated 29 March 1944 as Company C, 753d Tank Battalion. Inactivated 9 January 1946 at Camp Patrick Henry, Virginia.

Activated 1 August 1946 at Fort Knox, Kentucky. Inactivated 15 October 1946 at Fort Knox, Kentucky.

Redesignated 20 March 1949 as Company C, 77th Heavy Tank Battalion, an element of the 7th Infantry Division, and activated in Japan. Redesignated 5 August 1950 as Company C, 77th Tank Battalion. Inactivated 10 November 1951 in Korea and relieved from assignment to 7th Infantry Division.

Redesignated 24 January 1962 as Headquarters and Headquarters Company, 3d Battalion, 77th Armor. Assigned 19 February 1962 to 5th Infantry Division and activated at Fort Devens, Massachusetts (organic elements concurrently constituted and activated; Company C activated at Fort Carson, Colorado).

CAMPAIGN PARTICIPATION CREDIT

World War II
- *Sicily (with arrowhead)
- *Naples-Foggia
- *Rome-Arno
- *Southern France (with arrowhead)
- *Rhineland
- *Ardennes-Alsace
- *Central Europe

Korean War
- *UN defensive
- *UN offensive
- *CCF intervention
- *First UN counteroffensive
- *CCF spring offensive
- *UN summer-fall offensive

DECORATIONS

*French Croix de Guerre with Palm, World War II, Streamer embroidered CENTRAL ITALY (753d Tank Battalion cited; DA GO 43, 1950)

*French Croix de Guerre with Palm, World War II, Streamer embroidered VOSGES (753d Tank Battalion cited; DA GO 43, 1950)

*French Croix de Guerre with Silver-Gilt Star, World War II, Streamer embroidered MOUNT MAJO (753d Tank Battalion cited; DA GO 43, 1950)

*French Croix de Guerre, World War II, Fourragère (753d Tank Battalion cited; DA GO 43, 1950)

*Republic of Korea Presidential Unit Citation, Streamer embroidered SEOUL (77th Tank Battalion cited; DA GO 35, 1951)

*Republic of Korea Presidential Unit Citation, Streamer embroidered KOREA (77th Tank Battalion cited; DA GO 22, 1956)

4th BATTALION, 77th ARMOR

AR
(157th Infantry Brigade)

LINEAGE

Organized 29 March 1944 in the Regular Army at Vitulazio, Italy, as Company D, 753d Tank Battalion. Inactivated 15 January 1946 at Camp Patrick Henry, Virginia.

Activated 1 August 1946 at Fort Knox, Kentucky. Inactivated 15 October 1946 at Fort Knox, Kentucky. Disbanded 25 February 1949. Reconstituted 5 November 1962, withdrawn from the Regular Army, allotted to the Army Reserve, and redesignated as Headquarters and Headquarters Company, 4th Battalion, 77th Armor (organic elements concurrently constituted). Activated 7 January 1963 with Headquarters at Germantown, Pennsylvania, and assigned to 157th Infantry Brigade. Location of Headquarters changed 31 January 1966 to Reading, Pennsylvania.

Home Area: First United States Army.

CAMPAIGN PARTICIPATION CREDIT

World War II
Sicily (with arrowhead)
Naples-Foggia
*Rome-Arno
*Southern France (with arrowhead)
*Rhineland
*Ardennes-Alsace
*Central Europe

Korean War
UN defensive
UN offensive
CCF intervention
First UN counteroffensive
CCF spring offensive
UN summer-fall offensive

DECORATIONS

*French Croix de Guerre with Palm, World War II, Streamer embroidered CENTRAL ITALY (753d Tank Battalion cited; DA GO 43, 1950)

*French Croix de Guerre with Palm, World War II, Streamer embroidered VOSGES (753d Tank Battalion cited; DA GO 43, 1950)

*French Croix de Guerre with Silver-Gilt Star, World War II, Streamer embroidered MOUNT MAJO (753d Tank Battalion cited; DA GO 43, 1950)

*French Croix de Guerre, World War II, Fourragère (753d Tank Battalion cited; DA GO 43, 1950)

457

Bibliography, 77th Armor

Butler, Frederic B. "Southern France Exploits of Task Force Butler." *Armored Cavalry Journal*. Part I in Volume LVII, Number 1 (January–February, 1948). Part II in Volume LVII, Number 2 (March–April, 1948).

Department of the Army
Korea, 1950. 1952.

Department of the Army. AMERICAN FORCES IN ACTION series.
Fifth Army at the Winter Line. 1945.
Salerno: American Operations From the Beaches to Volturno. 1944.

Miller, John, jr., O. J. Carroll, and M. E. Tackley. *Korea 1951–1953.* Washington: 1956.

Unit Members. *Bayonet, a History of the 7th Infantry Division.* Tokyo, Japan: 1951.

————. *The Seventh Infantry Division in Korea.* Atlanta, Georgia: 1954.

UNITED STATES ARMY IN THE KOREAN WAR
Appleman, Roy E. *South to the Naktong, North to the Yalu.* 1961.

UNITED STATES ARMY IN WORLD WAR II
Cole, Hugh M. *The Ardennes: Battle of the Bulge.* 1965.
Garland, Albert N., and Howard McGaw Smyth. *Sicily and the Surrender of Italy.* 1965.

81st ARMOR

HERALDIC ITEMS

COAT OF ARMS

Shield: Per fess enhanced or and sable, in chief a chevron in point embowed between two fleurs-de-lis vert and in base a battle-axe and key in saltire of the first.

Crest: On a wreath argent and vert between two branches of oak proper a tower or charged with an escutcheon per pale tenné and azure and surmounted with a lion's head erased gules.

Motto: *Supero Omnia.*

Symbolism: The gold of the shield is the color for armor. The fleurs-de-lis symbolize the Normandy and Northern France Campaigns. The chevron in point embowed recalls the Battle of the Bulge during the Ardennes-Alsace Campaign. The key (occurring frequently in the civic arms of the towns of Rheinprovinz) symbolizes the Rhineland Campaign; symbolic of the successes of this campaign, it allegorically represents the "Key to Victory" in Europe. The battle-axe, a favorite Teutonic weapon, signifies the Central Europe Campaign.

The red lion's head is adapted from the arms of the Duchy of Luxembourg, and the gold tower alludes to the successful mission in that area. The oak leaves symbolize honor, victory, and valor, and the shield, in the colors of the Luxembourg Croix de Guerre, alludes to the award of that decoration.

DISTINCTIVE INSIGNIA

The distinctive insignia consists of the shield and motto of the coat of arms.

LINEAGE AND HONORS

LINEAGE

Constituted 28 August 1941 in the Army of the United States as 81st Armored Regiment and assigned to 5th Armored Division. Activated 1 October 1941 at Fort Knox, Kentucky.

459

Regiment broken up 20 September 1943 and its elements reorganized and redesignated as follows: Regiment (less 3d Battalion, Band and Maintenance, Service, and Reconnaissance Companies) as 81st Tank Battalion and remained assigned to 5th Armored Division; 3d Battalion as 707th Tank Battalion and relieved from assignment to 5th Armored Division; Reconnaissance Company as Troop E, 85th Cavalry Reconnaissance Squadron, Mechanized, an element of the 5th Armored Division; and Band, Maintenance and Service Companies disbanded.

81st Tank Battalion inactivated 8 October 1945 at Camp Myles Standish, Massachusetts. Redesignated 18 June 1948 as 81st Medium Tank Battalion. Allotted 25 June 1948 to the Regular Army. Activated 6 July 1948 at Camp Chaffee, Arkansas. Inactivated 1 February 1950 at Camp Chaffee, Arkansas. Activated 1 September 1950 at Camp Chaffee, Arkansas. Inactivated 16 March 1956 at Camp Chaffee, Arkansas. Relieved 3 February 1962 from assignment to 5th Armored Division.

707th Tank Battalion assigned 12 July 1945 to 7th Armored Division. Inactivated 8 October 1945 at Boston Port of Embarkation, Massachusetts. Redesignated 4 November 1950 at 94th Medium Tank Battalion, allotted to the Regular Army, and remained assigned to 7th Armored Division. Activated 24 November 1950 at Camp Roberts, California. Inactivated 15 November 1953 at Camp Roberts, California. Relieved 3 February 1962 from assignment to 7th Armored Division.

Troop E, 85th Cavalry Reconnaissance Squadron, Mechanized, redesignated 16 June 1945 as Troop E, 85th Mechanized Cavalry Reconnaissance Squadron. Inactivated 11 October 1945 at Camp Kilmer, New Jersey. Converted and redesignated 18 June 1948 as 505th Replacement Company, allotted to the Regular Army, and assigned to 5th Armored Division. Activated 6 July 1948 at Camp Chaffee, Arkansas. Inactivated 1 February 1950 at Camp Chaffee, Arkansas. Activated 1 September 1950 at Camp Chaffee, Arkansas. Inactivated 16 March 1956 at Camp Chaffee, Arkansas. Relieved 3 February 1962 from assignment to 5th Armored Division.

81st Tank Battalion, 94th Medium Tank Battalion, and 505th Replacement Company consolidated, reorganized, and redesignated 3 February 1962 as 81st Armor, a parent regiment under the Combat Arms Regimental System.

CAMPAIGN PARTICIPATION CREDIT

World War II
   Normandy
   Northern France

Rhineland
Ardennes-Alsace
Central Europe

DECORATIONS

Luxembourg Croix de Guerre, World War II, Streamer embroidered LUXEMBOURG (81st Tank Battalion cited; DA GO 44, 1951)

1st BATTALION, 81st ARMOR

RA

(1st Armored Division)

Constituted 28 August 1941 in the Army of the United States as Company A, 81st Armored Regiment, an element of the 5th Armored Division. Activated 1 October 1941 at Fort Knox, Kentucky.

Reorganized and redesignated 20 September 1943 as Company A, 81st Tank Battalion, and remained assigned to 5th Armored Division. Inactivated 8 October 1945 at Camp Myles Standish, Massachusetts. Redesignated 18 June 1948 as Company A, 81st Medium Tank Battalion. Allotted 25 June 1948 to the Regular Army. Activated 6 July 1948 at Camp Chaffee, Arkansas. Inactivated 1 February 1950 at Camp Chaffee, Arkansas. Activated 1 September 1950 at Camp Chaffee, Arkansas. Inactivated 16 March 1956 at Camp Chaffee, Arkansas.

Redesignated 3 February 1962 as Headquarters and Headquarters Company, 1st Battalion, 81st Armor; concurrently, relieved from assignment to 5th Armored Division, assigned to 1st Armored Division, and activated at Fort Hood, Texas (organic elements concurrently constituted and activated).

CAMPAIGN PARTICIPATION CREDIT

World War II
*Normandy
*Northern France

*Rhineland
*Ardennes-Alsace
*Central Europe

DECORATIONS

*Luxembourg Croix de Guerre, World War II, Streamer embroidered LUXEMBOURG (81st Tank Battalion cited; DA GO 44, 1951)

461

2d BATTALION, 81st ARMOR

RA
(1st Armored Division)

LINEAGE

Constituted 28 August 1941 in the Army of the United States as Company B, 81st Armored Regiment, an element of the 5th Armored Division. Activated 1 October 1941 at Fort Knox, Kentucky.

Reorganized and redesignated 20 September 1943 as Company B, 81st Tank Battalion, and remained assigned to 5th Armored Division. Inactivated 8 October 1945 at Camp Myles Standish, Massachusetts. Redesignated 18 June 1948 as Company B, 81st Medium Tank Battalion. Allotted 25 June 1948 to the Regular Army. Activated 6 July 1948 at Camp Chaffee, Arkansas. Inactivated 1 February 1950 at Camp Chaffee, Arkansas. Activated 1 September 1950 at Camp Chaffee, Arkansas. Inactivated 16 March 1956 at Camp Chaffee, Arkansas.

Redesignated 3 February 1962 as Headquarters and Headquarters Company, 2d Battalion, 81st Armor; concurrently, relieved from assignment to 5th Armored Division, assigned to 1st Armored Division, and activated at Fort Hood, Texas (organic elements concurrently constituted and activated).

CAMPAIGN PARTICIPATION CREDIT

World War II
  *Normandy
  *Northern France

*Rhineland
*Ardennes-Alsace
*Central Europe

DECORATIONS

*Luxembourg Croix de Guerre, World War II, Streamer embroidered LUXEMBOURG (81st Tank Battalion cited; DA GO 44, 1951)

462

4th BATTALION, 81st ARMOR

AR

(191st Infantry Brigade)

LINEAGE

Constituted 28 August 1941 in the Army of the United States as Company D, 81st Armored Regiment, an element of the 5th Armored Division. Activated 1 October 1941 at Fort Knox, Kentucky.

Reorganized and redesignated 20 September 1943 as Company D, 81st Tank Battalion, and remained assigned to 5th Armored Division. Inactivated 8 October 1945 at Camp Myles Standish, Massachusetts. Redesignated 18 June 1948 as Company D, 81st Medium Tank Battalion. Allotted 25 June 1948 to the Regular Army. Activated 6 July 1948 at Camp Chaffee, Arkansas. Inactivated 1 February 1950 at Camp Chaffee, Arkansas. Activated 1 September 1950 at Camp Chaffee, Arkansas. Inactivated 16 March 1956 at Camp Chaffee, Arkansas. Relieved 3 February 1962 from assignment to 5th Armored Division.

Redesignated 15 March 1963 as Headquarters and Headquarters Company, 4th Tank Battalion, 81st Armor; concurrently, withdrawn from the Regular Army, allotted to the Army Reserve, assigned to Sixth United States Army, and activated at Salt Lake City, Utah (organic elements concurrently constituted and activated). Assigned 10 August 1963 to 191st Infantry Brigade. Reorganized and redesignated 18 September 1963 as 4th Battalion, 81st Armor.

Home Area: Sixth United States Army.

CAMPAIGN PARTICIPATION CREDIT

World War II
  *Normandy
  *Northern France

*Rhineland
*Ardennes-Alsace
*Central Europe

DECORATIONS

*Luxembourg Croix de Guerre, World War II, Streamer embroidered LUXEMBOURG (81st Tank Battalion cited; DA GO 44, 1951)

463

Bibliography, 81st Armor

Unit Members. *History of the 81st Tank Battalion.* N.p.: 1947.

————. *Paths of Armor, Normandy, Northern France, Ardennes, Alsace, Rhineland, Central Europe.* A history of the 5th Armored Division. Atlanta, Georgia: 1950.

————. *The Road to Germany, the Story of the 5th Armored Division.* Paris: 1944.

————. *The Victory Division in Europe, Story of the Fifth Armored Division.* Europe: 1945.

UNITED STATES ARMY IN WORLD WAR II

Blumenson, Martin. *Breakout and Pursuit.* 1961.

Cole, Hugh M. *The Lorraine Campaign.* 1950.

————. *The Ardennes: Battle of the Bulge.* 1965.

MacDonald, Charles B. *The Siegfried Line Campaign.* 1963.

MacDonald, Charles B., and Sidney T. Mathews. *Three Battles: Arnaville, Altuzzo, and Schmidt.* 1952.

ARMY LINEAGE SERIES

Tentative List of Volumes
Armies and Corps
Artillery
Aviation
Engineers
Infantry (revised edition)
Medical
Separate Brigades and Divisions
Service and Support Organizations
Signal and Military Police

465

Name Index

Unit Index

U. S. GOVERNMENT PRINTING OFFICE : 1969 O - 314-902